# PROFILING
# POLITICAL LEADERS

# PROFILING POLITICAL LEADERS

## Cross-Cultural Studies of Personality and Behavior

EDITED BY Ofer Feldman
AND Linda O. Valenty

 PRAEGER

Westport, Connecticut
London

**Library of Congress Cataloging-in-Publication Data**

Profiling political leaders : cross-cultural studies of personality and behavior / edited by
Ofer Feldman and Linda O. Valenty.
    p.  cm.
    Includes bibliographical references and index.
    ISBN 0–275–97036–1 (alk. paper)
    1. Personality and occupation—Cross-cultural studies.   2. Political leadership—
Psychological aspects—Cross-cultural studies.   3. Political psychology—Cross-cultural
studies.   I. Feldman, Ofer, 1954–   II. Valenty, Linda O.
BF698.9.O3P76   2001
303.3'4'019—dc21        00–052866

British Library Cataloguing in Publication Data is available.

Library of Congress Catalog Card Number: 00–052866
ISBN: 0–275–97036–1

First published in 2001

Praeger Publishers, 88 Post Road West, Westport, CT 06881
An imprint of Greenwood Publishing Group, Inc.
www.praeger.com

Printed in the United States of America

The paper used in this book complies with the
Permanent Paper Standard issued by the National
Information Standards Organization (Z39.48–1984).

10 9 8 7 6 5 4 3 2 1

# Contents

# Tables, Figures, and Appendixes

## TABLES

## FIGURES

## APPENDIXES

# Preface

*Profiling Political Leaders: Cross-Cultural Studies of Personality and Behavior* seeks to contribute to the growing interest in the field of personality and politics. The focus of this volume is the examination and application of a variety of methods designed to profile political leaders from divergent societies. It is innovative in the sense that this is the first scholarly attempt, in one volume, to examine the utility of these methods in the analysis of linkages between personality, political motivation, and behavior in countries such as China, Japan, Israel, Iran, Russia, New Zealand, Germany, Canada, and the United Kingdom.

Our original idea was to publish a volume that included several case studies of American political leaders. We, the editors, have agreed, however, to follow the advice of Dr. James T. Sabin, Director of Academic Research and Development at Greenwood Publishing Group, to dedicate a separate, full volume to the study of American political leadership. In retrospect, Dr. Sabin's advice was very useful and timely, and we thank him for that and for supporting our project as a whole.

The second volume, *Political Leadership for the New Century: Personality and Behavior among American Leaders,* is forthcoming from the same publisher. These volumes should be read together, as they combine contributions from international scholars concerned with cross-cultural perspectives on political leadership and communicate across national and disciplinary boundaries with contributing authors from a variety of societies and disciplines, including history, political science, psychology, social psychology, and communication. The two-volume set presents chapters that speak to each other in their attempt to find answers to similar queries using differing perspectives and diverse research methods. Finally, both volumes aim to stimulate broad general appeal and professional interest in the linkages between personality and political behavior.

While working on this project and preparing these two volumes, we have attempted to keep several audiences in mind. The volumes are aimed primarily at scholars of political science, psychology, political psychology, sociology, contemporary history, and cross-cultural studies who are interested in an interdisciplinary approach to the study of political leadership and the research methods that support those studies. However, each or both of the edited books can serve as textbooks for courses in the above fields or for courses specifically dealing with political behavior and psychology, political sociology, personality, political leadership, cultural studies, or social psychology. In addition, the volumes are accessible to the general reader who is interested in analyses of some of the most highly visible political figures of recent years. It has been our goal to provide depth and breadth in the collected research, and we are delighted that what has resulted is a survey of the state of the art with contributions from a truly distinguished group of political scientists, psychologists, and political psychologists, with seasoned backgrounds and experience in understanding the interaction between leadership and personality, on the one hand, and political behavior, attitudes, and culture, on the other. We hope that these two books will provide a stimulus for additional cross-cultural research on political leadership, personality, and behavior.

We would like to offer our sincere appreciation to the contributors for their chapters and for their responses to our endless harassment for revisions. Linda Valenty would also like to thank her children, Bethany and Luke, for their steadfast love and understanding during the completion of these volumes. Finally, Ofer Feldman owes the biggest debt to his wife, Rie, and sons, Utai and Iri, who were a constant source of support and encouragement throughout the whole project.

# Introduction

## Ofer Feldman and Linda O. Valenty

The study of political leadership presents a challenge to researchers from both political science and psychology. Although studies are available in the general assessment of the effects of personality in political decision making and processes, the present book distinguishes itself among others of this genre by offering analyses of political leaders from around the world and demonstrating the use of a variety of analytic methods to further understanding of the political personality and its function from an international, comparative perspective. The contributors to this volume were specifically asked to explain and evaluate current methods—and their application—available for the assessment and examination of relationships between personality, motivation, decision making, leadership style, and behavior among political leaders and across divergent cultures.

The collected research presented in the following chapters describes and analyzes theoretical issues related to political leadership; examines available methods and the cross-cultural application of these methods in the analysis of political leadership (including thematic content analytic methods used in the measurement of motive imagery and integrative complexity); presents techniques that may combine one or more of the extant methods or develop a novel approach to the assessment of the political personality; and/or evaluates psychodiagnostic and psychobiographical methods and their application in profiling the personalities of political leaders. Chapters utilize case studies of those who are undoubtedly among the most powerful and significant leaders of the twentieth century—Mao Zedong of China; Nobusuke Kishi of Japan; Tony Blair of the United Kingdom; David Lange of New Zealand; Sayyed Mohammed Khatami of Iran; Yitzhak Shamir, Yitzhak Rabin, Shimon Peres, and Benjamin Netanyahu of Israel; Helmut Kohl of Germany; and Joseph Stalin, Boris Yeltsin, Aleksandr I. Lebed, Vladimir Zhirinovsky, and Vladimir Putin of Russia.

The present volume surveys state-of-the-art research on psychological profiling and the analysis of political leadership. It illustrates the role of cultural and political context, including historical circumstances, environmental factors, and socialization agents that affect and shape political leadership and performance in divergent cultures. Its approach is multidisciplinary with contributors from the fields of political science, psychology, political psychology, social psychology, and history.

## OVERVIEW OF THE BOOK

The goal of this volume is to present and examine the application of methods designed to profile political leaders across cultures and within differing societies. Each of the 14 chapters assembled in this book presents an approach, a method or a mixture of methods designed to analyze political leadership; presents the case study of a leader—a president, prime minister, or a monarch—or leaders in a given society; and evaluates the benefits, merits, or problems associated with the adopted method as well as its potential utility for future investigations. The chapters together provide a broad social scientific view of political leadership from different perspectives (multicultural, multidisciplinary, and multimethodological). The book is divided into three parts: "Assessment of Personality and Leadership: Content Analytic Techniques," "Profiling the Political Personality: Psychodiagnostic and Psychobiographical Approaches," and "The Cultural Context: Applications from East to West."

In Part I, the four chapters present research methods designed specifically to evaluate personality "from a distance." Political leadership and behavior are analyzed using thematic content analysis to uncover motive imagery, integrative complexity, and operational codes. Authors explain and then apply methods that have been developed to profile personality and predict political behavior with case studies from Canada, the United Kingdom, Russia, and Iran.

Chapter 1, by Peter Suedfeld, Lucian Gideon Conway III, and David Eichhorn, examines Canadian prime ministers. Suedfeld and his associates summarize research that utilizes the archival records of prime ministers to focus on two types of variables: cognitive (integrative complexity) and motivational (motive imagery). In so doing, the authors trace scholarly output, political events, and related findings. Levels of complexity are discussed in relation to political crises and ideological differences. The authors also evaluate research that relates levels of complexity and motive imagery to electoral success. They discuss a variety of causal factors related to expert ratings of prestige and accomplishment for Canadian prime ministers and proceed to present new research on associations between levels of complexity and prestige scores. Although the authors observe that the determination of precise factors capable of predicting leadership success is a complex process, they acknowledge that some reliable correlates have emerged. Finally, they note that it has become clear that research must deal with a specific structural and cultural context and that these multidimensional systems will benefit by the expansion and application of variables that seek to measure social competence, personality, and the congruence between leader policy and public demand.

In Chapter 2, Mark Schafer and Stephen G. Walker use operational code analysis to determine propensities for Prime Minister Tony Blair's leadership in the foreign policy domain. The Verbs In Context System (VICS) of operational code content analysis is explained and employed to analyze Blair's speeches. The authors proceed to expand the operational code construct—a fairly static conceptualization used to build indexes of philosophical and instrumental beliefs and to create a continuum measuring cooperation and conflict behavior. They develop a more "domain-specific" and dynamic operational code conceptualization that allows resulting profiles to account for contextual changes in cognitive and affective attributes. Schafer and Walker compare Blair's diagnostic, choice, and shift propensities toward democracies and dictatorships and use their results to investigate the "democratic peace" phenomenon. They present evidence that supports cultural explanations for peace between democracies, a more dynamic view of personality as it operates within political context, and the presence of institutional role variables associated with the office of prime minister. Schafer and Walker discuss their findings with reference to more dynamic conceptualizations of "personality-in-situation."

In Chapter 3, Linda Valenty and Eric Shiraev utilize speech and interview data to content-analyze motivational pattern and integrative complexity for former Russian president Boris Yeltsin and his closest contenders in the 1996 Russian presidential contest. Special attention is given to retired Russian army lieutenant general and later governor of Krasnoyarsk Aleksandr I. Lebed, a political figure who gained prominence during and after the 1996 electoral cycle. Valenty and Shiraev compare Lebed's motivational and cognitive profile to the profiles of Yeltsin, Zyuganov, Yavlinsky, and Zhirinovsky, all contenders in the 1996 Russian presidential contest. Their motivational and cognitive findings indicate that Lebed was capable of a certain amount of adjustment when the stakes were high and the goal required it. Lebed's motivational patterns are discussed with reference to potential for rigidity in approach to negotiation and in perceptions of independence versus interdependence. Integrative complexity scores are evaluated, indicating differentiation and some integration in Lebed's evaluation of national issues, as well as some contextual declines in levels of complexity and increases in rigidity when Lebed was operating from within the government and under conditions of stress. Lebed's motivational and integrative complexity profile is compared to results from other Russian leaders, and implications are discussed.

In Chapter 4, Tanyel Taysi and Thomas Preston evaluate the personality and leadership style of Iran's President Khatami, elected in 1997 and the driving force behind reforms aimed at reconciliation with the West. Utilizing the Personality Assessment-at-a-Distance content analytic technique, these authors analyze Khatami's spontaneous interview responses across differing time periods, audiences, and substantive topic areas. Taysi and Preston explore relationships between content analytic results and Khatami's working style and political personality. Results are discussed with reference to Khatami's general foreign policy preferences and his leadership style in both domestic and foreign policy. General expectations are presented regarding his use of advisory systems, advisors, and information in policy making. The authors discuss the suitability of the Personality Assessment-at-a-Distance technique as a tool for improving understanding of world leaders. In particular, they cite the technique's empirically supported measures of leader characteristics, its ability to generate data for use in comparing Khatami with other Iranian leaders, and its tendency to avoid the danger of Western bias in its analysis.

Part II of this book focuses on psychodiagnostic and psychobiographical approaches in examining the political personality. Authors explain and then utilize methods that have been developed to profile personality and predict political behavior in countries such as the United Kingdom, Russia, China, and Israel and in the European region. These methods assess personality using psychobiographical analyses and a psychodiagnostic approach built upon the DSM-IV (*American Psychiatric Association's Diagnostic and Statistical Manual of Mental Disorders*, 4th ed.).

In Chapter 5, Juliet Kaarbo expands the current research on prime ministers by focusing on individual differences and isolating personality factors as potential determinants of policy outcomes. Kaarbo evaluates relationships between prime ministerial leadership style, identification of governmental policy alternatives, and choices between these identified policy alternatives. Kaarbo distinguishes components of leadership style, theoretically develops the link between leadership style and cabinet decision-making processes, and examines empirical evidence for this association. Comparative data are drawn from Western European prime ministers and British prime ministers. The chapter also evaluates the limitations and utility of the approach and discusses the influence of institutions as compared to individuals, in so doing addressing the enduring debate on this issue.

In Chapter 6, Dean Keith Simonton analyzes similarities between modern heads of state and historic hereditary monarchs. He reviews seminal research on monarchs and modern heads of state from the perspective of psychology, sociology, history, and political leadership. Simonton finds evidence for strong variation in personality and leadership style across hereditary monarchs and relates this variation to genetic proclivity, role-modeling effects, and gender. This preliminary discussion is then used to determine the relative influence of historical activity, individual characteristics, and personality attributes upon political leadership and perceptions of greatness, both for historic hereditary monarchs and for modern heads of state. The chapter concludes with a discussion of the essential similarity of predictive independent variables in determining performance and eminence in monarchs and modern heads of state and an argument that this comparison may help to develop a more comprehensive understanding of political leadership.

In Chapter 7, Michael Sheng uses psychoanalytical theories of pathological narcissism in a pathbreaking effort at the systematic analysis of Mao Zedong's personality and its role in China's political and cultural history. Sheng argues that Mao was afflicted by narcissistic personality disorder, basing this determination upon diagnostic criteria delineated in the DSM-IV and relating the disorder to Mao's political behavior. Sheng further discusses literature that examines the behavioral manifestations of the disorder (including depression, paranoia, anti-social self-isolation, and exuberance in pursuit of unrealistic, grandiose fantasies), connects the genesis of the pathology to detailed biographic information, and finally relates theory to practical political behavior with a series of illustrative incidents. Sheng analyzes the effect of emotional disturbance on political choices and evaluates the psychoanalytical approach for use in cross-cultural leadership studies and as an interpretive framework capable of utilizing materials that have been ignored in more conventional studies.

Psychohistorical and psychobiographical perspectives are employed by Juhani Ihanus in Chapter 8 to provide an integrated profile of prominent Russian leaders from Stalin to Putin. Ihanus begins by tracing the development of psychohistory and psychobiography as research methods and proceeds to describe the evolution of leadership in Russia while constructing a rich historical and cultural context to that evolution. Biographic information is provided for each of the leaders who are evaluated. The interaction of society and dictator is analyzed with specific reference to Stalin. Boris Yeltsin is discussed with emphasis on the association between political behavior, public perceptions, and public expectations. Zhirinovsky is evaluated from the perspective of the needs of the Russian people and the interaction of those needs with political and social reality, while Putin—Yeltsin's "crown prince"—is discussed as a modern leader with charisma that translates well technologically. Ihanus provides a critique of psychohistorical and psychobiographical methods, finding them useful in the assessment of the interaction between cultural context and political outcomes.

In Chapter 9, Shaul Kimhi employs a qualitative method labeled behavior analysis to develop a psychological profile for former Israeli prime minister Benjamin ("Bibi") Netanyahu. The method is clinically derived and has pragmatic application as it builds from empirical data regarding a variety of behaviors, including precise political behavior, to suggest a global personality type. Data are generated with content analytic techniques based upon primary as well as secondary sources. Kimhi, a clinical psychologist, discusses results that indicate that egocentricity, ambition, determination, aggression, and manipulation are key components of Netanyahu's personality profile. He goes on to analyze Netanyahu's behavior under stress, his high levels of cognitive function, his charisma, and his leadership style. Kimhi also analyzes detailed biographic information that may underlie much of the personality findings. Finally, Kimhi discusses an overall finding of narcissistic personality disorder, the effects of this personality type upon leadership style, and its potential in the creation of serious administrative problems. The method itself is determined to be useful in the attempt to provide explanations for Netanyahu's meteoric rise to power as well as his failure as a prime minister. Although behavior analysis has its own unique limits, it also provides some unique advantages over other qualitative methods.

Part III of this volume consists of five chapters, each of which focuses upon the multicultural application of personality analysis and profiling techniques. Specific reference is made to cultural context: methods are evaluated with an eye to their utility within the particular culture that is the focus for the chapter and with reference to multicultural application. Political leaders in Japan, Israel, New Zealand, Germany, and the United States, respectively, are evaluated.

In Chapter 10, Shigeko Fukai examines the case of Prime Minister (1957–1960) Nobusuke Kishi of Japan, a powerful political figure and unindicted Class A war criminal who rose to the pinnacle of power in Japan within nine years of his release from prison. Kishi's unique position in Japan's political history includes his transformation of Japan's prewar economy from a free-market orientation to a highly controlled economic system geared for war mobilization, his status as a member of Tojo's war cabinet, his postwar influence in propelling political innovations that succeeded in altering the formal and informal systems of postwar party politics, his position as prime minister, and finally his resignation after his forceful support of the revised United States–Japan Security Treaty culminated in the May–June Crisis of 1960. Kishi's political style was both autocratic and hawkish, and his leadership held typical and extraordinary components. Fukai uses Jean Blondel's typology to analyze Kishi's leadership style, his response to environmental pressures, his societal and political influence, and his relevant personality characteristics before, during, and after World War II. Fukai also provides an evaluation of the Blondel typology for use in the examination of character, leadership, political behavior, and the interaction between institutional and environmental influences and leader response.

In Chapter 11, Yael Aronoff evaluates Israeli prime ministers Yitzhak Rabin, Yitzhak Shamir, Shimon Peres, and Benjamin Netanyahu to determine the role that ideology, perceptions of time, and cognitive complexity play in explaining whether and to what extent political leaders change their attitudes and policy predispositions toward an international enemy in response to new information. Aronoff uses personal interviews with decision makers and their aids, transcripts from television interviews, newspaper interviews, and communications at party central committee meetings to analyze attitudes and policy preferences toward the Palestinian Liberation Organization (PLO). Although each of these prime ministers once supported hard-line policies, Rabin and Peres of the Labor Party experienced a shift in attitude and policy, eventually negotiating an agreement in which the PLO was recognized. The Likud Party's Shamir and Netanyahu vigorously opposed this change. Aronoff's analysis evaluates the influence of ideology on image of the enemy, perception of the *intifada*, reaction to the *intifada*, and ability to negotiate agreement with the Palestinians for each of these prime ministers. She determines that individual time horizons help to explain rates and mechanisms of attitudinal and policy change among those with similar ideological leanings and that perceptions of time may influence an individual's potential for a reevaluation of the image of the enemy. Finally, Aronoff discusses surprising findings about the role of individual cognitive systems in attitudinal transitions.

In Chapter 12, John Henderson focuses on David Lange, prime minister of New Zealand during a time of policy change and political upheaval (1984–1989). Henderson analyzes the interaction of personality and political behavior from the perspective of his own experience as director of Lange's Policy Advisory Group and as director of the Prime Minister's Office. He uses the analytical framework originally developed by James David Barber to analyze American presidents and applies this method to Prime Minister Lange. Lange's management of an extensive economic restructuring and his support for the adoption of anti-nuclear foreign policy in New Zealand provide counterpoint to descriptions of his personal affect, policy preferences, love of the political "stage," and patterns of interaction with staff and supporters. In his analysis Henderson argues that the Barber typology is useful in explaining the administration of David Lange as well as his resignation as prime minister. Henderson notes that Barber's framework is capable of crossing cultures and, as such, can provide a basis for understanding and predicting the performance of leaders in parliamentary systems.

In Chapter 13, Astrid Schütz uses content analytic techniques and quasi-experimental analysis to evaluate the utility of the social psychological theory of self-presentation in understanding German chancellor Helmut Kohl. She presents a taxonomy of self-presentation strategies used by political figures, uses content analysis to identify particular strategies, and conducts a quasi-experimental analysis to evaluate the effect of self-presentation strategies. Schütz discusses the use of self-presentation theory to analyze political communication and proceeds to create and apply an expanded version of the theory to evaluate Kohl and his competitor in 1987, Social Democrat Johannes Rau. In the second part of her analysis, Schütz builds upon previous research to evaluate the impact of self-presentation strategies on German students viewing the 1990 chancellery debates between Kohl and Social Democrat Oskar Lafontaine. She discusses the implications of results that may indicate that aggressive styles of self-presentation create positive perceptions of strength in the German electorate. Finally, Schütz considers the advantages of evaluating self-presentation theories with content analysis in conjunction with quasi-experimental analysis and recommends supplementation with biographic data.

In Chapter 14, Stanley Renshon provides a conceptual overview that ties together and examines the common threads of the various chapters. To accomplish this, he uses a case study of noteworthy American political leader John McCain—senator from the state of Arizona and recent candidate for the Republican nomination for the presidency. Renshon argues that this particular case material is an important way of addressing the comparative use of trait theory. He notes that trait theory, in one form or another, has become the dominant paradigm and the most widely used approach for leadership analysis, both in the United States and elsewhere. When considered in light of the international transplantation of American election technology, he argues that it is clear that trait theory is poised to become the dominant way in which leaders are understood and analyzed by both professionals and citizens. Accordingly, Renshon critiques trait theory, explaining that it cannot alone carry the theoretical or explanatory load. Using the McCain case study as an easily understood and accessible illustration, he demonstrates the problems of trait theory as a method of analysis and offers comparative psychoanalytic theory as an important adjunct, indeed, a viable alternative. Drawing on his previous work with comparative psychoanalytic theory,

Renshon presents a theory that relies on public, accessible information to discern the core elements of a leader's character structure and its relationship to his leadership performance. Central to this analysis is the independent role of each of the three major determinants of leadership success: a leader's character and psychology, the general tasks of leadership and those that might be specifically required by historical circumstance, and the cultural and political contexts in which these elements unfold. Finally, Renshon addresses future research and the role that political leadership plays in modern societies. He deals with the importance of cross-cultural studies and perspectives in developing a better comparative model of psychological function and political behavior, and in enhancing our understanding of the tasks of political leadership.

Taken as a whole, this volume addresses the role of a nation's culture and politics in framing the association between psychological profile and leadership performance. Each chapter calls attention to the fact that the behavior of leaders is only a subset of the behavior of people. Cross-cultural comparative research on leadership should be applied within the broader study of cultural and national differences and characteristics, with acknowledgment of and understanding that the behavior and function of leaders within societies can shed light on the (accepted) behavior and norms of the societies themselves. It is our sincere hope that readers will find this book useful and that it will stimulate further research into political leadership around the globe.

Part I

# Assessment of Personality and Leadership: Content Analytic Techniques

Chapter 1

# Studying Canadian Leaders at a Distance

Peter Suedfeld, Lucian Gideon Conway III,
and David Eichhorn

## INTRODUCTION

Canada is the second largest country on earth in size; it spans the North
American continent from sea to sea to sea (the Atlantic, Pacific, and Arctic Oceans). Its population, about 31 million in 1999, ranks 34th out of
227 nations in the world (U.S. Census Bureau, 2000). Formerly a British
colony and still a member of the Commonwealth, it has played an independent role in world affairs during the twentieth century. This role
has included prominent leadership in the United Nations (UN), the
North Atlantic Treaty Organization (NATO), the World Trade Organization, and many other international organizations, and significant participation in both world wars, the Korean War, and international
peacekeeping under the UN aegis (an activity invented by Lester Pearson
and first commanded by General E.L.M. Burns, both Canadians).

Thus, Canada is a substantial presence on the world stage, if for no
other reason than that its political leaders are worth studying. Another
justification for such studies is that Canada makes for an interesting comparison with both the United States, its neighbor—with which it shares
a long border, a dominant language and political culture, and British-
derived legal principles but from whose presidential political system it
differs widely—and other parliamentary systems, such as the British,
again with both significant similarities and differences. Third, of course,
one would expect that the leaders of any country would be of professional interest to the scholars of that country. Under some governments,
it might be risky to turn this interest into actual research, but that is not
the case in Canada any more than in the United States or Britain.

Yet, Canadian political psychology barely exists; and to the extent that it does, it largely ignores the psychological study of political figures. Many qualitative biographies and histories describe their subject's childhood, social relations, and personality, sometimes going on to speculate about the effects of these variables on the leader's political positions and actions. The kinds of scientific studies—quantitative (e.g., Simonton, 1987b) or, if qualitative, taking a systematic approach to the dissection of psychological variables (e.g., Renshon, 1996b)—that have proliferated in the study of American presidents, political figures of international importance (Post, 2001), and even the rank-and-file legislators of various nations (DiRenzo, 1974; Feldman, 2000; Hermann, 1977) are absent from the Canadian social science literature.

Even the ranking and rating of the chief executives,[1] long a popular activity in the United States (from Schlesinger, 1948, to Faber & Faber, 2000), began only relatively recently in Canada. Ballard and Suedfeld (1988) published the first such study, with rankings on 10 evaluative scales submitted by 97 Canadian historians and political scientists. More recently, a panel of 25 noted Canadian historians and political scientists, overlapping with Ballard and Suedfeld's experts, ranked all of the prime ministers (PMs). Although the reasons underlying the rankings were not reported, the resulting book (Granatstein & Hillmer, 1999) describes the issues faced by each PM and analyzes his (or, in one case, her) performance both before and after taking office. The authors being historians, there is relatively little in the way of psychological explication, although some interpretation of the PMs' goals, interests, priorities, and personality is presented. Table 1.1 shows the rankings by the experts in the two studies.

It may be worth noting that, in spite of the dearth of psychological research on Canadian PMs, Canada has not escaped the scandal of psychodiagnosis at a distance. The Canadian version of the 1964 Goldwater "diagnosis" scandal (Rogow, 1970) was much tamer: one of Canada's most prominent psychiatrists produced a diagnosis of Lucien Bouchard, then going into a federal election as the leader of the separatist Bloc Quebecois. The diagnostician had never met his subject, and the diagnostic category—"aesthetic personality disorder"—was one that he had invented himself (Martin, 1997). As in the Goldwater case, the implication was that a combination of egomania, rigidity, intolerance, and inability to control his temper when frustrated made Bouchard a dangerous politician.

## PSYCHOLOGICAL STUDIES OF CANADIAN PRIME MINISTERS

Below, we summarize research on two variables, one cognitive (integrative complexity) and one motivational (motive imagery), that have

**Table 1.1**
**Rankings of the Canadian Prime Ministers**

| Prime Minister | Term in Office | Rank | |
| --- | --- | --- | --- |
| | | B&S | G&H |
| Sir John A. Macdonald | 1867–1873, 1878–1891 | 1 | 2 |
| Alexander Mackenzie | 1873–1878 | 10 | 11 |
| Sir John Abbott | 1891–1892 | NR | 17 |
| Sir John S. Thompson | 1892–1894 | NR | 10 |
| Sir Mackenzie Bowell | 1894–1896 | NR | 19 |
| Sir Charles Tupper | 1896 | NR | 16 |
| Sir Wilfrid Laurier | 1896–1911 | 2 | 3 |
| Sir Robert Borden | 1911–1920 | 5 | 7 |
| Arthur Meighen | 1920–1921, 1926 | 9 | 14 |
| W. L. Mackenzie King | 1920–1926, 1926–1930, 1935–1948 | 3 | 1 |
| R. B. Bennett | 1930–1935 | 11 | 12 |
| Louis St. Laurent | 1948–1957 | 7 | 4 |
| John Diefenbaker | 1957–1963 | 8 | 13 |
| L. B. Pearson | 1963–1968 | 6 | 6 |
| P. E. Trudeau | 1968–1979, 1980–1984 | 4 | 5 |
| Joe Clark | 6/1979–3/1980 | 12 | 15 |
| John Turner | 6–9/1984 | NR | 18 |
| Brian Mulroney | 1984–1993 | NR | 8 |
| Kim Campbell | 6–10/1993 | NR | 20 |
| Jean Chretien | 1993–Present | NR | NR |

NR = not rated.
*Sources*: B&S: Ballard & Suedfeld, 1988; G&H: Granatstein & Hillmer, 1999.

been studied in the archival records of the PMs and research on the factors related to their short-term electoral success and long-term expert ratings of prestige and accomplishments.

## Integrative Complexity

Perhaps no other psychological variable has received as much attention with respect to Canadian PMs as integrative complexity, a structural (rather than content) aspect of information processing. Complexity scores comprise two components: *differentiation*, the recognition of more than one dimension of, or legitimate perspective on, an issue; and *integration*, the recognition of relationships among these dimensions or perspectives through, for example, syntheses, trade-offs, compromises, or higher-level conceptual schemata (Schroder et al., 1967; Suedfeld et al., 1992). Differentiation is necessary, but not sufficient, for integration. The dimension is scored on a scale from 1 (both differentiation and integration are absent) to 7 (high levels of both are present).

### PMs in Crisis

A defining part of many leaders' careers is how they respond when the going gets tough. Many crises require the expenditure of resources necessary to reach and maintain high complexity. Such resources include internal characteristics (energy, attention, and thought) and external variables (sources of information, time, money, and personnel). Severe and/ or prolonged stress, which often accompanies the occurrence of crises, can deplete the resources available to the individual (the "disruptive stress hypothesis"; e.g., Suedfeld & Tetlock, 1977), inducing lower levels of complexity.

According to the cognitive manager model (Suedfeld, 1992), optimal information processing and decision making involve an efficient allocation of the resources available. An effective cognitive manager devotes resources to solving a given problem to the extent that the resources are available, necessary to solve the problem, and not needed for dealing with more important decisions.

These hypotheses were examined in crises faced by three PMs (Ballard, 1983).[2] The first was Sir John A. Macdonald's handling of the 1884 death sentence of Louis Riel, defeated leader of a Metis (denoting a mixture of white and Indian ancestry) rebellion. This sentence, supported in English Canada, was criticized in Quebec. This posed a serious problem for the Anglophone prime minister, who had, until then, generally managed to satisfy his Quebec constituents (ethnically, linguistically, religiously, and ideologically different from the majority).

The second crisis was faced by William Lyon Mackenzie King during World War II. His government had passed conscription in 1940, with the proviso that conscripts would not be sent overseas. A 1941 amendment, dropping this restriction over very strong objections from French Canadians, had never been implemented. In 1944 Canadian casualties in Italy and France were so heavy that volunteers could not make up the difference. King's problem was similar to Macdonald's: how could he send conscripts into battle in Europe without splitting the country? King, who depended upon the support of Quebec Liberals, was in a true quandary.

The third event was the October Crisis of 1970. Trudeau (himself a Francophone Quebecois) was faced with an escalating terrorist campaign by Quebec separatists. After several years of bomb-setting, the terrorists

Table 1.2
Mean Crisis Complexity of Prime Ministers Macdonald, King, and Trudeau

| Prime Minister | Crisis Phase | | | |
| --- | --- | --- | --- | --- |
| | Non-Crisis | Pre-Crisis | Crisis | Post-Crisis |
| Macdonald | 1.9 | 2.4 | 1.8 | 3.0 |
| King | 1.6 | 2.8 | 1.6 | 2.4 |
| Trudeau | 2.3 | 1.7 | 1.4 | 1.9 |

kidnapped a British official stationed in Montreal and then the provincial minister of labor. At this point, there was considerable support for separation (but not necessarily for terrorism) among some segments of the Quebec population, particularly the youth, labor unions, intellectuals, and media personalities. Trudeau had to decide what compromises were possible, politically acceptable, and morally defensible and how to suppress terrorism without alienating moderate Quebecois.[3]

All three PMs showed a decline in complexity from the period when the crisis first began to develop (the "pre-crisis" phase) to the interval between the occurrence of the proximal precipitating event and the announcement of the PM's decision. Two of the three, Trudeau being the exception, also increased in complexity from an earlier, non-crisis period to the pre-crisis phase, indicating the increased mobilization of cognitive resources to deal with the problem (Table 1.2). Trudeau's very high complexity in the baseline phase is noteworthy. Compatibly with the resource depletion-recovery hypothesis, the complexity of all three PMs increased after the crisis was over. The results are consistent with data on international, rather than domestic, crises (Suedfeld & Rank, 1976; Wallace & Suedfeld, 1988; see also Conway et al., 2001).

Wallace and Suedfeld (1988) scored the integrative complexity of the Canadian statesman Lester B. Pearson in speeches made before and after his becoming PM in 1963. Pearson's pre-crisis, crisis, and post-crisis integrative complexity scores were computed across three historical events.

At the outbreak of the Korean War in 1950, Pearson was minister of external affairs. Although Canada was to take a significant part in the conflict, his complexity level remained approximately the same across all three crisis phases.

The resolution of the 1956 Suez invasion was, to a great extent, Pearson's handiwork, for which he received the 1957 Nobel Peace Prize. Pearson actually increased in complexity during the crisis, as he successfully negotiated an end to the fighting and established the concept and the reality of UN peacekeeping. His complexity decreased once the conflict was settled.

During a serious political division (both within Canada and vis-à-vis the United States) over American policy in Vietnam, when as PM he had to maintain the support of both the Canadian public and Canada's most important ally, Pearson followed the same course as the PMs in Ballard's study. His complexity dropped during the crisis and recovered after the crisis was over.

These different patterns are reminiscent of other research showing that a stress-induced reduction in complexity is not the only possible course of crisis decision making. Indeed, whether or not complexity drops during crises has been shown to predict whether international confrontations are ended by peaceful (complex) or violent (simple) solutions (Conway et al., 2001).

Ballard (1983) suggested that all of the crises examined in her study were resolved through simple solutions, with the PM's selecting a drastic, unidimensional strategy rather than a compromise. This may explain the similarities among her examples and their differences from Pearson's complexity pattern. On the other hand, Pearson's complexity during the one crisis that occurred during his prime ministerial term (which he did not resolve in any unidimensional way) changed in the same way as those of the three PMs in the Ballard study. This explanation is compatible with other findings that the chief executive's psychological resources are depleted more than those of subordinate officials (Wallace et al., 1993).

Some individuals may have unusual ability, whether acquired or innate, to raise and maintain their level of complexity during stressful experiences. Such individuals tend to remain in high office longer than counterparts who are more susceptible to disruptive stress. Among stress-resistant problem solvers have been the Duke of Wellington, Andrei Gromyko, and Lester B. Pearson (Wallace & Suedfeld, 1988). In fact, none of the scores of the other 20 historical figures in Wallace and Suedfeld's study ever reached as high as the level of Pearson's lowest complexity score (Pearson's lowest score = 3.89; next highest = 3.45).

## Party Differences in Integrative Complexity

Although any political opinion can be stated at any level of complexity, people to the left of the political center in both the United States and Great Britain tend to be more complex in their thinking than those on the right (Suedfeld & Epstein, 1973; Tetlock, 1983, 1984; Tetlock et al., 1985). This was not true of university political groups in British Columbia, Canada. There, members of the two major centrist parties (Progressive Conservative [PC] and Liberal) wrote more complex essays (on the relationship between equality and freedom) than members to the left (New Democratic Party [NDP]) and right (the populist provincial Social Credit Party) (Suedfeld et al., 1994).

What about Canadian PMs? Suedfeld et al. (1990) looked at the campaign speeches of leaders of the two major parties (Conservative and Liberal) covering the 10 elections from 1945 to 1974. Consistent with research in other nations, the campaign speeches of Liberal Party leaders exhibited significantly higher integrative complexity than did those of their Conservative counterparts. Four explanations present themselves (Suedfeld et al., 1990).

1. Incumbents are more complex than challengers. Those responsible for current policies and outcomes need to acknowledge shortcomings while emphasizing successes, temper ideology with pragmatism, and recognize the limitations of their power. All of this calls for differentiated and integrated viewpoints. Challengers need only to mount strong attacks on existing policies and extol their own alternatives (e.g., Suedfeld & Rank, 1976; Tetlock et al., 1989).

   In another of the few psychological studies of Canadian politicians, Pancer et al. (1992) found this to be the case in the Canadian Parliament. Members of whichever was the governing party made more complex speeches than the opposition. Further supporting the hypothesis, when neither party had a majority so that policy making was shared, members of both parties increased in complexity. Last, complexity was related to the time since the last election (and the approach of the next one): the speeches of government members became more, and those of opposition members less, complex as their campaign roles—defense and criticism, respectively—loomed more saliently.

   Because in the era under study by Suedfeld et al. (1990) Liberals won 8 of the 10 elections, incumbency and party membership were confounded. The higher complexity of Liberals may, in fact, have reflected the higher complexity of incumbents.

2. Repeated electoral losses may leave politicians with a chronic sense of threat. Because the stress associated with this threat may reduce complexity, consistently losing parties—regardless of political orientation—may be more likely to exhibit low complexity. It is possible that Conservatives developed a chronic sense of threat that, in turn, reduced the complexity levels of their leaders.

3. Tetlock's value conflict model (1983) suggests that two main political values, freedom and equality, are frequently in conflict. The purpose of government in many areas is to navigate the tensions and trade-offs between these two ideals. According to Tetlock's model, conservative positions tend to elevate freedom at the expense of equality, while liberals value both at about the same level. The former value hierarchy requires less interactive or trade-off (complex) thinking. This is less persuasive because the two Canadian parties are almost equally centrist in ideology: Liberals may value equality, and Conservatives freedom, a little more—but not much. Thus, the trade-off requirements seem to be about the same for both.

4. Liberals may consider it desirable to project an image of high complexity (moderation, willingness to compromise) more than conservatives. Consequently, the difference found in the analysis is due to contrasting impression

management strategies (Tetlock, 1981). This is an interesting hypothesis but a difficult one to test, and the role of impression management in complexity is controversial (Suedfeld et al., 1992).

The last study concentrating on leaders' complexity analyzed speeches during the federal election of 1997 (Suedfeld, 2000). This was a particularly interesting election, because there were five major parties contending for seats in Parliament, and there were significant ideological and geographic differences among them.

The speeches of the party leaders in most cases reached only the category of low differentiation. This was in the same range as all but two Canadian party leaders in 10 elections between 1945 and 1974. The two exceptions were Lester Pearson in 1958 and Pierre Trudeau in 1972, both of whom scored around 2.3 (Suedfeld et al., 1990). The overall differences among the 1997 leaders were not striking.

We then disaggregated integrative complexity across topic domains to see whether topics of particular importance or sensitivity to particular parties were addressed with complexity levels that were different from those for less crucial subjects. Two topics, federal–provincial relations and the economy, elicited particularly high complexity from most leaders. These are always hot topics in Canada, partly because of the amorphous nature of authority and finance. They become particularly controversial during federal elections, when Quebec's drive for more and more autonomy, its status compared to that of the other provinces, and the fiscal relations between the federal and provincial governments are especially salient.

We found fairly low overall complexity (M = 1.1) in the speeches of Alexa McDonough of the social democratic New Democratic Party (NDP), similar to young NDP supporters assessed in an earlier study (Suedfeld et al., 1994). She did not show the predicted high complexity when discussing issues of great concern to her party, such as health, social, and job-creation programs (all at 1.5 or below).

Another surprise was that Gilles Duceppe, the leader of the separatist Bloc Quebecois, did not rise to highly complex levels in speaking about national unity (1.4), although he did show high complexity (2.4) in discussing relations between the federal and provincial governments.

Preston Manning of the conservative populist Reform Party functioned overall at a level perhaps more appropriate for an incumbent than a challenger, M = 1.7, the same as the PM (see below). Manning showed particularly high complexity in dealing with the economy (2.6) and intergovernmental relations (2.1), areas where the Reform Party had a unique platform: enthusiastic about private enterprise, on the one hand, and about decentralization, on the other.

The other two parties are more pragmatic than ideological (Suedfeld et al., 1994). It was expected that Jean Chretien, the incumbent PM, would function at a fairly high level, as he and his party had been responsible for (and had to defend) policies in all important domains. His complexity scores (M = 1.7, without major cross-domain fluctuation except for low scores of 1.3 concerning the campaign and in criticizing other parties) supported this prediction.

Jean Charest (Progressive Conservative Party, devastated in the previous federal election) was deeply concerned with, and especially complex about, rebuilding his party, a topic that no other leader addressed at length (1.9). He also reached high levels overall (M = 1.6), especially in discussing the economy, a major campaign issue of his party (2.6).

The next major political utterance after the election[4] was the Speech from the Throne, which is delivered by the governor-general of Canada (the representative of the monarch) at the opening session of each new Parliament. The speech is written by representatives of the government— that is, the party that has a majority in the Parliament—and reflects the concerns and thinking of its leaders.

With the 1997 election over and the government again safely in their hands, the Liberals could turn their attention from their immediate political fate and think in a relatively complex way about the rapidly approaching future. The Throne Speech showed substantially higher complexity (M = 2.9) than had the campaign speeches of any of the party leaders. This was true even on health care policy (2.2), where the government had serious problems. It reached solid differentiation on most topics, approached integration on prospects for the twenty-first century (3.5), and created opportunities for the next generation (3.4).

### Motive Imagery

Suedfeld et al. (1990) also applied other content analytic methods to materials produced by federal party leaders—potential and actual prime ministers—and popular media in the period identified above. Besides the campaign speeches of the leaders, they analyzed excerpts from the country's major newspapers, comic strips, major magazines, and popular songs.

The material was scored for imagery representing the seminal motives of power, affiliation, and achievement. The scoring systems had originally been developed for analyzing responses to Thematic Apperception Test (TAT)-type pictures and were later modified to be usable with written or spoken passages taken from archives (Winter, 1983).

Integrative complexity and affiliation imagery were significantly and moderately highly correlated (r = 0.47) in campaign speeches; neither variable had a direct relationship with electoral success. It would be interesting to investigate the relationship in more detail, for example, to correlate the two variables in specific passages or within specific topic domains. It is possible that the correlation is an artifact of the complexity–party or complexity–incumbency link; it is also possibly an outcome of some idiosyncrasy of the Canadian political landscape.

Power was the dominant image for every politician, with achievement second. In the media, power was also predominant, except for popular songs, which emphasized affiliation. Media sources scored higher than the politicians on both power and affiliation and lower on achievement.

Politicians' power orientation was expected, both on intuitive grounds and based on previous U.S. research (Winter, 1987). What was not predicted was that power imagery would be even higher in the mass media materials. However, as the difference was mostly accounted for by one media source, the comics, the finding may not apply to wider aspects of popular culture. The media also scored higher than politicians on affiliation imagery, but the difference was due to the high affiliation levels of comics and songs. Affiliation imagery was low in newspapers and magazines.

The researchers were surprised by the relatively high level of achievement motivation revealed in political speeches. This motive involves a concern with excellence and accomplishment, a desirable, but not ubiquitous, orientation among politicians. The fact that it loomed so important in the campaign materials speaks well for Canadian politicians and/or for how they view the preferences of their constituents.

## WHAT MAKES A CANADIAN PRIME MINISTER SUCCESSFUL?

As indicated earlier, psychologists and historians have recently become interested in rating the various prime ministers in terms of their "prestige" or "significance." However, such ratings beg the question: What is it, exactly, that makes a Canadian PM great? What situational and psychological factors contribute to the short-term (getting elected) and long-term (e.g., being held in high historical esteem) success of PMs?

### Short-Term Success: Winning Elections

In Suedfeld et al.'s study (1990), the dependent variable was straightforward: success in the next election for the party and its leader (who would then become, or continue to be, PM).

There were no obvious hypotheses. The electorate may respond favorably to politicians whose professed goal is innovation and excellence (achievement), a friendly and supportive government (affiliation), or the ability to shape events (power). Although social scientists tend to be biased in favor of high complexity (Suedfeld, 1992), there is no evidence that it is either morally or pragmatically more desirable or that the voters would share the experts' bias (Suedfeld & Tetlock, 1991).

In fact, there was no clear-cut, straightforward relationship between any of the independent variables and electoral success. The winning party's leader did not convincingly differ from that of the losing party on either integrative complexity or any of the three motives.

Suedfeld et al. (1990) also tested the match between the PM hopefuls' imagery and the popular media. A "matching" hypothesis suggests that leaders whose speeches reflected motivational patterns similar to those of the citizenry (as indirectly measured from popular, mass media) would be most likely to succeed.

None of the scores for the three individual motives supported the "matching" hypothesis. However, the summed score of the three types of motive imagery, which the researchers labeled "motive richness," did support the hypothesis. There was a significant positive correlation ($r = 0.54$) between the motive richness of the speeches of victorious leaders and that of the combined mass media samples. In particular, the winners' correlations with newspaper articles were significant: for power imagery, $r = 0.71$, and for integrative complexity, $r = 0.72$. No significant correlations were found for leaders of the losing party.

This suggests that winning politicians evidence an overall level of dynamic imagery that is in accord with the *Zeitgeist*. Although the theoretical nature of this finding is somewhat ambiguous, Winter (1987) found similar support for a "matching" hypothesis in American elections, using a related composite score of the three motive imagery measures. As in the Suedfeld et al. (1990) study, Winter also failed to find significant relationships with success for the three motives taken individually. Thus, the finding may represent something that is real, replicable, and valid beyond Canadian politics.

### Long-Term Success: The Judgment of History

As mentioned previously, Ballard and Suedfeld (1988) asked experts on Canadian politics (37 historians and 60 political scientists) to evaluate each PM on 10 Likert-type scales assessing the PMs' environmental circumstances, personality characteristics, and historical prestige/significance (see Table 1.1). An objective measure of success, length of term in office, was significantly correlated with current prestige and significance of overall accomplishments. Of primary interest here, however, is the question: Which characteristics predicted the prestige and significance ratings of the PMs?

Both situational and personality factors were found to be important predictors. This should not be a surprise; person-by-environment interactions almost always provide the best explanations of behavior (see, e.g., House et al., 1991).

On the situational side in the Canadian cases, those PMs who were rated as having faced particularly difficult circumstances were judged to be the most prestigious and to have accomplished the most significant things. This finding, which is in accord with research on U.S. presidents, makes intuitive sense. Leaders who govern in easy, prosperous times may be well liked and may be credited for not "messing things up," but heroes must overcome obstacles.

There was one exception to the above trend. Anyone who aspires to become a highly rated Canadian PM or American president should be careful not to hold office during an economic depression. One of the most poorly rated PMs, R. B. Bennett, governed during the Great Depression, Canada's most difficult economic time, according to the historians and political scientists sampled. Herbert Hoover, the U.S. president during the same time period, also suffers greatly in the eyes of history. Thus, research on both sides of the 49th parallel suggests that the relationship between difficulty and historical success is modified by the nature of the difficulty. Economic crises are bad news for a leader's future historical standing; other crises, including wars, are good news.

There are at least two possible reasons for this. Economic problems may simply be harder to solve; and it is the solving, not the mere existence, of the crisis that results in a post-retirement halo. Being helpless in the midst of a severe crisis is hardly likely to bring widespread historical recognition. The Great Depression in particular (although not uniquely) was a worldwide phenomenon, from which no national leader could protect or save his country apart from the rest of the international economic community.

An alternative, but related, reason for the difference between economic and non-economic crises is that they may lead to different attributions of responsibility. Domestic crises, where citizens expect the government to have more control, may tend to inspire harsher judgments. Thus, when a serious economic downturn happens, people may be more likely to blame the government. Such a response may be particularly ironic, because the government probably has minimal control over fluctuations in the economy. Because of the complexities of economics, citizens may be blaming their leader for a problem that his or her policies did not create and cannot directly solve.

On the other hand, a government that does solve the crisis may be seen as merely solving a problem that it had created or, at least, permitted to develop. In contrast, where the government is "thrown into" a crisis clearly caused by others, the leader is less likely to be held accountable for the crisis and more likely to be respected for a "significant accomplishment" if he or she solves it. Of course, this is merely speculative, but future research would do well to examine more fully the reasons underlying why this particular type of difficulty moderates the difficulty–historical success relationship.[5]

The personality cluster correlated with current prestige and perceived accomplishments comprised strength, activeness, effectiveness, innovativeness, flexibility, and—interestingly—being dishonest with the public. The first five are not surprising, although the inclusion of flexibility may reflect the pro-complexity bias of social scientists: others may judge firm adherence to principles more impressive. But the sixth is, indeed, intriguing.

This finding could have multiple causes. Ballard and Suedfeld (1988: 300) suggest: "Perhaps it takes a certain amount of deception or reticence for a good PM to get on with the job. PMs who are 'too' honest may be seen as naive or garrulous, or excessive honesty may be viewed as part of an ineffectual personality configuration." Indeed, it may be that leaders prone to dishonesty *are* more effectual in government; U.S. presidents high in Machiavellianism were more likely to get acts passed during their administration (Simonton, 1986c; but Machiavellianism was approximately equally correlated with both legislative defeats and legislative victories). Although the exact description of the Machiavellianism measure used in his study is not given by Simonton, in general one aspect of the theoretical construct has been a willingness to use deceit for personal gain (see, e.g., Fehr et al., 1992). Thus, willingness to lie has its advantages in the political arena. Certainly, recent presidents noteworthy for frankness—Jimmy Carter leaps to mind—have not enjoyed great prestige.

An alternative and perhaps less cynical interpretation suggests that the difference lies not in the honesty of various PMs but rather in the way that their other traits are perceived. Because historians and the general public alike distrust politicians in general, it may be that, independently of how honest their statements actually are, certain types of PMs are more likely to be viewed as dishonest. Our dishonesty detection mechanisms are imperfect, even in hindsight. Uncompromising positions may be interpreted as being honest due simply to their straightforwardness ("They must believe what they say to be true; otherwise, why are they so definite?").

On the other hand, flexible statements may seem "wishy-washy"— even when they are perfectly sincere attempts at compromise. Indeed, perceived flexibility in policy implementation and perceived honesty in public dealings were negatively related (Ballard & Suedfeld, 1988). The two most flexible PMs (King and Macdonald) were rated as the least honest; conversely, the two least flexible PMs (Mackenzie and Meighen) were rated as the most honest (Ballard & Suedfeld, 1988). Tetlock et al. (1993) reported similar perceptions of highly complex (and therefore flexible) decision makers in a non-political context. Of course, people who are willing to be flexible may actually be more willing to shade the truth.

It is also possible that these perceptions are unique to experts. In a study using 1,076 undergraduate students from the United States, Canada, and Britain, Pancer et al. (1999) found integrity to be one of the three descriptive factors contributing most to the overall evaluation of political figures. Veteran leaders (Mulroney, Bush, and Thatcher) were evaluated more heavily on their perceived integrity than less established figures. More in agreement with the experts, charisma and competence were the other two major factors. Perhaps dishonesty is most likely to be rationalized (and valued) from a cold, objective, analytical, social science perspective.[6]

### Complexity and Historical Judgments: A Re-Analysis

As suggested earlier, the integrative complexity levels of the campaign speeches of potential or actual PMs predicted the winner of the election (Suedfeld et al., 1990). However, does integrative complexity help us understand which PMs are likely to be viewed as prestigious in the eyes of history?

Although no direct study of the relationship between Canadian PMs' complexity and prestige has been reported, for this chapter we performed new analyses combining data from two previous studies (Ballard & Suedfeld, 1988; Suedfeld et al., 1990). Suedfeld et al. (1990) reported the integrative complexity of five PMs' campaign speeches from 1945 to 1974. These PMs included those rated by the respondents in Ballard and Suedfeld's (1988) study as fairly prestigious and successful (King, Trudeau, Pearson), as well as those rated as less successful (Diefenbaker, St. Laurent). For all PMs except King, scores from multiple time periods were reported. In these cases, we now summed the multiple scores to obtain a single integrative complexity score for each PM.

The resulting scores suggest that more complex leaders were more likely to be viewed positively through the eyes of history. The two least successful PMs in the group had the lowest mean complexity scores (Diefenbaker, 1.48, and St. Laurent, 1.58). Trudeau had the highest score (1.97), with Pearson next (1.85). King, the most successful of the five, scored just above St. Laurent (1.6). The correlation between complexity and prestige rating was $r = 0.60$, and between complexity and rated significance of accomplishments, $r = 0.53$.

These correlations were derived from a tiny sample, and the results may be due to chance. Therefore, they should be interpreted as nothing more than suggestive findings calling for further study. However, this result is consistent with three strands of previous research.

First, one of the findings to emerge from the Ballard and Suedfeld

(1988) study is that, like dishonesty, flexibility in policy implementation is associated with historical accolades. Although flexibility ratings and integrative complexity were essentially unrelated in the five PMs under scrutiny here (r = 0.19), integrative complexity theory posits that flexibility frequently involves balancing or accommodating different viewpoints. This is one hallmark of complex thinking.

Second, research on U.S. presidents suggests that those presidents who are rated as intellectually brilliant are higher on historical "greatness ratings." Although, of course, complexity and intelligence or brilliance are different constructs, complexity is positively correlated with some aspects of both intelligence (Suedfeld & Coren, 1992) and academic performance (McDaniel & Lawrence, 1990).

Last, research on revolutionary leaders suggests that, while low complexity is an adaptive characteristic during the revolution, longevity in power after a victorious revolution is predicted by an ability to shift to higher levels of complexity (Suedfeld & Rank, 1976). The present results deal with elections, not revolutions; nevertheless, both sets of findings suggest that long-term success is associated with higher levels of complexity.

Although King, the most prestigious PM of the five under scrutiny here, scored only in the middle of the pack in complexity, other evidence suggests that it may be premature to judge him as generally low in complexity. As reviewed earlier, Ballard (1983) analyzed three PMs during non-crisis, pre-crisis, crisis, and post-crisis times. Averaging across all four times, King's integrative complexity score was considerably higher than his campaign speech average, at approximately 2.1. In contrast, Trudeau's crisis-study mean complexity was approximately 1.8, slightly lower than his campaign speech average. Indeed, King's complexity score in the pre-crisis phase rose above the 2.7 mark—suggesting that he was reliably capable of reaching the level of differentiation. Sir John A. Macdonald, the other PM evaluated in Ballard's (1983) study—and the most highly rated PM in Ballard and Suedfeld (1988)—had scores similar to King's, approximately 2.2. A similar study on various different international figures also included pre-crisis, crisis, and post-crisis complexity scores for Pearson during three separate crises in his tenure as PM (Wallace & Suedfeld, 1988). Pearson, who scored high relative to the other PMs in the Ballard and Suedfeld (1988) study, maintained consistently high levels of integrative complexity throughout all three crises, with a mean score of 4.3.

## DISCUSSION

Social scientists seek to understand what leadership entails, so that we might better understand interpersonal processes and the workings of history and politics. We try to identify and measure the cognitive and social characteristics that contribute to personal success or failure in demanding situations and how these characteristics interact with aspects of the situation. Among these aspects, crucial to political behavior but often ignored by psychologists, is the formal and informal structure that frames the conditions of governing. These templates differ across nations, one good reason to study not only individual countries but systemic prototypes such as presidential versus parliamentary institutions (Kaarbo, 1997).

The importance of the events faced by a given leader is highlighted by the difference between performance during ordinary versus extraordinary situations. Crisis situations tend to highlight the successes of a flexible or complex thinker, and good performance in times of serious trouble perhaps outweighs less than admirable aspects of behavior or character. It would be enlightening to compare leader success and personality during periods that are relatively devoid of extraordinary events, to round out the picture painted by investigators who have concentrated on the crisis behavior of leaders.

It may never be possible to define or predict precisely what combination of factors contributes to the making of a successful leader. Nevertheless, some predictors, or at least correlates, have had demonstrable reliability, and more specific factors will no doubt become apparent as the research continues. One major step has been the recognition that the topic is multidimensional. The behavior or faculties that one wishes to predict or examine may be a useful over-arching category for organizing this research area. Another is the level of challenge faced by a given leader. We have seen that measures of cognitive processing, such as integrative complexity, are sensitive to situations that severely challenge the leader, his or her followers, and the nation. In these situations, complexity of thought shows up sharply against the backdrop of subsequent successes and failures.

In ordinary circumstances, however, cognitive measures such as complexity may become less useful, while measures of social competence and personality become more meaningful. For instance, the intuitive appeal of the motivational matching hypothesis derives from its attempt to capture the harmony between leader policy and public demand that should theoretically underlie leadership success in election outcome and longevity in office.

As psychologists we should bear in mind that the behavior of leaders is only a subset of the behavior of people. The cross-cultural or international comparative study of leadership should take its place within the broader study of cultural and national differences and characteristics (e.g., in decision making) (Weber & Hsee, 2000).

## ACKNOWLEDGMENT

The preparation of this chapter was aided by a grant from the Social Sciences and Humanities Research Council of Canada to the first author.

## NOTES

1. Although this term is not in use for the Canadian PM, who is both the executive and legislative leader, we use it as a simple label to identify heads of government, including presidents, PMs, and chancellors.

2. The historical synopses are based on Granatstein & Hillmer, 1999.

3. The outcomes of the crises were as follows: (1) Macdonald confirmed the sentence, and Riel was hanged. Although Macdonald's Conservative Party lost seats in Quebec in the next election, it retained power. (2) King sent 16,000 draftees overseas. His major supporter in Quebec, Louis St. Laurent (the next PM), helped to persuade Quebecois that he was forced to take this step by the massive casualty list. Quebec voted for King's Liberal Party, which won the next election. (3) Trudeau imposed martial law in Montreal, with hundreds of separatists—by no means all terrorists—arrested. The labor minister was murdered by his kidnappers, which united much of the country against them; the kidnappers were caught and tried, the terrorist (although not the separatist) movement disappeared, and Trudeau's Liberal Party won the next election.

4. The Liberals won the 1997 election, with a commanding parliamentary majority. The Reform Party took second place as the official Opposition, the Bloc kept the majority of seats from Quebec, and both the NDP and the Progressive Conservatives increased their representation, but not by very much.

5. Economic depression is also the only form of national crisis that does not lead to consistent complexity decreases among non-political or, at least, non-governmental elites. This group—novelists, scientists, journalists, artists, and the like—shows a drop in the complexity of its letters, articles, speeches and so on, during times of war but not in bad economic times (Porter & Suedfeld, 1981; Suedfeld, 1985).

6. This argument is weakened by recent opinion polls in the United States that showed that a large segment of the public believed President Clinton to be a liar but nevertheless thought he was doing well in his official role.

Chapter 2

# Political Leadership and the Democratic Peace: The Operational Code of Prime Minister Tony Blair

Mark Schafer and Stephen G. Walker

## INTRODUCTION

Tony Blair's ascendance to the office of prime minister marked the beginning of a new generation of political leadership in British politics. He followed the post–World War II generation of British leaders in the United Kingdom, which reached the zenith of its influence during the Thatcher era and did not really recede until Blair's Labour Party unseated the Conservative Party government led by John Major. When leaders change, it is normal and easy to ask, What difference does a leader make? Answering is harder than asking this question, however, which requires both a comparative and a theoretical perspective. Contemporary operational code analysis offers both of these analytical vantage points.

The study of a leader's operational code has been characterized as "the most widely used concept relating to the link between belief systems and international relations. . . . [O]ver two dozen studies have used it in an attempt to explain the foreign policy choices of leaders . . . [and] . . . in virtually every case, tended to find the concept very useful as a research technique" (Smith, 1988: 20, 22). While this assessment is somewhat dated, it does suggest that operational code analysis may be useful in profiling Tony Blair's leadership propensities in the foreign policy domain. The operational code construct is a complex set of elements defined initially by Leites (1951, 1953) as the conceptions of political strategy in Bolshevik ideology that functioned as expressions of the Bolshevik character. This initial conceptualization defined these beliefs as parts of the leader's personality that expressed motivational biases as well as represented the appraisal of political realities. It was an approach to the study of political personality as well as a cognitive model of the leader's worldview (Smith, 1968).

In his review of the Leites studies of the Bolsheviks, George (1969) reconceptualized a leader's operational code as simply a political belief system in which some elements (philosophical beliefs) guide the diagnosis of the context for action, and others (instrumental beliefs) prescribe the most effective strategy and tactics for achieving goals. His work and the subsequent work by others (e.g., Holsti, 1970; Walker, 1977) focused on images of "other," rather than "self," as the most important beliefs and on the processes of cognition, rather than affect (George, 1969, 1979). This exclusive focus on beliefs at the expense of extra-cognitive aspects of personality in the 1970s placed operational code analysis within the general cognitivist research program in world politics (Tetlock, 1998).

A re-analysis of the operational code typology developed by Holsti (1977) redirected attention in the 1980s to self-images and affective dynamics, a focus equally consistent with the prototypical study of the Bolsheviks by Leites (Walker, 1983, 1990). These two models converged during the 1990s in the study of cognitive attributes with affective tags as valenced ($\pm$) indexes of a leader's diagnostic, choice, and shift propensities (Walker et al., 1998, 1999). In this synthesis, a leader's philosophical beliefs represent reality and indicate a leader's diagnostic propensities, while instrumental beliefs express identity and indicate a leader's choice and shift propensities among different goals and courses of action.

George's (1969) original formulation of the five philosophical and five instrumental beliefs is still used as research questions to profile a leader's operational code (see Figure 2.1). But contemporary operational code analysis no longer relies on answers to these questions in the form of hermeneutic interpretations of a leader's speeches and other public statements. The Verbs In Context System (VICS) of content analysis has been developed to extract indexes of a leader's philosophical and instrumental beliefs. The indexes are constructed from coding the positive ($+$) and negative ($-$) valences of verbs uttered by the leader and then scaling them into positions on a continuum of cooperation and conflict behavior divided into words and deeds. These indexes form a kind of "belief system," but they do not have the kind of cognitive consistency postulated by George (1969, 1979) and Holsti (1977; see also Converse, 1964).

Any properties of centrality and interdependence are partly artifacts of the mathematical logic of the indexes. That is, the indexes for philosophical beliefs are statistical aggregations at different levels of generality for words or deeds attributed to "others" in the political universe, and the indexes for instrumental beliefs are their counterparts based on words and deeds attributed to "self" in the political universe (see Figure

**Figure 2.1**
**George's Ten Questions about Operational Code Beliefs**

---

**The Philosophical Beliefs in an Operational Code**

P-1. What is the "essential" nature of political life? Is the political universe essentially one of harmony or conflict? What is the fundamental character of one's political opponents?

P-2. What are the prospects for the eventual realization of one's fundamental values and aspirations? Can one be optimistic, or must one be pessimistic on this score; and in what respects the one and/or the other?

P-3. Is the political future predictable? In what sense and to what extent?

P-4. How much "control" or "mastery" can one have over historical development? What is one's role in "moving" and "shaping" history in the desired direction?

P-5. What is the role of "chance" in human affairs and in historical development?

**The Instrumental Beliefs in an Operational Code**

I-1. What is the best approach for selecting goals or objectives for political action?

I-2. How are the goals of action pursued most effectively?

I-3. How are the risks of political action calculated, controlled, and accepted?

I-4. What is the best "timing" of action to advance one's interests?

I-5. What is the utility and role of different means for advancing one's interests?

---

2.2). Collectively, they measure aspects of a generalized "self" schema and a generalized "other" schema, which are capable of disaggregation by domain and target. While it is possible to argue that the generalized indexes are useful in some theoretical contexts (e.g., Wendt, 1999; Walker et al., 1999; Walker, 2000), it is not the perspective taken in this study of Prime Minister Tony Blair.

Instead, we move from a general conceptualization of a single operational code for a political leader to a domain-specific conceptualization that allows for the existence of different "states of mind" in different contexts (Walker, 1995). The former assumes that a leader's operational code beliefs form a coherent worldview and response repertoire that are internally consistent and relatively static. The latter assumes more of a "personality-in-situation" perspective that treats both cognitive and affective attributes of a leader's personality as dynamic.

Happily, we do not have to take a position here on which general approach to the study of leaders is more fruitful, a question that has become rather controversial (see Eysenck & Eysenck, 1985; Mischel, 1977). Our analytical tools allow us to treat these differences as more

**Figure 2.2**
**Indexes for a Leader's Operational Code**

---

### DIAGNOSTIC PROPENSITIES

| Elements | Index* | Interpretation |
|---|---|---|
| D-1. NATURE OF THE POLITICAL UNIVERSE (Image of Others) | % Positive minus %Negative Other Attributions | +1.0 friendly to −1.0 hostile |
| D-2. REALIZATION OF POLITICAL VALUES (Optimism/Pessimism) | Mean Intensity of Transitive Other Attributions divided by 3 | +1.0 optimistic to −1.0 pessimistic |
| D-3. POLITICAL FUTURE (Predictability of Other Tactics) | 1 minus IQV** for Other Attributions | 1.0 predictable to 0.0 uncertain |
| D-4. HISTORICAL DEVELOPMENT (Locus of Control) | Self Attributions divided by [Self plus Other Attributions] | 1.0 high to 0.0 low self-control |
| D-5. ROLE OF CHANCE (Absence of Control) | 1 minus [Political Future × Historical Development Index] | 1.0 high role to 0.0 low role |

### CHOICE AND SHIFT PROPENSITIES

| Elements | Index | Interpretation |
|---|---|---|
| C-1. APPROACH TO GOALS (Direction of Strategy) | %Positive minus %Negative Self Attributions | +1.0 high cooperation to −1.0 high conflict |
| C-2. PURSUIT OF GOALS (Intensity of Tactics) | Mean Intensity of Transitive Self Attributions divided by 3 | +1.0 high cooperation to −1.0 high conflict |
| S-3. RISK ORIENTATION (Predictability of Tactics) | 1 minus Index of Qualitative Variation for Self Attributions | 1.0 risk acceptant to 0.0 risk averse |
| S-4. TIMING OF ACTION (Flexibility of Tactics) | 1 minus Absolute Value [%X minus %Y Self Attributions] | 1.0 high to 0.0 low shift propensity |
| a. Coop. v. Conf. Tactics*** | Where X = Coop. and Y = Conf. | |
| b. Word v. Deed Tactics | Where X = Word and Y = Deed | |
| C-5. UTILITY OF MEANS (Exercise of Power | Percentages for Exercise of Power Categories a through f | +1.0 very frequent to 0.0 infrequent |
| a. Reward | a's frequency divided by total | |
| b. Promise | b's frequency divided by total | |
| c. Appeal/Support | c's frequency divided by total | |
| d. Oppose/Resist | d's frequency divided by total | |
| e. Threaten | e's frequency divided by total | |
| f. Punish | f's frequency divided by total | |

---

*All indexes vary between 0 and 1.0 except for D-1, D-2, C-1, and C-2, which vary between −1.0 and +1.0. D-2 and C-2 are divided by 3 to standardize the range (Walker, Schafer, & Young, 1998).

**The Index of Qualitative Variation is the number of different pairs of observations in a distribution over the maximum possible number of different pairs for a distribution with the same number of cases and the same number of variable categories (Watson and McGaw, 1980:88).

***Coop. = Cooperation; Conf. = Conflict.

localized methodological and empirical questions within a particular study. The logic of the VICS indexes allows us to calculate them first for a leader's general operational code and then disaggregate them for different domains of the political universe.

## POLITICAL LEADERSHIP AND THE DEMOCRATIC PEACE

The political domains that interest us are defined by the current interest in the "democratic peace" phenomenon—the general contention that democracies are more peaceful than other kinds of regimes in the conduct of foreign policy. This assertion rests partly on the rhetoric of the cold war between the United States and the Soviet Union and, more generally, on twentieth-century liberalism's crusade at the end of both World War I and World War II to make the world safe for democracy. There are also more serious philosophical and empirical grounds for making this claim. Kant's philosophical argument that democracies are more peaceful and the empirical findings of several social scientists have both made it a more credible intellectual position and refined the basis for making the argument (e.g., Doyle, 1986; Russett, 1993; Maoz, 1998).

It turns out that democracies are more peaceful when the meaning of this statement is limited to "democracies never (or rarely) fight one another," which excludes more universal generalizations that (1) they fight less than other kinds of states or (2) engage less frequently in lower levels of conflict behavior (e.g., join alliances, exercise economic sanctions, or engage in covert actions). While this empirical finding is rather robust (Maoz, 1998), it is not yet clear what causal mechanisms account for this generalization (Elman, 1997). Two general theoretical accounts have populated the research in this area.

One explanation suggests that the pattern of peace is due to the increased institutional accountability of democratic regimes to the societies that they govern. In other words, public opinion and electoral punishment deter leaders of democratic states from making a decision for war. While they will fight when attacked, pairs of democracies are unlikely to fight with one another because these mechanisms of accountability are operating in both states. They are totally or at least partly absent in disputes between pairs of non-democracies or mixed pairs of states (Russett, 1993).

The other explanation is a cultural one that emphasizes the norms of democratic domestic politics with their emphasis on deliberation and negotiation rather than the coercion and threats that characterize domestic politics in non-democratic regimes. In this account a transfer effect occurs in the conduct of international politics between democratic states. Because they share the same norms and because these norms emphasize the peaceful settlement of disputes, two democratic states are less prone to escalate a conflict to war between them than a pair of dictatorships or a mixed pair of states (Russett, 1993; Dixon, 1994). This cultural explanation appears to have more empirical support than the institutional one (Russett, 1993).

The cultural explanation is also couched in terms of shared normative beliefs, which makes it congenial to further explanation by political psychologists (Hermann & Kegley, 1995). It also raises some research questions about the intervening processes and mechanisms that link cultural norms and state behavior. A particularly crucial one is whether the leaders of democracies have actually internalized these beliefs about the political universe and the most effective strategies and tactics of political action. More generally, is there variance among democratic leaders on these dimensions, and are they substantively important? For example, are leaders of parliamentary democracies less war-prone than leaders of presidential democracies? (Elman, 1995).

While we cannot address the more general question of variance across leaders and types of democracies with a single-case research design, we can ask the more limited question of whether Prime Minister Tony Blair has internalized the logic of the democratic peace argument in his operational code beliefs. In order to do so, we turn now to the description of his general operational code and then to a comparison of his philosophical and instrumental beliefs regarding relations with democracies and non-democracies.

The comparisons are guided by the following hypotheses, which we infer from the democratic peace argument's cultural explanation for why democracies do not fight one another (and why democracies do fight non-democracies). We do not address the institutional explanation, because we do not have data on public opinion or elections, which are the mechanisms that inform this explanation. If the logic of the cultural explanation is correct, then we hypothesize that:

H-1. A democratic leader will internalize the belief that democracies are committed to the peaceful resolution of disputes.

H-2. A democratic leader will internalize the belief that non-democracies are not committed to the peaceful resolution of disputes.

From these two hypotheses we draw the following general test implication that if a democratic leader does internalize these beliefs, then a democratic leader's operational code ought to be more cooperative and/or less conflictual toward other democracies than toward dictatorships.

Specifically, regarding relations with other democracies, a democratic leader should have philosophical beliefs that manifest a more friendly image of "other" (P-1), greater optimism in realizing fundamental political values in dealing with "other" (P-2), and higher predictability by "other" (P-3). The leader's philosophical belief in the ability to control historical development (P-4) is less likely to be affected one way or the other, because it reflects the power relationship between self and other rather than their relations of hostility or friendship toward one another. The belief in the role of chance (P-5) may be lower, because its index is partly influenced by (P-3) the higher predictability of "other" (see Figure 2.2).

Also, if "other" is a democracy, then a democratic leader's instrumental beliefs about "self" should manifest a higher cooperative strategic approach (I-1) and a more cooperative tactical (I-2) intensity, a more acceptant risk orientation (I-3), and a lower propensity to shift between cooperation and conflict tactics (I-4a). The propensity to shift between words and deeds (I-4b) is less likely to differ in dealing with democracies, because words and deeds may be either cooperative or conflictual. Finally, we would expect that a democratic leader's use of different means (I-5) would be more highly skewed toward appeal/support statements, promises, and rewards in dealing with other democracies, because of the more cooperative orientation at the levels of tactics and strategy.

## RESEARCH METHODS

In order to test these hypotheses, sampling frames were developed from public sources of the prime minister's speeches. They included only those speeches that contained at least 1,500 words to provide enough data per speech to construct the operational code indices. Each speech was then coded using the VICS procedures. Space does not permit an extensive discussion of the coding procedures here (see Walker et al., 1998), but a brief description is appropriate. The recording unit is the verb-based utterance, which finesses the potential complication of some speakers using very long sentences and others using short sentences. Each verb is identified in context. The utterance is identified as a self utterance (I, us, we, Britain, etc.) or an other utterance (they, you, Israel, Hussein, etc.). The verb is identified as a transitive or an intransitive verb and as a positive/cooperative or negative/conflictual attribution. If the verb is transitive, it is categorized as a word or deed and placed in the appropriate verb category: cooperative words in either appeal or promise; cooperative deeds in reward; conflictual words in oppose or threaten; and conflictual deeds in punish.

Two coders spent, on average, six hours in training. They were tested against pre-coded samples; errors and disagreements were discussed and corrected. This process continued until inter-coder agreement reached at least 90%, at which time the coders were assigned speeches from the sample. Throughout the coding process, we randomly sampled sets of 20 utterances from each coder and conducted inter-coder reliability tests. These averaged 94% agreement.

We used two different sources of speeches by Prime Minister Blair for our sampling frames; both sources are official government Web sites that make complete-text speeches given by Blair available on the Internet. From the first set (www.parliament.uk) we drew speeches given by Blair in the House of Commons. From the second set (www.number-10.gov.uk) we drew speeches that were given in other venues, such as to various domestic audiences and in international settings. Together, these sources represent the full range of speeches given by Blair during his first term in office (from 1997 to the present). In all, 17 speeches were randomly selected and coded. For the analyses below, we included only material that made reference to international topics by Blair, thus omitting utterances that he made regarding the domestic domain.

## TONY BLAIR'S GENERAL OPERATIONAL CODE

The index scores for the prime minister's general operational code can be found in Table 2.1. How does Tony Blair view the political universe? To answer this question, we turn to his scores on the philosophical indexes of his operational code. Blair has a view of the political universe ($P-1 = +.02$) that is balanced between cooperation and conflict and a similarly mixed, though leaning slightly to pessimistic, outlook on the prospects for realizing fundamental political goals ($P-2 = -.07$). Blair sees the political future as very unpredictable ($P-3 = .03$), though he sees himself as having a high degree of control over historical developments ($P-4 = .78$). Rounding out his philosophical indexes, Blair attributes a very high role to chance in the international arena ($P-5 = .98$); this index is influenced heavily by his view of politics as unpredictable.

The values for P-1 and P-2 are notably lower compared to those reported elsewhere for U.S. presidents (see Walker et al., 1998, 1999; Schafer & Crichlow, 2000; Dille, 2000; Walker & Schafer, 2000). While generally thought of as having similar outlooks and objectives in global politics, as manifested by the special "relationship" between the United States and the United Kingdom (Wolfers & Martin, 1956), these initial data on Blair suggest a more complex situation. At the very least, these data suggest that comparative analysis of U.S. presidents and U.K. prime ministers would be interesting and appropriate, though certainly beyond the scope of the present chapter (Waltz, 1967).

Given these views of the political universe, how does Blair think "self" ought to behave? To assess this part of his operational code, we turn to the index scores for the instrumental indexes. Blair believes that a very

Table 2.1
The General Operational Code of Prime Minister Blair

| Philosophical Questions | Index |
| --- | --- |
| P-1  Nature of the Political Universe | +.02 |
| P-2  Prospects for Realization of Political Values (optimism/pessimism) | −.07 |
| P-3  Predictability of Political Universe | .03 |
| P-4  Belief in Ability to Control Historical Development | .78 |
| P-5  Role of Chance | .98 |
| **Instrumental Questions** | |
| I-1  Approach to Goals (Direction of Strategy) | +.72 |
| I-2  Pursuit of Goals (Intensity of Tactics) | +.43 |
| I-3  Risk Orientation (Diversity of Tactics) | .16 |
| I-4  Timing of Action | |
| I-4a  Flexibility of Cooperation/Conflict Tactics | .26 |
| I-4b  Flexibility of Word/Deed Tactics | .47 |
| I-5  Utility of Means | |
| Appeal | .45 |
| Promise | .21 |
| Reward | .21 |
| Oppose | .06 |
| Threaten | .05 |
| Punish | .02 |

cooperation-oriented direction is the best strategy to pursue (I-1 = +.72). He further believes that definitely cooperative tactics are appropriate (I-2 = +.43), though his score on this index is somewhat more moderate than his score on I-1. Blair is fairly risk-averse (I-3 = .16), meaning that he diversifies his choice of tactics well. However, he is more apt to diversify his tactics across word and deed categories, where his score is in the medium range of diversity (I-4b = .47), than he is across the conflict and cooperation categories, where his score is in the low range of diversity (I-4a = .26).

In terms of specific tactical categories (I-5 utility of means indexes), Blair sees very high utility in the appeals/support category (.45). Indeed, he relies on this type of tactic more than twice as often as the next most frequently used tactic. He relies on rewards (.21) and promises (.21) quite a bit as well, with both falling into the high range of the scale. All three of the conflict categories of tactics, however, are in the low to very low range. Of these three, Blair is more likely to rely on the oppose/resist category (.06), though this is closely followed by threats (.05). He finds the least utility in the punish tactic (.02), which he uses less than half the time of either of the other two conflict categories.

Overall, even though Blair assesses the political universe as mixed between conflict and cooperation, he perceives that the best way to proceed is by pursuing cooperative tactics. He sees himself as having quite a bit of control in the political arena, but he also sees politics as fairly unpredictable. Rhetorical responses are his favorite means of action: appeal/support was the most common tactical category overall, while the corresponding category on the conflict side, oppose/resist, was the most commonly used of the three conflict categories. Finally, unlike his scores for the first two philosophical indexes, Blair much more closely resembles typical U.S. presidents with his scores on the first two instrumental indexes (Walker et al., 1998, 1999; Schafer & Crichlow, 2000; Dille, 2000; Walker & Schafer, 2000).

## DEMOCRATIC VERSUS NON-DEMOCRATIC OPERATIONAL CODES

We now turn to our main substantive research question—the ways in which Prime Minister Blair's operational code may differ in relations with democratic and non-democratic regimes. For each utterance we coded whether Blair was discussing a democratic or non-democratic "other." For "self" utterances (the basis for his instrumental indexes), this meant coding the target of the action by Blair, or the grammatical object of the sentence. For "other" utterances (the basis for his philosophical indexes), this meant coding the regime type of the grammatical subject of the sentence. The interpretation of these coded utterances is similar to the interpretation of the general operational code indexes discussed above, but with more targeted information. The philosophical indexes now differentiate Blair's views of democratic actors from his image of non-democratic actors in the political universe. The instrumental indexes now indicate how Blair thinks he should act toward democratic targets versus non-democratic states.

In his general operational code above, we simply aggregated all utterances across all coded speeches to derive his index scores. However, now we have a question that requires statistical comparison, and so we rely on the speech as the unit of analysis as we have done elsewhere (Walker et al., 1998, 1999). Here, we technically use the regime-type part of each speech as the unit of analysis. After differentiating each utterance by regime type, we then aggregated those utterances by speech, thus (potentially) resulting in a democratic and a non-democratic operational code for each speech.

Although we sampled a total of 17 speeches by Blair, it is not the case that he spoke of democratic and non-democratic actors in every speech. Thus, in some speeches we were not able to compute a democratic operational code, and in others we could not compute a non-democratic operational code. The analyses that follow are based on 15 speeches in the democratic domain and 8 speeches in the non-democratic domain. Each utterance was used in no more than one of the regime-type operational codes, thus resulting in orthogonal data. We report p-values for one-way Analysis of Variance (ANOVA) results for each index, with the regime-differentiated speech as the unit of analysis and regime type as the grouping variable. The p-values are one-tailed tests for directional hypotheses and two-tailed for non-directional tests (the latter are noted in Table 2.2).

The upper half of Table 2.2 presents the results of Prime Minister Blair's philosophical indexes for democracies and non-democracies. On three of the five indexes, Blair has a very different assessment of politics across the two regime types. On the nature of the political universe (P-1), the prime minister sees democratic actors as being fairly friendly (+.37), but non-democratic actors as definitely hostile (−.42). The difference between these two regime types is significant, $F(21,1) = 12.23$, $p = .001$. This dissimilarity between regime types is mirrored in his assessment of his prospects for realizing fundamental political goals (P-2). Blair is somewhat optimistic in this area when considering democracies (+.22) but somewhat pessimistic for non-democracies (−.33); these two are also statistically different, $F(21,1) = 12.007$, $p = .001$. There is also a divergence in Blair's belief in his ability to control historical development (P-4). When dealing with democracies, he has a high belief in his ability to control (.81), whereas with non-democracies his belief in his control is only medium (.54). Blair sees himself as much more of an influential player capable of controlling democracies as compared to non-democracies. These differences are significant, $F(21,1) = 13.54$, $p > .001$.

The two remaining philosophical indexes do not differ across regime type. Interestingly, he sees non-democracies as somewhat more predictable than democracies (P-3; .31 vs. .46), though the scores are not statistically distinct, $F(21,1) = 1.477$, $p = .238$ (two-tailed). His scores on the role of chance (P-5) show virtually no difference across regime types; Blair sees the role of chance as similarly high for both democracies and non-democracies (.75 and .77, respectively).

Overall, it is clear that Blair sees the political universe in differentiated terms when it comes to democracies and non-democracies. As hypothesized, Blair sees democracies as friendly and is optimistic about political prospects with them. Not surprisingly, given his role in Europe, he sees

Table 2.2
**Indexes of Prime Minister Blair's Democratic and Non-Democratic Operational Codes**

| | Democratic | Non-Democratic | F(21,1) | p* |
|---|---|---|---|---|
| *Philosophical Questions* | | | | |
| P-1 Nature of the Political Universe | +.37 | −.42 | 12.234 | .001 |
| P-2 Prospects for Realization of Political Values (optimism/pessimism) | +.22 | −.33 | 12.007 | .001 |
| P-3 Predictability of Political Universe | .31 | .46 | 1.477 | .238 |
| P-4 Belief in Ability to Control Historical Development | .81 | .54 | 13.540 | < .001 |
| P-5 Role of Chance | .75 | .77 | .050 | .412 |
| *Instrumental Questions* | | | | |
| I-1 Approach to Goals (Direction of Strategy) | +.78 | +.20 | 16.526 | < .001 |
| I-2 Pursuit of Goals (Intensity of Tactics) | +.47 | +.03 | 28.663 | < .001 |
| I-3 Risk Orientation (Diversity of Tactics) | .24 | .25 | .012 | .915 |
| I-4 Timing of Action | | | | |
|    I-4a Flexibility of Cooperation/Conflict Tactics | .17 | .65 | 15.942 | < .001 |
|    I-4b Flexibility of Word/Deed Tactics | .46 | .36 | .849 | .367 |
| I-5 Utility of Means | | | | |
|    Appeal | .46 | .40 | .395 | .268 |
|    Promise | .22 | .12 | 5.663 | .013 |
|    Reward | .22 | .08 | 8.978 | .004 |
|    Oppose | .06 | .10 | 1.785 | .098 |
|    Threaten | .03 | .20 | 14.523 | < .001 |
|    Punish | .01 | .09 | 11.480 | .002 |

*One-tailed p-values for directional hypotheses except for P-4 and I-4, which are two-tailed p-values for non-directional hypotheses.

himself as having great influence and control in the domain of democracies. Non-democracies, on the other hand, are seen as unfriendly and posing obstacles to his political goals. Blair sees himself as having much less control over non-democracies than over democracies.

We turn now to the prime minister's instrumental indexes to assess his strategic choice propensities across the two domain types. Scores and statistical tests for Blair's instrumental indexes are presented in the lower half of Table 2.2. Several of the mean scores are statistically different across regime type, thus supporting the general hypothesis that Blair operates differently when dealing with democracies and non-democracies. As hypothesized, the direction of Blair's strategic orientation (I-1) is much more cooperative with democracies than with non-democracies. For democracies, Blair is very cooperative (+.78); with non-democracies he still operates on the cooperative end of the strategy continuum, but his score is only somewhat cooperative (+.20). These two mean scores are statistically different, $F(21,1) = 16.526$, $p < .001$. Likewise, in terms of the intensity of his tactics (I-2), Blair is much more cooperative with democracies than non-democracies (+.47 vs. +.03), and these mean scores are also statistically different, $F(21,1) = 28.663$, $p < .001$. This tendency shows up further in the flexibility of Blair's tactics in terms of cooperation and conflict. Blair has a low propensity to shift away from cooperative tactics with democracies (.17), whereas with non-democracies he shows a high level of flexibility to shift between conflict and cooperation (.65); $F(21,1) = 15.942$, $p < .001$.

The remaining significant instrumental indexes for Blair are all in the I-5 category (utility of means). Blair is significantly more likely to make promises and give rewards to democracies than to non-democracies, while he is more likely to make threats and punishments to non-democracies. All of these means are statistically different across regime types at the $p < .05$ level or higher (see Table 2.2). One other utility of means index approaches significance. Blair has a slight propensity to issue more oppose/resist statements to non-democracies than to democracies (.10 versus .06); $F(21,1) = 1.785$, $p = .098$.

Interestingly, Blair finds the tactic appeal/support to be equally useful across regime types; the difference in these means is not significant, $F(21,1) = .395$, $p = .268$. This is the transitive verb category that Blair uses more than any other—it clearly is his dominant tactical choice—and he finds it equally useful when dealing with both democracies and non-democracies. Blair is also similar in his approach to the two different regime types in terms of his risk orientation (I-3) and in terms of the flexibility of his tactics between words and deeds (I-4b). These latter two non-significant indexes show that Blair uses a similar pattern of mixing his tactics across democracies and non-democracies.

Overall, in terms of the prime minister's instrumental indexes, the results are very much as hypothesized from the cultural explanation for the democratic peace. The general pattern is that Blair tends to be more cooperative in his choice and shift propensities toward democracies than toward non-democracies. This pattern shows up in the direction of his strategy (I-1), in the intensity of his tactics (I-2), in his cooperative-conflictual shift propensity (I-4a), and generally in the utility of means categories (I-5). Blair tends to be similarly risk-averse (I-3) across regime types, and he diversifies his word-deed choice propensities similarly for democracies and non-democracies as well. His favorite utility of means category (I-5 appeal/support), where he makes normative "should"- and "ought"-type statements, dominates his transitive verb categories similarly for both democracies and non-democracies.

## CONCLUSION

The preceding analysis of Prime Minister Tony Blair's operational code sheds some light on two topics of general interest. One is the debate among psychologists over whether "personality" ought to be conceptualized as relatively static or more dynamic across situations. A closely related question is whether situational variables "swamp" the impact of personality variables in explaining the behavior of states. Situational variables in the foreign policy universe often include such staples as the balance of power and other materialistic elements that define an occasion for decision. The other topic of general interest is how the democratic peace operates. The related question here is, What mechanisms, institutional or cultural, actually account for the lawlike regularity that marks the absence of war between democratic states?

Although it is difficult to generalize with much confidence from a case study because of the limitations in observing covariance for a single case, it is nonetheless possible to draw some tentative conclusions (King et al., 1994). By disaggregating the observations of Tony Blair's operational code into different domains of the political universe, we were able to compare his diagnostic, choice, and shift propensities toward democracies and dictatorships. In doing so, we found evidence that supports the cultural explanation for the democratic peace and a less static view of personality.

The VICS indices for the philosophical beliefs in Blair's operational code diverged sharply and significantly in the hypothesized directions regarding democracies versus non-democracies, indicating a friendly versus hostile image of "other" and an optimistic versus pessimistic orientation toward the realization of fundamental values. Similar strong patterns of support were evident in the VICS indexes for instrumental beliefs. Blair was significantly more cooperative in both his strategic and tactical choice propensities toward democracies. His shift propensity between cooperation and conflict was significantly lower in dealing with democracies, and he believed that promises and rewards were significantly more useful in relating to democracies, while threats and punishments were significantly more useful in dealing with non-democracies.

These findings are consistent both with the cultural explanation for the democratic peace and with a more dynamic conceptualization of "personality-in-situation" (Smith, 1968). The cultural explanation is supported because it appears that Blair has, indeed, internalized the logic and beliefs of the democratic peace argument. The dynamic conceptualization of "personality-in-situation" (Smith, 1968) is supported because Blair clearly has different modal "personalities," manifested as belief systems (Greenstein, 1987: 2–3), when operating in situational contexts that differ by regime type. It appears prudent, therefore, as a methodological procedure to disaggregate the VICS indexes for a leader's general operational code whenever the data permit and the research questions call for it.

However, we cannot conclude that personality variables "wash out" of the analysis because we do not have independent measures of situation and personality variables (Greenstein, 1987). The operational code beliefs that we attribute to Blair could be shared cultural beliefs among the British elite or institutional role variables associated with the office of prime minister. The intensity and persistence of these beliefs could also be individual differences associated with the prime minister himself. Different British leaders could be socialized more or less effectively into their roles and associated norms, including the norms associated with differentiating between democracies and non-democracies in conducting international relations.

Without a bigger sample of leaders from among the British elite, it is not feasible to address these questions more directly. Therefore, we caution against generalizing widely from these results for Prime Minister Tony Blair regarding the relative influence of personality versus situation as sources of a leader's behavior because of the possibility of "selection effects" associated with the non-random sampling of Blair as our case study (Geddes, 1990).

## ACKNOWLEDGMENT

We are grateful to Scott Crichlow, Scott Payne, and Wendy Theodore for their research assistance in coding and entering data.

Chapter 3

# The 1996 Russian Presidential Candidates: A Content Analysis of Motivational Configuration and Conceptual/Integrative Complexity

Linda O. Valenty and Eric Shiraev

## INTRODUCTION

The measurement and evaluation of motives as applied to political leaders and performed utilizing existing speech and interview data have a rich and enduring history in political psychology (cf. the works of Hermann, 1980b, 1984a; Winter, 1991a, 1992a; Winter & Carlson, 1988; Winter & Stewart, 1977; Winter et al., 1991; among others) Similarly, the measurement and evaluation of cognitive style and structure as applied to political leaders and performed using speech and interview data have also received detailed attention in the literature (cf. the works of Santmire et al., 1998; Suedfeld & Bluck, 1988; Suedfeld & Rank, 1976; Tetlock, 1983, 1985; Tetlock & Boettger, 1989; Tetlock & Tyler, 1996; Walker & Watson, 1992; Wallace et al., 1996; among others). Most of these studies dealt with such issues as individual cognitive complexity—as an underlying factor—in crisis management, conflict resolution and negotiations, foreign policy decision making, and leadership behavior. These studies demonstrated that leaders' cognitive styles, expressed as differing levels of conceptual/integrative complexity in particular, are linked to different behavioral outcomes in domestic and foreign policy fields.

   The current study utilizes both lines of theoretical development to perform a content analysis of motivational pattern and conceptual/integrative complexity for former Russian president Boris Yeltsin and his closest contenders in the 1996 Russian presidential contest: Gennadi Zyuganov, Aleksandr Lebed, Grigory Yavlinsky, and Vladimir Zhirinovsky. This chapter compares motivational profiles and conceptual/integrative complexity for each of these prominent Russian politicians and then proceeds to give particular focus to a political figure who gained prominence during and after the 1996 electoral cycle: retired Russian army lieutenant general and later governor of Krasnoyarsk, Aleksandr I. Lebed. To accomplish this particular part of the analysis, data are drawn from interviews within chronological divisions spanning the major epochs of Lebed's professional life.

Lebed became a primary focus for this research due to his popularity with the Russian people, general acknowledgment that he was one of a handful of serious contenders for the presidential elections in 1996, and his tenuous relationship with the Russian establishment in general. Lebed's strong presence in Russian politics created a nexus that was at once unpredictable and charged. The Russian people, occupied with the experience of rapid and inexorable movement from a highly controlled economic and political matrix to free market competition, have endured this transition as a rather chaotic evolution absent the support of fully developed democratic institutions. As a result, the necessity for strong leadership has been extraordinarily apparent. At the same time, under Yeltsin, the government suffered from a physically unstable leader and ongoing conflictual internal arrangements, continually vulnerable to critiques from Lebed and others. Further, General Lebed's presidential candidacy in 1996 engendered a surge of public support.

His candidacy, his third-place finish in the June 16 first round election, the influence of his decision to throw his support to Yeltsin in the runoff election (in the presence of similar offers from both Yeltsin and Zyuganov), his subsequent appointment to and then ouster from an official role as secretary of the Security Council and national security advisor in the Yeltsin government, and his successful election on May 18, 1998, as governor of Krasnoyarsk[1] all indicated that this particular political actor merited attention.

### The 1996 Russian Presidential Elections

The first Russian presidential campaigns of the post-Soviet era occurred early in the evolution of the country's multiparty system. By late 1995 the developing Russian party system was extremely fragmented, polarized, and unstable. A wide range of ideological perspectives and societal interests was represented, and many leaders had strong personal followings. In the December 1995 Duma elections, 43 parties and electoral blocs competed, and 18 garnered at least 1% of the party-list votes. The communist parties in particular (there were several currents in the communist movement) gained 30% of the party-list vote (Stavrakis 1996: 14). Gennady Zyuganov's Communist Party of the Russian Federation led the way with 22%, and although Vladimir Zhirinovsky's Liberal

Democrats had lost some support since the 1993 elections, they still were able to place second with 11%.

President Boris Yeltsin, however, consistently maintained a position that was "above politics" and specifically outside party lines (White et al., 1996: 135). This nonpartisan demeanor was specifically designed to consolidate the millions of Russians who did not identify with any of the competing parties vying for electoral support at that time (White et al., 1996). However, in January and February 1996, Yeltsin's prospects for re-election looked dim: only 8% of those polled in January 1996 pronounced themselves "satisfied" or "mostly satisfied" with their life, fewer than 1% considered the political situation "favorable" or the economic situation "good," and only 6% said they were planning to vote for Yeltsin (Treisman 1996), whose popularity had declined steadily since 1992 (White et al., 1996: 167–70).

It was widely believed and suggested by some of Yeltsin's advisors that the only way that he could stay in office would be to cancel the presidential elections. Instead, Yeltsin executed one of the most surprisingly deft political turnarounds in recent history, winning a plurality in the first-round presidential balloting on June 16 (competing with nine other candidates) and constructing a majority win by July 3 in the two-candidate runoff between himself and Zyuganov.

The results of first-round balloting were that Boris Yeltsin received 35%; Gennady Zyuganov, an early strong favorite, made it into the runoff with 32%; former general Aleksandr Lebed collected 14.5%; Grigory Yavlinsky received 7.34%; Vladimir Zhirinovsky got 5.70%; and no other candidate (including Bryntsalov, Fyodorov, Gorbachev, Shakkum, and Vlasov) carried as much as 1% of the vote. According to exit polls of first-round and runoff voters, economic issues (i.e., high prices, inflation, low wages) were foremost in voters' minds, followed at a considerable distance by the war in Chechnya and concern about crime and corruption (Mitofsky, 1996).

Prior to the required runoff election (Russian presidential elections require that the winner receive more than 50% of the vote), Lebed publicly announced his support for Yeltsin and received an appointment as secretary of the Security Council in Yeltsin's cabinet. This unexpected maneuver seriously hurt Zyuganov's presidential aspirations. With 69% of the Russian electorate turning out to vote, Yeltsin won 53.83% of the second-round runoff election votes to Zyuganov's 40.31%, 4.82% voted against both.

## RESEARCH DATA AND METHODOLOGY

The present data derive from publicly available interviews given by Russian president Boris Yeltsin and his closest contenders in the 1996

Russian presidential contest: Gennadi Zyuganov, Aleksandr Lebed, Grigory Yavlinsky, and Vladimir Zhirinovsky (see Appendix 3.1). Interviews and the question- and-answer portions of press conferences were selected as the running text from which to measure motive imagery and conceptual/integrative complexity, primarily because they represent a sample of material that is unlikely to have been prepared by staff or for specific audiences. Thus, the assessment of motives and conceptual/integrative complexity is more likely to be representative of the interviewee's extemporaneous thought. Comparison data for these five leaders are limited to the time period prior to the 1996 election during which each was an acknowledged presidential candidate.

As Lebed is a primary focus for this chapter, his cognitive style was also examined across several time periods. Each of the relevant time periods is evaluated by scoring all available interviews and pooling the results within each time division (see Appendix 3.2). Motive data were then standardized across time periods and within motivation. The standardization procedure for all motive data utilizes a mean of 50 and a standard deviation of 10, allowing for reliable comparisons across candidates and between time periods.

The motive imagery scoring system was originally developed to evaluate motives on the basis of individual results of the Thematic Apperception Test, in which subjects were asked to interpret pictures (McClelland et al., 1953; Atkinson, 1982). However, it has been extensively used to analyze other types of verbal and written material (Donley & Winter, 1970; Hermann, 1979, 1980b; Winter, 1994b; Winter & Stewart, 1977; Winter et. al., 1991; among others). The current study uses the integrated system developed by Winter for scoring motives in running text (Winter, 1991a, 1992a, 1994a). This method was developed to measure motive imagery labeled as achievement, affiliation-intimacy, and power. Motive imagery is scored in images per 1,000 words. A brief description of the three motivations would include the following (see also Winter, 1991a, 1994a).

### Achievement

Imagery is scored based upon indications of a distinct concern with and standard of excellence in performance, goals, competition, and accomplishment.

### Affiliation/Intimacy

Imagery is scored based upon indications of concern with establishing, maintaining, or restoring friendly relationships or affiliative activities, expression of positive, friendly, or sympathetic feelings toward other individuals or groups, and/or friendly, nurturant acts.

## Power

Imagery is scored based upon indications of concern with control, impact, influence, prestige, or glory. The focus is upon outer effect rather than inner capacity and can include persons, groups, institutions, or countries.

Interviews were also evaluated for conceptual/integrative complexity. Scorers were trained using a comprehensive manual and practice scoring materials (Baker-Brown et al., 1992). The method has its roots in Kelly's personal construct theory and is "a cognitive structure variable, essentially independent of the content of thought" (Suedfeld et al., 1990: 28). Lowest scores on the continuum indicate a rigid, unidimensional, value-laden perspective and interpretation of events; scores increase according to emerging tolerance for other perspectives. Highest scores are reserved for speech that clearly exhibits an ability to evaluate events from a global perspective—understanding and accepting alternative viewpoints while discerning the way in which levels of the given problem or concept dynamically interact. Scoring units are evaluated on a scale from 1 to 7 (for a detailed analysis of the method, see Suedfeld et al., 1992; Baker-Brown et al., 1992). A brief synopsis would include:

- Score of "1"—no evidence of differentiation or integration.
- Score of "2"—transitional, showing some evidence of emerging differentiation.
- Score of "3"—moderate to high differentiation—but no integration.
- Score of "4"—transitional, showing some evidence of emerging integration.
- Score of "5"—moderate to high differentiation and moderate integration.
- Score of "6"—transitional indicating the emergence of an organizing principle; individual is working with several levels of schemata and understands alternatives as dynamic.
- Score of "7"—presence of a global perspective regarding the nature of the relationship between multiple, specific, and embedded levels of the issue or event—high differentiation and high integration.[2]

As conceptual/integrative complexity focuses on structure, not content, there is no presumption that higher scores are necessarily better or superior; they represent a more complex argument, not always a qualitatively better or more accurate position (Baker-Brown et al., 1992).

The basic scoring unit for conceptual/integrative complexity is the section of the text (in this case, the interview) devoted to one idea. The section might be a single answer, several consecutive answers to similar questions, or one section of a long answer that deals with two separate issues. Five interviews were chosen randomly from each candidate's available interviews during the time period in question, and all scorable units within each of the five interviews were scored.

The grand mean of scores from the five interviews represents the complexity score for each candidate. Documents were scored by trained scorers who demonstrated category agreement of .85 or above with the calibration materials that had been pre-scored by experts. Inter-coder reliability, was at .85 or above for all three motives and .90 or above for conceptual/integrative complexity scoring. In an effort to further ensure reliability, scorers were kept unaware of the purpose of the study, and all of the documents were randomized and supplied to scorers in random packets.

## MOTIVE IMAGERY COMPARISON ACROSS RUSSIAN LEADERS

Table 3.1 compares Yeltsin, Zyuganov, Lebed, Yavlinsky, and Zhirinovsky. It is apparent that Lebed lands closer to Zhirinovsky and Zyuganov on the motive imagery continuum, scoring high in power and low in affiliation. Yeltsin, alternatively, scores higher in achievement and affiliation and lower in power than any of the other four leaders. Yeltsin's comparatively high score in affiliation and comparatively low score in power are perhaps interesting for Western observers. Hermann's 1980 study of Soviet leaders indicated that those who scored high in affiliation and low in power were relatively more favorable to detente than those who scored low in affiliation and high in power (Hermann, 1980b). In another study, Hermann (1980a) was able to show that, based upon press conference transcripts of 45 world leaders who scored high in the power motive imagery, the high power motivational profile predicts a proclivity for independence and confrontational foreign policy. In the same study, those who scored high in affiliation were more likely to attempt cooperation and perceive interdependence in international policy (1980a). In 1991 Winter et al. found that Mikhail Gorbachev and George Bush scored high in affiliation and average in power imagery. The authors related the high affiliation, low power motivational pattern to the relatively low levels of aggression (absent a significant stimulus, i.e., the annexation of Kuwait by Hussein or the imminent dissolution of the Soviet Union) during the tenures of Bush and Gorbachev.

This pattern may also extend to campaign style. Content analysis has demonstrated that Yeltsin's campaign messages demonstrated extremely low levels of negativity—only 2.4% of Yeltsin's total assertions contained criticisms of his opponents or their platforms. This was significantly

Table 3.1
Motive Imagery and Complexity: Top Five Russian Presidential Candidates

|  | Raw Scores | | | Standardized Scores | | | C/I Complexity Score |
|---|---|---|---|---|---|---|---|
|  | Ach. | Aff. | Power | Ach. | Aff. | Power | C/I Complexity |
| Yeltsin | 9.05 | 6.47 | 7.33 | 64.56 | 67.57 | 38.82 | 1.526 |
| Zyuganov | 4.62 | 1.71 | 10.95 | 45.91 | 44.89 | 53.74 | 2.053 |
| Lebed | 4.99 | 2.09 | 12.30 | 47.47 | 46.70 | 59.31 | 3.476 |
| Yavlinsky | 6.59 | 1.30 | 7.56 | 54.28 | 42.94 | 39.77 | 3.571 |
| Zhirinovsky | 2.71 | 2.34 | 12.07 | 37.87 | 47.89 | 58.36 | 1.914 |

lower than the "negativity" scores of his top opponents (Sigelman & Shiraev, 1998).

## Conceptual/Integrative Complexity Comparison across Leaders

Given that higher levels of integrative complexity indicate an acknowledgment and attempt to reconcile differing perspectives, it is of some interest that both Yavlinsky and Lebed score significantly higher (p < .01) than any of the other candidates for the Russian presidency in 1996. These scores suggest that both Lebed and Yavlinsky were processing information from a variety of perspectives and attempting to speak substantively to the needs of the divergent groups that they were courting in their quest for the electoral win. They each also make some effort to explain the tension between and interdependence of alternative views.

Zyuganov's scores fall into the middle range of this field of candidates. He has some emergent differentiation of perspectives and dimensions, recognizing the potential for looking at the same issue in different ways, but he rarely fully differentiates and does not integrate—since he does not differentiate between perspectives, he cannot then acknowledge the dynamic mutual influence and interdependence of alternative ways of evaluating the situation.

Yeltsin and Zhirinovsky score lowest on the integrative complexity continuum, indicating that their respective approaches to the national election were more rigid and value-laden, with little effort to differentiate between perspectives and very simple right versus wrong analyses of issues—although from widely divergent policy viewpoints.

These results would generally replicate the Tetlock and Boettger (1989)

Table 3.2
**Power Imagery Minus Achievement Imagery: Top Five Russian Presidential Candidates**

|            | Raw Scores | Standardized Scores |
|------------|:----------:|:-------------------:|
| Yeltsin    | −1.72      | −25.74              |
| Zyuganov   | +6.33      | +7.83               |
| Lebed      | +7.31      | +11.84              |
| Yavlinsky  | +.97       | −14.51              |
| Zhirinovsky| +9.36      | +20.49              |

study, which indicated that Soviet reformist politicians in the late 1980s scored significantly higher on the integrative complexity continuum than did the more traditionalist leaders of the Communist Party. Lebed and Yavlinsky were generally supporting reform agendas, while Yeltsin and Zyuganov were both attempting to support their version of the status quo, and Zhirinovsky was espousing an ultra-nationalistic rigid platform.

### Power Minus Achievement across Leaders

Subtracting achievement from power can give the analyst some further view into the likelihood of the individual leader's pursuing achievement at the expense of negotiation—or, being motivated by personal power without reference to the "best" or ideal policy. The standardized results in Table 3.2 indicate that Lebed is closer to the center on this measure than either Yeltsin or Zhirinovsky, who represent the two extremes. Yeltsin and Yavlinsky's negative scores indicate that achievement colors their approach to problem resolution. This pattern has been shown also to be predictive of a certain proclivity toward the frustration of policy goals and an inability to pursue practical negotiation (Winter & Carlson, 1988). Zhirinovsky's profile indicates that his drive for power may overwhelm any sense of what is best for the country or what represents rational or ideal policy. Yeltsin's concern with achievement may interfere with negotiation toward pragmatic settlement, while Zhirinovsky is less able to give up personal power for laudable goals. Here, then, is some indication that Lebed might be better able to effectively implement pragmatic policy than either Yeltsin, Yavlinsky, or Zhirinovsky (for further information on the power minus achievement measure, see Winter, 1997, 2000).

As this analysis gives individual attention to Aleksandr Lebed and determines associations between psychological and behavioral variables for this particular political actor, we proceed to the case study.

## THE CASE STUDY: ALEKSANDR LEBED

### Aleksandr Lebed: Some Biographical Notes

Lebed's rapid ascent onto the international political scene drew the attention of many. Lambeth (1996: iii–iv) evaluated him as "a respected professional of strong authoritarian bent and unsure devotion to the idea of democracy, yet one who has spoken out strongly against crime and corruption, appears committed to a market economy, and is less aggressively nationalistic than many Western accounts have suggested." Some preliminary insights into the personality of this potentially important Russian political figure may be gained from a look at known highlights from his life.

Lebed was born to a working-class family in Novocherkassk, a Cossack area in the Rostov Oblast of southern Russia. When he was still fairly young, he was involved in an infamous incident during which Soviet troops fired on demonstrators in 1962. In Lebed's words:

We were sitting in a chestnut tree, and then a round of fire from an automatic weapon hit the people who were sitting above me and below me. I jumped down from the tree by myself and without getting a running start I jumped over such a high wall that to this day I am surprised whenever I walk past it. That was on 1 June, the Day of Protection of Children, in 1962. (Interview, FBIS-SOV-95-089)

He claimed that he attended the demonstration "out of childhood curiosity. My mother locked me in and I crawled out through the window on the street, and so forth" (Interview, FBIS-SOV-95-089). This incident did not, however, affect Lebed's perception of the army; he explained that many soldiers disagreed with the order, one had committed suicide, and the final disposition of the incident was sufficiently punitive as to imply that eventually the army acted "extremely correctly and I would say nobly" (Interview, FBIS-SOV-95-089).

Lebed graduated from the Ryazan Higher Airborne Forces School with the rank of army lieutenant. He served as a paratrooper early in his career and was later chosen to command the first battalion of the 345th Airborne Regiment in Afghanistan. He earned the Order of the Red Star as a result of his combat successes during 1981–1982. He attended the highly prestigious Frunze Academy—a senior military service school—and then commanded the Tula airborne division between 1985 and 1991.

During the August 1991 attempted coup, Lebed supported Boris Yeltsin rather than the communist hard-liners. However, he explained that

the White House and the president were the least of my concerns. I had to avoid provocation and bloodshed. . . . I was ordered to take the battalion and organize the protection and defense of the building of the RSFSR [Russian Soviet Federative Socialist Republic] Supreme Soviet. Without any details. The battalion arrived there and was located on the embankment. I did not know our assignment, the battalion commander did not know, there was a crowd surrounding the battalion. The men were confused, people were grumbling at them and cursing them. Everyone was nasty . . . I did not defend the White House, and I refused the status of its defender in September, 1991. (Interview, FBIS-SOV-95-089)

Despite his denials, Lebed was rewarded for his loyalty. Defense Minister Grachev soon appointed Lebed commander of the Russian 14th Army, stationed in Moldova (Lambeth, 1996: 15). However, many in Russia felt that he should have been appointed commander of the air force and that his denials of heroism in the failed coup could have had an impact on the subsequent appointment (FBIS-SOV-95-089).

### Privatization of the 14th Army

Lebed's independence and initiative almost immediately propelled him into controversy. Although he had been ordered to maintain neutrality, he got involved in a dispute between Moldova and the Trans-Dneister Russian Republic. This region, populated by a large number of Russians, had recently declared independence from Moldova. Unrest evolved into fighting, and Lebed determined that he would end this "wild, stupid war" with a strong artillery offensive against Moldovans who were approaching Tiraspol, the city chosen by the Russians as the capital of their new republic. Some claimed that he was, in effect, defending the Soviet empire; Lebed maintained that he saw an obligation to protect this outnumbered group of Russians from slaughter. He did effectively end the fighting but in so doing also declared his independence from Moscow's control. The minister of defense (Grachev) reorganized the 14th Army Group's headquarters and effectively eliminated Lebed's position. Although Grachev offered Lebed a position as deputy commander for training in the Transbaikal Military District, Lebed resigned in protest to this reassignment as well as to the Russian military campaign in Chechnya. When Yeltsin announced the resignation, Lebed's reply was, "I guess that Yeltsin got sick and tired of me, and I am sick and tired of him as well" (Gordon, 1996; Lambeth, 1996).

### From Candidate to Kingmaker

With his military life ostensibly behind him, Lebed began to focus upon the presidency. Early in the electoral season, Lebed aligned with Skokov, a former aide to Yeltsin. This alignment did not particularly help Lebed, and his popularity suffered. However, Lebed took a note from Western politics and hired "high powered political consultants" to package his candidacy and create sophisticated, modern political advertising that portrayed him as virulently anti-crime and above corruption (Gordon, 1996). The strategy worked, and Lebed became a significant player in the power game of electoral politics. The 14.5% of the vote that his candidacy garnered during the first round of presidential elections in Russia represented twice as many votes as for his nearest contender, Grigory Yavlinsky, and nearly three times as many votes as for Vladimir Zhirinovsky. The runoff election created an opportunity for Lebed to exercise his political strength and lend his support to Yeltsin, thereby all but ensuring a Yeltsin presidency (Reuters, July 9, 1996).

### National Security Advisor and Secretary of the Security Council

On June 18, 1996, Yeltsin appointed Lebed to the post of national security advisor to the president and secretary of the Security Council. Yeltsin may have anticipated that these roles and political power might pacify Lebed and that Lebed could be of some help in reforming and restoring the seriously troubled Russian military ("The Yelstin–Lebed Alliance," 1996). Alternatively, Yeltsin may have been willing to overlook what he knew would be long-term problems in exchange for short-term votes and a presidential win. Lebed immediately claimed that the new post was "not a matter of an alliance" with Yeltsin but a new course for the country. With Lebed's new political power, Defense Minister Pavel Grachev's departure was swiftly accomplished. The day following his appointment, Lebed described events as follows:

Between nine and ten this morning Generals Barynkin, Shulikov, Tsvetnov, Kharchenko, and Lapshov; Elena Agapova, the minister of defense's press secretary; and particularly, touchingly, the Georgian Minister of Defense Vardiko Nadibaidze were in the restroom of the minister of defense's office trying to persuade the Minister of Defense to put the troops on alert in order to put pressure on the president.

I took measures myself. The measures were, are, and will be preventative, to prevent all possible conflicts or wars, or if there are any going on now, their swift and sure suppression. . . . I gave the order to the duty general of the central command post of the General Staff and forbade him from passing on any orders from the Minister of Defense to the troops. A telegram was sent from the headquarters of the Moscow Military District with my signature. The telegram was about my appointment and removing Grachev, and there was a request to the troops to remain calm and continue with planned military training; and to the generals not to bother spending public funds on condolence telegrams or the money would be charged to them. (Interview, June 19, 1996, FBIS-SOV-96-119)

This move illustrated the maddening independence with which Lebed had historically conducted himself. Lambeth (1996: 17) describes it as "an attitude regarding compliance with the will of his superiors that is ambiguous at best." It is interesting to note that Lebed's explanation for the removal of Grachev indicated that it was necessary to "prevent all possible conflicts or wars" rather than to solidify his own power base or even remove the disloyal. He perceived the stakes as enormous, just as the stakes in Moldova had been when he had to "end this wild, stupid war" rather than maintain neutrality, as he had been ordered.

In several interviews, Lebed insisted that he had informed Yeltsin that he "was no good as a boy for his retinue" and that he would support his own ideas. By Thursday, October 17, 1996, Lebed had been accused of conspiring to create a private army to stage a coup. President Yeltsin dismissed Lebed, stating in a television address, "I have told Lebed to learn to work with other state bodies and leaders . . . he did not learn his lesson" (Specter, 1996). Lebed took the dismissal in relatively good humor, claiming that he had thought that he would last only two months instead of four and later publicly taking his wife to see a play entitled *Ivan the Terrible*, explaining that it would help him to "learn how to rule the state" (Specter, 1996).

### Governor of Krasnoyarsk

By May 1998 Lebed had managed to win the post of governor of Krasnoyarsk, a very large (it meets the Arctic in the north and almost reaches the border of Mongolia in the south) and industrially powerful region in central Siberia, from incumbent governor Valery Zubov. With his brother Alexei already governor of the neighboring republic of Khakassia, Lebed would seem to be well positioned for his anticipated next run for the presidency. However, controversy erupted in Krasnoyarsk as Lebed, in January 1999, fired director Konstantin Protopopov and chief editor Irina Tretyakova of the regional television and radio station in Krasnoyarsk. He had complained during his election that the local television news was favoring the incumbent governor, Valery Zubov. After firing the executives, he placed "police cordons outside the regional television and radio company" to prevent the executives from returning (Associated Press, 1999).

The following sections describe Lebed's motive profile during each of the above time periods and in comparison to other Russian leaders. As Table 3.3 illustrates, Lebed's motive profile over time is fairly stable but does demonstrate a rather interesting evolution.

### Lebed's Imagery

#### Achievement

A high level of achievement imagery is generally associated with a tendency to modify actions based upon experience from previous actions and a tendency toward risk calculation combined with an avoidance of extreme risks (Winter, 1997). The negotiating style is cooperative, and

Table 3.3
Aleksandr Lebed: Motive Imagery and Integrative Complexity from 1995 to 1999

| | Raw Scores | | | Standardized Scores | | | C/I Complexity Score |
| --- | --- | --- | --- | --- | --- | --- | --- |
| | Ach. | Aff. | Pow. | Ach. | Aff. | Pow. | Complexity |
| Lebed as General/Commander of 14th Russian Army | 5.84 | 2.34 | 12.84 | 46.09 | 48.07 | 59.12 | 2.15 |
| Lebed as Candidate for the Russian Presidency | 4.99 | 2.09 | 12.30 | 34.63 | 46.42 | 52.34 | 3.48 |
| Lebed as Secretary of the Security Council and National Security Advisor | 6.88 | 5.14 | 12.03 | 60.11 | 66.51 | 48.95 | 2.22 |
| Lebed after Ouster: Post-Security Council Time Period | 6.58 | 2.56 | 12.60 | 56.07 | 49.52 | 56.11 | 2.95 |
| Lebed as Governor of Krasnoyarsk | 6.36 | 1.04 | 10.79 | 53.10 | 39.48 | 33.48 | 2.70 |

such people primarily seek out technical experts when they need advice. Politically, individuals who exhibit this personality profile are likely to experience frustration, as they are driven by idealistic and perfectionistic goals and have a decreased ability to practice practical political negotiation (Winter, 1997). Lebed's achievement imagery is higher than his affiliation/intimacy imagery but low in comparison with his high scores in power imagery.

An evaluation of the standardized scores over time indicates that achievement imagery initially decreased after Lebed's military career evolved into a political career. Once he joined the government, his achievement imagery increased and remained above the mean, even after dismissal. There was a slight decrease in achievement imagery after his removal from Yeltsin's cabinet and then again after his successful bid for the governor's seat in Krasnoyarsk; however, his scores have remained higher than at any previous time in his professional life.

### Affiliation/Intimacy

Affiliation imagery is associated with a cooperative and friendly style except when there is a perceived threat. Under conditions of threat the high affiliation motive profile will tend to become defensive/hostile. This type will look to friends for help when help is needed, is inclined to search for a peaceful solution, and is vulnerable to scandal (Winter, 1997).

Affiliation imagery is very low overall for Lebed. There is, however, a noticeable increase in affiliation imagery during Lebed's time as Yeltsin's advisor. After his departure, affiliation imagery dropped to previous levels and then dipped below any previously recorded levels after his election as governor.

### Power

Those who have high power scores in their motivational profile tend to exercise leadership; are impulsive if they lack responsibility; negotiate with exploitative, aggressive tactics; generally seek out help from political "experts"; and are charismatic, aggressive, and independent in foreign policy (Winter, 1997). Lebed utilizes power imagery in interviews at quite high levels during all five time periods. However, power imagery does slightly decrease during Lebed's run for the presidency and after his appointment as Yeltsin's advisor, and then when measured as governor, his power imagery decreases again, below any previously recorded levels.

### Power Minus Affiliation

Lebed's changes over time may also be evaluated from a power minus affiliation perspective. Winter's (1993) study indicated that an aggressive response to crisis is related to high levels of power motivation and low

**Table 3.4**
**Aleksandr Lebed: Power Imagery Minus Affiliation Imagery from 1995 to 1999**

|                                                                 | Raw Scores | Standardized Scores |
| --------------------------------------------------------------- | ---------- | ------------------- |
| Lebed as General/Commander of 14th Russian Army                 | 10.50      | +11.05              |
| Lebed as Candidate for the Russian Presidency                   | 10.21      | +5.92               |
| Lebed as Secretary of the Security Council and National Security Advisor | 6.89       | –17.56              |
| Lebed after Ouster: Post-Security Council Time Period            | 10.04      | +6.59               |
| Lebed as Governor of Krasnoyarsk                                | 9.75       | –6.00               |

affiliation. The opposite configuration—low power and high affiliation—would then be related to a tendency toward peaceful resolution of crises. Table 3.4 indicates that Lebed's power-to-affiliation ratio changed significantly over the years. Standardized scores indicate that during the time that he was a part of Yeltsin's government and when he won a major election and achieved a respected political office—governor of Krasnoyarsk—there was a shift across the mean so that power minus affiliation resulted in negative scores. Despite his posturing, Lebed has responded to successful bids for political roles with an adjustment in motivational imagery that indicates a willingness to respond with goals that include relatively peaceful and pragmatic solutions to problems that he has encountered during these periods.

### Conceptual/Integrative Complexity

While the comparison across leaders (Table 3.1) indicated that Lebed was comparatively more complex in his verbal communication during his candidacy for the Russian presidency, his conceptual/integrative complexity scores (Table 3.3) have declined since that time. There was a significant change ($p \leq .01$) in scores from general to candidate and then again when he joined Yeltsin's cabinet. His most integratively complex communications to date occurred while he was running for the presidency in 1996. His scores increased while out of the government and positioning himself for a run for the governor's office in Krasnoyarsk but declined again once he assumed office.

These changes indicate an increasingly rigid policy perspective and a decrease in processing other viewpoints once Lebed is in political office.

His dismissal of the management of the regional radio and television stations in Krasnoyarsk and especially the method and use of the police cordon to keep the executives out may be practical evidence of this increased rigidity and decreased acceptance of differing opinions. Indeed, as governor, Lebed's affiliation imagery has been the lowest measured in the five time periods covered by the current study. However, although his power imagery continues to be quite high when compared to that of other presidential candidates, as governor, Lebed has achieved his lowest recorded score in the five measured time periods, again indicating some power imagery adjustment to the role of government insider.

## DISCUSSION AND CONCLUSION

The attraction of the outsider in troubled political times has been duly noted in recent American elections, as indicated by the success of Carter in 1976, Reagan in 1980, Clinton in 1992, Governor Ventura in 1998, and the influence of Ross Perot and the Reform Party in 1992 and 1996. Lebed is seen by the Russian people as just that, an outsider who is not responsible for the chaos that has beset the Russian economic and political landscape.

Two quotes by interviewers are particularly interesting in this context. Fleming Rose in Tiraspol writes:

An hour and a half in the presence of General Lebed leaves an impression of a man who is more than a political figure who will be here today, gone tomorrow. With a firm gaze which does not wander from his interlocutor and a voice which with its vibrating bass far exceeds everything that modern hi-fi technology can produce and which must be able to make even the most unruly soldiers follow orders, Aleksandr Lebed radiates a charisma and a rebellious independence which could under the right circumstances, mobilize the Russian soul to acts of heroism. (FBIS-SOV-95-092:84)

Along these same lines, Yefim Bershin, special correspondent for *Literaturnaya Gazeta*, exclaimed to Lebed during an interview: "Your entry into Tiraspol was somewhat similar to the entry into Jerusalem. At least, there were a good many cries of 'Hosanna' " (FBIS-SOV-95-101: 67).

Russians may have been attracted to Lebed as a potential savior, as one of their own, firmly anti-corruption, defiantly anti-crime, determined to reform the system and to restore his country's honor. The motivational profile indicates that Lebed is capable of a certain amount of adjustment when the stakes are high and the goal requires it. Power minus achievement scores indicates an ability to practice pragmatic politics, while power minus affiliation scores predicts that some internal situational adjustment can occur and may enhance Lebed's ability to "rise to the occasion" when his country needs him to. However, and importantly, the high power imagery when combined with low affiliation is predictive of independence and confrontational foreign policy, as well as associated with leaders who are less likely to attempt cooperation and perceive interdependence in international policy (Hermann, 1980b). Lebed, therefore, might be expected to be rigid in his approach to negotiation and resist definitions of interdependence between Russia and other nations. His perspective is likely to be characterized by strong nationalistic responses to what Lebed might believe to be the appropriate international provocation. Indeed, during the 1990s Lebed persistently maintained anti-Western and anti-American views, as reflected in is numerous television appearances and newspaper and radio interviews. He vigorously opposed American involvement in the conflict in Bosnia (1991–1996), condemned North Atlantic Treaty Organization (NATO) actions against Serbia doing the Kosovo crisis in 1999, and was among the most vigorous opponents of NATO expansion (Shiraev & Zubok, 2000).

Integrative complexity scores show that this Russian politician is capable of differentiation and some integration in his evaluation of national issues, but the level of complexity declines significantly and his approach becomes more rigid when Lebed is operating from within the government and under conditions of stress. Overall, these results suggest a psychological profile of a leader with strong cognitive resources and some ability to adapt situationally. However, if Lebed were to attain the Russian presidency, his impulsivity when combined with a proclivity toward rigidification of thinking while in office could result in increased international tension and might involve the country in conflictual situations in the interest of what Lebed would perceive to be national honor.

## APPENDIX 3.1: MATERIALS CODED FOR YELTSIN, ZHIRINOVSKY, ZYUGANOV, AND YAVLINSKY

**Boris Yeltsin**

| April 20, 1996 | FISC (Federal Information Systems Corporation) |
| April 21, 1996 | FISC* |
| April 30, 1996A | FBIS-SOV-96-084 |
| April 30, 1996B | FISC |
| May 17, 1996 | FBIS-SOV-96-098* |
| May 29, 1996 | FBIS-SOV-96-104 |
| May 31, 1996 | FBIS-SOV-96-106* |
| June 5, 1996 | FBIS-SOV-96-109 |
| June 10, 1996 | BBC* |

*Indicates that interview was randomly selected for integrative complexity coding.

June 14, 1996          FBIS-SOV-96-116
June 26, 1996          FISC*

## Vladimir Zhirinovsky

May 2, 1996            FBIS-SOV-96-086*
May 20, 1996A          BBC
May 20, 1996B          BBC
May 22, 1996           BBC*
May 23, 1996           BBC
May 26, 1996           BBC
June 5, 1996           BBC*
June 6, 1996           ABBC
June 6, 1996           BFBIS-SOV-96-116
June 11, 1996          Cable News Network, Inc.*
June 13, 1996          FISC
June 16, 1996          BBC*

## Gennadi Zyuganov

April 23, 1996         FISC*
May 12, 1996           BBC*
May 17, 1996           BBC
May 22, 1996           FISC*
June 11, 1996          FISC*
June 14, 1996A         Cable News Network, Inc.
June 14, 1996B         Cable News Network, Inc.*
June 16, 1996          BBC

## Grigory Yavlinsky

March 3, 1996          BBC
April 29, 1996         BBC*
May 7, 1996            BBC
May 12, 1996           BBC*
May 20, 1996           BBC
May 28, 1996           BBC*
June 6, 1996           FISC
June 10, 1996          BBC*
June 13, 1996          Russian Public TV
June 16, 1996          BBC*

## APPENDIX 3.2: CODED INTERVIEWS AND PRESS CONFERENCES WITH ALEKSANDR LEBED

### Lebed as Commander of the 14th Russian Army

| | |
|---|---|
| February 4, 1994 | FBIS-SOV-94-024* |
| July 21, 1994 | FBIS-SOV-94-140 |
| September 8, 1994 | FBIS-SOV-94-174 |
| September 12, 1994 | FBIS-SOV-94-176 |
| September 15, 1994 | FBIS-SOV-94-179* |
| November 8, 1994 | FBIS-SOV-94-216 |
| November 23, 1994 | FBIS-SOV-94-226 |
| January 13, 1995 | FBIS-SOV-95-009 |
| January 27, 1995 | FBIS-SOV-95-018* |
| February 2, 1995 | FBIS-SOV-95-022 |
| February 22, 1995 | FBIS-SOV-95-035 |
| February 23, 1995 | FBIS-SOV-95-036 |
| February 24, 1995 | FBIS-SOV-95-037* |
| March 6, 1995 | FBIS-SOV-95-043 |
| March 17, 1995 | FBIS-SOV-95-052* |
| April 11, 1995 | FBIS-SOV-95-069 |
| May 9, 1995 | FBIS-SOV-95-089 |
| May 25, 1995 | FBIS-SOV-95-101 |

### Lebed as Presidential Candidate

| | |
|---|---|
| March 22, 1996 | FBIS-SOV-96-057* |
| March 24, 1996 | BBC |
| March 28, 1996 | AFBIS-SOV-96-061* |
| March 28B, 1996 | FBIS-SOV-96-061 |
| April 9, 1996 | BBC |
| April 25, 1996 | FBIS-SOV-96-081 |
| May 13, 1996 | FISC* |
| May 24, 1996 | BBC |
| May 29, 1996 | FBIS SOV-96-104* |
| May 30, 1996 | FBIS-SOV-96-105 |
| June 13, 1996 | BBC* |

### Lebed as Yeltsin's Security Advisor

| | |
|---|---|
| June 18, 1996 | FISC |
| June 19, 1996A | FBIS-SOV-96-119* |

| June 19, 1996B | FBIS-SOV-96-119 |
| June 21, 1996 | FBIS-SOV-96-121* |
| July 11, 1996 | FISC* |
| August 12, 1996 | FISC |
| August 16, 1996 | FISC |
| September 3, 1996 | FISC* |
| September 12, 1996 | FBIS-SOV-96-178* |

## Lebed during the Post–Security Advisor Time Period

| October 17, 1996 | FBIS-SOV-96-061 |
| October 18, 1996 | Nezavisimaya Gazeta |
| October 21, 1996 | FBIS-SOV-96-205* |
| October 22, 1996 | AFBIS-SOV-96-206 |
| October 22, 1996 | BFBIS-SOV-96-207 |
| November 24, 1996 | FBIS-SOV-96-228* |
| January 1, 1997 | FBIS-SOV-97-047 |
| January 14, 1997 | FBIS-WEU-97-010 |
| January 15, 1997 | FBIS-SOV-97-012 |
| January 18, 1997 | FBIS-SOV-97-013* |
| January 28, 1997 | FBIS-SOV-97-019 |
| February 3, 1997 | FBIS-SOV-97-025 |
| February 8, 1997 | FBIS-SOV-97-027* |
| February 12, 1997 | FBIS-SOV-97-036* |
| February 17, 1997 | FBIS-SOV-97-033 |

## Lebed as Governor of Krasnoyarsk

| June 7, 1998 | FBIS-SOV-98-158 |
| September 1, 1998 | FBIS-SOV-98-244 |
| September 3, 1998 | FBIS-SOV-98-246* |
| September 4, 1998 | Burrell's Information Services* |
| September 9, 1998 | FBIS-SOV-98-252 |
| September 29, 1998 | FISC* |
| January 27, 1999 | FISC |
| March 31, 1999 | FISC* |

## NOTES

1. A region of Siberia that is approximately one-fourth the size of the United States.

2. Definitions adapted from Baker-Brown et al. (1992).

Chapter 4

# The Personality and Leadership Style of President Khatami: Implications for the Future of Iranian Political Reform

Tanyel Taysi and Thomas Preston

## INTRODUCTION

The Islamic Republic of Iran, formed in 1979 after a revolution that shook the world, is now experiencing a period of reform, opening, and reconciliation with the West that would have been unthinkable even five years ago. The driving force behind the changes occurring in Iran is the Iranian president, Sayyed Mohammed Khatami, elected in a resounding victory over the conservatives in 1997. The election of Khatami, a reform-minded cleric, shocked the conservative technocrats who had been in control of the government since the revolution and who still retain most of the key power positions within the Iranian government.[1] At present, the country is locked in a battle over the future of the Islamic Republic of Iran. That reform must occur is clear, especially after the sweeping victory of reform candidates in the *Majlis* (Senate) elections in February 2000. Equally obvious is the fact that the ruling conservative clergy are growing ever more worried and defensive of the reformer's gains. This is well illustrated by their actions prior to the last elections, disqualifying many reform-minded candidates and going so far as jailing reformist candidates on trumped-up charges. After the elections revealed the depth of their political losses, the Conservatives responded by organizing challenges to numerous election results, succeeding in replacing several democratically elected reformers with hard-liners. Further, Conservatives have become more open in their challenges to the reformers' efforts, jailing reformists on trumped-up charges, "silencing" others in more sinister ways (Burns, 2000b).

What can we expect in the future? How significant a role can President

Khatami play in this battle over reform? In this chapter, we examine these issues by exploring the political personality and leadership style of President Khatami, utilizing Margaret G. Hermann's (1983, 1999) Personality Assessment-at-a-Distance (PAD) content-analytic technique in the context of the particular political environment in which he operates. The resulting profile of Khatami's personality and the implications of his scores across numerous individual characteristics upon his foreign and domestic policy styles are discussed.

Next, we examine Khatami within the Iranian political context, exploring the degree to which we would expect his leadership style or personality to have an impact upon Iranian reform efforts or policy. As Greenstein (1969) correctly observes, constraints within the political environment (the degree to which it allows restructuring) serve to diminish the impact of leader personality upon policy. On the other hand, where constraints are less severe and restructuring possible, leaders may have a truly significant impact upon events. By placing Khatami properly within the Iranian political context (taking note of his power position vis-à-vis others, the nature of the constraints upon his actions, etc.), we should be better equipped to interpret how his personality and style are likely to affect both policy and reform efforts in Iran. Finally, a comparison of Khatami's profile with a previously developed profile of Ayatollah Khamenei, the supreme leader of Iran, is offered.

## USING PAD TECHNIQUE TO UNDERSTAND PRESIDENT KHATAMI'S PERSONALITY AND LEADERSHIP STYLE

In this section, we present a personality profile of President Khatami and explore the possible impact of his individual characteristics upon his political behavior and leadership style. Before discussing his profile, however, it is useful to briefly discuss the methodology underpinning it. The Khatami profile was generated using Hermann's (1983, 1999) PAD approach. This method utilizes content analysis of the spontaneous interview responses by political leaders across differing time periods, audiences, and substantive topic areas to construct detailed personality profiles of individuals according to seven different traits: the need for power, in-group bias (ethnocentrism), belief in ability to control events (locus of control), complexity, self-confidence, distrust of others, and task/interpersonal emphasis (see Table 4.1 for definitions and coding categories).[2]

The trait analysis in PAD is quantitative in nature and employs frequency counts—assuming that the more frequently leaders use certain words and phrases in their interview responses, the more salient such content is to them. The focus of PAD analysis is upon what percentage of the time in responding to interviewers' questions, when leaders could exhibit particular words or phrases, that they do, in fact, use them (Hermann, 1999). The PAD approach has previously been used to construct detailed profiles of more than 120 political leaders in over 40 different countries. These data for a sizable number of leaders not only allow us to set out the range of each characteristic, thereby demonstrating what constitutes high and low scores for leaders, but also provide the means to compare empirically and interpret the scores for world leaders across these traits (see Table 4.2).[3] Quantitative analyses of the large data set reported in Hermann (1999) demonstrate not only that there is substantial variation across all of the trait scores in the set but also that these traits are statistically distinct from one another. Thus, the 122 leaders and the 87 heads of states become meaningful norming groups that can be used in the same way as such groups are used in most standard inventories to put a particular leader's scores into perspective (Hermann, 2000).

In terms of inter-coder reliability and validity, the PAD technique has demonstrated across numerous studies the ability to achieve inter-coder agreement for all seven traits ranging from 0.78 to 1.00 between sets of coders and Hermann (e.g., Hermann, 1980a, 1980b, 1980c, 1984a, 1987b; Hermann & Hermann, 1989). Currently, profiles generated by coders are not included within the larger data set until they achieve inter-coder reliabilities with Hermann on all traits that are 0.90 or higher (Hermann, 1999).[4] Further, in a series of studies, Hermann (1984b, 1985, 1986, 1988) developed profiles of 21 leaders and, based on their scores, indicated on a series of rating scales the nature of the leadership behaviors that these individuals should exhibit. These ratings were compared with those made by former government personnel and journalists who had had the opportunity to actually observe and interact with these particular leaders. As Hermann (1999: 40) observes, the correlations between the two sets of ratings average 0.84 across the set of leaders, suggesting that the profiles derived from PAD provided "similar types of information on which to judge behavior as had the other raters' experiences with the actual figures." Regarding the use of translated material for coding purposes, several tests were conducted to see if there would be a difference between a native speaker's coding text in the original language (in this case, French and Russian) compared with Hermann's using translated text. Across these studies, inter-coder reliability averaged .92 across the traits (Hermann, 1980b, 1987a, 1987b).

The PAD technique also has a long track record of use in previous research on political leaders (Hermann, 1980a, 1980c, 1984b, 1987b, 1989, 1995; Hermann & Preston, 1994, 1999; Kaarbo & Hermann, 1998; Preston & 't Hart, 1999; Preston, 1996, 1997, 2001; Winter et al., 1991). In particular, a growing body of empirical research has focused upon whether or not the actual leadership styles and behavior of policy makers were

Table 4.1
PAD Definitions and Coding Categories for Personal Characteristics

| Individual Characteristic and Definition | Coding Categories | Score Used |
|---|---|---|
| *In-group Bias*—View of the world in which one's own nation holds center stage; strong emotional ties to one's own nation with emphasis on national honor and identity. | Focus on nouns/noun phrases referring to nations or governments; coded nationalism if speaker identifies with nation or government mentioned and noun is modified by favorable term, term denoting strength, or phrase suggesting importance of national honor or identity; also coded nationalism if speaker does not identify with nation or government mentioned and noun is modified by a hostile term, term suggesting weakness, or phrase denoting meddlesomeness in affairs of others. | Percentage of references to own or other nations/governments meeting criteria. |
| *Belief in Ability to Control Events*—View of the world in which individual perceives some degree of control over situations he/she is involved in; government can influence what happens in or to nation. | Focus on verbs (action words); coded for this characteristic if context of verb indicates speaker (or group speaker identifies with) is accepting responsibility for initiating or planning the action. | Percentage of verbs meeting criteria. |
| *Need for Power*—Concern with "establishing, maintaining or restoring one's power, i.e., one's impact, control, or influence over others" (Winter, 1973: 250). | Focus on verbs (action words); coded need for power if verb context meets any of the following six conditions included in Winter's (1973) need for power coding scheme: (1) indicates strong, forceful action; (2) indicates giving of help when not solicited; (3) indicates an attempt | Percentage of verbs meeting six criteria. |

60

to control others; (4) indicates an attempt to influence, persuade, or bribe others; (5) indicates an attempt to impress others; (6) indicates concern for one's own reputation or position.

| | | |
|---|---|---|
| *Conceptual Complexity*—Ability to differentiate the environment. Degree of differentiation that person shows in describing or discussing other people, places, policies, ideas, or things. | Looked in content for set of words indicating a high degree of differentiation or high-complexity words (e.g., may, possibly, sometimes, tends) and set of words indicating a low degree of differentiation or low-complexity words (e.g., always, only, without a doubt). | Percentage of high-plus low-complexity words that were high in complexity. |
| *Distrust of Others*—General feeling of doubt, uneasiness, and misgiving about others; an inclination to suspect and doubt the motives and actions of others. | Focus on nouns/noun phrases referring to groups that speaker does not identify with; coded for distrust if context shows indications of doubts or misgivings or suggests particular group is going to harm speaker or group with which speaker identifies. | Percentage of nouns meeting criteria. |
| *Self-Confidence*—Person's sense of self-importance or image of his/her ability to cope with the environment. | Focus on pronouns referring to self (e.g., myself, I, me, mine); coded for self-confidence if self is seen as instigator of activity, authority figure, or recipient of positive feedback. | Percentage of self-references meeting criteria. |
| *Task/Interpersonal Emphasis*—Relative emphasis in interactions with others on getting the task done vs. focusing on feelings and needs of others (an interpersonal emphasis). | Looked in content for set of task words (e.g., results, goal, solution, achievement) and set of interpersonal words (e.g., sensitivity, understanding, appreciation, coordination). | Percentage of task plus interpersonal words that were task words. |

*Source:* Based on Hermann, 1983.

Table 4.2
PAD Profile of Iranian President Khatami and Potential Comparison Groups

| | Khatami PAD Scores | 122 World Political Leader Set | Score in Relation to 122-Leader Set | 87 Heads of State | Score in Relation to 87-Leader Set |
|---|---|---|---|---|---|
| In-group Bias | .56 | Mean = 0.43 Low < 0.34 High > 0.53 | High | Mean = 0.42 Low < 0.32 High > 0.53 | High |
| Need for Power | .70 | Mean = 0.50 Low < 0.38 High > 0.62 | High | Mean = 0.50 Low < 0.37 High > 0.62 | High |
| Complexity | .52 | Mean = 0.45 Low < 0.32 High > 0.58 | Medium-High | Mean = 0.44 Low < 0.32 High > 0.56 | Medium-High |
| Task Orientation | .59 | Mean = 0.62 Low < 0.48 High > 0.76 | Medium | Mean = 0.59 Low < 0.46 High > 0.71 | Medium |
| Self-Confidence | .83 | Mean = 0.57 Low < 0.34 High > 0.80 | High | Mean = 0.62 Low < 0.44 High > 0.81 | High |
| Belief in Ability to Control Events | .46 | Mean = 0.45 Low < 0.33 High > 0.57 | Medium | Mean = 0.44 Low < 0.30 High > 0.58 | Medium |
| Distrust of Others | .58 | Mean = 0.38 Low < 0.20 High > 0.56 | High | Mean = 0.41 Low < 0.25 High > 0.56 | High |

Data for leader sets supplied by Social Science Automation.

consistent with those expected (based upon the psychological literatures), given their specific PAD trait scores (Preston, 1996, 2001; Preston & 't Hart, 1999). This extensive archival research across multiple leaders has provided strong empirical support for the validity of the PAD scores themselves and their link to leader style and behavior.

In generating our Khatami profile, we sought to use responses as spontaneous as possible by focusing solely upon interview and press conference material gathered from the Foreign Broadcast Information Service (FBIS) and CNN (see Appendix 4.1). Over 50 interview responses were then randomly selected and coded according to the procedures described above (see Table 4.1) for each trait.[5] An additional measure gauging leaders' policy experience or expertise developed in Preston (1996) was also incorporated into the profile. This measure takes into account the nature of leaders' prior policy experience and expertise by looking to their prior policy positions (both official and unofficial) that involved a given policy area, the degree to which they focused upon specific policy areas in their past jobs, and the extent to which they possessed other relevant policy experience.[6] Given Khatami's background and experience, we find that he should be considered to have high expertise/prior experience in domestic politics and low expertise/prior experience in foreign affairs. In Table 4.2, Khatami's PAD profile and scores across a number of individual characteristics are presented alongside several potential comparison groups (122 world political leaders and 87 heads of state).

What interpretations are possible, given these scores? In Table 4.3, several analytical interpretations of Khatami's profile scores are provided using models developed by Hermann et al. (1996), Hermann (1999), and Preston (2001). These models combine to predict Khatami's general foreign policy preferences, his likely leadership styles across both domestic and foreign policy realms, and general expectations regarding his likely use of advisory systems, advisors, and information in policy making. While the interpretation of high and low scores is fairly straightforward (i.e., leader behavior expected to be consistent with individual's possessing either high or low score on this trait), medium scores require more explanation and interpretation. Medium scores for traits suggest that in certain contexts (i.e., topic/policy areas, time periods, before specific audiences), a leader may evidence behavior typical of individuals possessing either high or low scores (Hermann, 1999).

Building upon the notion of leadership style as a function of responsiveness to constraints, openness to information, and motivation described in Hermann et al. (1996), Khatami (high power needs and medium belief in own ability to control events) would be expected to alternate between challenging and respecting constraints, depending upon the situational context. In addition, his medium score on task/ interpersonal focus (i.e., emphasis upon getting a task done versus emphasis on group maintenance motive) suggests that Khatami would focus on both problem and relationship in differing contexts. Finally, Khatami's high scores on both complexity and self-confidence suggest an openness to information and sensitivity to context.[7]

As outlined in greater detail in Table 4.2, when challenging constraints *and* focusing upon the problem (task over group maintenance emphasis), Khatami would be expected to exhibit the *active independent* general foreign policy style. In contrast, when challenging constraints but focusing upon group maintenance, a *directive* style would be expected of Khatami. On the other hand, when respecting constraints and focusing on the problem, Khatami would be characterized by the *opportunistic* foreign

Table 4.3
Interpretations (Predictions) of Khatami Political Style and Behavior Based upon PAD Profile Scores and Existing Scholarship

| Author | Focus of Analysis | Khatami PAD Scores of Relevance | Interpretation |
|---|---|---|---|
| Hermann, Preston, & Young (1996); Hermann (1999) | Leadership style as a function of *responsiveness to constraints, openness to information,* and *motivation.* | High Power and *Medium* Belief in Ability to Control Events = *Tendency to shift between challenging and respecting constraints, depending on the context.* | *When challenging constraints and focusing on problem,* adopts *Actively Independent* style (focus of attention is on maintaining one's own and the government's maneuverability and independence in a world that is perceived to continually try to limit both). |
| | | | *When challenging constraints and focusing on relationships,* adopts *Directive* style (focus of attention is on maintaining one's own and the government's status and acceptance by others by engaging in actions on the world stage that enhance the state's reputation). |
| | | Moderate Task = Motivation for seeking office is *focused upon **both** problem and relationship, depending on the context.* | *When respecting constraints and focusing on problem,* adopts *Opportunistic* style (focus of attention is on assessing what is possible in the current situation and context, given what one wants to achieve and considering what important constituencies will allow). |
| | | Self-Confidence and Complexity *Both* High = Open to contextual information. | *When respecting constraints and focusing on relationships,* adopts *Collegial* style (focus of attention is on reconciling differences and building consensus—on gaining prestige and status through empowering others and sharing accountability). |

| Preston (2001) | Leadership style as a function of *need for control and involvement in the policy process and sensitivity to context.* | High Power, High Complexity, and Limited Prior Experience or Expertise in Foreign Policy = *Magistrate-Observer policy style.*<br><br>High Power, High Complexity, and Extensive Prior Experience or Expertise in Domestic Policy = *Director-Navigator policy style.* | *In foreign policy making, exhibits Magistrate-Observer style.* Decision making centralized within tight inner circle with preference for hierarchical advisory structures designed to enhance personal control. Tendency to set general policy guidelines, but to delegate policy formulation and implementation tasks to subordinates. Reliance upon views of expert advisors rather than on own policy judgments. High cognitive need for information but limited personal interest/background in policy area. Heavily dependent upon expert advice to make sense of context and for policy recommendations. Reduced sensitivity to potential outside constraints on policy and less awareness of (search for) information and advice from relevant outside actors. High self-monitor.<br><br>*In domestic policy making, exhibits Director-Navigator style.* Decision making centralized within tight inner circle with preference for hierarchical advisory structures designed to enhance personal control. Preference for direct personal involvement throughout policy process and tendency to actively advocate own policy views, frame issues, and set specific policy guidelines. Tendency to rely more on own policy judgment than those of expert advisors. High general cognitive need for information and high personal interest/background in policy area. Active collector of information from policy environment. Great sensitivity to potential outside constraints on policy and enhanced search for information and advice from relevant outside actors. High self-monitor. |

policy style but would shift to the *collegial* style when both respecting constraints and focusing upon relationships (Hermann, et al., 1996; Hermann, 1999). Khameini, on the other hand, would be expected to exhibit a classic *evangelical* style.

Preston (2001), in contrast, focuses upon the impact of individual leader characteristics upon their likely structuring of advisory systems, selection of advisors, and use of information and advice in their decision making. As outlined in detail in Table 4.2, Khatami's high power and complexity scores but low prior policy experience/expertise in foreign affairs would result in a *magistrate-observer* leadership style in that policy arena. On the other hand, Khatami would be expected to possess a more active, dynamic *director-navigator* leadership style in domestic policy making given his high scores for power, complexity, and prior domestic policy experience/expertise. At the same time, the Preston model would suggest that, in addition to these overall leadership style characteristics, Khatami's medium score on belief in ability to control events would result in a cautious general style (whether in domestic or foreign policy), given his lack of faith in his ability to manage or control either policy or the political situation.

This description of Khatami would clearly not be at odds with the observations (and frustrations) of his followers over the past four years in Iran. Khatami's high distrust of others would also be expected to result in further caution regarding building political alliances with others (or foreign, non-Iranian actors). The moderate score on task suggests that Khatami is calculating and monitors his environment to determine the optimum time to focus upon either task accomplishment or maintaining his interpersonal/group relations. This would be expected of a high-complexity individual who is generally sensitive to environmental context. It is also consistent with the observations of followers that Khatami's style is a highly self-monitoring one. Finally, Khatami's high score on in-group differentiation (ethnocentrism) suggests that he may, despite his high complexity, be vulnerable to stereotypical thinking regarding adversaries and opponents, thereby making negotiations and bargaining (whether domestically or internationally) more problematic.

## THE IRANIAN POLITICAL CONTEXT

While Khatami enjoys unprecedented support in the Iranian populace, many wonder why the promised changes of his campaign have yet to materialize. While Khatami is president, he does not have absolute power and is severely limited by the power of other actors in this system. Indeed, the Iranian political system is marked by a substantially uneven distribution of power that is divided between institutional political power and religious power. Khatami must answer to the *Rahbar*, or supreme leader, who wields a large amount of power.[8] Ali Khamenei, a notorious hard-liner who had been moving his way up in the religious and institutional political power circles for decades, has been the *Rahbar*, a lifelong appointed position, since 1989. Although Khatami enjoys unprecedented public support and has been a favorite among the people and within the political arena for decades, he is severely constrained in his actions and policy recommendations by the hard-liners such as Khamenei (Eteshami, 1995).

As the situation in Iran has become progressively more unstable over the past year, Iranians and Westerners alike have expressed frustration at Khatami's lack of progress toward reform. What must be kept in mind are the considerable roadblocks erected by hard-liners against Khatami's reform efforts, actions that have provoked extreme civil unrest. For example, August 1999 saw a riot unprecedented in size since the 1979 revolution over the hard-line clergy's decision to shut down five newspapers that were sympathetic to Khatami or reform in general. Politically motivated jailings of reformers, censorship, murders, and corruption are occurring with increasing regularity. As a result, the political situation in Iran has become increasingly tense, with many citizens feeling that promised reforms are not occurring fast enough. In fact, there have been ominous rumblings about a second revolution if Khatami is not allowed by the clergy to implement his reform policies. At the same time, the hard-liners have expressed the view that violence by the conservatives to prevent many of these reform efforts from succeeding is justified (Burns, 2000b).

In order to understand the nature and scope of the constraints that Khatami is operating under, it is useful to turn to Greenstein's (1969) discussion of the three situational contexts that allow an individual's actions (action dispensability) to affect events. First, *the likelihood of personal impact increases to the degree that the environment admits of restructuring*. Situations in which modest interventions are able to produce disproportionate results are considered unstable (Greenstein, 1969: 42). An unstable environment allows for more leeway; a closed environment, for less. However, it is important not to confuse this type of instability with political instability. Many of the situations considered politically unstable, such as what is occurring in Iran right now, do not admit to restructuring (Greenstein, 1969: 43).

The political environment in Iran at the moment is exceedingly closed in nature. Hard-liners who occupy key positions of power are going out of their way to ensure that any intervention that Khatami makes does not produce disproportionately large results. Given the current power struggle occurring between the reformists and the hard-liners, Khatami (in his role as president) is constrained even more than usual because he is seen as a threat by the others operating within the system. Thus, his every action is scrutinized, leaving him little room to maneuver. If he does manage to produce a desired result from an action, the hard-liners retaliate with a counter-move that negates Khatami's action. For instance, if Khatami attempts to improve freedom of the press, hard-liners retaliate by closing down several newspapers, thus restricting the press to an even greater degree than before.

The power struggle occurring between the reformists and the hard-liners, contrary to popular belief, is not new. There have been problems between reform-minded individuals and hard-liners since the revolution, as hard liners attempted to block any restructuring of the environment that would lead to a decrease in their power (which would inevitably occur if reforms were successful). This power struggle began while Ayatollah Khomeini was still alive and was helped along by Khomeini's notorious refusal to take a concrete stand on many issues. After Khomeini's death in 1989, it became greatly intensified (Eteshami, 1995). The reformers, who were seeking to make the system more open and democratic, saw Khomeini's death as an opportunity to begin making concrete changes (Eteshami, 1995). In contrast, the hard-liners, also known as the Fundamentalist Islamic Republicans, realized that their days could be numbered once Khomeini expired, and they grew nervous. At this point they began to crack down on reform-minded individuals, setting a clear precedent for how reformists who attempted to change the system would be dealt with.

Prior to his death, Khomeini appointed Ayatollah Montazeri, a well-respected cleric, as his successor. However, Montazeri resigned as *Faqih* designate in 1989 under extreme pressure and harassment from hard-liners due to personal differences between himself and Khomeini; Khameini and Rafsanjani Montazeri openly called for reforms, freedom of press and speech, an admission of past mistakes, and the implementation of democracy in Iran. He believed that an honest, hard look at changes that needed to be made must occur if the Islamic Republic of Iran was to continue on the correct path (Eteshami, 1995). Instead of Montazeri's reforms seeing the light of day, Rafsanjani and Khamenei ensured not only that they would not occur but that Montazeri would never occupy a position of power again. The past 20 years have been characterized by a similar pattern of public strong-arming and the removal of reform-minded individuals by the same hard-liners who are in power positions today (Khamenei is now the supreme leader). Given the history of how key power players dealt with anyone who tried to restructure the environment, it is clear that Khatami is operating in an environment that is extremely closed to restructuring.

The second situational circumstance offered by Greenstein (1969) is that *the likelihood of personal impact varies with the actor's position in the environment*. In order to shape political events, an action must be performed by an actor who occupies a strategic place within that environment (Greenstein, 1969: 44). Thus, actors occupying lower and middle governmental/power positions are not able to implement much change, since they are severely inhibited by others. Khatami, by nature of his placement as president of Iran, is less constrained than he would be if he held a position of less power. However, although president, he has less power than some may think and is constrained by several other actors. Executive powers are not only in the hands of the president. The *Rahbar* actually has more powers than the president and is able to impeach the president if he feels that he is acting in a manner that is not in the best interests of the Islamic Republic (Eteshami, 1995). The specific powers of the Iranian president include the ability to choose the country's ministers; to direct the nation's economic, foreign, political, and public policies; to chair the National Security Council (formulating foreign policy); and to serve as the executive branch representative on the council of the three branches of the government—executive, legislative, and judicial.

Foremost among the institutional actors serving as a constraint on Khatami's influence is the *Faqih Rahbar*, or supreme leader—at present, Ayatollah Khamenei. While the president can exercise direct and indirect power in numerous ways, Khamenei is able to effectively block Khatami through the powers of his office. The impressive array of formal powers held by the supreme leader include:

- Supreme commander of armed forces
- Power to determine the general policies of the Islamic Republic of Iran (with the expediency council)
- Ability to supervise the implementation of policies
- Ability to order referenda
- Power to declare war and peace and general troop mobilization
- Power to appoint and dismiss:
  1. Members of the Council of Guardians
  2. Head of the Judiciary
  3. Director of radio and television networks
  4. Chief of staff of armed forces
  5. Commander in chief of the Guardians of the Islamic Revolution
  6. Commander in chief of the military and security forces
- Resolve differences and regulate relations among the three branches of the government
- Resolve (through the Expediency Council) problems that cannot be solved by ordinary means

- Sign decree naming the president after popular elections
- Power to impeach the president

By retaining the power of appointment and dismissal of most of the key positions within the government, the *Rahbar* holds much more real power than the president, who is able only to choose his ministers. Besides these two players, several other institutional bases of power can serve as constraints upon Khatami's influence, such as the Council of Guardians (12 members), the *Majlis* (270 members), the Expediency Council (20 members), the Assembly of Experts (83 members), the chief justice (head of executive), National Security Council (11 members), cabinet (23 members), and various other foundations, Friday prayer posts, and Islamic associations.

Finally, the third circumstance offered by Greenstein is that *the likelihood of personal impact varies with the personal strengths of the actor*. In other words, the greater the actor's experience and skill as a politician, the less need for either a favorable position or a manipulable environment. Further, the greater the skill, the greater the likelihood that the actor himself or herself will contribute to making the best of a bad situation and make his or her position favorable and the environment more manipulable (Greenstein, 1969: 45). The fact that Khatami has been elected, remained in power, diffused tense situations, and successfully implemented some changes in the face of such severe constraints testifies to the strength of his skill as a politician.

Khatami has been active in the Iranian government since the Islamic Revolution, but his interest in politics goes back to pre-revolutionary times. His political career became serious in 1982, when he was appointed minister of Islamic culture and guidance. Khatami occupied this post for 10 years, quietly building his skills, along with a reputation for honesty and fair dealings. In 1992 he left this post in much the same way as Montazeri "resigned" as *Faqih*-designate. However, this 10 years in office was invaluable to Khatami's political acumen building, as he was able to gain invaluable insight into the behind-the-scenes dealings of the hard-liners, as well as what one could and could not do if one hoped to stay in power. After 1992 Khatami was pushed out of the spotlight into the position of head of the National Library in Tehran. During this time in the notorious backwater of the dusty halls of the library, far removed from any position of real significance, Khatami, rather than becoming angry and frustrated, thrived in this environment. He used this time out of the spotlight to hone his already keen political skills (http://tehran.stanford.edu/khatamistory).

Khatami chose to run for president reluctantly, only after it became clear that there was no viable opposition to the government-endorsed candidate, Nateq-Nouri. Khatami ran a Western-style campaign, with little popular support at the beginning. A ragtag bunch made up of former radical revolutionaries, reform-minded officials, and technocrats constituted his only supporters. However, using his political acumen to advantage, that soon changed. Khatami traveled tirelessly around the country, giving in-depth interviews and making himself accessible to the people, especially women and students. He talked about hobbies, such as table tennis and swimming. Khatami swiftly gained popularity at a rate that stunned even his closest advisors. Building on the support of the younger generation of Iranians and women voters, he rode the wave to victory, gaining an amazing 70% of the vote. The conservative establishment was stunned. Khatami literally came out of nowhere, easily toppling Nateq-Nouri, whom they fully believed would be victorious.

When Khatami is examined in the context of Greenstein's three propositions, the extent of the constraints under which he is acting becomes clear. The Iranian political environment is closed, and there is little opportunity for Khatami to effect any real change. Khatami is not a predominant leader (with the authority to personally commit resources or change policy). The nature and position of the other leaders within the Iranian political arena (especially Ayatollah Khamenei) constrain Khatami. However, that Khatami has managed to accomplish as much as he has despite these constraints suggests that an examination of his personality, leadership style, and skills as a politician is useful in exploring Khatami's role in future reform efforts.

## KHATAMI IN CONTEXT

How well, then, does Khatami's observable behavior fit in with the predictions forwarded by the PAD assessment? Further, how does Khatami's style compare with the style of his "key opponent" in the current power struggle, Ayatollah Khamenei? Khatami's profile produced a high power score and a medium score for his belief in their ability to control events. According to Hermann, leaders who are not as high in their belief in their ability to control events as they are in their need for power will challenge constraints but do so behind the scenes (Hermann, 1999). They will challenge some restraints and respect others. Thus, one would expect Khatami's leadership style to be one in which reform efforts and policy change are made in a low-key manner, avoiding extreme (or highly controversial) reform efforts. Not surprisingly, Khatami's leadership style is very non-confrontational, avoiding open clashes with conservatives at all costs. Khatami's specific tactics are to parade his own Islamic credentials while offering oratorical strikes against the conservatives, stopping short of giving them enough reason to sack him (Burns, 1999a). He attempts changes that have a good chance of succeeding and stays clear of policy changes, such as normalization with the United States, that would not be supported by the domestic political environment in Iran.

In his first year in office, Khatami smoothed foreign relations with the Gulf states and Turkey. Recently, Khatami managed to begin a dialogue with Italy, Britain, Egypt, and China. However, relations with the United States are simply not within his control, given domestic political constraints. As a result, he has been very cautious, avoiding any real attempt at normalization. At the same time, sensing opportunity in the domestic environment, Khatami has attempted numerous reform efforts. Censorship of books and newspapers was lifted, and citizens have obtained greater personal freedoms. However, the outgoing conservative-dominated Parliament cracked down on Khatami's efforts after their resounding loss in the *Majlis* (Senate) elections in March 2000. Although Khatami has made some progress in his cultural openings, it has been a rocky path, with most of his moves continually blocked by the hard-line conservatives (Burns, 1999a).

Khatami's scores for self-confidence and complexity are both high. When a leader displays equal scores for these two traits, his or her behavior depends on whether the scores are high or low compared to those of other leaders. Khatami manifests high scores for both. According to Hermann (1999), leaders who are high on both are open and strategic, focusing attention on what is feasible at any given time. Leaders with these scores are very open to contextual information. High self-confidence leads to high levels of patience and allows leaders to bide their time to see what will succeed. Leaders of this type also have a clear sense of what they hope to accomplish but are sensitive to their environment to a degree that they do not attempt something that has no chance of working. Finally, the behavior of such leaders may appear to the outside observer and their own constituents as erratic and opportunistic, appearing indecisive and chameleon-like. However, when one understands the goals and political contexts of these leaders, their actions begin to make more sense.

In Iranian politics, nothing is as it seems. Improvisation, role-playing, and deception are key to any Iranian politician (Sciolino, 1999). Layer upon layer of meaning is attached to every word, every action (Milani, 1999). As a result, it is imperative for anyone hoping to be successful in Iranian politics to be a chameleon, never showing his or her true intentions. Khatami's high self-confidence and complexity allow him an edge in this respect. Being already predisposed to environmental sensitivity, Khatami has mastered the art of chameleon politics, enabling him to stay in power in an environment that (necessitates) this trait.

This chameleon-like sensitivity to both domestic and foreign context is well illustrated by Khatami's ability to adjust his speech to suit a given audience. For example, during Khatami's recent visit to the United

Nations (UN), he had nothing negative to say about the United States and criticized Israel only mildly (Sciolino, 1998c). Indeed, his interview with CNN in January 1998, in which he recommended an exchange of cultures with the United States and praised the American people (if not the government), was seen by most (aside from the U.S. government) in a positive light (Sciolino, 1998a). However, Khatami's speech a few weeks later at Ayatollah Khomeini's tomb was far less conciliatory, as he attacked the United States in no uncertain terms (Sciolino, 1998b). Of course, this led to great confusion among analysts, since this rhetoric was completely at odds with his gentler tone during the CNN interview. Not surprisingly, the U.S. government reacted negatively to Khatami's apparent mercurial attitude to U.S.–Iranian relations—not appreciating the necessity of such behavior, given the Iranian political context. Even at home, Khatami's constituency is often frustrated by these contradictions. However, even though his pursuit of reform efforts has been slow and his rhetoric at times contradictory, Khatami's constituents appear to understand the nature of Iranian politics and its constraints upon the president's actions. It is recognized that Khatami must play a very complicated political game in order to succeed. Indeed, despite their frustrations, Khatami is seen by most of his supporters as having stayed on course with his reforms, despite the odds against him, and of promoting a political opening with the West. For Western observers, it is equally important that they not react to seemingly contradictory statements (as the United States did) but recognize both Khatami's style and the requirements of the Iranian political context when assessing the Iranian president. In this, PAD profiling offers analysts useful insights into his patterned, not erratic, behavior.

Finally, Khatami's mid-range scores for task focus indicate that he is motivated by both problem and relationship, depending on the context. Not surprisingly, Hermann (1999) and others (Byars, 1972, 1973; Hermann & Kogan, 1977; Bass, 1981) have found that leaders who fall in this "middle range" are those most often defined as charismatic leaders, a title that has been used to describe Khatami quite often. Leaders of this type focus on the problem when it is appropriate and upon building relationships when that is appropriate. For instance, when Khatami was running for office and on several occasions when there was no crisis occurring, he focused on the morale, feelings, and needs of the Iranian people. By portraying himself as an intellectual and good-natured man who sees himself as a philosopher first and a politician second, he is making sure that Iranian citizens see him more as a friend who cares as opposed to a politician far removed from their everyday lives (http://tehran.stanford.edu/khatamistory). Although most other power holders in the Iranian government drive luxurious cars and live in mansions, Khatami, whose popularity is, in no small part, based on his reputation for honesty and fair dealings (in contrast to the corruption and extravagance of others), drives an older car and lives in a modest house with his family. Posters portraying Khatami most often show him smiling, in contrast to the dour hard-liners glaring out from hooded eyes on their posters.[9]

However, on certain occasions, especially during domestic political crises, Khatami shifts easily toward a focus upon solving problems rather than maintaining interpersonal relationships. In such contexts, Khatami, not hesitating to severely chastise (or even threaten) his constituents, appears much more like a mullah defending the religious basis of the Iranian republic than the good-natured philosopher of non-crisis situations (Demick, 1999). For example, during a critical challenge to his power in 1999, when the streets of Iran erupted into the worst rioting since the revolution of 1979, Khatami shifted seamlessly from interpersonal to task focus. The riots, triggered by tough new press law and the closing of *Salaam* (a reformist newspaper) by the hard-liners, began with a peaceful demonstration on July 7, 2000, at Tehran University. In retaliation, the security police and vigilantes stormed the student dormitory with tear gas and killed a student, which led to further demonstrations that spread outside Tehran and turned to rioting. The situation became increasingly tense as hard-liners accused Khatami of an inability to control the people, as well as a more general inability to govern. While the students and other rioters were very much members of Khatami's constituency, calling for greater freedom and democracy, he refused to meet with the students or encourage their rioting (Sciolino, 1999). In an interview on Iranian radio and television he warned that unruly elements would be dealt with swiftly and harshly. Further, he called for students to be vigilant about any conspiracy against the basis of the Islamic Republic, as well as the country in general. Not long afterward, Khatami reversed focus and again sought to strengthen his relations among his constituents.

In contrast, Ayatollah Khamenei, Khatami's key conservative opponent, is high in both power and belief in ability to control events. As Hermann (1999) notes, leaders who are high in both tend to challenge environmental constraints and push the limits of what is possible. In Khamenei's case, this willingness to challenge environmental constraints has taken the form of resisting the clear (and increasingly strident) calls from the majority of Iranian citizens for social and political reform. Ironically, Khamenei's own intransigence (and that of the ruling clergy as well) has actually helped to create the very political context and base of popular support that has allowed Khatami to challenge the hard-liners' control. Khamenei also scores much higher in self-confidence than in complexity, leading to the expectation that he would tend toward the behavior of the ideologue who is closed to contextual information and driven by causes. Such leaders tend to be unresponsive to clues from their environment and often re-interpret feedback from the environment to fit their pre-existing views of the world. Further, Khamenei's scores also suggest that he would not be above using devious or coercive tactics to obtain what he wants. [10]

As is readily apparent from even a cursory look at Iranian politics, these predictions for Khamenei's behavior are supported by his actions. Unwilling (or unable) to discern the momentum in the political environment for change, Khamenei has acted to block Khatami's reform efforts in particularly blunt, heavy-handed ways—oblivious to the popular reaction to his actions. His jailing of reformists, disqualification of popular election results going against the hard-liners, and outspoken threats of violence to prevent reform from succeeding demonstrate both his lack of sensitivity to the political context and his refusal to see the reality of the current political situation (Burns, 1999b). But ironically, in Khamenei's ideologically driven, closed style resides Khatami's strongest ally in his struggle for reform, for Khamenei lacks the chameleon-like political ability and sensitivity to context possessed by Khatami. As a result, Khamenei is less likely to be able to adapt to a changing political environment or to subtly position himself to undercut the reformers among the populace. Of course, this style also represents a danger for Khatami, since leaders with Khamenei's characteristics are less likely to
seek compromise with opponents and are more likely to actually follow through on their threats of violence to stop policies threatening their positions.

## CONCLUSION

This brief analysis of President Khatami's personality and leadership style within the Iranian political context should illustrate the value of Personality Assessment-at-a-Distance (PAD) as a tool for improving our understanding of world leaders. Not only does the technique provide empirically supported measures of leader personal characteristics, but since the comparison data are based upon a population of over 120 world leaders, it avoids the danger of Western bias in its analysis (Hermann, 1999). Further, as our analysis of Khatami demonstrates, our expectations regarding his style and political behavior found substantial support in the case study materials. By matching these predictions with the Iranian political context—essentially placing the leader in context—our PAD analysis provides a more nuanced, overall portrait of Khatami and allows us to interpret his behavior based upon clear measurements of his personal characteristics rather than though mere intuition. It also allows for comparison between the likely styles of Khatami and his main opponent, Ayatollah Khamenei. As noted above, such comparison provides analysts with a sense of how this conflictual relationship between the two, so critical for the future of Iranian reform, might take shape in the future.

Finally, it should be noted that this brief sketch of Khatami using PAD merely scratches the possible analytical surface. Although beyond the scope of this chapter, more extensive PAD profiling would allow topic- and audience-specific scores, indications of change across time, and comparison with a population of profiled Iranian leaders, which would further serve to place Khatami in context. Nevertheless, our analysis of Khatami should provide the reader with a sense of the application and utility of the PAD approach to profiling leaders.

## APPENDIX 4.1: KHATAMI INTERVIEWS CODED BY PAD

| | |
|---|---|
| March 17, 1997 | FBIS-NES-97-107 |
| May 27, 1997 | FBIS-NEW-97-102 |
| August 15, 1997 | FBIS-NES-97-227 |
| August 20, 1997 | FBIS-NES-97-232 |
| August 24, 1997 | FBIS-NES-97-236 |
| August 24, 1997 | FBIS-NES-97-236 |
| October 31, 1997 | FBIS-NES-97-304 |
| November 20, 1997 | FBIS-NES-97-324 |
| November 24, 1997 | FBIS-NES-97-328 |
| December 14, 1997 | FBIS-NES-97-348 |
| December 14, 1997 | FBIS-NES-97-348 |
| December 28, 1997 | FBIS-NES-97-362 |
| December 29, 1997 | FBIS-NES-97-363 |
| January 7, 1998 | CNN Interview by Christianne Amanpour |
| July 1, 1998 | FBIS-NES-98-182 |
| September 27, 1998 | FBIS-NES-98-270 |
| September 24, 1998 | FBIS-NES-98-267 |
| February 1, 1999 | FBIS-NES-99-032 |

*Source*: World News Connection, a service of the National Technical Information Service, www.fedworld.gov.

## NOTES

1. For an in-depth analysis and history of the division of powers in Iran, see Eteshami (1995).

2. Analysts can develop adequate assessments of leadership style based upon 50 interview responses of 100 words or more in length (although the more re-

sponses coded, the better). To ensure that the description of style is not context-specific, the coded responses should span the leader's tenure in office, occur across different types of interview settings, and focus on a variety of topics (Hermann, 1999).

3. As Hermann (1999: 32) explains, both leader samples include those who have held positions of authority from 1945 to the present. The 87 heads of state represent some 46 countries from all parts of the globe; the 122 leaders are drawn from 48 countries and include (in addition to the 87 heads of state) members of cabinets, revolutionary leaders, legislative leaders, leaders of opposition parties, and terrorist leaders.

4. Of the authors, Preston was trained by Hermann and has contributed profiles to the data set. Taysi was trained by Preston.

5. The PAD scores for power, self-confidence, distrust of others, in-group bias, and belief in ability to control events were coded by Taysi. She has achieved .70–.80 inter-coder reliability with Preston on a substantial number of randomly selected Khatami documents. The scores for complexity and task were generated using the automated profiler+ system—which Hermann and Young at Social Science Automation report generates data at a .80 inter-coder reliability (comparing machine-coded results with those of expert coders of the same documents). See Hermann, 1999; Young, 2000; Hermann, 2000 for more details or visit www.SocialScience.net. Interview material coded for this profile is available from the authors.

6. This measure was designed for and used exclusively for studying U.S. presidents in past research. The authors recognize that this limits the validity of the measure in this particular case and envision it as more of a plausibility probe to determine whether the indicators employed still provide useful guidance for analysts regarding prior policy experience/expertise among foreign leaders. For more details of this measure, see Preston (1996).

7. Although Khatami's complexity (.52) is considered medium relative to the 122 leader data set, empirical research by Preston (1996, 2001) has clearly demonstrated through archival research that U.S. presidents with scores < .50 exhibit behavior consistent with the expectations for high-complexity individuals (i.e., high need for information, extensive differentiation of environment, willingness to consider multiple perspectives on policy issues/information, low use of analogy and stereotypes, etc.). Therefore, this score is considered high in this study.

8. The titles *Rahbar*, supreme leader, and *Faqih* are interchangeable.

9. It is quite out of the ordinary for a political poster in the Islamic Republic of Iran to present a smiling image.

10. Khamenei PAD scores courtesy of M. G. Hermann and Charles Snare. Those interested in Khamenei's specific scores should contact SocialScience.net for more information.

Part II

# Profiling the Political Personality: Psychodiagnostic and Psychobiographical Approaches

Chapter 5

# Linking Leadership Style to Policy: How Prime Ministers Influence the Decision-Making Process

Juliet Kaarbo

## INTRODUCTION

Political leaders adopt a variety of ways of managing the policy-making process around them. This is true of prime ministers in parliamentary democracies as well as their counterparts in other types of political systems. Prime minister leadership style—the leaders' work habits, how they relate to those around them, how they like to receive information, and how they make up their minds—may, in part, be a reaction to situational imperatives or to the institutional structure in which they reside. Yet two prime ministers may have dramatically different styles in response to similar situational and institutional constraints. This is because leadership style is also a reflection of individual characteristics—a leader's personality and beliefs.

What leaders are like can have a profound effect on the policies chosen by their governments (George & George, 1956; Holsti, 1970; Walker, 1977; Hermann, 1980a; Winter, 1992b; Hermann & Kegley, 1995). In particular, how they manage the advisory process and structure the policy-making system influences the options that are debated and the decisions that are made (Janis, 1972; George, 1988; Burke & Greenstein, 1990; Hermann & Preston, 1994). Thus, the link between a leader's style and policy outputs lies in the nature of the policy-making process. Indeed, I argue that leadership style has the most direct impact on the decision-making process and that policies are influenced through this process.

The link between leadership style and policy is often assumed, but the mechanism for this relationship is typically left theoretically underdeveloped and empirically untested. This chapter traces the relationship between style and process in the context of prime ministerial leadership. Prime ministers are certainly constrained in their attempts to directly affect policy. While they are often *"first* among equals," they are part of a cabinet that has the constitutional authority to make collective decisions. Since they do not enjoy the electoral mandate of presidents who are placed into office by the public, they are further constrained by their political party, which can replace them. Despite these constraints, prime ministers can and do make choices regarding the structure and process of cabinet decision making. These choices can have powerful effects on the policies chosen by the cabinet. This chapter examines empirical evidence for this first link—how prime ministers' individual leadership styles affect cabinet decision-making processes. Evidence from a comparative study of Western European prime ministers and from a collection of studies of British prime ministers is used in this preliminary investigation.

## THE IMPORTANCE OF PRIME MINISTER LEADERSHIP STYLE

Most past research on prime ministers has not focused on the role of individual differences or personality factors. Instead, students of comparative politics have generally attributed differences in prime minister leadership style to variation in structure, not to variation in the characteristics of individuals. Structural factors that affect a prime minister's style include the centralization of power in the constitution, the prime minister's control over patronage, the importance of a cabinet committee system, and the procedures for hiring and firing cabinet ministers (Andeweg, 1993; Rose, 1991; Weller, 1985). Since these structures tend to vary across political systems, scholars have typically adopted a country-by-country approach (e.g., Blondel, 1980; Plowden, 1987; Rose & Suleiman, 1980; Jones, 1991), rather than an approach that compares individuals. The consensus in this literature is that structures pose constraints within which prime ministers must work; as Rose (1980: 43–44) succinctly puts it, "[P]olitical circumstances are more important than personality."

Lacking in this consensus is recognition that, within certain constraints, leaders still have choices regarding the way that they deal with those constraints (Greenstein, 1969). While collective authority may dilute the effects of a leader's individual characteristics, it certainly does not eliminate them. Indeed, leadership in groups with equal members is an important variable for explaining group processes (Levine & Moreland, 1990). As Cartwright and Zander (1968: 301) note, "[T]he nature of a group's leadership clearly makes a difference to many aspects of its functioning. The early work on leadership . . . provided striking evidence that the same group of people will behave in markedly different ways when operating under leaders who behave differently." Indeed, within countries, there is significant variation in the approach that individual prime ministers adopt to cope with, or even challenge, existing institutional structures. Prime ministers may even choose to ignore the very rules and norms that supposedly constrain them.

Prime ministers can shape the decision-making process in a number of ways—they can, for example, establish subcommittees or interministerial consultation groups, absent themselves from important meetings, make certain decisions on their own, allow issues to be placed on cabinet agendas, and block the moving of a decision from an inner cabinet to a full cabinet. These choices can affect the nature of the decision-making process, including the number and duration of cabinet conflicts, the locus of the conflict (i.e., is the conflict between different ministers in the same faction or between different ministers from different factions?), the issue area of the conflict, which cabinet members are included in the final decision-making unit (i.e., does an inner cabinet consistently make the decisions, or does the whole cabinet tend to be involved?), the number of formal votes taken, the decision-making rule that is employed, the number of proposals introduced in and considered by the cabinet, and the number and extent of cabinet reshuffles and resignations. These characteristics of the process may all be affected by the prime minister's leadership style. The nature of this decision-making process, in turn, can shape the final policy decision.

## THE ELEMENTS OF PRIME MINISTER LEADERSHIP STYLE

A prime minister's leadership style can be conceptualized through five important elements, each of which may vary from individual to individual.[1] These elements are similar to those employed by students of the U.S. presidency (see, e.g., Hermann & Preston, 1994). Indeed, to construct this framework, research on the American president was adapted to the parliamentary context through slight modifications. The most "unique" element of the framework concerns prime ministers' relationships with their political parties, reflecting the particular importance of party management in parliamentary democracies.

The first component of leadership style is the *interest and experience* that the prime minister has in a particular issue area. In her discussion of German chancellors, Mayntz (1980: 146) terms this "selective volunteerism," by which she means that leaders "will actively set policy goals and formulate directives in one or a very few selected fields." Empirically, prime ministers' interest and experience have varied. In interviews of several government ministers, Müller et al. (1993: 227) found more prime ministers interested in having an influence in the overall government organization and in economic affairs, than in influencing foreign or defense affairs. Yet, more prime ministers were interested in foreign affairs than in social affairs. Prime ministers' experiences in different issue areas also vary. As Elgie (1993: 64) observes, prime ministers come to the office with different experiences as former ministers, members of Parliament, or bureaucrats, and these experiences affect the prime ministers' skill in different areas. Interest and experience may affect how involved a prime minister is in policy making. The more salient the arena for leaders, the more they want to be involved in shaping policy and the more control they want over the nature of any policy (Hermann, 1980a, 1984a). Thus, a prime minister's interest and experience are an important element for a prime minister's style and its effect on policy making.

A prime minister's *motivation for leading* is also an important part of leadership style. A prime minister may come to politics to promote a particular cause or a general ideology or to win popular approval or personal gain. Motivation for leading may be reflected in the leader's task orientation—whether or not the individual has a goal or process orientation. Research in organizational psychology suggests that, while both are important to successful management, leaders tend to emphasize one task—either goals or interpersonal relations—over the other (Cartwright & Zander, 1968; Bass, 1981; Hargrove, 1989). A prime minister's task orientation depends on whether the prime minister stresses information and the policy goal and focuses discussion on the issue or whether the prime minister stresses relations, either interpersonal or political, among cabinet ministers.

Conflict is a pervasive part of cabinet life, especially in highly factionalized, single-party cabinets and coalition cabinets ('t Hart, 1994). Prime ministers' *strategy for dealing with conflict* is, therefore, an important part of their leadership styles. Prime ministers use a variety of strategies for dealing with disagreement. Some act as advocates and impose their own personal positions, thus playing a more forceful role in the proceedings than those who choose to arbitrate the conflict or to seek consensus. The latter demands that the leader take a more facilitative role and broker a decision through negotiation. Prime ministers can also decide not to become involved in conflict, choosing instead to remain above the fray.

The prime minister's *strategy for managing information* is another important element of leadership style. As Giddings (1995: 46) notes: "[T]he process by which prime ministers prepare themselves for meetings may be more significant in determining the decision-making outcome than the meeting itself." Although information in a cabinet setting is usually channeled through individual ministries, the form in which the prime minister likes to review the information can vary. Prime ministers may want all the basic facts to interpret themselves, or they may want summaries and policy options only. Furthermore, the prime minister may use the prime ministerial staff to gather information independently or rely only on ministerial information networks.

The final element is the prime minister's *strategy for dealing with party factions and other parties* that might be in the cabinet. Leaders usually do not see all others around them equally or behave similarly toward them (Dansereau et al., 1975). This would be most true for prime ministers with factions challenging their leadership. The management of party relations by a prime minister is extremely important. As Weller (1985: 11) states: "[P]rime ministers are party leaders; they hold the former position only as long as they hold the latter." In the cabinet context, dealing with party factions or other parties in a coalition is not just a party matter; it is a government matter as well and often affects the policy-making process and policy outputs. Factions and coalition partners within the prime minister's party may be considered an opponent by the prime minister. In such a case, the prime minister's strategy for dealing with party relations might be competitive, and the prime minister may use policy making to gain ground against them. The strategy for managing party relations is the final component included in the framework for prime ministerial style and, as previously mentioned, is unique to the context of prime ministerial leadership.

Previous research indicates that variation on each of these elements in the framework of leadership style occurs both within and between political systems (Kaarbo, 1997; Kaarbo & Hermann, 1998). Furthermore, these elements appear to be independent of each other; pairs of prime ministers who share one element differ on other elements. Yet, there do seem to be patterns of leadership style, consistent with theoretical expectations. Prime ministers who adopt an advocacy role, for example, often are goal-oriented and filter information for themselves. Finally, preliminary research suggests that these elements of leadership style are related to more basic, underlying characteristics of individuals such as conceptual complexity, belief that one can control what happens, need for power, and need for affiliation (Kaarbo & Hermann, 1998). A representation of the relationships between individual characteristics, leadership style, the decision-making process, and policy outcomes is offered in Figure 5.1.

## LINKING PRIME MINISTER LEADERSHIP STYLE TO DECISION-MAKING PROCESSES

Prime minister leadership style may affect the decision-making process in a variety of ways. Here I suggest a few hypotheses on the nature of this relationship. These hypotheses are somewhat speculative since, as argued above, the relationship between style and process is often as-

**Figure 5.1**
**Relating Leadership Style to Individual Characteristics and Policy Making**

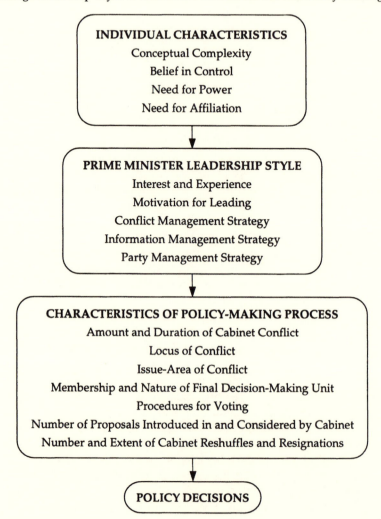

sumed but rarely made explicit. Such speculation, however, is important in order to establish theoretical expectations and to demonstrate the utility of the above conceptualization of leadership style. Following this discussion of expectations, I conduct a preliminary examination of the relationship between style and process with empirical evidence that is available from comparative and British political studies.

Each of the five elements in the framework of leadership style might directly affect decision-making processes. We might expect, for example, that for prime ministers who are interested and experienced in foreign policy, conflict in the cabinet would more likely occur in the foreign policy issue area since that is where the prime minister's attention is directed. It also makes sense that interested and experienced prime ministers would feel more confident to make decisions alone or in a small "kitchen cabinet" and that there would be tension between these prime ministers, who want to direct foreign policy themselves, and their foreign ministers. This tension might even lead to several cabinet reshuffles and resignations involving the foreign ministry.

A prime minister's motivation for leading could also directly affect the decision process. For example, a leader whose task orientation is focused on the group and interpersonal relations would be expected to experience less conflict in the cabinet than a leader who is focused on a policy goal, as interpersonal or political harmony motivates the group-oriented leader. For this reason, a group-motivated leader would more likely see decisions made by the cabinet as a whole, with a consensus decision rule.

A prime minister's strategy for managing conflict can also be linked to the policy-making process. A prime minister who is an advocate of his or her own position will likely see higher levels of conflict and conflict between the prime minister and other ministers. Conflict that occurs in cabinets led by arbitrators, on the other hand, would more likely be between ministries or factions, since arbitrators allow conflict to occur but do not take a side themselves. A consensual strategy might produce less conflict and see decisions taken in the cabinet as a whole with a consensus rule since the prime minister is most interested in hearing and integrating all positions. A prime minister who chooses to manage conflict by not becoming involved might, in fact, see lower levels of conflict, as decisions, even contradictory ones, would be taken in ministries. It is also more likely that such a prime minister would more likely favor the use of a majority rule—choosing to side with whatever minimum winning coalition first emerges—since this is one way to avoid conflict and get a quick decision.

A prime minister's strategy for managing information can also be expected to have direct effects on processes. If, for example, a prime minister is involved in managing the information and establishes independent sources of information, decisions might more likely occur without advice from the cabinet, or, if the cabinet is involved, the process would be characterized by a higher level of considered proposals as additional information is being introduced by the prime minister.

Finally, the strategy for managing party relations can be linked to the policy-making process. Prime ministers who are competitive with other factions in their party, for example, will likely experience higher levels of cabinet conflict between factions, entertain fewer proposals from challenger factions, and be more likely to engage in opportunistic reshuffles of the cabinet positions.

## ASSESSING THE LINK BETWEEN PRIME MINISTER LEADERSHIP STYLE AND DECISION-MAKING PROCESSES

The relationship between prime ministers' leadership style and decision-making processes can be examined by looking at how actual cabinets made decisions under leaders with different styles. To assess this relationship, two types of evidence are reviewed below. First, a comparative survey of cabinet ministers across Western Europe tapped ministers' perceptions of elements of prime ministers' leadership style as well as perceptions of cabinet policy-making processes. Although this survey was administered by other researchers and for somewhat different purposes, the ministers' responses can be mined for evidence of the link between style and process. Separate questions in the survey asked ministers to assess their prime ministers' styles and their cabinets' decision-making processes. Second, a collection of studies on British cabinets, along with my previous and independent classification of British prime ministers' leadership styles, can be used to assess the style–process relationship across leaders within a single political system.

### Evidence from Comparative Analyses

A significant and unique study on cabinet decision making in Western Europe allows for a comparative investigation of the relationship between leadership style and decision-making processes. In their edited volume *Governing Together: The Extent and Limits of Joint Decision-Making in Western European Cabinets*, Jean Blondel and Ferdinand Müller-Rommel (1993) present data collected for the purpose of comparing the differences in structures and decision-making processes of single-party and coalition cabinets. The data consist of answers to a survey administered in interviews to 400 cabinet ministers and ex-ministers in 12 European countries.[2] With this study, "cabinet behavior can thus be compared across Western Europe in a way that had not previously been possible" (Blondel & Müller-Rommel, 1993: 16).

Of special interest here are the data collected on ministers' views of prime ministers' styles and aspects of the cabinet decision-making process. These data are presented in the chapter "Prime Ministers and Cabinet Decision-Making Processes" by Müller et al. (1993). Two specific elements of prime minister leadership style are included in the study—the prime minister's field of interest in policy making and the prime minister's strategy for dealing with conflict. Field of interest was ascertained by asking ministers if the prime ministers under whom they served were particularly interested in foreign affairs, economic problems, or social policy; were more concerned with overall government organization; or were not interested in any specific aspect of cabinet life. To ascertain the prime minister's strategy for dealing with conflict, ministers were asked if the leaders exercised influence by seeking consensus or forcefully imposing their own solutions.

The study reports mixed evidence on the relationship between these elements of prime minister leadership style and certain cabinet decision-making processes. Perhaps most surprisingly, the amount of conflict in the cabinet, as perceived by the ministers, was not related to the leader's style. "Disagreements are not more or less prevalent whether prime ministers are involved in economic affairs, in foreign affairs, in both, or in neither. They are no more and no less prevalent whether prime ministers are concerned or not with the overall governmental organization. The style, consensual or forceful, does not appear to have an incidence either" (Müller et al., 1993: 246). As previously discussed, we might have expected more consensual prime ministers to see less cabinet conflict compared to prime ministers who advocate their own position, but this is apparently not the case in this study. Unfortunately, the ministers were not asked the locus of conflict, and thus we cannot assess if a prime minister's field of interest might lead to conflict in some parts of the cabinet but not in others or not in the cabinet as a whole.

The minister survey does, however, provide evidence on how prime minister leadership styles influence the collective and hierarchical nature of the cabinet decision-making processes. Ministers were asked how often they or their colleagues participated in cabinet discussions on matters beyond their departmental jurisdiction. The more frequent this practice, the more collective, as opposed to departmental, the decision making appears. The study finds that, not surprisingly, prime ministers with consensual strategies of conflict management were associated with cabinets with collective decision-making processes and that prime ministers with forceful strategies were associated with departmental decision-making processes. Thus, the prime minister's style does seem to affect the collective nature of cabinet decision-making processes, although the authors point out that this is not a perfect relationship. They also report a complex relationship between a leader's field of involvement and collective decision-making processes:

Prime ministers who are concerned with all or most fields of government are more likely to be found in collective cabinets in contrast to those who are not involved in either foreign affairs or the economy, but the relationship stops at this point: the level of prime ministerial concern with the general organization of the government is the same irrespective of the extent to which the cabinet is collective. Moreover, collective cabinets are more likely to be headed by prime ministers who are involved in foreign affairs than by prime ministers interested in the economy. (Müller et al., 1993: 247–48)

Thus, it appears that a prime minister's area of interest and strategy for managing conflict can affect the collective nature of cabinet decision making.

The study also reports a strong relationship between prime minister style and the hierarchical nature of the cabinet. Ministers were asked if cabinet conflicts were solved by prime ministers' stepping in and making an authoritative decision, or a "prime ministerial decision." Prime ministers whose field of interests was economic and foreign affairs were much more likely to impose decisions than were prime ministers not interested in these fields. Furthermore, very few prime ministers with consensual styles and the vast majority of prime ministers with forceful styles imposed prime ministerial decisions on the cabinet. Thus, a prime minister's interest in policy making and strategy for dealing with conflict does seem to directly affect how decisions are made at the cabinet level.

Finally, this comparative study allows us to examine the relationship between a prime minister's style and the centrality of the cabinet. Ministers were asked if the cabinet tended to be the arena in which issues were debated and decisions were taken. Prime ministers who were interested in economic and foreign affairs were associated with cabinets that were more central to the decision-making process, compared to prime ministers whose interests lay in overall government organization. The authors of the study also report a strong relationship between prime ministers' strategies for conflict and the centrality of the government, although the nature of the relationship is somewhat surprising, as prime ministers with forceful styles were associated with cabinets that were central to the decision-making process, and prime ministers with consensual styles were associated with cabinets that were not particularly central. It is possible that the consensual prime mininsters' tactic for preserving consensus involved delegating authority to the departments, and thus the cabinet was less important. Forceful prime ministers, on the other hand, might see the cabinet as the arena in which they could exercise control, thus making it more central to the policy-making process.

This unusual study on cabinet decision-making processes across several European parliamentary systems affords us a look into the relationship between style and process. Consistent with expectations, a consensual conflict management style is associated with more collective cabinets, and a forceful style is associated with cabinets in which decisions are often imposed by the prime minister. Also consistent with expectations, the prime minister's particular interest can affect policy making. Interest in foreign affairs seems to have an especially important relationship to cabinets that are collective and central to the decision-making process but that are also subject to prime ministerial impositions (perhaps limited to the area of foreign affairs). Most surprisingly, neither field of interest nor conflict management style seems to be related to levels of cabinet conflict in this comparative study.

### Evidence from Great Britain

More evidence on the relationship between prime minister leadership style and decision-making processes comes from single-country studies. Students of British politics have been particularly interested in the continuities and changes of cabinet life. In previous research (Kaarbo, 1997; Kaarbo & Hermann, 1998), I have assessed the leadership styles of most postwar British prime ministers along the dimensions presented above. The key differences that emerged from this assessment are presented in Table 5.1. This previous research allows us to examine the relationship between elements of British prime ministers' leadership styles and dynamics of cabinet decision-making processes.

Numerous comparisons of the importance of cabinets to policy making across certain prime ministers' administrations offer opportunity to assess the impact of prime minister leadership style on this aspect of the policy-making process. The number of cabinet meetings, for example, declined under Margaret Thatcher by two-thirds (Thomas, 1998: 188). Under John Major, both the number and length of cabinet meetings rose (Seldon, 1994: 161–62). Compared to Thatcher, Major's government had fewer ad hoc cabinet meetings and fewer ad hoc committees to compete with the cabinet for a central position in policy making (Seldon, 1994: 162–65; James, 1999: 109). Under Major, however, more authority lay in the hands of departments, away from the full cabinet but also away from the Prime Minister's Office, which was more significant under Thatcher (Seldon, 1994: 157; Thomas, 1998: 44). These differences in the centrality of the cabinet possibly stem from the differences in Thatcher's and Major's areas of interest, motivations for leading, and information and conflict management strategies. This relationship would be consistent with the findings from the comparative study reported above.

Evidence on the importance of the cabinet and its relationship to prime minister style can also be found in a set of case studies of cabinet decision-making processes by Martin Burch and Ian Holliday (1996). Burch and Holliday examined 14 cases across four prime ministers (Harold Wilson, L. James Callaghan, Thatcher, and Major). In each case, the authors assessed whether or not the issue took an "orthodox" pathway through the cabinet system, where the final decision was made, and how much overall impact the cabinet system had on the policy that was chosen. The majority of cases under Callaghan followed an orthodox route,

**Table 5.1**
**Classification of British Prime Ministers' Leadership Styles**

---

AREA OF INTEREST

| *Domestic* | *Foreign* | *Government Organization* |
|---|---|---|
| Attlee | Eden, Thatcher | Major |
| | (& most others) | |

EXPERIENCE IN FOREIGN AFFAIRS

| *High* | *Moderate* | *Low* |
|---|---|---|
| Eden, Macmillan | Major | Thatcher |
| Douglas-Home, | | |
| Callaghan | | |

MOTIVATION FOR LEADING

| *Goal-Oriented* | *Political Relationship-Oriented* |
|---|---|
| Attlee, Heath, | Major, Eden, Wilson, |
| Thatcher | Macmillan, Callaghan |

STRATEGY FOR MANAGING CONFLICT

| *Advocate* | *Arbitrator* | *Consensual* |
|---|---|---|
| Thatcher | Attlee | Major |

STRATEGY FOR MANAGING INFORMATION

| *Departments as Sources* | *PM/Independent Sources* |
|---|---|
| Attlee, MacMillan, Major | Eden, Wilson, Thatcher |

STRATEGY FOR MANAGING PARTY RELATIONS

| *Competitive* | *Non-competitive* |
|---|---|
| Thatcher | Major |

---

*Sources*: Barber, 1991; Burch, 1995; Clarke, 1992; Doherty, 1988; Giddings, 1995; Hanrieder
& Auton, 1980; Helms, 1996; Hennessey, 1986; Jones, 1985; Kavanagh, 1994; King, 1985;
Little, 1988; Norton, 1994; Ridley; 1991; Sampson, 1982; Shell, 1995; Shepherd, 1991;
Smith, 1999; Thomas, 1998; Young, 1991.

the majority of cases under Thatcher took unorthodox pathways, and cases under Wilson and Major were evenly split. Final decisions in the Wilson cases tended to be made in the cabinet, final decisions in the Callaghan cases ranged from the Parliament to a cabinet committee to the cabinet, final decisions in the Thatcher cases occurred either in a cabinet committee or informally, and final decisions in the Major government tended to be taken in a cabinet committee. The overall impact of the cabinet system was moderate in the Wilson cases, showed a wide range in the Callaghan and Major cases, and tended to be minimal in the Thatcher cases (although more so at the beginning of her administration and less so near the end). Thus, these cases also show different policy-making processes under prime ministers with different leadership styles.

The amount of conflict in the British cabinet also varies across administrations and may be related to prime minister leadership style. James (1999) argues that the majority of postwar British cabinets (under Harold Macmillan, Edward Heath, Callaghan, Winston Churchill, Clement Attlee, Harold Wilson [from 1974 to 1976], and Alec Douglas-Home) experienced strong collegiality and low levels of conflict, while some (under Anthony Eden, Major, and Wilson [from 1964 to 1970]) experienced moderate collegiality and levels of conflict, and one (under Thatcher) was characterized by weak collegiality and high levels of conflict. Thatcher, of course, stands out on this dimension, and the conflictual nature of policy-making processes in her cabinets may be related to her strategy for managing conflict (advocate) and her strategy for managing party relations (competitive). Cabinet conflict may lead to early termination, before general elections. The only prime ministers to have resigned early, not due to health reasons, are Wilson, Attlee, and Thatcher (Woldendorp et al., 1993). The latter two prime ministers share the goal-oriented element of prime minister style and thus might be expected to generate competitors and be forced to resign. Conflict may also lead to frequent reshuffling of ministers' portfolios, a prerogative of the prime minister. From Attlee to Thatcher, reshuffling was most common in the Heath, Attlee, and Thatcher cabinets and least common in the Eden and Douglas-Home cabinets (Woldendorp et al., 1993). Again, the prime minister's goal orientation is the element shared by those prime ministers with more reshuffles.

Thus, this research on cabinets under various British prime ministers also suggests a link between leadership style and cabinet processes. In particular, the importance of the cabinet to policy making (measured a number of different ways) varied across prime ministers with different areas of interest, motivation, and strategies for managing conflict and information. The amount of conflict in the cabinet (also based on a variety of indicators) varied across prime ministers with different task orientations and strategies for managing conflict and party.

### Discussion

While an examination of this evidence from the comparative study and from studies of British cabinet decision making has provided an opportunity to look at the often-assumed, but rarely investigated, link between leadership style and policy-making processes, this examination must be considered quite preliminary. Several concerns present themselves. First, the relationships between style and process may be overstated if the measures of the variables are not completely independent of each other.

While great care was taken to use different answers in the ministerial survey to assess style versus process and to use different sources (or parts of sources) to assess the styles of British prime ministers versus cabinet decision-making processes, we cannot be certain that they are truly independent. Survey respondents, for example, may have inferred their perception of the leaders' approach to conflict, based on their perception of the level of conflict in the cabinet. Experts on British politics, too, may have deduced a prime minister's motivation for leading from the importance that the cabinet played in policy making, or vice versa. This concern should not, however, be applied to this investigation as a whole. Some variables, such as leader's interest and the frequency of cabinet meetings, are likely to be measuring independent phenomena. Moreover, the relationships were not as perfect as one would expect if the measurement were skewed in a way to support the hypotheses. In the minister survey, for example, respondents clearly had independent visions of a prime minister's approach to conflict and the level of conflict in the cabinet, since there appeared to be no relationship between the two.

Second, while some of the evidence suggests that style and process covary, the causal direction of this relationship remains unknown. Leadership style may not affect the process, as argued, but process may produce leadership style. Rather than directing the process, prime ministers may adapt to the decision-making process around them. They may, for example, adopt different strategies for managing conflict, depending on how central the cabinet is, which may be influenced by the other cabinet ministers' styles, situational changes, or institutional procedures. This concern is more applicable to the strategies for managing conflict, information, and party relations, as the evidence for these aspects of leadership style often comes from the leader's behavior during his or her prime ministership, at a time in which the prime minister may have, indeed, adapted to the cabinet environment. This is less of a concern for other aspects of leadership style, such as a leader's experience, interest, and motivation for leading, as the evidence for these elements usually comes from a portrait of the leader prior to assuming office.

Finally, the relationships that surfaced in this evidence may be spurious. Other factors, such as institutional procedures and power structures, party strength and accountability networks, or situational requirements—factors that have nothing to do with individual characteristics—may have determined both leadership style and policy-making process in patterned ways. While these factors certainly change across time, from Thatcher to Major, for example, evidence demonstrating variation in style and process from single countries that hold some of these conditions constant provides more confidence that how the individual chooses to respond to institutional and situational constraints is somehow connected to underlying individual differences.

## CONCLUSIONS

This last concern, of course, brings up the enduring debate on the role of institutions as compared to the role of individuals—a debate that applies generally to the social sciences as well as specifically to the study of political leadership. While most personality theorists agree that the interaction of situations, institutions, and individual characteristics contributes to individual choice and behavior, the study of prime ministers has largely privileged the institutional explanation. Research suggests, however, that leadership style, given institutional and situational constraints, may still vary due to underlying differences across individual leaders. Furthermore, this study indicates that leadership style may have a direct impact on the policy-making process.

More research is necessary, however, to address the above concerns. In particular, quality data on cabinet life under prime ministers facing similar external constraints are needed to investigate how the choices that prime ministers make in managing those around them affect the policy-making process. These data could take many forms. A survey of cabinet ministers, similar to the one administered in the Blondel and Müller-Rommel (1993) project, could incorporate more of the elements of prime minister leadership style and additional questions on the policy-making process. Evidence could also be collected from newspaper or other "cabinet-watcher" sources. The Blondel and Müller-Rommel study did include such evidence on cabinet conflict (e.g., duration of conflicts, how conflicts were resolved, who was involved in the conflict), but, unfortunately, the data were presented only across countries, not across prime ministers. Finally, a set of carefully selected case studies of prime ministers with similar and different styles facing similar and different policy problems could be collected to assess the style–process relationship. While labor-intensive, these methods of data collection could help address some of the above concerns, particularly the issues of independence of measurement and spuriousness. A study of leaders whose styles could be completely measured prior to assuming office, such as foreign ministers or party leaders who later become prime minister, could address the direction of causality problem.

Additional research is also needed on the link between process and policy, which is also often assumed but rarely examined (George, 1980; Hermann, 1980; Janis, 1972). While a prime minister's leadership style may be directly related to policy (e.g., a prime minister who shows a competitive strategy for dealing with party factions might also favor policy that is competitive or zero-sum with other political actors), it is more likely that leadership style affects policy indirectly through the process. For example, a prime minister can structure the process so that few alternative proposals are considered. Proposals that are never considered will obviously not emerge as policy output. On the other hand, if the prime minister's leadership style allows for a large number of proposals to be considered, and if the prime minister arbitrates among those proposals and encourages compromises, the resulting policy will be a hybrid of the proposals.

To further specify the indirect effects of leadership style on policy, it is necessary to know the content of the proposals, the actors who advocate those proposals, or both. For example, if we know that the prime minister has a competitive strategy for managing party relations, and if we know what policy a challenger faction advocates, we can predict that this policy advocated by this faction will not emerge as the final decision. Knowing only which policies are considered and which factions are advocating them is not enough. Leadership style is the necessary factor that tells us which policy will eventually win out and why.

Leadership styles—of prime ministers, presidents, and authoritarian leaders—are an important factor for understanding politics and policy. A leader's approach to managing actors and information links the individuals at the highest level of government, the institutional and structural constraints they face, the policy-making process, and the options that become policy. While this effort was a preliminary investigation of one aspect of this complex chain (the style–process connection), it offers validity to this often assumed relationship.

## NOTES

1. For a more detailed discussion of these elements and evidence of variation across British prime ministers and German chancellors, see Kaarbo (1997) and Kaarbo and Hermann (1998).

2. The following countries were included in the Blondel and Müller-Rommel study: Britain, Ireland, France, Belgium, the Netherlands, Germany, Denmark, Norway, Sweden, Finland, Austria, and Italy. For further descriptions of the ministerial survey, see the editors' introductory chapter and Appendix I in Blondel & Müller-Rommel (1993).

Chapter 6

# Kings, Queens, and Sultans: Empirical Studies of Political Leadership in European Hereditary Monarchies

Dean Keith Simonton

## INTRODUCTION

Political leadership may adopt many forms, depending on the specific system of government. Yet almost every political system has a special spot reserved at the top for that leader who can be considered the nation's head of state. This is the individual who has the primary responsibility for the formulation and execution of policy, both at home and abroad. In modern times, especially in the world's democracies, the nation's leaders are most likely to have titles like prime minister or president. Moreover, the individuals who possess these titles are usually elected to their position, either directly or indirectly, and have their powers constrained by a written constitution or at least by historical convention and legal precedent. As part of these conspicuous constraints, such heads of state can be peacefully obliged to leave office, whether by term limits imposed on their tenure or by outright defeat in the voting booth. As Benjamin Disraeli once put it when he was appointed prime minister of Great Britain, "Yes, I have climbed to the top of the greasy pole" (*Who Said What When*, 1991: 256). Finally, any citizen of the country can rise to the nation's highest spot, at least nominally. Native-born children in the United States, for example, can say, "I want to be president when I grow up" without fear that some playmate or parent will say, "But that's impossible."

Yet in the history of world politics, presidents and prime ministers represent a relatively uncommon category of political leadership. In fact, prior to World War I, monarchs—from the Egyptian pharaohs and the Chinese emperors to Russian tsars and Ottoman sultans—dominated political history. All told, there were at least 13,000 monarchs in the world, a figure that easily exceeds even the most inclusive list of prime ministers and presidents (Tapsell, 1983). But why should these rulers still interest us? After all, the institution is almost obsolete, surviving in only a few places in the world in its pure form.

I begin this chapter by examining the justification for using hereditary monarchs in empirical studies of political leadership. I then review what such research has discovered about the nature of political leadership, with special emphasis on leader performance. Finally, those findings are compared to what has been learned in research on presidents of the United States.

## ADVANTAGES

Despite their rarity in recent world history, monarchs actually have several assets as subjects of empirical investigations into political leadership. These assets emerge from the following five distinctive features of monarchy.

First, although some monarchies were elective or operated by appointment or adoption, the majority of these were hereditary, typically following a parent–child or grandparent–grandchild line of succession. One immediate consequence of this succession is that hereditary monarchs can rule their nations for a very long time—sometimes close to an entire life span. Usually their tenure in office is limited only by how long they live after ascending to the throne. This gives hereditary monarchs an incredible opportunity to leave their mark on the history of their nation. No president of the United States served longer than Franklin Roosevelt, and yet his mere dozen years pales in comparison to the 72 years that Louis XIV was king of France. In general, monarchs typically rule three to four times longer than presidents or prime ministers (Sorokin, 1926).

Second, because the right to rule is determined by inheritance, it often became possible for women to govern whole nations. To be sure, many countries forbid female succession, as in the Salic law that ensured that no queen would rule France or Bourbon Spain. Even so, a sufficient number of nations permitted such succession as to fill history with the names of great women leaders. Obvious examples include Margaret of Denmark and Norway, Isabella I of Spain, Elizabeth I of England, Catherine the Great of Russia, and Maria Theresa of Austria. This situation contrasts greatly (and sadly) with the dearth of female prime ministers and presidents. For every Margaret Thatcher, Golda Meier, or Indira Gandhi there are dozens of queens and empresses who stood at the apex of their political system.

Third, in hereditary monarchies it is possible to gauge whether political genius is born or made. The pedigree of most royal families is extremely well established, permitting the determination of how genetic relatedness influences the leadership qualities of monarchs. This also differs greatly from the situation that prevails in democratic heads of state. The Pitt family among British prime ministers or the Adams, Harrison, and Bush families among U.S. presidents are the exception rather than the rule. Certainly, democratic systems have no counterpart to the current imperial line of Japan, which dates back over a millennium.

Fourth, for much of the history of the world's hereditary monarchies, there were few, if any, constraints on their political powers—as implied by the term "absolute monarch." To be sure, the kings of feudal times were often little more than "first among peers," their power being heavily contingent on the goodwill of their vassals. Moreover, in more modern times "constitutional monarchs" evolved, the constraining powers of parliaments largely reducing kings and queens to mere figureheads, as is the case in European monarchies today. Even so, for significant periods of history the world's monarchs enjoyed executive, legislative, judicial, and military powers that some modern heads of state would envy. Probably only contemporary dictators come close to this degree of control over their nation's affairs. As a result, absolute monarchs provide an ideal opportunity to gauge the relation between the ruler's personal qualities and the nation's welfare.

Fifth and last, of all systems of government, monarchy was the most widely distributed geographically and historically. Indeed, the emergence of monarchs is among the first things that define the transformation of a culture into a bona fide civilization (Carneiro, 1970). As a consequence, monarchical leadership provides an ideal vehicle for expanding any comparative study of political leaders. Although monarchs are unique in many ways, they still may share a lot of common characteristics with more modern heads of state. These shared attributes should give hints about those aspects of political leadership that are most likely to be cross-culturally and transhistorically invariant (Simonton, 1990). Whenever an empirical finding transcends time and place in this fashion, it is more likely to remain true well into the future as well. Such results would have a higher likelihood of still remaining valid even when subsequent governmental innovations introduce totally novel types of political leadership.

These assets will become more apparent when I review what has been already learned in empirical studies of hereditary monarchs.

## RESEARCH

Frederick Woods conducted the first scientific study of monarchs in 1906. His specific focus was the distribution of intelligence and morality in royal lines. He showed, for example, that intellect and virtue were positively correlated, a finding later replicated by Edward L. Thorndike (1936) in a follow-up study published decades later. From the standpoint of political leadership, however, another inquiry by Woods (1913) has even more interest. Woods assessed the leadership qualities of hundreds of European hereditary monarchs and then evaluated the general state of the nation during each ruler's reign. He reported a positive correlation between the two—the first empirical demonstration that political leaders may really matter.

More than a decade later, the eminent sociologist Pitirim Sorokin (1925, 1926) published a two-part study of monarchs and other kinds of rulers, making statistical comparisons with respect to various personal qualities, such as ability and life span. Yet after the publication of these two papers there appears something of a hiatus in the literature, modern forms of leadership taking precedence. In fact, sometimes monarchs would be deliberately excluded as unsuitable subjects. An example is Cox's (1926) inquiry into the relation between intelligence and achieved eminence in a sample of 301 historical personalities. Although she included 109 eminent leaders, not one was a hereditary monarch. Rulers like Elizabeth I of England, Philip II of Spain, Louis XIV of France, Peter the Great of Russia, and Charles XII of Sweden were summarily dismissed because Cox believed that their status in the annals of history was ascribed rather than achieved!

Nonetheless, psychologists have recently returned to monarchs as exemplars of political leadership. David Winter (1993) included 300 years of the British monarchy as part of a larger investigation into how the outbreak of war is associated with leaders who exhibit high power motivation but low affiliation motivation. I conducted a single-case, time-series analysis of King George III of Great Britain to determine whether his mental breakdowns could be attributed to sources of personal and political stress during his reign (Simonton, 1998a). However, below I would like to focus on a series of studies that were originally inspired by the pioneering work of Woods (1906, 1913) and Sorokin (1925, 1926). These investigations concern how political leadership is associated with (1) individual differences across hereditary monarchs and (2) longitudinal changes across the course of each monarch's reign.

## Individual Differences in Monarchical Characteristics

One fact has been established beyond any doubt: kings, queens, and other monarchs vary tremendously in personality, including those attributes associated with leadership. For instance, when Woods (1906) rated the intellect of royalty on a 10-point scale, Catherine the Great of Russia was honored with a score of 10, whereas Charles II of Spain received a mere 1. Likewise for virtue, the scores could range from 10 for

Gustavus Adolphus of Sweden to 1 for Peter the Cruel of Castile and Leon. Two questions can be asked about this substantial cross-sectional variation. First, what are the origins of these individual differences? Are they genetic or environmental? Second and most critical, what is the connection between individual differences in the monarch's personal qualities and his or her long-term eminence as the nation's ruler?

### Are Great Leaders Born or Made?

Hereditary monarchy is founded on that twofold premise that (1) certain leaders possess superior "kingly" characteristics and that (2) these personal assets can be passed down to their offspring in a "like father, like son" or "chip off the old block" fashion. This doctrine of "royal blood" was tested in a sample of 342 hereditary monarchs who represented 14 distinct European nations, from Scandinavia to Spain and from France to the Ottoman empire (Simonton, 1983). These rulers, along with their parents, grandparents, and predecessors, were then assessed on the following variables: intelligence, morality, leadership, eminence, life span, reign span, and ultimate eminence in history. The intelligence and morality ratings were adapted from Woods (1906), and the leadership ratings came largely from Woods (1913), while the eminence scores came from a measure of how much attention the monarch receives in encyclopedias, biographical dictionaries, and histories (see Simonton, 1991a, for a psychometric evaluation of such measures).

If these personal characteristics are subject to the laws of genetic inheritance, then certain patterns should emerge in the correlations. For instance, a monarch's genetic similarity to a grandparent should be only half as great as to that of a parent. Thus, Queen Elizabeth I should be two times more similar to Henry VIII than to Henry VII. Detailed analysis revealed that this was true for two attributes, intelligence and life span. Hence, cognitive ability and biological longevity appear to be passed down royal lineages in a genetic fashion. Yet other monarchical characteristics were not transferred in this manner. In particular, the transfer of morality and eminence from generation to generation was more consistent with what would be predicted from role-modeling effects. For example, the degree to which two monarchs were similar on these characteristics was more strongly determined by the amount of contact that the persons had than by their degree of genetic relatedness. In the case of assessed leadership, in fact, monarchs were actually more similar to their grandparental than to their parental predecessors. Furthermore, the degree of intergenerational similarity was sometimes contingent on gender, in a fashion inconsistent with any known genetic hypothesis. Specifically, the historical eminence of a king bears a consistent correlation with the eminence of his father, should he also have been king, but the eminence of a queen has no such relation. This result suggests that role-modeling effects are stronger for same-sex parent–child relationships and transfers of power.

Despite all of these complexities, one broad generalization persists: hereditary monarchy provides an effective means of maintaining the quality of political leadership across consecutive heads of state. For no attribute was the predecessor–successor correlation negative. Therefore, if one monarch is highly accomplished, so will the family member who follows. Such is the situation when a dynasty is at its acme of political power and influence. Yet this very continuity can work in a dysfunctional manner as well. Inferior rulers will be more likely followed by other inferior rulers, until the ruling dynasty is finally overthrown. This pattern is commonplace in hereditary monarchies. Indeed, the Chinese historian Pan Piao and the Islamic thinker Ibn Khaldun constructed their philosophies of history around this very observation.

### Are Great Leaders the Right Person or Merely at the Right Place and Time?

The foregoing analysis assumed that rulers' personal qualities bear some connection with their political leadership. This assumption is compatible with Thomas Carlyle's (1841: 1) belief that "[t]he history of the World is but the Biography of great men." Yet not everyone believes that the head of state's individual attributes have any genuine causal relevance. A classic example is Leo Tolstoy, who devoted a large part of the Epilogues of his *War and Peace* to debunking the great person theory of history.

A king is history's slave. History, that is, the unconscious, general, hive life of mankind uses every moment of the life of kings as a tool for its own purposes. In historic events, the so-called great men are labels giving names to events, and like labels they have but the smallest connection with the event itself. Every act of theirs, which appears to them an act of their own will, is in a historical sense involuntary and is related to the whole course of history and predestined from eternity. (Tolstoy, 1862–1869/1952: 343–44)

If the great leader has not control over the course of events, then it is clearly irrelevant what his or her intentions may be. A well-meaning monarch can reign over national disasters, while an ill-intentioned monarch can still govern during times of prosperity and triumph.

Especially interesting is Tolstoy's claim that the "so-called great men" are merely names for events—that they constitute historically impotent eponyms. This assertion resonates in a curious fashion with an observation made by Sorokin (1926: 533) in his statistical study of monarchs: "The duration of life of the great monarchs is higher than that of the average ones." In hereditary monarchies, how long a ruler lives should be the primary determinant of how long he or she reigns. Furthermore, the longer the monarch's reign, the more historical events will tend to appear, independently of what the ruler actually seeks as a matter of personality or policy. Finally, the greater the number of events, the higher will be the monarch's utility as an eponym, as a Tolstoyan label for a period in history. Is it any accident, for example, that history is often sliced up in phrases like the Elizabethan Age, the Age of Louis XIV, or the Victorian Age? After all, Elizabeth, Louis XIV, and Victoria were all monarchs who governed their countries for an unusually long period of time.

Tolstoy's eponymic theory was tested on the same 342 monarchs used in the preceding investigation (Simonton, 1984b). To the original set of measures—eminence, leadership, intelligence, morality, reign span, and life span—was added another, the degree of historical activity during each ruler's tenure on the throne. This assessment was a simple count of all events that were included in a large collection of historical chronologies, such as wars, battles, revolts, rebellions, riots, laws, reforms, epidemics, famines, economic booms and busts, and so forth.

This tabulation of historical activity accounted for 39% of the variation in leader eminence, a figure far higher than for any other predictor. In addition, the single best predictor of historical activity was how long the monarch reigned, 18% of the variance being thus explained. Finally, as hypothesized, the most potent predictor of reign span was how long the monarch lived. Hence, the outcome is the following Tolstoyan causal chain:

Life Span $\rightarrow$ Reign Span $\rightarrow$ Historical Activity $\rightarrow$ Leader Eminence

What about the monarch's qualities of leadership, intelligence, leadership, or morality? All of these personal attributes were relevant, but to a very weak degree and often in a surprising manner. The following three points deserve emphasis:

1. Intelligence had an impact on leader eminence, reign span, and life span but explained only 5%, 2%, and 4% of the variance, respectively. This predictive power is superior to that of any of the other two leader traits. Yet only in the case of life span was the association positive and linear. Especially striking was the U-shaped relationship between intelligence and reign span. Those monarchs who have the longest tenures in office are either very bright or very dull. The former probably have the wit to outsmart various conspiracies that might arise, whereas the latter are likely mere figureheads in the hands of powerful ministers.

2. The monarch's assessed leadership predicts only reign span and accounts for solely 2% of the variance. Presumably, those with superior skills as politicians will be less threatened by the danger of usurpation.

3. The ruler's rated morality predicts both leader eminence and historical activity, yet with two quirks. First and perhaps a bit sadly, the monarch's ethical caliber has the most minimal predictive usefulness, smaller than any other factor examined. Morality accounted for only 0.7% of the variance in historical activity and only 0.5% of the variance in leader eminence. Hence, in both cases, the leader's "virtues and vices" explain less than 1% of the variance in either variable. Second, in both instances the function is described by a U-shaped curve. The monarchs who have the most eponymic value and enjoy the greatest eminence are those who are either very good or very bad—saint or sinner. In contrast, those who are, like Shakespeare's Hamlet, "only indifferent honest," are more prone to end up in obscurity.

Of course, an advocate of Carlyle's great leader theory might object that the historical activity measure contains many events that are the direct result of the ruler's leadership. The monarch may decide to conquer a neighboring country and even personally lead the armed forces on the battlefield. Yet, curiously, a detailed analysis of this composite index revealed an empirical weakness in this argument. Those events over which the leader had considerable control had about the same impact on his or her eminence as those over which he or she had no control whatsoever (e.g., whether or not the ruler was commanding the troops in battle). Even more strikingly, it also did not matter whether the events were good or bad, so long as they were notable. Thus, military defeats counted the same as military victories, major governmental reforms as much as unfortunate episodes of corruption, and so forth. In fact, the more eminent monarchs were more likely to have suffered a violent death, an event that they certainly did not consider positive. All in all, in line with the eponymic theory, the most critical factor in the determination of leader eminence is simply whether the monarch provides a convenient historiographic label for a period of salient events.

Before I leave this subject, two additional empirical findings are worth noting. The first is a null result: female monarchs did not differ from male monarchs in any important way. Queens were neither better nor worse than kings or sultans. The second finding is evidence for the biblical warning "He who lives by the sword dies by the sword." Those who obtained the throne by violent means were more likely to leave it in the same manner. England's Richard III is a prototypical example.

## Developmental Changes in Monarchical Expertise

As noted earlier in this chapter, hereditary monarchs can reign for a very long time. From the perspective of political leadership, however, this may not be an asset. On the one side, the ruler may succeed to the throne at too young an age to exhibit effective leadership. To be sure, a regency will be imposed if the monarch is excessively young, but even at attaining majority, the youth may lack sufficient maturity. This possibility was recognized by the authors of the U.S. Constitution when they specified that the president had to be at least 35 years old. On the other side of the age dimension, a ruler may govern far past his or her prime. As the infirmities of age set in, the country may be as much the loser. In support of these conjectures, an extensive literature suggests that achievement in many domains is often a curvilinear, single-peaked function of age (Simonton, 1988a).

Two studies have examined whether such a function also holds for monarchical leadership.

### The Reigns of Long-Tenured European Monarchs

The first inquiry began with the 342 monarchs studied in the previous investigations but then took those 25 who governed their nations the longest (Simonton, 1984a). These 25 still represented over a dozen countries and covered from 1072 to 1780 of European history. All of the sampled monarchs had ruled at least 36 years, and the average reign span was an impressive 43 years (excluding periods under regents). The reigns of each monarch were then divided into consecutive 5-year age periods, following the procedures used in previous studies of the age–achievement relation (e.g., Quètelet, 1968; Lehman, 1953; Simonton, 1977). Into these time-series units were tabulated several kinds of events that assessed various aspects of foreign and domestic affairs. After introducing several control variables as well, each of these assessments was subjected to a trend analysis to determine how the state of the nation changed over the course of the monarch's reign. Several significant trends were identified.

In the first place, as the monarch ages, the nation over which he or she rules has a lower likelihood of invading another nation or conquering foreign territory. In fact, as the ruler gets older, the nation is actually more likely to lose territory to the conquests of neighboring states. The number of military victories also declines as the monarch gets older, at least if the ruler's personal contribution to the nation's military success is considered. In other words, older kings are less likely to lead their nation's troops in battle. Older monarchs also appear to be less accomplished in diplomacy, because the number of important treaties declines as well. Moreover, at the domestic level, matters tend to deteriorate in several respects as the monarch ages. Toward the later years of the reign the monarch has to cope with increasing disturbances involving either the populace or members of the royal family. In fact, only one national condition appears to increase during the course of the monarch's reign: literary activity! That is, the latter part of a monarch's reign is more likely to be graced by a large number of literary masterworks. Perhaps this reflects a shift in the ruler's interests, cultural activities replacing political ambitions.

Even more fascinating, however, are the two curvilinear functions—both U-shaped rather than inverted-U. These single-trough functions were found for national defeat and losses of territory by conquest, with the low point around the monarch's 42nd year. Another way of putting this is to say that monarchs who are in their mid-40s are most likely to preside over a nation that has a strong military. Interestingly, this is about the same age at which generals are most likely to emerge victorious on the battlefield (Simonton, 1980). This peak also corresponds to the specific experience of Louis XIV. The peak of French military might occurred around 1680, when the king was 42 years old, while French hegemony suffered a serious decline during the War of the Spanish Succession, when the monarch was in his early 60s and early 70s.

### The Reigns of British Kings, Queens, and Regents

The above investigation was the first ever to examine how the monarch's age might affect the quality of political leadership that he or she displays. This meant that it had one or more methodological inadequacies, a common problem with pioneering studies. Perhaps the most irksome difficulty is the fact that it did not distinguish between chronological and career age. Recent theoretical and empirical work has shown that this is a crucial distinction (Simonton, 1997). Chronological age is the number years that the person has accumulated since birth, whereas career (or professional) age is the number of years that the individual has accumulated in a particular career (or profession). For monarchs, the latter would be a count of the number of years that they have been sitting on the throne. General developmental changes due to the maturation process are captured by chronological age, whereas longitudinal changes specific to mastering a profession are registered by career age. In particular, career age has more to do with the acquisition of domain-specific expertise. Empirical investigations demonstrate that the two sets of age trends do not have to coincide with each other (Simonton, 2000).

To test whether this distinction is useful in the area of political leadership, data were collected on all kings, queens, and regents who governed England from 1066 to 1811, that is, from William the Conqueror to George III (Simonton, 1998b). This period was again sliced into consecutive five-year periods, producing 110 time-series units. For each unit the leader's chronological age and career age (i.e., the number of years the ruler had been governing) were calculated. Also for each unit the events corresponding to 17 criteria of leader performance were tabulated, including both foreign and domestic affairs. The time-series analysis revealed a complex set of trends, as the following three examples illustrate:

1. The monarch's activity as a legislator and reformer is a function of chronological age but not career age. In particular, such involvement is a curvilinear, inverted-U function of the monarch's actual age, with peaks at 45 for legislation and at 42 for reforms. These age optima fit nicely with the tendency for creative achievement to peak in the early to middle 40s (Simonton, 1988a) and for creativity in leaders to be strongly associated with legislative activity (Simonton, 1988b). This hints that the ruler's achievements in these performance areas may operate according to the same processes that underlie creativity in the arts and sciences (Simonton, 1997).

2. The monarch's responsibilities as the nation's commander in chief are associated with career age, not chronological age. Specifically, war years, battles fought, battle victories, invasions of other nations, and territorial gains are all curvilinear, single-trough functions of how long the ruler has reigned. The low points all fall somewhere around the 20th year of the reign. Hence, these monarchs are most likely to engage in military activities toward the beginning and the end of their tenure on the throne, regardless of how old they happen to be.

3. Various disturbances provoked by the aristocracy, such as baronial revolts, are functions of both chronological and career age. On the one hand, the frequency of aristocratic disturbances is an inverted-U function of chronological age, with the peak at age 43. On the other hand, these disturbances are related to career age according to a backward-J curve, with a trough at the 22nd year into the reign. Although it is difficult to interpret what these two trends imply about political leadership, that may not be a very interesting issue anyway, given that such disturbances are peculiar to hereditary monarchies. Certainly, most presidents and prime ministers do not have to worry about such outbreaks. So it suffices to note that occasionally the leader's performance can be a joint function of both chronological and career age.

At the same time, it also should be recognized that most performance indicators are a function of either chronological age or career age but not both.

## COMPARISONS

Although I have published a half dozen articles on hereditary monarchs, my research on political leadership has primarily concentrated on a totally different form of the phenomenon: the performance of U.S. presidents. This work began in the early 1980s (e.g., Simonton, 1981, 1985b, 1986a, 1987a) and culminated in a book on *Why Presidents Succeed* (Simonton, 1987b), which was then followed by several studies that built upon the theoretical and empirical framework developed in that book (e.g., Simonton, 1988b, 1993, 1996, in press). As a consequence of that work, I have to come to appreciate that certain generic findings transcend the specific type of political leadership. To a very large extent, the performance of a head of state is governed by the same principles no matter whether the leader is a hereditary monarch or an elected chief executive. Most strikingly, the factors that predict the historical eminence of monarchs are conceptually similar, if not identical, to those that predict the assessed greatness of U.S. presidents. Consider the following five findings.

1. The most powerful single predictor of presidential greatness is how long the person served in office (Simonton, 1981, 1991b, in press). This is true even if statistical control is introduced for whether or not the president had been re-elected to a second term (Simonton, 1986b). In other words, the positive association holds even if the analysis is confined to either one- or two-term chief executives. In contrast, the number of times that a president was elected (or re-elected) to office has no correlation with presidential greatness once tenure duration is partialed out. Hence, it is not a mere matter of the long-tenured presidents having been certified by the American voter as excellent political leaders. This result closely parallels the finding that reign span correlates with a monarch's eminence more highly than any other variable except for the index of historical activity for which it is a conceptual proxy (Simonton, 1984b).

2. Those presidents who were assassinated in office are rated more highly in greatness than those who were not (Simonton, 1986b, 1996, in press). Similarly, monarchs who died a violent death are more eminent than are those who died naturally (Simonton, 1984b). Although the latter variable is more inclusive, that may just reflect the fact that monarchs, especially kings, had the option of personally leading their armies into battle. No president of the United States has tried to imitate King Gustavus Adophus of Sweden, who was shot leading a cavalry charge at the Battle of Lutzen. Perhaps if a president had died in such fashion, he also would have gained in assessed greatness. In partial support of this conjecture, U.S. presidents are more likely to have higher greatness ratings if they had been national war heroes prior to entering office (Simonton, 1986b, 1996, in press). George Washington and Andrew Jackson are prime examples.

3. Although no study has yet tested whether an inclusive index of historical activity would predict presidential greatness, research has shown conclusively that those who had served as commander in chief during wartime tend to receive higher evaluations in posterity's eyes (Simonton, 1986b, 1991b, in press). Specifically, presidential greatness assessments are positively correlated with the number of war years during the president's administration. This positive association still holds even after statistically controlling for the number of years that the president served in office (which correlates with both presidential greatness and number of war years, and thus could be a source of spuriousness). Ob-

vious instances are Abraham Lincoln, Woodrow Wilson, and Franklin Roosevelt. This finding overlaps the relation between historical activity and monarchical eminence to the extent that the events of war tend to dominate the annals of history. "War makes rattling good history; but Peace is poor reading. So I back [Napoleon] Bonaparte for the reason that he will give pleasure to posterity," said a character in *The Dynasts* by Thomas Hardy (1903–1908/1978: 88).

4. Presidential greatness is a curvilinear, U-shaped function of a measure of dogmatism (Simonton, 1986b, 1987b). The latter measure assesses where the chief executive stands on a bipolar dimension that ranges from the rigid and idealistic at one pole to the pragmatic and flexible at the other. Where the former types are very moralistic, the latter types are so driven by political expediency that they are often perceived as Machiavellian wheeler-dealer politicians. Thus, this functional association is quite similar to the U-shape relation that holds between a monarch's historical eminence and his or her assessed morality or virtue.

5. Although the U.S. presidents have been assessed on dozens of cognitive, motivational, and personality attributes, only one has emerged as a consistent predictor of presidential greatness, namely, the chief executive's intelligence (Simonton, 1986c, 1988b; cf. McCann, 1992; Simonton, 1992). Similarly, intelligence correlates more strongly with monarchical leadership—and with more aspects of the phenomenon—than did any other individual-difference factor besides life span (Simonton, 1983, 1984b). Both of these findings fall right into line with the more general finding that intelligence is the personal quality that most consistently predicts leader performance in the greatest variety of circumstances (Simonton, 1995). In other words, the strong predictive value of intelligence for both monarchical and presidential performance goes beyond the confines of political leadership. In all likelihood it represents something intrinsic to the very nature of the performance of all types of leaders (Simonton, 1985a).

Investigations by other researchers have identified similar universals. For example, Winter (e.g., 1973, 1991b) has shown how the motivational makeup of leaders determines their performance in a manner that may transcend the peculiarities of any given leadership position. In particular, power motivation is associated with aggressive and dominating behavior in all kinds of leaders, including monarchs and U.S. presidents (Winter, 1987, 1993). When these results are combined with findings concerning the determinants of presidential greatness, it becomes clear that monarchical leadership does not really constitute a freakish form of leadership. To be sure, a king, queen, or sultan may have entered office in a fashion alien to democratic systems and may even enjoy privileges and responsibilities unknown to a duly elected president or prime minister. Nevertheless, at bottom, they remain human beings who are attempting to exercise political leadership. As such, they provide useful exemplars of this very important phenomenon.

Chapter 7

# Mao Zedong's Narcissistic Personality Disorder and China's Road to Disaster

Michael M. Sheng

## INTRODUCTION

Mao Zedong, the Chinese Communist Party (CCP) leader, was undoubtedly one of the most powerful and significant political leaders of the twentieth century; he ruled more than one-fifth of the world's population in 1949–1976. Yet, he remains a mystery a quarter of a century after his death. Seemingly a great leader, why did he launch the fantastically bizarre "Great Leap Forward" (GLF) in 1958–1960, during which more than 30 million people died of starvation? Why did he decide to split with his Soviet ally, when he was provoking a confrontation with the United States in the Taiwan Straits in 1958? Why did he wage one political campaign after another in the 10 years of so-called Great Proletarian Cultural Revolution? During that revolution the Chinese people and economy suffered a great deal, and Mao nearly destroyed the CCP and its state power, things that he had fought hard to establish.

## RESEARCH METHOD

This study uses psychoanalytical theories on pathological narcissism, particularly those of Otto Kernberg (1975, 1985) and Heinz Kohut (1971, 1977, 1978, 1985) to examine the behavioral pattern of Mao. The working hypothesis is that Mao was afflicted by narcissistic personality disorder, which, in turn, was responsible for much of his destructive behavior.

This diagnostic evaluation of Mao's personality is derived first on the basis of the American Psychiatric Association's *Diagnostic and Statistical Manual* (DSM-IV), which lists nine diagnostic criteria:

1. Has a grandiose sense of self-importance.

2. Is preoccupied with fantasies of unlimited success, power, brilliance, and so on.

3. Believes that he or she is "special" and unique and can be understood only by, or should associate with, other special, high-status people or institutions.

4. Requires excessive admiration.

5. A sense of entitlement, that is, unreasonable expectations of especially favorable treatment or automatic compliance with his or her expectations.

6. Is interpersonally exploitative, that is, takes advantage of others to achieve his or her own ends.

7. Lack of empathy: unwilling to recognize or identify with the feelings and needs of others.

8. Is often envious of others or believes that others are envious of him or her.

9. Arrogant, haughty behavior or attitudes.

A person has to have at least five of the above to be diagnosed as a patient with narcissistic personality disorder. Clinicians treating this category of patients consistently emphasize self-esteem, which takes two forms: grandiosity and inferiority (Derksen, 1995: 89–90).

The DSM-IV, however, has its limits as a diagnostic tool for the evaluation of a past or distant political figure such as Mao. That is because each individual story about Mao's behavior is anecdotal, and each of the criteria does not have quantitative measurements. What measure of self-importance is "grandiose" and therefore pathological? Thus, it is difficult to make a convincing case without a systematic analysis of the genesis and dynamics of Mao's personality. Therefore, I turn to two distinguished theoreticians and practitioners in psychoanalysis, Kernberg and Kohut. (For more information about the evolution and application of clinical theories and the two men's roles in them, interested readers can consult Mishne, 1993.) Both men emphasize the grandiosity-inferiority structure of narcissistic patients, as Kernberg (1975: 227) put it, the "curious apparent contradiction between a very inflated concept of themselves and an inordinate need for tribute from others." Kohut goes further to draw a line between the "defensive structure" and "compensatory structure"; while the function of the former is to cover over the primary defect in the self, the latter is to compensate for it (Kohut, 1977: 3–4). Along this line I postulate that central to Mao's pathology was the co-existence of grandiosity and inferiority/insecurity; the latter was the primary pathogenic defect, while the former was a defense mechanism against the latter. Mao's psychic structure was a result of an inability to maintain narcissistic equilibrium by regulating his self-esteem. This inability led to his oscillations between depression, paranoia, and antisocial self-isolation, on one hand, and exuberance in pursuit of unrealistic grandiose fantasies, on the other. To understand the dynamics of Mao's personality, I now examine the genesis of Mao's narcissism.

## SPLITTING: THE GENESIS OF MAO'S PERSONALITY PATHOLOGY

Mao was born in 1893 to a peasant family in central China, with an overprotective mother and a harsh father. The contrast of parental demeanor toward the child can be pathogenic. Mao's mother was a loving person of Buddhist conviction whose indulgence of her first son was enhanced by cultural elements particular to a Chinese woman. Like any newlywed, she was nobody in the Mao family hierarchy until she proved her "worthiness" by giving birth to a male offspring, who proved her fertility and established her status as the future mother-in-law and the matriarch (Wolf, 1970). Her over-supply of gratification to young Mao might have encouraged him to feel that he and the outer world were the same; he was at the center of an "all-good" world, worthy of and entitled to the treatment that he was receiving. This archaic, grandiose self is modified in a child's normal psychic development when the aim-inhibiting and ego-controlling elements, such as the parent saying no to the child, are gently introduced into his or her developmental process.

This normal process, however, did not occur in Mao. Feeling that he and the outer world were "all-good," the sudden entry of the harsh and critical father presented an opposite world, making him feel that he and the world were "all-bad." Mao's parental imagoes were in such startling contrast that the young mind of Mao failed to absorb the outside stimuli gradually and gently to accomplish the developmental task of integration to form a healthy and balanced self. Instead, the process of "splitting" was taking place as a defense mechanism: The young Mao's mind compartmentalized the "all-bad" world and himself in one box and the "all-good" world and himself in another. To avoid the devastating feeling of a worthless self in a cruel world, he would retreat into the "all-good" compartment, where he could fantasize a worthy self in a perfect world, which was a regression into his archaic narcissism.

Like any analysis of the initial pathogenic arrests of a grown-up, the above analysis is necessarily speculative. To substantiate it, I will now examine Mao's diametrically opposite parental images first, followed by his opposing self-concepts.

### An "All-Bad" Father

From very early in his life, the young Mao became rebellious against his father and, thus, against the prevailing cultural norm as well. When Mao was 27 years old, his father died; he did not even bother to go home for the funeral. Considering the Confucian norm of the day that demanded the son to stay home mourning the father for three years, Mao's behavior was clearly against the dominant social-cultural values. While in his early 40s, he told Edgar Snow that his father was a "severe taskmaster" and a "hot-tempered man" who made Mao work in the field in the day and do his bookkeeping at the night and yet gave Mao no money and the "most meager food." The old man also beat Mao "frequently." "I learned to hate him," Mao said (Snow, 1968: 130–38).

Mao's aggression toward his father was an effort to escape from the grasp of the darkness of his father imago; and yet, he actually internalized his father's values and attitudes. Just as so many people who were abused early in their life become abusive, Mao turned out to be a harsh and distant father to his own children. His angry censure of his second son was so severe and scary that it triggered the junior's first episode of schizophrenia. Mao avoided seeing his daughters, who lived in the same compound; he allowed them to come to visit him only a couple of times in a year. When he was dying, none of the three surviving children were present at his deathbed (Li, 1991: 163–68; Guo, 1993: 33–41).

### An "All-Good" Mother

Although he acted just like his father, he preferred to fantasize about being the angel in the perfect world of his mother. In contrast to ignoring his father's death, when his mother was dying, he rushed home; he wrote a lengthy oration and two couplets for her funeral. He praised his mother with every virtue of womanhood and motherhood, from her "hatred of injustice," and "impartial love for all," to the "purity of her inner and outer world" and her ability to manage the family. In his mind, his mother exemplified a virtuous and "spotless" world, in which *he* was at the center (*Mao Zedong Nianpu*, 1993: 45–52). The contrast between Mao's parental imagoes is emblematic of the "splitting" process early in his life. His idealizing transference with his mother evolved into transference with the communist cause, which supposedly represented the ultimate good for China and the world. His utopian visions and unrealistic policies, however, were nonetheless defense mechanisms against the darkness of his father imago, which was responsible for his insecurity and paranoia. His aggression toward his father was to evolve into various political campaigns against all sorts of real and imagined enemies.

### SPLITTING: MAO'S CONFLICTING SELF-CONCEPT

Parallel to the conflicting parental images, Mao also exhibited diametrically opposed self-concepts from very early in his life: he was full of a grandiose sense of self as the hero of the universe; at the same time, he hated and condemned himself. In a poem he wrote at age 17, the young Mao was flirting with the idea of death. But he would not die an ordinary man; he would die a hero; only the green mountains would embody the timeless hero that he was to be (*Mao Zedong Nianpu*, 1993: 8). In his later poems, he routinely fantasized about being the timeless and limitless hero of the universe who could cut the legendary Kunlun Mountain in half with his sword or sweep the universe clear like the typhoon.

His grandiose fantasies demanded a world of perfection, and yet, he was incapable of facing his own imperfection; he needed to project it onto an external object. He became critical and contemptuous of others by demanding no less than perfection. He told Snow that he and his friends were all "serious-minded" young men, having "no time for love or romance." Once he was in a fellow's house, and the host instructed a servant to buy some meat and prepare a meal. "I was annoyed," Mao said, "and did not see that fellow again. My friends and I preferred to talk only of large matters—the nature of men, of human society, of China, the world, and the universe!" (Snow, 1968: 147).

At age 22, he wrote: "China's predicament ahead is to be a hundred times greater than ever before, and its salvation is out of question unless there is an unusual hero. . . . If one is not a holy legend, he can't succeed single-handedly; thus . . . my urgent need is to find friends." He advertised in a local newspaper to seek like-minded friends. Although we know that Mao was successful in gathering a small group of radical students around him in his home province, he felt that none of those fellows were really desirable friends. He was lonely, but he blamed the others and wanted to leave.

My spirit can hardly be bounded. In the end, I still can't see this quarter as a learning place; I don't feel the freedom of will here, the quality is too low, people in charge too evil. My useful body and invaluable time are consumed here gradually. Thinking what has faded and gone, my heart is truly in great pain. . . . I want to leave for a better place in order to fulfill my great promise. (Schram, 1992: 83–84)

Soon after, his dark side surfaced, and he felt himself worthless and hypocritical; he hated himself and was deeply depressed. He wrote: "I am frightened morning and night and ashamed to face up [to the ideal of] the superior man." In his private journal entitled "Self Condemnation," he imagined that a "guest" had come to his room, pointing a finger at him, while condemning him:

I see that you have but one crude skill, and yet, you make a treasured gift of it. You have not achieved any measure of virtue, and yet, you wish to make a show for the crowds, gathering your kind around you and putting on airs by rolling up your sleeves and raising your eyebrows. You do not have the capacity for tranquillity; you are fickle and excitable. Like a woman preening herself, you know no shame. Your outside looks strong, but your inside is truly empty. Your ambitions for fame and fortune are not suppressed, and your sensual desires grow daily. You enjoy all hearsay and rumor, perturbing the spirit and misuse time, and generally delight in yourself. (Schram, 1992: 72–74)

The tone of this self-condemnation is apparently that of his father, and yet, the substance of the values was that of his mother imago. He could not balance the good and the bad of himself; he could only fantasize about being the hero of the universe or hate and condemn himself. He created the "guest" who was really the idealized other part of himself.

His emotional turbulence and unrelenting inner conflict made his childhood and adolescence very difficult. Although he demonstrated his intelligence early in his life, he had disciplinary problems. He skipped school and ran away from home when he was about 10 years old, and at age 19, he quit school to pursue "self-study" on his own in the provincial library. He went back to school later, but at the age of 27. He wrote to a friend: "I hate school to the extreme all my life, and I have thus decided not to go to school any more." He decided to study on his own again, but he did not know what to study. While fellow students moved on—Luo Zhanglong, for instance, was to graduate from the Department of Philosophy at Beijing University and become a professor—Mao was still struggling with himself. His career pursuit was disastrous; having just confessed that he hated school, he took a position at the elementary school in Changsha in September 1920. He stayed for only a year; that position was the only professional job that he ever held. He was destined to be a rebel, a leader of his own cult.

Mao seemed to have a vague recognition of his problem. In 1920 he wrote: "I am too full of emotions, suffering from vehement feelings; my mind thus can't quiet down, and my effort can't last for very long. . . . Driven by my emotions, I always feel it difficult to lead an orderly life" (*Mao Zedong Nianpu*, 1993: 59). Later, he said that he had the "tiger spirit" as well as the "monkey spirit" in him. He tried to put a positive spin on his emotional conflict in terms of "dialectics," his "yin" and "yang" sides were never harmonious, and he did not know that the root of his emotional problems was the unconscious, low self-esteem and self-hatred, the hidden "ying" side of his personality (Sheng, 1998: 9–11).

## THE SYMPTOMATOLOGY OF MAO'S NARCISSISTIC PATHOLOGY

The inner conflict between the two bipolar self-objects in Mao's psychic structure was disabling in a vicious, cyclical manner. To escape from depression and insecurity, he needed grandiose fantasies and adulation; and yet, the more he inflated his ego, the greater his paranoia and insecurity. He learned to project the "all-bad" self onto an external object and to depreciate it, so that he could feel good about himself in the struggle against evil. He was adamant in denial of his own mistakes, no matter how conspicuous they were, and intolerant of disagreement, no matter how trivial the issue in question might be. To deal with the negative result of one defense mechanism, he had to activate another defense mechanism; the complex of various defense mechanisms formed the basics of the symptomatology of Mao's narcissistic personality disorder.

## Mao's Insecurity and Need for Admiration

Dr. Li observed that Mao was haunted by constant fear of disloyalty of not only other ranking leaders of the CCP but also his lowly service staff members—namely, his bodyguards, barber, cook, secretaries, physicians, and nurses. He expected those people to repeat all their conversations and activities to him in detail, encouraging them to criticize each other; he permitted no secrets (Z. Li, 1994: 81). Dr. Li's observation of Mao's paranoia of just about everyone concurred with that of bodyguard Li. Li had been Zhou Enlai's bodyguard, but was reassigned to serve Mao in 1947, when Li was merely an uneducated peasant teenager. Upon being told his new assignment by Wang Dongxing, Mao's chief security officer, Li slipped and said that he was afraid that he would not do the job right, and he had not been with Zhou for long. Mao made Wang repeat every word that Li had said, which weighed heavily on him. On the first day Li came to serve him, he never uttered a word to him; his eyes bypassed him as if he was not there. When they were crossing a river, Li tried to help Mao, but he refused to take Li's extended hands. Li felt that Mao was angry with him but didn't know why; the young man was very anxious. That night, Mao finally spoke to Li; he asked why Li was reluctant to come to serve him. Li was clever and said that he wanted to fight the enemies on the battlefront and didn't feel good about staying behind as a bodyguard. Mao did not believe Li: "[A]ny other reasons? Say, prefer to be with Zhou Enlai." Mao obviously was very nervous about how Li regarded him, and he wanted approval/adulation from everybody (Li, 1991: 25–29).

To make sure that the supplies of flattery were forthcoming, Mao often lavishly rewarded those who lauded him. In the summer of 1956, Mao traveled by air for the first time, and Hu Ping, an air force colonel, was the pilot. Hu flattered Mao, and Dr. Li was soon to discover "a strong correlation between the flattery Mao received and the speed with which the flatterers were promoted." Hu became the chief of China's air force general staff. Later, when Mao became suspicious of Hu after the Lin Biao affair in 1971, Hu was jailed (Z. Li, 1994: 131).

One of the occasions that Mao loved the most was standing on the Tiananmen, receiving a mass parade on the National Day or May Day. In anticipation of a coming celebration, his insomnia was always particularly acute, Dr. Li observed. Virtually sleepless for a few days, Mao would be unusually energetic and excited on the day; then he would fall ill and be miserable for a few weeks (Z. Li, 1994: 88–92). Apparently, the cheering crowds chanting "Long Live Chairman Mao" and the military parade marching to the rhythm of "The East Is Red" gratified Mao's self-image as a great man.

### Mao's Arrogance and Intolerance

At the same time, Mao was pathologically intolerant of any disagreement, no matter how trivial the issue in question might be. In 1956 Mao wanted to swim in the Yangtze River, but Wang Dongxing worried about his safety. Eventually, Mao agreed to send two security officers, Mr. Han and Mr. Sun, to the Yangtze River to "investigate." When Han told Mao that the river was too dangerous for swimming, Mao pounded his fist on the table and exploded, "I bet you didn't even go into the water. How could you know? How can you serve as captain of our guards? *Gun dan!*" [get your balls out of here, or fuck off]. Then Mao turned to Sun, who knew he had to lie: "Chairman, you can swim there." Mao immediately smiled. Han was transferred soon after, while Sun remained as Mao's guard (Z. Li, 1994: 159–60).

Equally telling of Mao's pathological intolerance of trivial disagreement and his absolute demand for conformity to his every whim is a story about him and his wife, Jiang Qing. He liked *hongshaorou* (fatty pork stewed in soy sauce) very much, and he had to have it twice a week, no matter what. One day in 1956, *hongshaorou* was supposed to be served, but Jiang Qing had ordered more healthful dishes to replace it. She had advised Mao that fatty pork had too much cholesterol to be good for him. This infuriated Mao, and he never ate from the same dish with his wife for as long as he lived (Li, 1991: 217–20).

### Mao's Denial

The newly emerged historical evidence makes it clear that Mao and the CCP leadership knew about mass starvation during the GLF. Mao, however, had to block himself from grasping the reality of the situation; he simply could not face it, even when the disastrous consequence showed up at his own dinner table. In the late 1950s food rationing was strictly enforced, and Mao's two daughters were often hungry. Bodyguard Li once hid a few cookies for one of the girls. When Mao found out (yes, he did bother to collect information about his daughters, even though he saw them only a couple of times in a year!), he censured Li with anger. One weekend, Li said to Mao: "Chairman, the girls are home. You haven't see them for weeks; could you let them have dinner with you tonight?" Mao agreed. When the dinner was ready, the two girls started swallowing their meals like "tiger and wolf," while Jiang Qing was shoveling food into their bowls. Mao watched them, gradually falling silent, putting down his chopsticks, staring at his daughters, "spellbound without emotion [*zhengzheng de chusheng*]" (Li, 1991: 163–68).

Bodyguard Li's intention in telling the story was to prove that Mao was a "selfless leader" who would suffer with the people. It may have been Mao's own urge to prove to himself that he was a man of moral incorruptibility. The problem, however, is that while millions of people were starving to death, the man ultimately responsible for it was playing the mental game of denial with himself. Instead of admitting the wrong of his policy and having the courage to correct it, Mao diverted his attention from the big policy issues to triviality: he gave up eating his beloved fatty pork for a while, and he did not allow his daughters to eat a few cookies. Mao's narcissistic vulnerability made it necessary for him to activate the defense mechanism of denial, and, thus, his reality testing under such circumstances was greatly compromised. When he was staring at his daughters, "spellbound without emotion," his cognitive ability seemed to shut down so that his fragile self could be preserved.

### Mao's Paranoia

With all the above-mentioned defense mechanisms activated at one time or another, Mao's fragile self was not strengthened; it was actually deteriorating, particularly when he was aging, and his sense of mortality intensified the unresolved inner conflict. In 1958, when the GLF was in full swing, Dr. Li observed Mao's intense paranoia for the first time; he was afraid that someone had poisoned his swimming pool in Chengdu. In the aftermath of the GLF, Mao was depressed. To pull himself out of depression, he decided to launch the "Great Proletarian Cultural Revolution," during which Mao's personality cult reached its peak.

Yet, it was also the time when Mao's paranoia was running progressively deeper. In 1965 he fell ill in Nanchang, and he told his physician, "There is something about this guesthouse, it's poisonous. There's something poisonous here. I can't stay here any longer." He ordered a move to Wuhan immediately. A few months later, however, Mao thought someone was in the attic of his guesthouse; he heard noises up there every night. When his guards caught two wildcats in the attic, he still insisted that someone was hiding there, and he left Wuhan immediately; he went to Hangzhou. "His paranoia persisted," Dr. Li observed. "After a few days anywhere, the anxiety set in and he had to be on his way. He did not feel safe in Hangzhou, either."

Mao went back to Beijing in July 1966, but he no longer felt safe even at home, and he complained that Building 1 in Zhongnanhai was poisoned. He moved to Diaoyutai, the former imperial fishing ground, but not for long. Mao felt insecure in Diaoyutai, too, so he moved to Room 118 in the Great Hall of the People. Mao lived in Room 118 for several months and continued throughout his life to take refuge there whenever he felt unsafe (Z. Li, 1994: 443–79). The bipolar co-existence of intense paranoia and grandiose fantasies exhibited in the last 10 years or so of his life testified to Mao's deteriorating narcissistic personality disorder, which, in turn, translated into China's chaotic and frenzied politics of the Cultural Revolution.

## THE POLITICAL CONSEQUENCES OF MAO'S PATHOLOGY

The game of power provided Mao with the ultimate means to inflate his grandiose ego; and yet, the grander he fantasized his role as "savior of the people" (*renming de dajiuxing*, a favorite title for Mao in CCP propaganda), the more paranoid of the "enemies of the people" he became. Consequently, the more power Mao accumulated, the more chaotic and irrational was Chinese politics. Oddly enough, irrationality or even madness of a political leader can be a plus in the politics of hate and in a cult. China's politics in the Mao years, characterized by the "class struggle," and Mao's personality cult both reached their peak during the Cultural Revolution. Mao was "mirror-hungry"; that is, he needed projection and transference, which led him to enjoy the cheering crowds of worshipers; the worshiping masses were "ideal-hungry"; that is, they needed inspiring ideals that they could not think up themselves. These complementary hungers made Mao's absolutist claims readily acceptable (Post, 1986). The more sincere and absolute he appeared, the more charismatic and appealing he became to his followers. Thus, Mao's "success" in winning political support could be better understood in a study of the group psychology of Mao's followers and the leader–follower dynamics than in the current study. A narcissistic leader cannot succeed without emotionally needy or damaged followers. Mao's self-grandiose fantasies as the "great leader" of "the people" and the neediness of "the people" reinforced each other in a pathogenic, cyclical manner, which may explain phenomena such as the "Great Proletarian Cultural Revolution" better than simply focusing on Mao's personality disorder alone.

However, certain personal qualities related to his pathology gave him political strength. Since his unsettling inner conflict made him restless, Mao seemed to have extraordinary energy and determination; he was constantly on the go and could never settle down with the status quo. His relentlessness and determination made him stand tall among his colleagues. Since he could not trust anyone but himself, he became the master of manipulation, which was essential, especially in the politics of cult and dictatorship. If Mao was ever "successful," it was before 1956; and it was not accidental that 1956 was the year of de-Stalinization. Elsewhere I have demonstrated that Mao tended to overestimate his strength and that of his party, and, thus, his policy tended to be radical and unrealistic. Stalin's advice pulled Mao back from dangerous adventures in several critical junctures in the CCP's history. Had there been no intervention by Stalin, Mao would have ruined the CCP several times over before 1949. Mao had good reasons to worship Stalin; Mao tried his best publicly and privately to assimilate Stalin's policy instructions. At every critical moment in the CCP policy-making history, Mao reported the situation to Stalin and sought Stalin's instruction. Mao never failed to follow Stalin's lead, willingly or otherwise. It is a myth of Mao's own creation that he alone was responsible for bringing the CCP to power (Sheng, 1998).

Mao's subordination to Stalin, however, must have caused tremendous discomfort. After the death of Stalin, especially after Khrushchev's de-Stalinization in 1956, the check-and-balance effect of Stalin on Mao was gone, and Mao was taking China down the path of destruction. Krushchev's anti-Stalin campaign excited Mao; it "lifted the lid" and "wiped out the blind faith" in Stalin, he said. He finally got a chance to vent his anger against the Boss and to argue for his own infallibility. On March 31, 1956, he summoned P. Yudin, the Soviet ambassador in Beijing, to chronicle Stalin's "mistakes" since the 1920s (Yudin, 1994: 134–44). In many ways, the Sino-Soviet split started in 1956, when Mao's fantasies of being the modern-day Karl Marx grasped him.

### The Origins of the Sino-Soviet Split

Mao's need to depreciate Stalin seemed to derive from the same root of his aggression toward his father. However, if his father-bashing conversation with Snow in the 1930s offered Mao an outlet to vent his hatred of his old man, his anti-Stalin conversation with Yudin in 1956 did more than that. It signified his obsession to become the leader of the world communist movement, which, in turn, drove him to prove that he could make China better than the USSR. Shortly after de-Stalinization, Mao's grandiose sense of his "historical responsibility" led him to attack openly the current Soviet leadership and the Soviet model of development. At a meeting on January 27, 1957, Mao accused the Soviet leadership of being *liling zhihun* (muddle-headed due to the pursuit for profit) and said that "the best way to deal with them is to give them a tongue-lashing" (*Mao Zedong waijiao wenxuan*, 1993: 280–83). At the same time, a Chinese delegation arrived in Belgrade. This mission was so secret that the Chinese ambassador to Yugoslavia was instructed to be the interpreter. The essential message was Mao's suggestion that due to the "very bad reputation of the Soviet Communist Party, not many [communist] parties will listen to them anymore." Therefore, "it will be better for the CCP, together with the Yugoslavian Party, to call for an international conference of communist parties to discuss and co-ordinate activities world wide." Tito politely rejected Mao's proposal. This must have offended Mao greatly: not long after, Mao ordered an assault on "Titoist revisionism," just before Beijing started a fierce ideological polemic against Moscow (Wu, 1991: 310–19). Mao's behavior in the world communist movement was clearly unprincipled and willful; and yet, he justified his rationalized rage in terms of protecting the purity of Marxist principles against "revisionism."

In the Stalin-bashing process, Mao reached such a state of euphoria that he even entertained the idea of a "true democracy" under the "proletarian dictatorship." In his lengthy talk with the Yugoslav delegation in September 1956, with Stalin's bloody purge in mind, Mao said that uniformity of people's minds embodies problems, because people are afraid of speaking out. "We thus must find some ways to encourage people to speak out. Our Politburo's comrades have recently been considering these issues" (*Mao Zedong waijiao wenxuan*, 1993: 251–62). This "being-better-than-Stalin" mood led to his call for the "hundred flowers" campaign, encouraging people to criticize the CCP and its cadres. But the euphoria did not last for very long. When the people started to criticize the CCP, including Mao himself, Mao turned the "hundred flowers" into the anti-rightist campaign, in which millions of innocent people who followed Mao's call to criticize the party were prosecuted.

When he was in an exhilarated mood fighting the "rightists," Khrushchev sent an invitation to him for the 40th anniversary of the Russian October Revolution. Before his departure, Mao was stricken by fancy, sending a request to the Kremlin that there be no ceremonial welcome when he arrived at Moscow's airport. Khrushchev, together with the entire Soviet Politburo, went to the airport to greet Mao nonetheless, displaying a ceremony for the most honorable state guest. While Khrushchev was personally escorting Mao to the Kremlin, Mao said: "Haven't I requested not to have ceremony for me? How come you still put up such a grand show?" Khrushchev explained that he and his colleagues did receive the message and discussed it; but they concluded that for as important a state guest as Mao, the welcoming ceremony could not be downgraded. Mao then said: "Well, in my view, when communism is finally realized, none of these things will matter any more" (Y. Li, 1994: 125–32; 1998).

Acting like the legitimate heir to Marx and Lenin, he talked at length about the theory of "dialectic materialism" with other participants such as Maurice Torez of France. Then, he asked his political secretary to sum up his thesis into a large paragraph to be included in the Joint Declaration of the Moscow Conference. When Mikhail Suslov came to ask Mao, with "extreme caution," if it was necessary to write this paragraph into the declaration since it was a familiar subject, Mao waved his hand lightly and stated: "[You] say it's familiar to everyone, I don't think so. If [you] say some people have known it, then, there must be others who don't. Would you believe me on this point?" The Soviets gave up (Y. Li, 1994: 125–32).

At the concluding session of the Moscow Conference of International Communist Parties, Mao announced, "In 1848, Marx and Engels issued the Communist Manifesto and launched a worldwide communist movement. Now, more than one hundred years later, the Moscow Declaration has summarized the experience of that movement and charted our future" (Z. Li, 1994: 224). Vividly, Mao was acting upon his fantasies as the latter-day saint of the communist faith.

## The Origins of the "Great Leap Forward"

Swept by his grandiosity, Mao stated that the "east wing" of socialism had prevailed over the "west wing" of capitalism, and before long, the productivity of the socialist camp would also surpass that of the capitalist world. He then designated a specific target for the communist world to reach: the USSR would overtake the United States in 10 years, and China would overtake Britain in 15 years (Y. Li, 1994: 146–47). Knowing very little about the West and disregarding the economic realities in China, his talk would have been harmless had it been just morale-boosting propaganda. But Mao was deadly serious.

As soon as he was back home, Mao "was gearing up to launch an all out drive to increase productivity," and he started to criticize lieutenants who were cautious and unwilling to promise a miracle. The more cautious and realistic economic planning adopted by the Eighth Congress of the CCP was thrown out the window by Mao single-handedly (Yan, 1996). At the Naning Conference in January 1958, he pushed his lieutenants onto his utopian path so hard that many were quickly stressed out. Before the end of the meeting, Huang Jing, the chairman of the State Technology Commission, experienced a psychotic episode and died soon after (Z. Li, 1994: 226–31). Several meetings followed in the months thereafter, and Mao kept pushing. The stage was set for the notorious GLF.

## The Origins of the Taiwan Straits Crisis of 1958

If Mao's domestic utopian policy was a projection of his fantasy of grandiose self onto the national scene, his grandiosity also led him into irrational adventures in the international arena. New evidence demonstrates that the Taiwan Straits Crisis of 1958 was an offspring of Mao's psychopathology, which led him to strive for power by taking charge of the "international struggle against western imperialism." Having learned the news about American intervention in Lebanon on July 15, 1958, Mao reversed the previous policy of peaceful coexistence single-handedly. He decided to attack the offshore islands, thus triggering the second Taiwan Straits Crisis. In appearance, Mao stood tall against "American imperialism." He said that "to assist the Arab people against invasion, we should not only give them our moral support, we shall give them substantive support as well. To attack Jinmen (Quemoy) and Mazu islands will have the effect of holding up the American imperialists." Mao, however, had no idea what American intentions were in Lebanon; nor did he know how the United States and its Guomindang (GMD) ally would react to the attack. Thus, his approach in conducting the military operation was *"zou yibu, kan yibu"* [take one step at a time, and then, watch the situation before taking the second]; he did not have a well-thought-out strategy, nor did he have a set of well-defined objectives (Xu, 1992: 197–239).

Having created military tension in the Taiwan Straits, Mao was nonetheless afraid of a direct confrontation with the United States. On August 21, he listened to General Ye Fi's report on military preparations. When the report ended, Mao was silent for a long while; and then, he suddenly asked: "You are going to use so many big guns. Are you going to kill the Americans?" Ye replied that the American advisors were everywhere in each battalion headquarters in the GMD military, and thus, it was inevitable that some of them would be killed. Mao fell in silence again for more than 10 minutes, and then, he asked: "Is it possible to avoid American casualties?" Ye's answer was negative. Mao did not utter a word, and the meeting ended right there. When the shelling started, the CCP wanted to cut off the supply line to the islands, but the U.S. Seventh Fleet intervened. On September 7, 1958, Ye told Mao that American warships were escorting the GMD supply ships to Quemoy; Mao ordered an attack on the GMD ships, but not the American warships. Ye then asked, If the Americans fired on the CCP forces, should the CCP fire back? Mao said firmly that without his personal order the CCP forces should not fire back on the Americans, even if they were fired upon (Ye, 1988: 654–55). If Mao did not want to have a few American advisors on the island killed to confront the U.S. naval force even when the Chinese military was fired upon, why did Mao decided to attack in the first place?

It appears that Mao's initial decision to attack after the Lebanon affair was driven by emotional impulse without strategic objectives and planning; his impulse derived as much, if not more, from his combative enmity against "U.S. imperialism" as from his grandiose ego, which was in competition against Khrushchev. Mao's close associates soon became aware of his intention to claim international leadership in the foreign policy arena by establishing policies independently of the USSR. When Mao was preparing and executing his military plan in the Taiwan Straits, he did not inform Moscow. This neglect was a gross violation of the letter and spirit of the Sino-Soviet Friendship and Alliance of 1950. The Soviets came to realize this change in Beijing's attitude as well. In July 1960 the Soviet Embassy reported back home: "Now it becomes clear that 1958–1959 was the period of a peculiar 'quest' of the Chinese leadership in the area of foreign policy" (Zubok, 1996: 233–34).

When the crisis reached its peak, the American threat of a nuclear strike against China alarmed the USSR. Gromyko, the Soviet foreign minister, rushed to Beijing on September 7. His Chinese counterpart told him that "inflicting blows on the offshore islands, the PRC has taken into consideration the possibility of the outbreak in this region of a local war of the United States against the PRC. And China is now ready to take all the hard blows, including atomic bombs." The USSR, the Chinese continued, should not take part in the conflict at this stage, even if the United States used tactical nuclear bombs. Only if the United States used larger nuclear weapons and risked broadening the war should the USSR respond with a nuclear counter-strike (Zubok, 1996: 225). Since Mao did not want to inflict any American casualties or permit firing upon U.S. warships, China obviously was not prepared for a nuclear war with the United States. Why did Mao lie and mislead the Soviets, who were supposed to provide China with a nuclear umbrella? The answer may lie in the events prior to the Gromyko visit.

In response to China's request for assistance in building nuclear submarines, the Soviets suggested that a Sino-Soviet joint fleet of nuclear submarines be established to combine Soviet technology with Chinese ice-free naval bases. On July 21, 1958, in the midst of the Taiwan Crisis, Mao received Moscow's proposal, and he exploded with anger. He accused the Soviets of wanting to control China's coastal line and of doubting Chinese ability to operate nuclear submarines. He was so emotionally disturbed and angry that Khrushchev rushed to China on July 31 in an attempt to appease Mao in person. Mao, however, would not listen, nor would he negotiate with the Soviets to gain terms favorable to China. Once he felt that the Soviets were looking down on him and China (he embodied China, of course,) he totally lost his composure as a statesman and his rationality. The meeting with Khrushchev turned into a bitter personal clash (Li, 1998).

As Kohut points out, the "fluidity of the borders of the self" often leads to "great narcissistic vulnerability with the tendency to perceive impersonal and accidental occurrences as personal slights." Mao expected no less than absolute respect and adoration, and thus, when Moscow offered the counter-proposal, he felt slighted. The Soviet proposal was a "deep personal affront, a frightening, inimical disturbance" of his "solipsistic universe" (Kohut, 1985: 54). He accused the Soviets of malicious intentions to take over the Chinese coastal line, and he was not happy until he saw the alliance destroyed. A year later, when Krushchev came to Beijing again for the 10th anniversary of the PRC, Mao engineered a confrontation between the CCP leadership and the Soviet delegation. The clash was so ugly that the Soviets informed Mao the next day that the USSR would rethink its promise to help the Chinese build a nuclear bomb (Y. Li, 1994: 160–64). Two months later, Mikhail Suslov delivered a report on the visit at a Politburo meeting. Suslov concluded that "The crux of the matter is that the Leadership of the CCP has recently developed tendencies to exaggerate the degree of maturity of socialist relations in China . . . There are elements of conceit and haughtiness." "[These shortcomings] are largely explained by the atmosphere of the cult of personality of com. Mao Zedong . . . who, by all accounts, himself has come to believe in his own infallibility" (Suslov, 1996–1997: 244–48). In retrospect, Suslov's remarks were not far off the mark. Soon after, Mao also managed to force Khrushchev to call back all Soviet advisors from China. The Sino-Soviet alliance was all but dead when the 1960s began.

## DISCUSSION AND CONCLUSION

I am a historian with considerable knowledge of Chinese history, culture, and society in general and the communist movement and Mao in particular. In my book on *Mao and Stalin* (1998), I use Erikson's theory of identification to explain the role of ideology in Mao's policy process and his relations with Stalin. Examining Mao's behavior in the post-Stalin era, however, I reached the conclusion that Mao's policies were so erratic and irrational that his personality or personality pathology has to be taken into account. I, nonetheless, have no formal training in psychoanalysis, and I thus would like to leave the reliability of my diagnosis open for discussion. I welcome any comments and suggestions. It is also advisable that in the future an inter-coder reliability study be applied with interdisciplinary collaboration or a team effort.

I am quite convinced, however, that Mao's emotional disturbance was severe enough to be easily recognized, as was its effect on the policy process, which he dominated. The evidence of Mao's pathogenic splitting is well documented; the intensity of his inner conflict between grandiose self and insecurity/paranoia is observable. With the latter as the dominant defect and the former the cover-up for the latter, Mao developed a series of defense mechanisms, that manifested themselves as various personality traits, such as intolerance of disagreement, need for excessive flattery, denial of his own mistakes, pursuit of grandiose fantasies, and so on. These personality traits greatly affected China's domestic and foreign policies in the Mao years.

This psychoanalytical approach to the study of Mao and Chinese politics has at least two benefits. First, although the debate will continue on whether the "agent" (such as Mao) or the structure (his historical environment) is more important in determining the course of history, there is little doubt that Mao dominated China's policy process single-handedly. Therefore, the personality and leadership style of Mao are crucial in our understanding of recent Chinese history. While the specifics of his personality or personality disorder can be debated, the study of his behavioral pattern and emotional life can shed new light on the origins and motivations of various historically important events. Second, the personality analysis, regardless of the tentative nature of the diagnosis, offers an interpretive framework that utilizes materials that are otherwise ignored by conventional political and social sciences studies. Various personality traits and the irrational behavior of Mao have been known since his death in 1976. Yet, this chapter is the first attempt to describe and analyze systematically Mao's personality and its role in China's politics. With the abundance of new materials on Mao published recently, a psychoanalytical study of Mao is especially timely.

## ACKNOWLEDGMENT

I wish to express my gratitude to Professors Fred Greenstein, Lucian Pye, and Robert Robins for their constructive comments and suggestions and their support and encouragement.

Chapter 8

# Profiling Russian Leaders from a Psychohistorical and a Psychobiographical Perspective

Juhani Ihanus

The tragedy of Russia is that we have inherited a state system and a mindset which relates to human life as to trash, to a prison camp trash.

—Aleksandr Lebed

Today, on April 21, 1999, presidential power collapsed.

—Aleksandr Lebed

## INTRODUCTION

In this chapter Russian political leadership is analyzed from psychohistorical and psychobiographical points of view. I apply psychohistorical perspectives and conceptions (child-raising mode, group fantasy, psychoclass, the leader as a delegate and a poison container) in connection with biographical information about childhood, youth, and family background, as well as about the roles and values of Russian leaders. In particular, psychological theories of charisma and group processes and developmental notions of self- and other-images are related to probing charismatic political leadership.

The chapter includes a short, historical overview of tsarist leadership and its legacy. Delegations of groups to leaders (or to fantasy-leaders) are seen in the context of the Russian "personal factor," the proclivity to prefer the leading personality over political parties and ideologies. The vicissitudes and forms of charismatic leadership and charismatic group immersion are followed through the Soviet political stage to the present situation by profiling leadership qualities and "governmentality" as represented by Stalin, Yeltsin, Zhirinovsky, and Putin.

Psychohistorical perspectives trace historical motivations to the development of human desires, emotions, fantasies, defenses, dependencies, and self-/object representations and relations. Psychohistory was first heavily oriented toward psychoanalysis and thus to unconscious motivations and intrapsychic undercurrents of historical (later also current) events. Rudolph Binion (2000: 133, 138) has called this applied psychoanalysis a "false start," since it easily led psychohistorians to neglect the close reading of historic records while reading into them psychoanalytic patient records. Clinical concern for the assessment and psychodiagnosis of personality tended to infiltrate psychohistorical-psychobiographical research, thus stressing individual psychological issues instead of large-scale human group processes and interactions.

Psychohistory, as formulated by Lloyd deMause (1975), one of its leading proponents, comprises the history of childhood, psychobiographical approaches, and group psychohistory. As the science of historical motivation, it has been introduced as the antidote to traditional history. In terms of its academic ranking, deMause (1975: 11) considered it necessary for psychohistory "to split off from history and form its own department within the academy in much the same way that sociology broke off from economics and psychology from philosophy in the late 19th century." Psychohistorical research has been carried out by many scholars other than historians. "The choice of problems—not the material studied—defines the discipline," deMause (1975) reminded his readers.

Political science, economics, and sociology have faced severe theoretical and methodological difficulties in trying to cope with psychological assumptions. While these fields have mainly kept political, economic, and social factors apart from psychological factors in interpreting history, psychohistory has reversed the paradigm: historical motivations can be studied only when we accept the fact that there are no political, economic, or social "forces," "organizations," or "systems" without the concomitant psychological, psychohistorical processes.

Freud (1921) already recognized the difficulties in carrying individual psychological conceptions over to analyzing "mass psychological" phenomena. Psychohistorians are in a demanding position because they need to use their own emotions, fantasies, identifications, and transferences as working tools in order to reach, discover, and recognize what is "out there" on the basis of what is "in here." Analyzing all the world "on the couch" means taking into account issues of the self and others in individual, group, nationwide, and even global interactions and communications. The research transferences of a psychohistorian should be open to detecting blind spots in one's own and others' previous research. Such transformative endeavors include cooperating in and co-constructing fruitful research projects (cf. Ihanus, 2000: 161–62).

Early researchers of budding psychohistory were psychoanalysts, psychiatrists, and psychologists who often lacked the skills for sound historical research. After World War II, many early psychobiographical studies focused on Hitler and the Nazis (cf. Elovitz, 2000: 134). For example, Erik H. Erikson (1950: 284–315) studied the appeal made by the imagery of Hitler to the unconscious passions of German youth. In the United States, Bronson Feldman (1952/1959) investigated the mythology of revolution and war as manifested by the popular cult of Lincoln the Liberator. Bruze Mazlish, Robert Waite, and William Langer were early academic historians positively tuned in to psychohistory. American political leaders such as Richard Nixon (Mazlish, 1972), Theodore Roosevelt (Davis, 1975), Henry Kissinger (Ward, 1975; Mazlish, 1976) and Jimmy Carter (deMause & Ebel, 1977; Mazlish & Diamond, 1979) have been case-studied from psychohistorical-psychobiographical perspectives. Historical records usually have a shortage of detailed data on childhood and sometimes even on youth. Thus, psychobiographical developmental interpretations often have to be made from scant data, but, related to the careful study of historical records, they may give intriguing and unique insights into the doings of man.

Different kinds of psychological theories may be used for psychohistorical and psychobiographical purposes. These theories were traditionally mostly psychoanalytic or, more broadly, psychodynamic. This theoretical orientation reached saturation in the 1970s. Since then there have been more eclectic trends, mixing and modifying earlier traditions with ego-psychological, object-relations, humanistic, and phenomenological as well as social-psychological and cognitive-psychological impacts in their links to personality, developmental, motivational, and social-interactional issues. In the future there may also be a shift toward more interdiscplinary research projects among psychohistorians. Because it is in the direction of our present-day desires, psychological, psychotherapeutic, and psychohistorical concepts "permeate all aspects of society, and have transformed the way that we see the world" (Elovitz, 2000: 137). Psychohistorical and psychobiographical studies are exciting, emotional-intellectual enterprises, for psychohistory may still be the only approach to history explicitly based on human love and on the displacement and re-enactment of mismanaged love onto historical (political, economic, social) arenas.

## LEGACY OF THE TSARS

Russian politics has a historical background of absolute autocracy that dates back as far as the realm of the Golden Horde. Later, with the advent of tsarism, autocracy was mixed up with influences from Oriental despotism and Byzantine obscurantism. In early Russia the term "tsar" was applied to the emperor of Byzantium and, during the Mongol Yoke, to the Mongol Khans. After the coronation of Ivan IV of Moscow in 1548, it was adopted as the official political designation for the Russian monarch. Even Peter the Great, who used the title emperor, was called tsar by the Russian people.

The tsars amassed the power of God, the fatherhood of families, and they represented the head of the body of Man and Society, governing the movements of all other parts of the body. For example, Peter the Great combined in his image the power of God and of the Warrior and Hero. He had many other mythical images—or ritualized Strong-Ego presentations, however—which changed according to the situations and were thus not self-identical. Among these were the Enlightener, the Educator, the Lawgiver, the Worker (who performed ordinary tasks), and the Titan (who constructed canals and erected cities, redirecting the flows of the water of Mother Russia) (Riasanovsky, 1985: 45–46; cf. also Hellberg-Hirn, 1998: 57–59, 64–65). The tsar and the people were as if wedded together, but the relationship between them was actually marred by a gulf, the tsar acting as an apocalyptic and messianic harbinger. This gulf was evidenced by Russian proverbs such as "It is too high to God, too far to the tsar" (*Da Boga vysoko, do tsaria daleko*; see Hellberg-Hirn, 1998: 64).

In his study of the scenarios of power during the three centuries of the Romanov dynasty, Wortman (1995) paid attention to the carefully presented and elevated symbolic and ceremonial sphere in which the Russian monarchs had a multitude of leader roles. They could be angelic, divine, Godlike or Christlike, erotic conquerors, benevolent, loving and kind, military commanders, pacifiers, fathers and mothers, models of moral perfection, of simplicity, of wisdom, omniscient and omnipresent, philosophers, religious guides, saviors, selfless, self-restrained, strong and forceful, for example. The divine, mostly superior qualities of the sovereign were also partly distributed to the power elite surrounding the sovereign (Wortman, 1995: 4; Hellberg-Hirn, 1998: 73).

Governmental systems have changed to some extent through "Europeanization," but the "personal factor" (one-person rule, the leading personality, presidential power, sovereign "governmentality") has persisted in the Russian mindscape, regardless of attempts at "collective leadership" or, later, at democratic decision making (on Russian leadership, see, e.g., Tucker, 1972: 205–25; Tucker, 1995b: 5–28). The state and its dominant institution, the presidency, are still carrying on the traditions of the old orders, in conflict with society and its democratic government (on the Russian presidency, see Huskey, 1999). The proclivity to place the leading personality above the political parties and ideological principles is strongly present, especially when democratization and the market-oriented economy have backfired, and political apathy and overt nationalism have been adopted again by many disappointed Russians.

The chaotic anything-goes mentality (*bespredel*) is largely felt in Russian society, and it often extends to politics as well (as unscrupulous acts, corruption, treachery, even murder).

Neither economic nor social forces (structures, systems) have created Russian realities by themselves without the impact of psychohistorical developmental, relational, and child-raising processes. Desires are molded into economies, ideologies, and policies. "Psychoclass" is not to be identified with economic class, nor is there any unilinear relation between an economic system and specific child-raising practices.[1] The Russians clung to the "ecstasy" of submission, the armor of regimentation, and the love of uniformity long after the autocratic rule of the tsars. The tighter the binding and the heavier the control, the "stronger" the labels given to the tsars (from Ivan the Terrible to Nicholas I, the "Iron Tsar"). These ties have formed the basis of attributions of charisma to rulers and of the emotional attachment of the group to the leader. The charismatic leader has literally been both desired and feared (on charisma, see Lindholm, 1990). Emotional submission has resulted in the emergence of a "we" group and the preferred exclusion of dyadic love relations. The leaders of large groups act as channels of group-induced aggression, but they also tend to desexualize sexual relationships, prohibit erotic-sensuous fantasies, and formalize and bureaucratize love (Kernberg, 1980: 39–40). During the Stalin period the official ideological Soviet "iconography of happiness" was considered the utmost guiding imagery of the nation.

As a representative, a leader embodies the "essentials" of a nation (power and control/weakness and loss of control). This linking of the leading person to the larger system is challenged during crises. In order to control excessive internal tensions and threats, the large group system becomes anxious of its borders, searching incessantly for external conspiratory enemies ("parasitic" Jews, "dirty" gypsies, Chechen "terrorists/bandits"). The rhetoric of law and order activates fantasies of salvation, victimization, scapegoating, and cleansing among the group. The need for more idealized and charismatic leaders is thus apt to arise in order to ensure continuous illusions of invulnerability and omnipotence.

For example, Nicholas II has been described as "sadly lacking in comprehension and will-power" in matters of state (Bolsover, 1956: 324; quoted also by Tucker, 1972: 209). During his coronation in May 1896, just before he was about to go through the ceremony of anointing with chrism ("holy oil") in the cathedral, the jeweled chain tore loose from his robe and fell at his feet. This was generally held as a bad omen. This was strengthened by the catastrophe occurring three days later during the coronation festivities when over 1,000 people died and many more were injured because of the too tightly pressed crowds (Iroshnikov et al.,

1992: 28–33, 122; Hellberg-Hirn, 1998: 74–76). The reputation of Nicholas II was shaken from the beginning, and the epithet "Bloody" was indelibly ascribed to him when, on "Bloody Sunday" in January 1905, workers who marched to the Winter Palace to ask for some alleviation from their plight were welcomed by bullets.

The Bolshevik regime replaced this "weak" tsar with a party dictatorship, actually with the oligarchy of the Leninist system. The charisma of Lenin came from the revolutionary, the argumentative thinker, and the clever father. The repressiveness was manifested in blood (of revolution) and sadomasochism (in thinking) and in the ruthless, "fatherly" persuasion of the chaotic masses, which were glorified as the "progressive" working class. Attempts to assert one's individuality were extirpated and brought forth the threat of exclusion from the "leading"—actually, led—revolutionary force. The homogeneity of this force was meant to be held together by repressing and finally eliminating individual expression and by reducing thinking to ideological absolute truths.

The legacy of the tsars and the killing of Nicholas II (an archaic parent imago) and his family were not adequately psychologically processed. It took a long time for the authenticity of the deaths and the burial place and time to be agreed upon. (The Russian Orthodox Church remained quite unconvinced of the authenticity.) The "sacred and charismatic persona of the emperor-tsar" (Stites, 1989: 80) had disappeared, but it has still haunted some hollows of the nation. The family's fate reminded people of the bloody past and hinted at the threat of regression. During the reburial of the tsar family in Peter-Paul Cathedral in St. Petersburg, Boris Yeltsin made a speech (on July 17, 1998) in which he referred to the execution of the family as "one of the most shameful events in our history." He linked the name of the Romanovs to "one of the most bitter lessons": "every attempt to change life through violence is doomed to failure."

## STALIN'S CHARISMATIC POWER AND PLEASURE

The disposal of the leader—in turn, a "poison container" and a "garbage can," then "trash" itself—has regularly been one of the main traumatic transitions in Russian psychohistory. It is also an indication of the tacit consent to keep old power structures as stable as possible. The fantasy-leader or the leader-father has been produced by the group's needs, but, sooner or later, the real leader has to face the fact that it is impossible for him to take care of the emotional conflicts of the group (displacement, disillusionment, hatred, rage), and he must try to "solve" them by intensifying his power, his savior image, and his purges, which deflect the deadly problems from himself onto others (deMause, 1982b: 174–75). Stalin's charismatic power and permanent urge to purge were seductive in pushing and pulling self-sacrificing persecutors and executors who, in their roles as their master's loyal servants and "watchdogs," were willing to inform on each other, to be punitively faithful (on the psychohistory of Stalin, see Ihanus, 1999).

There was no gratitude, only victimization among the charisma-ridden masses (summarily executed). This totalitarian control had a deadly triple-bind "love rule": "I am bad, but you must love me, and you will die, because you have to love me." The leader-lover was the only officially permitted (actually forced) "erotic" object. Love could be only "patriotic" and procreative (for multiplying the workforce) (Ihanus, 1999). In 1923 Stalin told Kamenev and Derzhinsky how he pursued his pleasure: "To choose the victim, to prepare the blow with care, to slake an implacable vengeance, and then to go to bed—there is nothing sweeter in the world" (quoted by Smith, 1968: 88). The "sweet revenge" ensured that no one was forgotten, that anyone could be targeted as an object.

This impersonal persecution had its developmental roots in Stalin's early personal experiences when he was subjected, as a child and later as a pupil and a student, to various punishments (beatings, bodily injuries, tough restrictions). The cruel methods of religious instructors, in particular, "schooled" him into an annihilating and programmatically atheistic worldview. Spying and prying into people's minds became part and parcel of the systematic inquisitions and forgeries, which could be seen as Stalin's displaced reenactments of the tortures and terrors of his childhood and youth. They were intensified through unconscious self-accusations and self-hatred. Stalin could trust no one, in his frenzied states not even himself. He used to work late at night and make sudden command calls to his "servants," who had to be prepared to follow every order. He tried in vain to manage his infantile terror by spreading Ultimate Terror all over. The lost souls were lost forever.

The parental, authoritative, all-knowing, and all-loving leader was first protective and supportive, promising benevolence and "warm love." Suddenly, he began to demand strict obedience and became persecutive, authoritarian, and finally totalitarian, threatening rejection, oppression, and terror. The "murder of being" was thus carried through in this "evil succession" (cf. Bollas, 1992). The despotic ruler commanded the personalities and alter personalities of his followers under his hypnotic spell.[2] The successful fantasy-leader has to be both masochistic and sadistic, but the only thing that he need not be is mature (deMause, 1982b: 176).

Stalin, the "pangovernor," was the master of conspiratorial theorizing and persecutory ideation and of cruel character assassination. As a patriarch, a liberator of nations, a great leader of peoples, the architect of socialism, and heir of Lenin, he was omniscient and could thus detect every crime, every anomaly and aberration. In his universe, where anything was possible, he needed the crowds of enemies who represented

Evil and who had to be forced to make forged confessions. The proof of their guilt had to be collected carefully, and when Stalin's mind was made up, his "slow-burning anger" (Tucker, 1990: 163) turned to exterminatory rage, the Great Purge, and a killed enemy appeased his own shame and self-hatred—but only for a while. As repetitions of the murder of the perpetrator's own childhood trust and hope, sadistic acts require stronger and stronger "doses," so that the manic exhilaration, triumph, and idealized self-image may be kept alive and distant from chronically depressive, estranged shameful states (cf. also Mollon, 1996: 178). Power intoxication, excitement, and the thirst for bloodshed promoted Stalin's pleasure and well-being. In his later years, however, he became more and more of a recluse, who hardly had a soul to talk to, ever more fearful of his countless enemies.

Under Stalin's limitless and "timeless" power, grandiose leadership accepted no individual desires and tolerated no fantasies, no private emotions, and no individual motives. Instead, it favored manipulable objects. "New man," stripped of any identity, was supposed to have been born. The modeling of *homo sovieticus* was accomplished through infantilizing, nationalizing, ideologizing, and mythologizing, as Mikhail Heller (1985) stated. Thus, the script of total control and terror was inscribed like a "natural" trance code on *homo sovieticus*. The original maxim of Plautus ("The unknown other is the wolf to man," later better known as "Man is the wolf to man") was taken to extremes.

Even Stalin had his comrade-wolves waiting for the end of his era. Khrushchev was among those who began the daily exercise of post-Stalin power and the representation of the superiority of the Soviet Union to the world. His charisma had more to do with framing "communism," the "cold war," the "Bomb," and the doctrine of the "inevitability" of the armaments race. His "love affair with the world" was a depressive (at times overly hilarious) submission to strong military force and mass production, the mightiness of which made "them" afraid of "us."

## THE RISE AND DECLINE OF YELTSIN'S PRESIDENCY

After the hard-line bunker mentality of the Soviet leaders, who did not give up their power until they were carried out dead, Mikhail Gorbachev was the first and last leader who represented the remnants of human-faced, down-to-earth socialism. His glasnost and perestroika, however, were already indicators of disintegration and ended in the collapse of the whole Soviet Union. The pseudo-rational renewals and the compulsive repetition of the old beliefs during Gorbachev's reign still showed evidence of the influences of ambivalent and intrusive child-raising modes, as described by deMause (1982a: 132–46). The new president was also influenced, to some extent, by the socializing mode (reflected in his "gradualist reform").

The intrusive child-raising mode, partly connected with the socializing mode, was clearly manifested in Boris Yeltsin's presidency, with its doses of compulsions, obsessions, anxieties, and addictions. In his autobiography, *Against the Grain* (1990: 18), he admits that his childhood was a "fairly joyless time," the only aim in life being to survive. As a child he was embedded in the generational chain of punishment practices: "My father . . . was rough and quick-tempered, just like my grandfather. No doubt they passed these characteristics on to me. My father's chief instrument of teaching good behavior was the strap, and he would wallop me good and proper for any lapses. . . . I always clenched my teeth and did not make a sound, which infuriated him" (Yeltsin, 1990: 17; see also Colton, 1995: 51). Later, Yeltsin said to a journalist: "I have not been trained in Hollywood. I am indeed a rather hard man" (Colton, 1995: 51). This obstinacy and moodiness were also present throughout his political career. From his heroic image atop a tank in August 1991 (during the attempted coup), he was finally reduced to a numbed and stubborn relic who continuously, as in anticipation of his own fate, abandoned political "objects" (first "promising" helpers, then "failed" rivals). Nobody is allowed, for long, to go on saving a Russia that vacillates between being a state and being in the state of collapse.

Yeltsin's difficulties in handing over power to his successor were clear, as he was following the old order of "institutional redundancy" and power duplication. Extensive bureaucracies already surrounded the tsars and, later, the general secretaries and Yeltsin's presidency, which was often in collision with the government headed by a prime minister. In addition to this, Yeltsin installed in the presidency competing power instances with overlapping responsibilities, thus maintaining a long chain of bureaucratic officials and steps of decision (Huskey, 1999: 8). The post-communist Yeltsin era still leaned heavily on the personality factor, the personalized patron. Stalin constructed the web of death camps and could trust nobody. Yeltsin trusted mostly the web of "family circles," a kind of "clan" of officials who were eager to "privatize" state power and property for their own purposes. The cause of the people is again quite different from the benefit of the power clan, and the power became ever more fragmented in Russian political and administrative practices (Huskey, 1999: 9).

As a leader-delegate, Yeltsin went through the motions of representation, led not so much by the voters but by new elite oligarchs who no longer belonged to the purely religious, economic, or political elite as such. It was more a question of a mediated elite that amasses and combines political and economic (not so much intellectual) assets. Characteristic of the present chaotic atmosphere in Russia is the fact that the members of the power elite do not even trust their own institutions. For example, research on the values of the Russian power elite showed that over three-fourths of the interviewed members of the political elite thought that politicians do not have any moral principles, and two-thirds of the members of the economic elite regarded their business companions as untrustworthy. The mass media elite was regarded with great suspicion (37% trusted it), but political parties received the lowest ranking (only 13% trusted them). Two-thirds of the elite (65%) trusted the Russian Orthodox Church, and the second place in trustworthiness was given to the Greens (59%) (Kääriäinen, 1999; on earlier Soviet elite, see Mawdsley & White, 2000).

Yeltsin's political leadership has been perceived ambivalently. His personality has been attributed with both dictatorial and democratic features. He pondered a long time over whether he would go on for a third presidential round. He was unwilling to give support to his possible followers. His rapid changes of prime minister, confusing as they may have looked, had, however, a certain logic. First, the older Chernomyrdin and then the younger Kirienko were both from the economic elite. The respected member-of-the-old-guard Primakov, with an espionage background, was from the highest political elite. He was allowed to act as a buffer between foreign investors, Russian oligarchs, parliamentary circles, and military circles. The next prime minister, Stepashin, came from military quarters and was about to overthrow Yeltsin in popularity. He was also too independent of the Yeltsin clan and was destined to leave the post quickly.

Vladimir Putin was, finally, the superloyal military man with a history of espionage, a sober mind, and a healthy body. He suited the clan and Yeltsin and forgave Yeltsin's personal economic scandals. People no longer hardly mention General Aleksandr Lebed, who helped Yeltsin in 1991, mediated in the Chechen peace accords, and through his candidacy in 1996 helped to diminish the popularity of Zhuganov and thus to open the way to Yeltsin's second presidential period. He was reminiscent of Russia's "trash" inheritance in the state and in the mind-set and defended human rights and individual dignity, but it turned out that he was not actually a boxer but rather a chess player, too humanistic for an army general.

Delegations to leaders have also changed. Psychological dilemmas are no longer derived from oedipal conflicts but from alienated feelings of emptiness, fragmentation, and abuse, from the "loss of memory," and from the absence of "others" and one's "self" (Lindholm, 1990: 84). The lack of social support, parental care, and emotional interaction has produced a vacuum, a *horror vacui* (horror of emptiness), which people try to fill with surrogates (religious ecstasy, charismatic cults, exalted reformative sects, obsession with healers, media stars, and leaders, and image-conscious politicians such as Vladimir Zhirinovsky).

## ZHIRINOVSKY'S JOKES

Lenin and Stalin were undoubtedly "great" Russian leaders (*vozhd's*) who ruled with an iron hand the masses of the mighty Russia. In the 1990s Vladimir Zhirinovsky tried to convince the Russian people that he would be the third *vozhd*. The Liberal Democratic Party was founded in March 1990 and elected Zhirinovsky its chairman. In fact, in April of the following year this party, which began amateurishly, [3] in jest, as Lenin's and Hitler's parties had begun, became the first officially registered alternative party in the USSR and thus soon the pioneer of a multiparty system in Russia. *Vozhdism*, represented by Zhirinovsky, is a geopolitically transformed and media-tailored continuation of national patriotism, with stereotyped conceptions of the Russian "national character," dictatorial poses, anti-Western propaganda, and populist rhetoric. From the beginning, Zhirinovsky was tuned in to media coverage through his egocentric, unpredictable declarations and scandalous exploitation of publicity, which were unusual amid the utter depersonalization and faceless nomenclature of the Soviet period (Solovyov & Klepikova, 1995: 4–8, 19–20).

Zhirinovsky has used media and psychological experts in planning to entrap different layers of Russian society (from pensioners to youngsters, from army ranks to environmentalists). These are the hurt and humiliated, the "orphans," for whom the "fatherless" (Zhirinovsky's father was a Ukranian Jew who died in 1946, the year Vladimir was born) leader is apt to become "a papa, a strict papa, because if a father is not strict his children are not obedient" (from Zhirinovsky's rally speech quoted by Solovyov & Klepikova, 1995: 40).

This papa has borrowed some of his leadership attitudes from the legacy of the tsars. People are given pathetic, nostalgic, and ritualistic promises by their Savior, but at the same time the apathetic masses are denigrated and shouted at. Zhirinovsky's apocalyptic-messianistic prophecies are like sermons delivered in front of the congregation, with the recurring hypnotic spell: I am the savior. The name of the prophet, Vladimir, is the "most ambitious and proud Russian name there is," meaning "possessor of the world" (*vladet' mirom*) (Solovyov & Klepikova, 1995: 26).

Like the earlier tsars of Russia, Zhirinovsky, pretending to be the emperor, has been given different leadership characterizations: "a political jester, an eccentric, a scandalmonger, buffoon, an upstart, a loudmouth, a demon, a magician, a shaman, a corrupter of the nation, an adventurer, a headless horseman, a populist, a prattler, a demagogue, a fascist, a

Nazi, a führer, and a Russian Hitler" (Solovyov & Klepikova, 1995: 2). As these numerous role names attest, Zhirinovsky's media leadership lives on publicity, however negative it is. Zhirinovsky has even feared that his political career would end if he were praised or treated with indifference.

This kind of Russian leadership emerged during the 1990s, with Zhirinovsky as its most famous example. Everything (boundaries, values, strategies, politics) can be changed by sleight of hand, according to the whims of the media hero. The persona transforms itself for different audiences, according to contradictory positions. Zhirinovsky may alternate—multiplying his alter egos—between being in favor of traditions and reforms, war and peace, anti-Semitism and cosmopolitism, dictatorship and democracy. As he exclaimed, "I'm either an anti-Semite or a Zionist . . . I'm either a communist or a fascist or something else!" ("Nobody Gave You the Right," 1994; see also Ihanus, 1994: 194; Solovyov & Klepikova, 1995: 163). In "trance thinking" opposites do not contradict; they merely exist simultaneously, side by side (deMause, 1982b: 189). In order to keep up the political show, with its many faces of potential destruction and benevolence, Zhirinovsky maintains and redesigns Russian "enigmatic unpredictability." Secrets, threats against enemies, and impulsive outbursts of dark humor and insults constitute a "joker" claiming to be able to destroy the "bad" and restore the "good."

Zhirinovsky as the "purifier" acts as the people's delegate showing the way from "bad" memories to Utopia, to the "last reconstruction of the world," the "last push to the south," when Russian soldiers untie their swaddling and "change into summer uniforms forever" (Zhirinovsky, 1993: 66). The purifying task given to Zhirinovsky and his geopolitical doctrine serves as a periodic cleansing, through wars, manic-depressive suicidal or regicidal acts, feelings of guilt about pursuits of pleasure and independence (see deMause, 1988). Russia's "trash," pollution, criminality, and disorder demand that the effective leader operate systems and rituals of cleansing.

In his media rituals and demagogic mass rallies, Zhirinovsky has willingly adopted the cleansing task and has been eager to search for enemies, impostors, and scapegoats, those "poison containers" (deMause, 1988) to be excluded, to be territorialized. He was never in power, he claims, when the misery and helplessness of Russia were created. He has, rather, handed over "new"/"old" values, on/off morality, promising the restoration of absolute power and also a Russianized consumption culture as a reward or "forepleasure," so that the poisoned "patient" (the dismembered Mother Russia) is forgotten in this jerky state of transition or collapse.

As a child Zhirinovsky craved his mother's love. She was "always at work" and spent most of her available time with her younger lover,

Vladimir's stepfather, who treated him badly, in a one-room communal flat in Almaty, the capital of Kazakhstan. Zhirinovsky's poverty seems to have been both economic and emotional. In his autobiography, he confesses, "I lived the greater part of my life without almost a single happy day. . . . It seems to have been my fate that I never experienced real love or friendship" (Zhirinovsky, 1993: 27). This sense of isolation from love, warmth, and tenderness was channeled to the "love" of politics, to the energetic attacking, beating, and lying that politics is about, as interpreted by Zhirinovsky.

Zhirinovsky's child-care center experiences are from the Stalin era, and he entered a boys' school the same year in which Stalin died. Like so many other Soviets, he was accustomed to hearing official love songs, such as "I have not seen Stalin but I love him." He was also accustomed to all-male groups at school, at Pioneer camps, at the university, and in the army.

Zhirinovsky's late, lonely, and ascetic sexual development (he had difficulties creating any emotional and reciprocal relationships with women) was coupled with his political fervor. He has used sexual metaphors for describing Soviet history and for comparing it to sexual "perversions": "The October Revolution raped the people, the Stalin era can be compared to homosexuality, the Khrushchev years to masturbation, and Brezhnev to impotence" (quoted by Kartsev & Bludeau, 1995: 93). Although his party has spoken in favor of family values, these values have been strictly patriarchal, even misogynist, fostering devotion to the home, children, cooking, and churchgoing for women, and family relations where the man is the head of the family (see Solovyov & Klepikova, 1995: 55). Zhirinovsky has enthusiastically recalled Stalin's sexual morals as promoting utmost purity, which has been lost through Western influences.

While claiming to be the defender of Russian sexual morals and despising Western sexual degeneration, Zhirinovsky has published a work called *Azbuka seksa* (The ABC of Sex) (Zhirinovsky & Jurovicky, 1998) in which he proposes, in a missionary tone, the establishment of a new Russian "sexually-oriented economy," which would make Moscow the mecca of the worldwide sex-tourism industry. Russia would show what a "world of total eroticism" would look like. Every year, 1.5 million 16-year-old girls will come to the Russian "virgin markets," which will accelerate the export of these virgins for the benefit of the national economy. No wonder Zhirinovsky promised as early as 1993 that his willful party would ensure that the days of "political impotence" would be over and that the whole nation, "for the first time," would "have a real orgasm!" (quoted by Kartsev & Bludeau, 1995: 93).

These sexual moral values belong to the age of virtual reality, which simulates ascetism/hedonism, with orgasms at the flip of a switch. The

Russian sexual reality is harsh, however, with 3 million abortions still being carried out yearly and with over half a million children on the streets or in inferior children's homes. The "as if" personality ignores facing such realities, is afraid of both intimacy and of losing control; its quasi-differentiated self is bound together with a hunger for narcissistically manipulable objects and fear of chronic depression, loneliness, and engulfment.

Thus, according to Zhirinovsky, politics is not only about attacking and beating but also about proving political potency, the illusion of sexual completeness, without engulfment or indecisiveness. The war against the Chechens was one such test that Yeltsin undertook with the support of Zhirinovsky and some other extremists.

## PUTIN THE WRESTLER

In order to improve his weakened position, Yeltsin launched a war in the Caucasus against Chechnya in 1994, on the eve of the New Year. The military campaign turned out to be a total disaster, in fact, a humiliating manifestation of the impotence of the Russian army, which finally annihilated the "center of power," the capital city of Grozny, and massacred civilians. Chechnya became effectively independent at the end of the 1994–1996 war with Russia, but by early September 1999 Russia was already launching a new military offensive against this breakaway republic. Islamic militants were blamed for lawlessness, kidnapping, banditry, and bombings in Russia.

The ailing and often out-of-touch Yeltsin still found the energy to assault this enemy, which had "no conscience, no pity nor self-respect, no faces, no ethnic origin nor religion" (Yeltsin on Moscow television after the bombing of a Moscow apartment house). After 14 years, large-scale military exercises, called *Zapad* (West), were mounted in the summer of 1999 to simulate attacks against Western countries. The "Bomb" as a secure, whole object (full of repressed separation anxiety and annihilation threats) was again cathected in fantasies and paraded in public. Yeltsin also hit out against U.S. President Bill Clinton in Beijing in December 1999, reminding him that Russia had a full arsenal of nuclear weapons.

With his strangulated communication, Yeltsin symbolically informed the Americans that the Russians still had a mission, missiles to be launched. This emotional reaction was related to the issue of world control, Russia's territorial borders, and Russian self-esteem. The "multipolar" rather than the "unipolar" world was Yeltsin's message. At the same time, the blitzkrieg situation once more gave him the opportunity to stress his strong presidency and to pave the way for his (and his clan's) choice for Russia's new president.

It was not Zhirinovsky, who had lost the interest of the larger audience, but another Vladimir, "possessor of the world," who suddenly became Yeltsin's crown prince. Vladimir Putin had decided that his "historical mission" was to solve the problem of Chechnya. Just as Yeltsin had been invited by Gorbachev in 1985 to Moscow to lead the estate department of the Kremlin, Putin had been invited by Pavel Borodin (not, as was thought, by the reformist Chubais) in 1996 to the same department, which later became the focus of high-level Kremlin corruption charges, which did not leave Yeltsin and his family or Borodin unscathed.

Yeltsin had achieved his success by sending out clear messages against corruption, privilege, and bureaucracy. He also skillfully exploited Russian nationalist feelings. When, on New Year's Eve in 1999 (again careful symbolic timing), Yeltsin gave presidential power to Putin, Putin's tough, no-compromise attitude toward the Chechen terrorists had ensured him high popularity. Such acclaim had not been witnessed since Yeltsin's heyday at the very height of his glory, when he was elected the first president of the Russian Federation in 1991 and when the Soviet Union ceased to exist on December 25, 1991.

Putin began to personify the new, "sober," educated, and self-determined Russia. His straightforward slogans, such as "terrorists should be destroyed in open-air toilets" and "corrupted officials should be eliminated like rats," delivered an image of a leader who would not give up in the face of foreign or internal pressures. Every poisonous placenta (Chechen bandits, cheating officials) in the womb of Mother Russia should be aborted. One of his first tasks as president, however, was to guarantee Yeltsin judicial immunity and to move his mentor Borodin onto diplomatic tasks.

The crown prince has not been ungrateful to his master, although he has softened Yeltsin's assault on President Clinton, for example, saying, "I would consider it absolutely incorrect to produce the impression that there has been a cooling of Russian–American relations" (Putin on December 9, 1999, Interfax). Putin does not have to remind the world about the "Bomb," but he has inherited from Yeltsin many delegations. He even goes beyond them in trying to re-enliven the national anthem of the USSR.

Putin's childhood background was a working-class home in Leningrad. His two older brothers died of hunger during the siege of Leningrad. After having seen an exciting spy film, he decided that spying was his intended career. He is said to have been bullied at school because of his small stature. Some boys teased him by locking him into the girls' toilet so that girls shouted and slammed him. His former teacher has said that the small Putin cried and swore to her that he would one day chase his attackers away (*Nezavisimaia Gazeta*).

In his student years, as an extreme act of sobriety, Putin and his friend gained fame by drinking six liters of milk. He has also excelled in wrestling and judo.[4] After graduating from the Law Department of Leningrad University, Putin received KGB training and undertook espionage tasks in the years 1975–1990 (e.g., in the DDR—Deutsche Demokratische Republik, or the GDR—German Democratic Republic). He then became the hardworking trustee of the mayor of St. Petersburg, Anatoly Sobchak. Putin is not at all ashamed of his KGB years, and, for him, the KGB has been an important part of Russian independence.

Putin's image and "cult" status have also been circulated effectively through the Internet where he and his co-workers have frequently posted information (e.g., www.russiaworld.com). There is something virtually modern and something tsar-old in the passionless, psychically and physically healthy leader icon of Putin. In the information society people will experience an increasing freedom of choice, more and more permutations of expressions and "interactive" situations. At the speed of electronic light, however, everyone is robbed of secure identities. Even charismatic ("healthy," "sober," "attractive") leaders can now be circulated globally through the "intimate" encounters staged by the current multimedia routines. The face of a charismatic leader has become an audiovisuoverbal "interface" with whom the voters are "closely" involved.

According to the opinion polls, many Russian women see Putin as handsome and sexy, while many men approve of his tough, unsmiling posture. When the Russian research institute Romin asked the voters' views of Putin, 25.4% of them saw in him a "wrestler," 16.3% a "boss," 12.9% a "patriot," 11.2% a "member of the intelligentsia," 10.0% a "reformer," 6.5% a "dictator," and 4.3% a "puppet," but only 0.7% saw him as a "bureaucrat" and 0.3% as a "loser." In Russia he is often called a "gray cardinal," a "real man," and a "rational terminator."

How far is he ready to go in securing the borders and teaching lessons to his adversaries? His "rational" and sporting image stands against fragmentation, terrorism, and alcoholism. However, his psychological bent is still oriented toward the Pavlovian tradition and Bechterevian reflexology, as can be concluded from his reference to dog psychology when speaking about Chechen rebels (interview in *Kommersant*): "You know, a dog senses when you are afraid of it and bites at once. So it is in this case. Only one way is possible—attack. You must hit first, but so that your adversary will not stand up again."

Inferiority problems may carry inhibitions against the living and unknown others, breeding rigidity, immobility, dullness, and cruelty against that which one's self secretly desires (cf. Reich, 1983: 18–19). Passionless, rational inhibition may already be fertile ground for secrets, for restrictions on opposition media, and for the "totally democratic" Kremlin art of fiction.

## CHARISMA AND THE LOVE OF DEATH

Charisma cannot be an internal, isolated quality. Like power, it becomes evident only in a relationship, in a mutual mingling of the charismatic leader and the follower (see Lindholm, 1990: 7). Lindholm (1990: 83, 85) gives two pictures of the conditions leading to charismatic succession. On the one hand, alienating modern conditions produce "anxious and narcissistic personalities," prone to searching for and accepting charismatic immersion (self-loss and merger). On the other hand, malleable individuals are channeled by "thought reform" techniques, "stripped of identity markers and ties with others," so that they voluntarily become seduced, hypnotized, "brainwashed," and engulfed by charismatic groups and leaders. These two "paths" of charismatic immersion are not mutually contradictory but converging. An individual (who has become a nobody) identifies with the group and the leader, who offer the protean individual a new revelation, a transpersonal and transcendental hope. According to Lindholm (1990: 87), "Postmodernist play ethic is more a precondition of than a defense against charismatic involvement."

In times of the collapse of old values, social ties, family structures, and self-esteem, charismatic leaders and groups may again revitalize desires and fears, common ideals that transgress the daily miseries. In a highly numbing and chaotic situation people tend to become more and more suggestion- and trance-prone and hypnotizable. They begin to dissociate (compulsively) rather than associate (freely). Dissociation is thus directed against transition, repetition against mobility, merging against individuation, regression against progression.

Disrupting the memory and twisting realities make people susceptible to dissociation, when they concentrate only on suggestions and hypnotic messages. The critical functions of the ego become numbed; "visionary" and "hallucinating" hypnotized tranceaction is apparently goal-directed, according to the suggestions of the "Other" (the Commander), and not intentional through the independent executive ego.

Charismatic immersion also reinforces archaic enjoyment, fatalism, millennial eschatological dreams, and morbid fantasies. When the daily living is catastrophic, the love of death takes the place of reality. One of the occult, eccentric thinkers in Russia's history, Nikolai Fedorovich Fedorov (1828–1903), taught that humankind was destined to work toward the universal resurrection of the dead. This "moral duty" was later repeated in the Cosmist (Russian cult) slogan, "Dead of all countries, unite!"

Lenin's embalmed corpse proved that he really was eternally dead (whereas Stalin was assumed to be eternally living even as a ghost). Sergei Jushenkov, a member of the Russian Duma, has vigorously maintained that "as long as the corpse of the bloody murderer is located in the mausoleum in the middle of Moscow, the country cannot develop in a civilized way." Western analysts, especially practitioners of transition-ology in Russian studies, have insisted that Russia' transition is possible only through neo-liberal, shock-therapy, and monetarist economic meas-ures (and their attendant politics). This view in itself surely incorporates the arrogance of biased Western attitudes and "America's post-cold-war triumphalism" (Cohen, 1999).

## CONCLUSION

In this chapter I have used the psychohistorical-psychobiographical approach to elucidate some continuities and changes of Russian political leadership and large-group processes. As often in this kind of research, the shortage of detailed data on childhood and child raising poses certain limits on detecting and studying developmental, motivational, and per-sonality patterns among individuals and groups in the historical as well as in the current context. Researchers on Russian studies should be very critical when using historical records because of the long tradition of official and unofficial truths and mixtures of the two. Close reading of Russian primary sources would be needed in the future to produce a broader and not such an impressionist picture of the emotional and mo-tivational basis of social action.

Political scientists have faced obstacles trying to incorporate psycho-logical theories in their quest to understand and even predict (and per-haps control) political behavior. Psychohistorical research can offer some clues for making better use of both historical research and psychological theories for such purposes. At present, unfortunately, psychological the-ories of charisma, leadership, and large groups are not very coherent.

Psychohistorians have abandoned the dominating impact of clinical-psychological orientations to some extent, which has resulted in the adoption of mostly eclectic theoretical positions and, lately, also in in-terdisciplinary projects. They use their own special methodology of dis-covery in these positions and projects, which requires them to make use of their own emotions, identifications, and transferences as research tools. To discuss the implications of these personal equations would re-quire more attention than has been hitherto the practice in scientific eval-uation. Psychohistorians do not possess any magical divining rods or predictive skills. Psychohistory has to depend on consistent concepts, the parsimony and coverage of theories, and empirically testable hypotheses.

It may be that, nowadays, psychohistorical-psychobiographical re-search, such as reported in this chapter, has heuristic value and func-tional applicability while pointing to historical and current issues concerning the self and others (loss of identity, fragmentation, regression, transition) at the crossroads of psychological development, personality formation, political behavior, and cultural transformation. The leap from intrapsychic to intra- and inter-group processes is, however, a tedious one, and it has not been unproblematic in my mini-case studies of Russian political leaders either. The individual psychological conceptions do not easily lend themselves to being linked to large historical and societal vistas.

The psychohistorical view cannot give priority to economic and political factors in approaches to Russia's dilemmas. Such issues are interspersed throughout with long-ingrained psychological coping strategies and defense mechanisms, with thought patterns, emotional constellations, group interactions, and mixtures of memories, dissociations, and repressed desires. Political behavior cannot be predicted solely on the basis of childhood background and the group fantasies of social actors. Still, psychohistorical-psychobiographical perspectives may well produce an understanding of the roots of displaced love projected onto the political stage and help to provide preventive measures against man's destructive love of death. This means remembering and opening up the past, and presenting new questions about our desires for the future. Arguably, the most difficult thing is not to predict the future but rather to assess the present, the actual state of affairs.

## NOTES

1. On "psychoclass," deMause (1982a: 139) states that it "is only partially related to economic class," while "political and religious movements correlate more closely to psychoclass than to economic class."

2. On the hypnotic spell of the charismatic leaders, see Atlas (1990). deMause (1982b: 176) stated that the sadistic leader often assumes responsibility

for the most destructive actions human beings can undertake, so that sadism normally found in each of us is not really sufficient to make an effective historical fantasy-leader. In addition, the leader must find enough gratification in "crazy" thought and action to allow himself to be a receptacle for the continuous psychotic projections of the group, including various levels of unreality, splitting, paranoid suspicion, grandiosity, violent rage and other forms of psychotic anxiety.

3. Sometimes such "crazy," "bizarre," or "amateurish" minority groups are delegated the task of acting out the majority's emotional state during the collapse period. Such groups are "able to hypnotize the public body far beyond their tiny size, because they reflect the main emotional conflicts of the moment of paranoid collapse" (deMause, 1982b: 185–86).

4. Putin (*Ot pervogo lica*, 2000: 21) has called judo "not only sport but philosophy. It means respect for those above, for an opponent; it is not for the weak."

Chapter 9

# Benjamin Netanyahu: A Psychological Profile Using Behavior Analysis

Shaul Kimhi

## INTRODUCTION

The present chapter describes the psychological profile (from a distance) of Israel's former prime minister, Benjamin Netanyahu.[1] In constructing the profile, a qualitative method called behavior analysis is employed (Kimhi, 1999). The method developed as a result of an attempt to create psychological profiles that are both clinically derived and politically pragmatic. Although qualitative profiles based upon personality theory have their own advantages and unique utility, the present intention was to produce a method built upon available empirical data rather than general presumptions driven by developmental personality theories. A parallel intent was to enhance the predictive ability of profiles that have been somewhat constricted by the use of limited psychological theories (e.g., theoretical psychology does not generally include dimensions that relate directly to political behavior and leadership style). Quantitative methods also have their advantages; however, results often focus upon narrower areas of interest selected from the larger personality.

The behavior analysis method observes specific behaviors that evolve into repeated patterns of behavior and synthesizes these tangible indicators into a global personality type. Much as the American Psychiatric Association's *Diagnostic and Statistical Manual* (DSM-IV) lists behaviors and provides a diagnostic personality type, the current method identifies behaviors in political leaders and then suggests a global personality type with precise reference to unique political behavior.

## RESEARCH METHOD: BEHAVIOR ANALYSIS

This method comprises three steps: collection (of any possible information on the leader's behavior), classification (into content categories),
and analysis (construction of the psychological profile). Behavior analysis
is based on behaviors described and reported publicly; the method utilizes measures of thoughts, feelings, and actions that have continuity over
time and between situations. Moreover, it makes a clear distinction between psychological hypotheses and findings based on gathered data.

### Data Collection: Sources

The sources for the present study are (1) books written by Benjamin
Netanyahu (Netanyahu, 1995, 1996); (2) volumes whose subject is Netanyahu (Vardi, 1997; Kaspit & Kfir, 1997a); and (3) a large quantity of
articles concerning Netanyahu that were published in Israeli newspapers
from 1985 to December 1997, including interviews that he granted to the
press. Among the 174 magazine and newspaper articles, 132 were classified into one or more content categories.[2] The other 42 articles were
deemed to be too general (e.g., a commentator's evaluation on Netanyahu's chances of winning the election), as they did not illustrate any of
the behaviors included in content categories.

Each written text that includes a relevant aspect of Netanyahu's behavior was marked as a unit of information, that is, a description of a
leader's behavior in a defined situation at a certain time. Such a description could entail one paragraph, a few, or even a full chapter. Every unit
of information was entered into the computer, with key words emphasizing both the general behavior (e.g., a tendency to mistreat his workers)
and the specific behavior (e.g., tardiness at a given meeting) described.

### Classification and Analysis

The units of information were classified according to two dimensions,
namely, content category and type of information. The classification into
content categories was accomplished in three stages. First, two researchers each independently proposed a list of categories for the analysis, each
category representing a psychological dimension (e.g., suspicion). Then
they discussed their respective lists and agreed upon a final list of 22
content categories (see Table 9.1). In the second stage, the two researchers
independently classified all units of information into these categories.
Each unit was assigned one (the most suitable) category. Classification
comparisons revealed a high degree of congruity ($r = .85$). Non-
congruent classifications were discussed and agreed upon. In the third
stage, all of the earlier categories were grouped into four major catego-

Table 9.1

Classification of Units of Information: Content Category and Type of
Information Sources

| General Content Areas | Content Category | Type of Information Sources | | | |
|---|---|---|---|---|---|
| | | Primary | Secondary | Others' Evaluations | Overall |
| **A** Distinguishing Traits | a. Egocentricity | 3 | 11 | 14 | 28(12) |
| | b. Ambition and determination | 3 | 8 | 11 | 22(4) |
| | c. Aggression and manipulation | 5 | 25 | 13 | 43(6) |
| | d. Credibility | 2 | 18 | 11 | 31(1) |
| | e. Interpersonal relationship | 1 | 10 | 6 | 17(6) |
| | f. Suspicion | 1 | 9 | 10 | 20(1) |
| **B** Functional Characteristics | a. Behavior under stress | 2 | 15 | 10 | 27(4) |
| | b. Cognitive functioning | 1 | 5 | 2 | 8(2) |
| | c. Appearance and rhetorical abilities | 1 | 17 | 3 | 21(5) |
| | d. Leisure life | — | 10 | 4 | 14(4) |
| | e. Relationship within a couple | — | 4 | 2 | 6 |
| **C** Leadership Style | a. Administrative style | 1 | 11 | 6 | 18(3) |
| | b. Working style | — | 7 | 12 | 19(1) |
| | c. Undemocratic nature | 1 | 12 | 3 | 16 |
| | d. Relation with the media | 4 | 11 | 11 | 26(4) |
| | e. Political worldview | 8 | 7 | 4 | 19(1) |
| | f. Political strategy | 3 | 2 | 3 | 8 |
| | g. Religiosity | — | 5 | 1 | 6(3) |
| **D** Family, Development, and Youth | a. Family, childhood, youth | 2 | 5 | 2 | 9(4) |
| | b. Military service | — | 5 | — | 5(2) |
| | c. Studies in the United States | — | 3 | — | 3(2) |
| | d Death of his brother | — | 4 | — | 4(2) |

*Note*: The numbers of units of information extracted from books are in parentheses; the
rest are from journals and magazines.

ries: distinguishing traits, functional characteristics, leadership style, and family and development. There was no disagreement on the classification of content categories into major categories.

Information came from three types of sources: primary sources, secondary sources, and commentary and evaluations.

1. Primary sources are based on direct observation of behavior, including interviews with the leader or books authored by him or her.
2. Secondary sources that are based on the impressions and perceptions of others, including books written about leaders and their background (such as biographies); articles describing leaders' behavior and characteristics (e.g., descriptions of meetings or a specific decision-making process); and written and verbal testimonies by people who had been close to leaders and could describe their behavior during differing situations and over periods of time.
3. Commentary and evaluations of the leader can be very diverse, ranging from political to psychological analyses of motives and personality. Unlike secondary sources, commentary and evaluation seldom consider specific behaviors in specific situations.

The predetermined criterion for including a content category in the data analysis was a combination of a minimum of three units of information of types 1 and 2. As Table 9.1 illustrates, most of our content categories easily met that criterion. The theoretical approach underlying the present study follows Maddi's (1989: 9) perception of personality as "a stable set of tendencies and characteristics that determine those commonalities and differences in people's psychological behavior (thoughts, feelings, and actions) that have continuity in time and that may not be easily understood as the sole result of the social and biological pressures of the moment." Maddi (1989) contends that any personality theory should deal with three points of reference: core of personality (the things that are common to all people); periphery of personality; and development of personality. For the purpose of psychological profiling of leaders, the second and third elements were determined to be most relevant.

Periphery of personality is generally learned rather than inherent and has a relatively circumscribed influence on behavior. It is used in the theories mainly to explain differences among people. The periphery includes three levels of statements, which are arranged hierarchically: (1) behavioral data—thoughts, feelings, and actions that have regularity in an individual; (2) peripheral characteristics or traits—patterns of behavior that tend to be consistent (e.g., stubbornness, cleanliness) and may explain much behavioral data; and (3) type—lifestyles or general orientations. The type is the combination of several dominant traits that appear together.

Development of personality explains how the leader's traits and typology evolved. The information about a leader's development is based on the testimony of others (i.e., biographical data); therefore, this point of reference should be considered as a hypothesis about development.

## DATA ANALYSIS: DISTINGUISHING TRAITS

### Egocentricity

A number of Netanyahu's behavioral patterns represent the dimension of egocentricity:

1. Personal success is more important to him than ideology, and he constantly strives for it. This pattern is demonstrated by his acceptance of help from U.S. contributors who held extreme views very different from his own (Kim, 1996a). He doesn't hesitate to exploit other people, including colleagues, in order to succeed. Journalist Yoel Markus describes Netanyahu: "[H]e is charismatic, driven, from an extremely ambitious family, egocentric, a lone wolf, the kind of person you might say has no God" (Markus, 1996).

2. Netanyahu sees himself as more perceptive than others. Thus, those who disagree with him don't understand historical/political processes correctly. According to the testimony of a journalist who interviewed him, Netanyahu is convinced that he discerns the historical processes that others do not and believes that it is his heroic task to rescue his homeland (Shavit, 1996).

3. His attitude toward people who work with him closely is self-centered. Some behaviors betray self-involvement to the point that others receive no consideration. This trait is also manifested in Netanyahu's manipulation of colleagues (Kim, 1997a).

4. A related and equally clear trait is Netanyahu's difficulty in appreciating perspectives other than his own (Benziman, 1993). Netanyahu's books and speeches presented no examples of attempts to understand or present perspectives other than his own.

5. Netanyahu has difficulty distinguishing between personal and public or political dimensions of his life. For example, at a meeting of senior Likud members after the Bar-On affair (a scandal in which high government officials were accused of trying to tamper with justice), he commented, "I receive a lot of support from all areas of the nation. They tell me to be strong and steadfast. 'We are with you; don't give up. Stand strong; truth will win.' Because this is what the success of the Jewish people, the success of the State of Israel, depends on, and they will never be defeated" (Verter, 1997).

6. Netanyahu is chronically tardy for meetings even with heads of state, interpreted by foreign leaders, politicians, and others as offensive, insulting, and even degrading (Benziman, 1997e). One can safely assume that the prime minister is aware of these reactions (some of them have been published in the press), but these reports have not influenced his behavior.

## Ambition and Determination

Ambition and determination are perhaps Netanyahu's most prominent character traits. Ambition is expressed in his desire to be the very best, to be first, to triumph over others, to reach the top (Horowitz, 1992: 6). He sets high goals and is not satisfied with partial successes. Netanyahu almost never despairs and never gives up. This stubbornness was demonstrated when, as Israel's ambassador to the United Nations (UN), he uncompromisingly struggled against the UN secretary-general and representatives, eventually winning in the decision to open UN files on Nazi crimes (Argaman, 1987: 46). He has displayed tremendous determination against all odds, reflecting strong willpower and a high degree of control. Professor Groesser at Massachusetts Institute of Technology (MIT), stated that Netanyahu was the most ambitious and focused man he had ever seen, with amazing willingness to work hard in order to achieve goals ("Netanyahu Sipur Haim," 1996: 7).

## Aggression and Manipulation

Netanyahu sees the game of politics as governed by the "laws of the jungle," where the strong survive and the weak fall by the wayside. To him, achievement of the goal justifies any political means (Sheory, 1985). This approach is manifested in both Netanyahu's behavior and his statements. In most cases, he does not act out of aggression, malice, or cruelty. His dominance and manipulation stem from cold, rational calculation, directed solely at achieving goals at any cost. For example, when he was putting together his cabinet, senior members of the Likud remarked that he was systematically settling accounts, humiliating and dominating party leaders. Individuals posing a threat to him were crushed (Verter, 1996b).

Several distinct, recurring behavioral patterns have been identified since Netanyahu's emergence into politics: (1) he preemptively attacks anyone perceived as an opponent or a rival. The attack may be direct or indirect (Golan, 1995); (2) he aims to shrink and diminish and, if necessary, dismiss those allies who might threaten him in the future. This is expressed in evasion and derision of prospective rivals, even allies who may threaten his future standing (Verter, 1997); (3) he utilizes assistants and colleagues to perform "deeds" that may arouse anger or dissent. Then, depending on results, he either supports them or denies any personal involvement (Kim, 1997a); (4) he forms and breaks pacts, drawing people closer or distancing himself from them, depending on current political needs or considerations. Today's ally may be tomorrow's rival, and vice versa (Markus, 1997b). He uses people for immediate needs, with no long-term loyalty or obligation.

## Credibility

The testimony of politicians, journalists, leaders, and public figures portrays Netanyahu as someone who makes and even signs promises that he does not keep. As a result, he is considered untrustworthy (Benziman, 1997b). Several leaders (e.g., President Mubarak, President Clinton) have accused Netanyahu of promising them things and then denying ever doing so. Journalist Benziman (1997d) reported that Clinton and his advisors were infuriated by Netanyahu's failure to fulfill promises that they claimed he made during his earlier visits to Washington (also see Benziman, 1997a).

Netanyahu's behavior indicates an attitude that duplicity is an agreed upon and accepted standard in politics. According to Barnea (1997), ministers often explain that their prime minister's amazing ability to survive is based on Netanyahu's introduction of a new political code, in which "bluffing" has become an acceptable form of deceit. This is not to say that he is a pathological liar (i.e., one who cannot discern between truth and lies), but rather a person who is convinced that in politics, any means are acceptable (Vardi, 1997: 225). Consequently, telling different people different things is accompanied by no psychological difficulty, sense of guilt, or pangs of conscience. In fact, more than once Netanyahu seemed surprised when accused of being untrustworthy. The result: even when he tells the truth, he sounds unconvincing.

## Interpersonal Relationships

Netanyahu's interpersonal relationships tend to be instrumental. He is not a good social mixer, nor is he a man who forms deep bonds with people. In general, he is closed and withdrawn, with very limited ability to empathize. Most of the people with whom he has social relationships are those he needs or who assist him (Galili, 1995). When these people cease to be of use to him, he terminates the relationship with them with relative ease (Verter, 1996a). This is not to say that he doesn't have friends with whom he stays in touch. However, interpersonal ties are not intimate and do not seem to involve emotional exchanges (Benziman, 1997c). This inability to empathize influences Netanyahu's interpersonal relationships with work colleagues: he tends to become entangled in conflicts and must constantly right relationships that have gone awry. Many of his relationships are more clearly based on mutual exploitation than friendship (Kim, 1996b).

## Suspicion

Another of Netanyahu's distinguishing traits is his suspicious nature (Benziman, 1997a). This suspicion that "the entire world is against him" is accompanied by feelings of victimization. His primary opponents are representatives of the former government, as well as the elite factions (the "princes") of his own party. From his behavior and speeches, it seems that it is precisely when he is under attack that he feels most at home. Apparently, feelings of victimization mobilize his inner resources, enabling him to fight and win in an effort to "show them" (Kim, 1997b).

Netanyahu's response to the "cassette affair" provides another example of this characteristic. After his wife received an anonymous phone call threatening that taped evidence of Netanyahu's betrayal of her would be publicized, he made a public statement, charging that "an unprecedented crime in the history of the state and the democracy has been committed" (Rozenblum, 1993).

Since Netanyahu's entry into political life, his levels of suspicion have increased. This tendency intensifies during crises, when he feels his position threatened. Individuals who are not members of his close staff are often automatically suspected of disloyalty and conspiring against him. The threat, as he sees it, is primarily personal.

## FUNCTIONAL CHARACTERISTICS

### Behavior under Stress

Benjamin Netanyahu's behavior under stress varies situationally. If stress can be anticipated and if its source is known, Netanyahu feels in control, is unlikely to improvise, and ensures backup for alternative plans. He remains calm during such crises and deals directly with problems, concentrating on the central issue. He remains optimistic even in difficult moments and recovers quickly from surprise punches. In television interviews he has demonstrated an excellent ability to handle difficult questions and to direct discussions.

When the crisis is unanticipated, and Netanyahu does not feel in control, he reacts in a pressured, frightened, and confused manner and may even lose his composure. For example, people who were close to Netanyahu at the time of the "cassette affair" mentioned above testify that he acted out of panic, "lost his cool," and failed to think things through (Galili, 1993). In such situations, he is willing to promise anything, sign any document (Markus, 1997a). He concedes to whoever puts pressure on him. When exposed to blackmail or extortion, he strenuously resists but will also concede dramatically. Israel Harel, a leader of the West Bank settlers, said in an interview after the Mashaal incident that Netanyahu had lost his senses, panicked, and given the Jordanians an outrageously exorbitant price (Harel, 1997). Military analyst Amir Oren's report stated that Netanyahu was so alarmed by the arrest of two Mossad agents in Amman that he himself proposed Ahmed Yassin's release to King Hussein, an offer that could not be retracted. In the end, it provided Yassin with the option of deciding for himself (Oren, 1997).

People who have worked closely with Netanyahu also report somatic reactions during stress: he will often withdraw during a crisis with a stomachache (Goren & Berkowitz, 1996: 87). This type of somatic reaction is indicative of a coping mechanism stimulated by feelings that Netanyahu is unwilling either to admit or to express.

## Cognitive Functioning

Netanyahu is a very talented and intelligent man. He is gifted with an extraordinary—some say phenomenal—capacity for learning and an excellent memory (according to Vardi, 1997: 217); he has the benefit of a broad education and possesses a strong ability for analytic and visual thinking (Admon, 1987: 22). Netanyahu is very well read in a wide range of subjects (art, history, and business), loves to quote (usually accurately) from books that he has read, and has a tendency to support his own views with those of outstanding historical figures (Vardi, 1997: 291).

Netanyahu is a person who needs constant stimulation. He seeks challenges that enable him to prove himself. He is a decisive person who hates routine work, prefers to set meaningful goals for himself, and is uneasy with free time. In an interview he said, "I enjoy the work load. I like periods of relief and calm, but not if they're too long. After a vacation of more than two days, I begin feeling uneasy, because time is passing without use" (Brezki, 1997: 44).

## Appearance, Charisma, and Rhetoric Abilities

Benjamin Netanyahu is an attractive and impressive man. He exudes self-confidence and charisma. He has great rhetoric ability and explains his views logically (Admon, 1987: 22). Netanyahu developed a flair for debate, logic, and powers of persuasion in his youth, such that his peers found him difficult to contend with. Netanyahu knew better than other government spokespersons how to explain Israel's position to an American audience, in polished English (Argaman, 1987: 46). His appearance and rhetoric abilities were part of his charm and served him well during his race for head of the Likud and, afterward, for prime minister (Markus, 1992).

## Leisure Life

Netanyahu loves the good life that status and power afford him ( e.g., Benziman, 1996). He lives lavishly: luxurious hotels, high-class restaurants, fine food, connoisseur wine, high-quality cigars, tailored clothes, and personal hairstyling before every public appearance or important meeting (Sheory, 1985). As part of this sense of entitlement, Netanyahu, after becoming prime minister, demanded considerable discounts or preferred treatment for himself and his family (cf. Goren & Berkowitz, 1996: 34).

### Couple Relations

Netanyahu has been married three times and divorced twice. In all three cases, he married strong, dominant women. This pattern of a controlling woman who commits herself to her husband's career is familiar to Netanyahu from his family of origin. According to people who knew Netanyahu, his first two marriages began in love and ended with the wife's decision to end the relationship (Kaspit & Kfir, 1997b: 22). Although he suffered from the separations, he recovered quickly and carried on. Netanyahu begins new relationships fairly easily but does not maintain them for long (Barnea, 1997). His present marriage took place after his girlfriend, Sara, became pregnant. According to people who knew Netanyahu, he had doubts about marrying her. She has received much press coverage herself (Grayevski et al., 1997). One journalist reports that Netanyahu never misses an opportunity to present himself as the perfect family man and devoted husband and father, dedicated to family values (Ashri, 1996).

## LEADERSHIP STYLE

### Administration and Work Style

Netanyahu is a centralist administrator who tends to work alone and to compartmentalize others. For example, according to the most senior state official's testimony on Netanyahu's work style: "He operates alone, he doesn't consult with experienced key advisors, and doesn't realize that one day he is going to need them" (Benziman, 1997e).

A journalist describes his administration style: he personally delegates tasks to his assistants, demands frequent reports on their activities, and rules with an iron hand. Staff must be loyal and disciplined (Aluf, 1996). His administrative style is aggressive. It is important for him to be at the top, to influence, to dominate. He loves to play commander in the "war room," drawing diagrams on a board (Vardi, 1997: 177). Netanyahu displays strong leadership ability and can successfully encourage people to follow him ("Netanyahu Sipur Haim," 1996: 9). He works well with a small, intimate, intelligent, and loyal staff. He gives his staff a feeling of importance, camaraderie, and intimacy, a sense of being an "elite unit" (Kaspit & Kfir, 1997a: 128).

Netanyahu's statements and behavior suggest an undemocratic character. This is acknowledged by his own ministers and cabinet members. He has been accused of using undemocratic manipulation to tilt the balance in the Likud Party. One journalist reports that, according to Likud supporters, soldiers for Netanyahu and Prime Minister Office General Manager, Avigdor Lieberman are like front-line troops who will follow him to hell and back, who will relentlessly pursue traitors on the home front and will do anything that Netanyahu demands of them—even commit suicide for him (Kim, 1997c). He does not consult others, except for his personal advisors. He utilizes yes-men who work for him without his having to be directly involved, makes conflicting promises, and uses behind-the-scene tactics that contradict his promises (Gilat, 1997: 3).

### Relations with the Media

The media suit Netanyahu's character; a man of words, Netanyahu has all the makings of a television star: a pleasant appearance, self-confidence, a superb talent for rhetoric, excellent English, intelligence, and strong logical abilities, which enable him to contend with any interviewer or rival (Sheory, 1985). He knows how to make the most of subject matter on which it is easy to find consensus (such as terrorism or the Holocaust). He has a knack for turning issues around to that which he would like to discuss, not necessarily what his interviewer or rival intended (Shalev et al., 1996: 2). His style: a simple message expressed briefly, clearly, and repeatedly (Galili, 1995). Supporters of a party rival, Ehud Olmert, say that Bibi Netanyahu lives in a completely imaginary reality. "From his point of view, the facts are only a marginal addition to what is publicized on TV and in the press" (Kaspit, 1997: 2). He knows how to use journalists to leak information when convenient, to pass messages to the media via others, and to manipulate the press to his advantage (e.g., to enter a convention hall exactly when the prime-time newscasts begin). He admits treating the television studio as a battlefield, in which he must defeat his rival, in one interview stating, "For me, television is a boxing arena. You stand opposite someone who wants to attack what you represent, and you have to decide when, what, and how to respond" (Brezki, 1997: 42).

### Political and Religious Worldview

His worldview regarding the Arab–Israeli conflict (as expressed in his speeches, interviews, and books) is as follows: (1) from a historical perspective, there is nothing more just than the return of the Jews to their homeland (Netanyahu, 1995: 174); (2) although it is in the right, Israel has failed to disseminate this information effectively, while Arab propaganda has presented false evidence of the nature of the conflict in Israel and abroad (Netanyahu, 1995: 15); (3) the Arab countries around Israel are not democracies, and therefore peace with them can be based only on a balance of fear and on Israel's ability to defend itself—Arab hostility will not disappear during this generation (Rozenblum, 1977); and (4) only a mighty Israel that maintains its convictions will eventually be accepted by the Arabs (Netanyahu, 1995: 354).

A leader's religious beliefs are not necessarily central to his or her personality. However, in Israel, where religion and politics go hand in hand, the religious convictions of a leader can have great political and personal significance. Netanyahu's life throughout his political career indicates a completely secular lifestyle (Benziman, 1996). His bond with religion is expressed primarily in a strong sense of historical continuity of the Jewish nation and respect for tradition, which were central to his family of origin (Goren & Berkowitz, 1996: 35). Once, during the election campaign, while on a visit to a synagogue, he kissed the cover of a Torah scroll, as customary, and then winked surreptitiously at the newspaper reporter who eternalized the moment (Vardi, 1997: 305).

## FAMILY AND DEVELOPMENT

Netanyahu's father, Ben-Zion, the eldest of the Milikovsky children, spent a large part of his life in the United States, dedicated to his career as a historian. Like his own father, Ben-Zion failed to integrate into the political or academic establishment and is described as an embittered man, feeling discriminated against because of his political opinions (Goren & Berkowitz, 1996: 35). Benjamin Netanyahu's mother, Celia, was born to elderly parents and was raised by her three older sisters. She grew up in Israel under difficult conditions during World War II. She was raised strictly and developed determinism and willpower. Throughout her married life with Ben-Zion, she devoted herself totally to his work. She was the drive behind his career and the dominant family figure (Doek, 1997). Celia was described as a cold woman who taught her children to use restraint, to hide their emotions, and to show strength. She also conveyed high expectations of success to her sons.

Ben-Zion Netanyahu's children were in awe of their father, who was distant from them. While he closed himself up in his study for hours, their mother enforced strict silence upon the children. The father pushed his children to succeed in school and kept them under spartan rule. The entire family was dedicated to the father's work (Goren & Berkowitz, 1996: 35). The family was socially isolated (Kaspit & Kfir, 1997a: 36). They had few friends and a limited social life and saw themselves as a closed unit facing a hostile world. There was an atmosphere of suspicion, bitterness, and a feeling of injustice (despite their successes) (Vardi, 1997: 50). The parents' message to their children: succeed at any cost, dedicate everything to your goal. Benjamin was described as a serious, exceptionally industrious, quiet, and withdrawn child. He was a very good, disciplined student and a voracious reader (Goren & Berkowitz, 1996: 36).

As a teenager, Benjamin Netanyahu was separated from Israel when the family moved back to the United States (one of many changes of location). During this time period, he demonstrated strong will, independence, and maturity. He dedicated all his time to studies, achieving honors with extraordinary self-discipline (Kaspit & Kfir, 1997a: 40). Netanyahu had excellent prospects: he was handsome, tall, athletic, and strong. Nevertheless, he was lonely and alienated, unfriendly, and unlikely to engage in heart-to-heart talks. He also displayed a strong desire to compete and win.

When he was 18, Netanyahu returned to Israel to serve his army duty. He was a good soldier: highly motivated, serious, ambitious, and totally obedient. He was described as a man of action, not of creativity, originality, or vision ("Netanyahu Sipur Haim," 1996: 6). He was a good officer, however, not outstanding in comparison with other commanders in their elite unit. He was described as strict but fair (Bashan, 1995: 10). In the army, Netanyahu did not make social contacts beyond those necessary in the line of duty. He was withdrawn and closed, although ready to help when needed (Horowitz, 1992: 6).

Benjamin Netanyahu's brother, Yoni, was three years older than he was. He was the talented and beloved son who "carried the family torch" and was earmarked from an early age to be a star, the hope of the family (Goren & Berkowitz, 1996: 35). Yoni often served as a father substitute to his younger brothers and was a central role model for them. He was the object of Benjamin's love and admiration and a model for emulation (Horowitz, 1992: 6). However, Yoni Netanyahu died in action during the Entebbe operation. For Benjamin Netanyahu, who was studying in the United States, this was the greatest blow that he had ever suffered. True to the developed character of the family, he reacted with emotional restraint. Feelings of grief and sorrow were channeled in a practical direction: in a relatively short time, the family dedicated itself to an unprecedented memorial to its son (Goren & Berkowitz, 1996: 36). The project became the center of Benjamin Netanyahu's life and served as a springboard to becoming a noted and international expert on terrorism. There is no doubt that Benjamin Netanyahu deeply grieved for his brother, but it is also impossible to ignore his exploitation of the memorial for his own self-advancement.

## PSYCHOLOGICAL EVALUATION

Benjamin Netanyahu's behavior reveals many of the characteristics of a narcissistic personality, including a tendency to megalomania (linking his personal fate to the national one); powerful ambition; total devotion to his goal (success at any price); failure to admit weakness and refusal to take the blame; manipulative relationships; using other people to attain his goals; taking from people; dishonesty in politics; a lack of personal and political ethics; great sensitivity to criticism; keen awareness of his appearance (American Psychiatric Association, 1994).

Netanyahu's suspiciousness (bordering on a paranoid tendency) displayed itself from an early age. Netanyahu notes conspiracy everywhere: whoever disagrees with him is by definition wrong and against him—the enemy. He has viewed the world as a cruel place, with no room for altruism, philanthropy, or true friendship, a continuous Darwinist struggle for survival. Netanyahu sees himself, like his father, as an outsider to the establishment, alienated and discriminated against. He has perceived all political colleagues as rivals and has taken revenge on those caught opposing him.

Netanyahu also possesses some of the characteristics of the authoritarian personality (Adorno et al., 1950; Stone et al., 1993): he tends to deny his weaknesses and to blame others (e.g., the media) for his failures; his relationships with people are manipulative and based, to some extent, on domination; he sees events and people in terms of power, for which he has very great passion; he is an aggressive leader. Netanyahu evaluates the world in stark contrasts. His politics of opposition is conservative and rigid. His primary platform is accentuated nationalism. He plucks the heartstrings of his public supporters, fans the fires of their instincts, promises to institute new social and government structures, and calls on his faithful public to rebel against the existing social order.

### Psychological Hypothesis

From a psychological point of view, it seems that the foundation for Netanyahu's conception of politics is based on several of his personality traits: (1) his inability to take perspectives other than his own into account; (2) the early familial environment in which the history of Zionism was seen as both a direct continuation of the path of ancestors who settled in the land of Israel and a means to right the historic injustice of the exile of the Jews from their land—in this context, Netanyahu identified deeply with the historical notion of a Greater Israel, which belongs to the Jews; (3) the central message of Netanyahu's upbringing that "nothing should stand in the way of determination," leading to a feeling of omnipotence when accompanied by a knowledge of goals and convictions; (4) Netanyahu's egocentrism, as clearly illustrated in his ability to sacrifice ideology for personal success.

Another hypothesis about the Netanyahu's family concerns the place that each child has in the family: there is some evidence that Netanyahu lived in the shadow of his older brother Yoni. Furthermore, Yoni's death altered Netanyahu's life. In the process of Yoni's commemoration, he revealed himself to the political world and became a well-known media figure.

## CONCLUSION

Benjamin Netanyahu is not likely to change dramatically. A narcissistic personality, like other personality types, is stable and unlikely to alter. Therefore, changes in leadership style are not expected. It is more likely that some of his character traits—suspicion, aggression in politics, megalomaniac perception of himself as savior of the nation from tragic mistakes, interpersonal relationship style, and lack of credibility—will be heightened while in a position of leadership. It seems that a good portion of Netanyahu's failures and mishaps in office was the product of his character, rather than lack of experience.

Many wonder at his meteoric rise to power, on the one hand, and his failure as a prime minister, on the other. His personality, as described here, provides a possible explanation. His character traits—ambition, determination, excellent media skills, superb rhetoric, and personal charm—were highly suited to the achievement of top political office. However, these traits are not sufficient for an effective administrator. Furthermore, additional traits that did not hinder his rise to the top—lack of credibility, impaired ability for interpersonal relationships, megalomania, aggression, suspicion, and egocentricity—represent a serious obstacle for a successful prime minister. Thus, the fascinating election campaign in 1996, which fueled the expectations of many, was followed by a flawed administration.

The use of behavior analysis to evaluate Netanyahu has allowed for the emergence of a unique and comprehensive psychological profile, based upon a content analysis of units of information categorized and compared by multiple researchers, tested for reliability, and based upon a large sample from a variety of sources. The method is somewhat limited since it is qualitative by nature and, as such, does not permit comparison between various leaders according to quantitative criteria (there are no standard scores to be compared).

Additionally, this method requires that a variety of secondary sources be utilized to control for the possibility of bias in the individual journalist. Nevertheless, the advantages of the behavior analysis seem to warrant its application in the construction of psychological profiles of political leaders.

### Epilogue

When this profile was prepared, Benjamin Netanyahu was Israel's prime minister. At that time, no one knew that he would be defeated a year later in the May 1999 election. The current analysis was not intended to serve as the basis for predicting whether Netanyahu would continue to occupy his position of power in the long run (as this is influenced by many factors, in addition to the leader's personality). However, based on Netanyahu's personality traits, as described here, it was possible to predict fairly confidently that his term in office would continue to be plagued by serious problems. These problems—poor teamwork; communication difficulties and problematic relationships with other important figures; hasty decision making (such as opening the tunnel in Jerusalem) or, alternatively, difficulty in making important decisions (concessions to the Palestinians in order to reach a peace accord)— were reflective of his administration. While it is clear that Netanyahu's personality traits contributed substantially to his fall, under certain conditions those same traits might induce him to return to the political arena.

## NOTES

1. It should be noted that the analysis was conducted before the May 1999 elections were announced, that is, when Netanyahu was prime minister. No major changes have been made since then.

2. Due to space limitation, the long list of 132 magazine and newspaper articles (with coded categories and type of information) is not presented in this chapter. Readers who would like the list should contact the author by E-mail: shaul; cashamir.org.il.

Part III

# The Cultural Context: Applications from East to West

Chapter 10

# Building the War Economy and Rebuilding Postwar Japan: A Profile of Pragmatic Nationalist Nobusuke Kishi

Shigeko N. Fukai

## INTRODUCTION

Nobusuke Kishi, prime minister of Japan (1957–1960), had an extraordinary career as a political leader in Japan. He was a leader of reform (*kakushin*) bureaucrats who advocated greater state control of the economy for war mobilization and countersigned the imperial ordinance proclaiming war as a member of Hideki Tōjō's cabinet. After Japan's defeat, he spent three years in prison as unindicted Class A war criminal. Only nine years after he was released from the prison, Kishi became the prime minister of Japan. His fall from power was even quicker, after his forceful passage of the revised United States–Japan Security Treaty inspired the massive protests that culminated in the May–June Crisis of 1960 (Shioda, 1996: 337). Not only for his prewar and wartime career but also for many of his postwar policy initiatives, Kishi was a controversial figure. For his vision, leadership, and political maneuvering, Kishi is variously called a superbureaucrat (Kobayashi, 1995: 183–84) and *Showa no yokai* (Showa's monster) (Iwami, 1994).

This chapter analyzes Kishi's leadership using Jean Blondel's (1987: 97) two-dimensional leadership typology, which is explained in the next section. This study focuses on the scope and the nature of Kishi's goals and intervention in society and is not a systematic study of his personality characteristics (Bass, 1981: 75–76). Then I review Kishi's bureaucratic and political career and analyze it in terms of Blondel's typology. By comparing Kishi's leadership style and effectiveness before and after World War II, I seek to highlight some aspects of the change and continuity in the Japanese political system and culture before and after the war. In the concluding section, I evaluate the utility of Blondel's typology in terms of explaining and predicting political behavior and the effectiveness of national leadership.

## BLONDEL'S TYPOLOGY

Using a two-dimensional typology, with each dimension divided into three groups, Blondel (1987: 97) classifies nine categories of leadership in terms of leaders' goals and their impact on society. Goals are defined as "a set of intentions which leaders effectively attempt to put in practice." They consist of the leaders' vision/view of their country and of their role in helping to realize this vision/view and "are not mere expressions of hope or desires that remain unfulfilled." Dimension I concerns change or no change aimed at by the leaders. In this typology, changes are viewed in a "neutral" manner ideologically but could be positive or negative (left or right; progressive or reactionary) (Blondel, 1987: 90–91). Those who simply want to stay in power are categorized as the status-quo leaders (Blondel: 1987: 80–82). Dimension II is related to the scope and range of intervention.

Another dimension to be distinguished is that of the international and internal fields: the latter is like a team sport, in which leaders attempt to build a "community," whereas the former is fought by several independent (in principle) actors and resembles poker or bridge, in which leaders are concerned with their position in the circle of world leaders and their country's position in the circle of nations. The distinction is useful in determining the character of transformers, who can aim at changes either in the international plane or in the internal plane. Someone like Woodrow Wilson may be seen to have aimed at the changes in the international plane, while preserving the status quo in the internal plane (Blondel, 1987: 91).

He calls those leaders who aim to deal with a broad scope of intervention as great leaders and classifies them into three categories: saviors, who seem to be able to solve a major problem facing the nation or the state, such as the threat of total annihilation; ideologues/revolutionary transformers, who are interested in bringing about major changes in the basis on which society is organized; and paternalists/populists, who wish to introduce some changes but do not want to upset the whole society. Paternalistic leaders often pursue the mix of reactionary and progressive policies. The vision and concern with the whole life and structure of the nation distinguish great leaders from mere policy makers who are concerned with an aspect of the life of the country. De Gaulle is classified as a savior operating on the international plane in 1940 and as a transformer operating mainly on the national plane in 1958.

Blondel defines those who aim at a moderate scope of intervention as ordinary heads of governments. Most heads of governments are policy makers whose activity and interest are limited and specific, rather than any of the three great leader types. In terms of Dimension I (change or continuity), they are classified into comforters, who calm a people worried by problems that are short of system collapse but serious, by assuring continuity of the system; and reformists, who are concerned with substantial changes in the structure of society. In between are redefiners, who redefine the agenda of the society to effect moderate change.

Blondel calls those who are concerned with a specialized scope of intervention policy makers and classifies them, according to the location on the scale of the continuity/change continuum, into managers, who deal with only some aspects of a policy area as problems arise in order to maintain the status quo; and innovators, who introduce and implement major reforms that effect a major change, like all aspects of economic policy. In between the two are adjusters, the agents of moderate change.

Blondel also draws attention to how the environment affects leaders' goals. A society under threat would demand comforters or protectors. If a nation's independence is threatened, leaders' goals would likely approach those of saviors, while normalcy would likely result in manager-type leaders. When there is dissatisfaction with some of the institutions or the policy directions, leaders have to become adjusters or innovators to ease tension in society. For the revolutionary/transformer type of leaders to emerge, societies must have very deep division and extraordinarily high levels of discontent.

In terms of Blondel's nine categories of leadership, how can Kishi be characterized? As Blondel cautions, these categories are not always exclusive or distinct but may overlap and should be considered in terms of a range rather than separate categories. How did Kishi's goals/ambitions and the environment interact to influence the direction and effectiveness of his leadership? The following section briefly reviews Kishi's childhood environment and upbringing to see how he developed his interest in politics. Then I review Kishi's bureaucratic career at the Ministry of Commerce and Industry and in Manchuria. Next I survey main events in Kishi's political career before, during, and after the war to see what his goals were, how he tried to accomplish them, and how the changing environment affected his goals and effectiveness before, during, and after the war.

## THE CASE STUDY: NOBUSUKE KISHI

### Formative Years: *Shishi* Ideal, National Socialism, Pan-Asianism

Nobusuke Kishi was born in 1896 as the second son of the Sato's, former samurai family, in Yamaguchi prefecture or Choshu. Choshu was the birthplace of numerous *shishi* (men of high purpose), including Shoin Yoshida and many other revolutionary leaders, who were the central driving force of the Meiji Restoration (Kishi, 1983b: 23–25). Tsurumi defines *shishi* as "men dedicated to the welfare of society as a whole as if it were their own." During the Tokugawa period, cultivation of this *shishi* spirit was an important goal of education of the samurai. This emphasis on the *shishi* ideal was based on the Confucian notion of how to govern the country. Yamaguchi prefecture has since produced many prime ministers in Japan (Tsurumi, 1970: 66).

Kishi's idea about himself and his vision of the country were nurtured under this patriotic, mission-oriented, and elitist political culture of his birthplace (Hosokawa, 1986: 10). Kishi's foundational political personality was formed under the tenacious pressure for keeping his family name in honor exerted by the closely knit Sato clan. His great-grandfather, Nobuhiro Sato, served as the governor of Shimane prefecture and was a friend of Shoin Yoshida, Hirobumi Ito, and other early Meiji leaders (Kishi, 1983b: 23–25). His father was a noncareer bureaucrat of the Yamaguchi prefectural government, but returned to the sake brewery business when Nobusuke was two years old (Hara, 1995: 3). Though his family had to live on a tight budget, his mother took special care not to spoil the children's pride by constantly reminding them of their samurai lineage. Under these circumstances, Nobusuke was raised as a cherished target of unusual communitarian educational zeal shared by the clan members (Hara, 1995: 6).

Kishi entered Tokyo Imperial University in 1917, the year of the Bolshevik Revolution in Russia and when Woodrow Wilson was waging a campaign against German authoritarianism and militarism. Many features of condemned German authoritarianism found their counterparts in Japan, where economic boom after Japan entered World War I generated inflation to threaten the middle- and working-class livelihood. Social unrest intensified as the gap between the rich and the poor grew to threaten the political foundation of the society. The rice riot in protest against the rising rice prices swept Japan, involving more than 700,000 mainly urban populaces (Tsurumi, 1970: 71). Socialism and liberalism were a growing influence in Japan, against traditionalist nationalism, deeply rooted among those conservatives determined to maintain the status quo of Japan's hierarchical order with the emperor at the apex. On the diplomatic front, the same year (1917) witnessed the Siberian expedition in the hope to contain the influence of Bolshevik Revolution.

In this environment, Kishi developed a strong interest in Ikki Kita's version of national socialism and Shumei Ohkawa's version of Pan-Asianism. Kishi acknowledges Kita's intellectual and ideological influence in shaping his political thoughts. So deeply impressed was Kishi that he stayed up all night to copy down Kita's secretly circulated *Nihon*

*Kaizo Hoan Taiko* [An Outline Plan for the Reorganization of Japan] (Kishi, 1983b: 184–85), which was not only to become a bible for the young officers who engineered the failed coup of February 26, 1936, but also to inspire some student radicals of the postwar left-wing movements (Tsurumi, 1970: 386).

Kita offered a set of concrete measures to reconstruct Japan, such as the abolition of the peerage system, nationalization of the imperial property, imposing limits on the people's private property rights, nationalization of the large capitals, and the distribution of the net benefits of the private firms to the workers and installing labor hour rules of an eight-hour day and no work on Sundays and national holidays. He also emphasized human rights for all nationals on the basis of equality and freedom. The redistribution of the world territories was another theme propagated in his book. Despite Kita's sharp criticisms of the emperor system, Kishi wrote in his memoir that Kita was among those who impressed him most profoundly and that he was a true revolutionary far above any right-wing fellows rising after him (Kishi, 1983b: 185).

Hara (1995: 27) observes that Kita's expansionist national socialism had been duplicated in Kishi's idea about the state and the course of action as a leader of reform bureaucrats and of Manchurian development and as a leader in charge of managing the Pacific War as a member of the Tōjō cabinet. However, in sharp contrast to Kita's ideas, Kishi's call, before and during the war, for the abolition of the peerage, reforms of the Ministry of Imperial Affairs, and the limitation on private property rights was motivated by the desire to preserve *kokutai* (national polity) (Kishi, 1983b: 186). In this sense, Kishi had elements of being a transformer on the domestic front, but his ultimate goal was to strengthen and preserve the existing imperial order.

Shumei Ohkawa's Pan-Asianism, the idea of uniting all the Asian nations under the leadership of Japan, also had a profound impact on Kishi in forming his ideas about Japan's role in Asia and the world. Drawing on Henry Cotton's *India in Transition* (1985), Ohkawa sought to demonstrate how ruthless squandering by the British had desolated India, how the resistance movement against Britain had evolved, and how Japan's resurgence as an independent Asian power gave a psychological boost to the forces for independence in India. Youthful Kishi was impressed by Ohkawa's ideas and self-confident way of making up his mind quickly and unambiguously, which he described as "unlike typical scholars who enlist alternative theories without identifying their own views" (Hara, 1995: 29).

If not typical, Kishi's upbringing and childhood environment represent one of the socialization patterns not uncommon among the prewar politicians of samurai lineage (Tsurumi, 1970: 64). He abundantly benefited from rich *kyoudobatsu* (clansmen, or persons from the same locality) relationships. His academic and career history represents a typical pattern of Japanese political leaders—on his graduation from the Law Faculty of Tokyo Imperial University, he became a bureaucrat and later a politician. He benefited from extensive *gakubatsu* (school and university classmates) ties.

On the other hand, he is atypical in many ways. In spite of his outstanding academic record, he chose the Ministry of Agriculture and Industry (divided into the Ministry of Commerce and Industry, to which Kishi belonged, and the Ministry of Agriculture in 1925) instead of the most prestigious Ministry of Finance or Ministry of Home Affairs, which were considered then as the most promising path to a political career. He was not a normal post-seeker but a hard-nosed, goal-oriented power-seeker, as will be seen. There are two types of power-seekers: those who seek power for the sake of power and the others who seek power as a means to achieve their goals derived from their larger visions. If a typical politician in contemporary Japan can be classified into the former category, Kishi seems to belong to the latter type.

### Kishi as a Bureaucrat

Kishi's bureaucratic career can be divided into two periods: domestic service years from 1920 to 1936 and Manchurian years from 1936 to 1939, when he was said to have grown into a politician.

#### *Kishi at the Ministry of Commerce and Industry (MCI)*

Kishi started his career amid the postwar depression, when, with the sharp decline in military demands, factory shutdowns and unemployment soared. In 1921, the largest-ever strike with some 30,000 workers broke out at the Kawasaki Shipyard in Kobe, and Takashi Hara, the first commoner prime minister, was assassinated (Hara, 1995: 39).

In 1922, the year the Japan Communist Party was born, Kishi was assigned to one of the most prized posts at the Document and Archives Section of the secretariat of MCI, where he met Shinji Yoshino, then section chief, to build the foundation of the "Yoshino/Kishi line relationship," which was to dominate the ministry (Kishi et al., 1981: 15). In 1926 Yoshino assigned Kishi to the job of managing the construction of the Japanese pavilion at the World's Fair in Philadelphia. Kishi was highly impressed, even shocked, by the material abundance and affluence of the United States. So vast was the gap with Japan, he felt, that the United States could not be a model for Japan. In contrast, he felt a sense of affinity with Germany, which he visited on his way home, as a have-not nation trying to overcome many problems familiar to Japan (Kishi et al., 1981: 12).

In October 1929, when he was an assistant section chief in the Documents section, Kishi led the opposition within MCI to a 10% pay cut for all civil and military officials ordered by the Osachi Hamaguchi cabinet as part of its deflationary program. This was the first occasion when Kishi collided head-on with his superior (Shioda, 1996: 82). This incident coincided with Yoshino's plan to send Kishi abroad to investigate the industrial rationalization movement in other countries. Kishi stayed for seven months in Berlin, studying and reporting on the industrial rationalization movement. His report had a direct impact on the course of Japan's industrial rationalization.

The Important Industries Control Law was enacted in 1931, which legalized so-called self-control (*jishu tosei*) in the form of treatylike cartel agreements among enterprises to fix levels of production, establish prices, limit new entrants into an industry, and control marketing for a particular industry. Hadley (1970: 330) notes that it produced a "cordial oligopoly" in the large-scale advanced sectors, in sharp contrast to the "cutthroat oligopoly" prevalent after World War II (Johnson, 1982: 109). Smeared by zaibatsu[1] banks' dollar-buying scandal, however, self-imposed control in industry failed in establishing a respectable record as expected by the planners (Johnson, 1982: 111).

### Kishi in Manchuria

On the strong request from the Kwantung Army to help its anti-zaibatsu industrialization campaign, which had gone awry, Kishi became the deputy director of the Industrial Department of the government of Manchukuo in 1936, to join the reform bureaucrats whom he had dispatched earlier from Japan (Kishi et al., 1981: 16).

At the first meeting with Chief of Staff Seishiro Itagaki of the Kwantung Army, Kishi demanded a totally free hand in the field of industrial economy. Itagaki accepted this demand, and since then the army has refrained from intervening in the implementation of the plan (Kishi et al., 1981: 29). Kishi took full charge of an ambitious industrialization plan, which involved large-scale infrastructure projects such as dam and power-line construction and land-reclamation to mining and start-up of the first aluminum industry in Japan. He invited Gisuke Ayukawa, leader of a "new zaibatsu," Nissan, to manage these projects (Kishi et al., 1981: 23; Iwami, 1994: 65–70). Kishi thus built extensive human ties and accumulated invaluable experience in implementing and, indeed, experimenting with new ideas in actually starting heavy industrialization from scratch. Kishi compared his experience in Manchuria to drawing a picture on a blank canvas.

On leaving Manchuria, Kishi made an oft-cited remark: "Politicians must be careful to have a political fund cleansed by a filter before receiving it" (Hara, 1995: 76). Hoshino observed that Kishi came to Manchuria as a brilliant bureaucrat and went back to Japan as a politician (Hara, 1995: 67).

### Kishi as a Politician: Before, during, and after the War

*Before and during the War*

During the period that Kishi was "drawing his picture" in Manchuria, a severe battle was under way in Japan over how to restructure the economy for war mobilization. The business community vehemently opposed state control espoused by reform-minded bureaucrats, and insisted on self-regulation rather than state control in order to expand production for war preparation (Johnson, 1982: 133).

In October 1939, amid this battle, Kishi was invited back to MCI as vice-minister to take charge of economic reconstruction in preparation for war (Kishi et al., 1981: 35). In July 1940 Fumimaro Konoe formed his second cabinet and requested Kishi to become MCI minister. Kishi declined the offer because, in Kishi's words, his appointment might look in the eyes of business leaders as if he, leader of reformist bureaucrats, had burst forth with a drawn sword by which to demand the immediate answer. To avoid such provocation, Kishi suggested that Konoe appoint someone from the business community (Kishi et al., 1981: 42). Konoe appointed as minister Ichizo Kobayashi, an outspoken leader selected by the business community, but said that he would consider Kishi as a de facto minister (Kishi et al., 1981: 44). The second Konoe cabinet included three of the five members of the Manchurian power center, Yosuke Matsuoka as foreign minister, Tōjō as army minister, and Naoki Hoshino as Cabinet Planning Board (PCB) president. The choice of Kobayashi may well have reflected a sense of alarm felt by the business community (Johnson, 1982: 148).

Upon Konoe's order, Kishi drafted plans for implementing the Economic New Structure for the MCI, in close conformity with the PCB's general plan published on September 13. Kobayashi accused the plan of being "red-tainted" in a speech at the Industrial Club (Kishi et al., 1981: 43). Fuming at this accusation, Kishi demanded a formal explanation as MCI minister. Kobayashi demanded Kishi's resignation (Kishi et al., 1981: 43). Kishi consulted with Konoe, who replied that "it is the order of things that the quarrel between minister and vice minister should be settled by the latter's resignation, isn't it?" (Kishi et al., 1981: 44). Kishi later confessed that he felt that he was still too young to understand what a political man was like (Kishi et al., 1981: 44).

In October 1941 Hideki Tōjō formed his cabinet and requested Kishi to become MCI minister. Before accepting the offer, Kishi wanted to know Tōjō's thoughts about war against the United States. Tōjō replied that he would try his best to avoid war against the United States but that no one could tell how history would turn. Kishi accepted the offer. He was 45 years old (Kishi et al., 1981: 49–50). On assuming the ministership, he undertook a thorough personnel change to facilitate smooth operation of ministerial work in emergency time. After appointing Etsusaburo Shiina, his longtime confidant, as vice-minister, Kishi asked all of Shiina's superiors to resign, and they did so (Kishi et al., 1981: 50). This started the practice for all classmates or seniors to resign when a new vice-minister takes over (Johnson, 1982: 66). In the 1942 general elections, Kishi was elected to the House of Representatives of the Imperial Diet.

MCI's mission encompassed a large area that included planned expansion of production, mobilization of resources, management of factories, regulation of consumption, and price control. The control associations for each industry were created, in theory, to integrate the public and private sectors for improved war production. Actually, however, they turned out to be quite ineffective, as they were dominated by the rampant *zaibatsu* profiteering from officially sanctioned cartels. Competition for, and sometimes hoarding of, materials pandemic among *zaibatsu* was joined by the army and navy to aggravate ineffectiveness of those cartels (Johnson, 1982: 153–54).

To overcome these defects of control associations and improve effectiveness of war production by centralizing control over it, MCI was converted into the Ministry of Munitions (MM) (November 1, 1943) (Johnson, 1982: 166). Kishi was a central figure in blueprinting and implementing this restructuring project (Hara, 1995: 94), which not only reduced MCI's jurisdiction but also demoted Kishi's own post from minister to vice-minister, an unusual behavior for the politically ambitious (Hara, 1995: 94). Evidently, what drove Kishi was something beyond immediate personal ambition.

Although he was regarded as a leading reform bureaucrat, Kishi's war mobilization plan was not based on total state control. From the Manchurian experience, he was keenly aware of the indispensability of the management skills of the private sector. The main actor in production must be the private sector, but only with the public sector, leadership, he thought, could the best of the private sector materialize.

Tōjō assumed the post of minister of MM along with the prime ministership and appointed Kishi as vice-minister of MM to be in charge of the actual operation of the ministry. Additionally, Tōjō appointed Kishi as a state minister with cabinet rank to give him authority to command the generals and admirals working in the ministry. Kishi asked Tōjō if he were aware that such an appointment would make him voice opposition if he disagreed with Tōjō's decision (Kishi et al., 1981: 63). Actually, this situation arose after Japan's disastrous defeat in Saipan in mid-1944, when Kishi voiced his opinion that Japan should consider ending the war, and, by rejecting Tōjō's request to resign, Kishi caused the fall of the Tōjō cabinet (Kishi et al., 1981: 68).

Standing up against Tōjō was a risky business, as he was known not to hesitate to use military police to harass or cause the death of those who opposed him (Hosokawa, 1986: 78). This action gave Kishi a reputation as a man of principle, although Kishi acted as part of a larger anti-Tōjō movement growing among former prime ministers and the imperial household (Hara, 1995: 98). Takeyo Nakatani and other parliamentarians had demanded that Kishi lead the movement to overthrow Tōjō. After the fall of the Tōjō cabinet, Kishi retired to Tabuse, his hometown in Yamaguchi prefecture, with his family (Nakatani, 1974: 234) and organized a local political association, the *Sonjo Doshi Kai*, purportedly to protect minimum living standards through local economic cooperation and to lessen the area's dependence upon central administration's control and support, as communications with the central government were increasingly difficult by wartime (Kishi et al., 1981: 72).

### After the War

Kishi spent three years and three months in prison before being released on Christmas Eve 1948. Kishi, however, did not have any sense of guilt about the war, which he defined as a defensive war compelled by the circumstances for national survival, instead of an aggressive war, as the victorious nations insisted (Kishi et al., 1981: 88, 310). The Tokyo tribunal was, in his view, a tragicomedy directed by the victorious nations and had nothing to do with international justice (Hosokawa, 1986: 90). Kishi agreed with the opinion of Ichiro Kiyose, Tōjō's defense attorney, that the "crimes against peace" were ex post facto laws that had not existed before the end of the war in international law, and hence the main point of the prosecution's argument was legally wrong (Hara, 1995: 122–23).

Viewing the U.S.–Soviet clash at the Paris Peace Conference in August 1946 as providing an opportunity for Japan to exploit, he wrote in his diary in prison that 80 million Japanese endowed with the best qualities in the East, even though defeated in war, should realize their historical mission and noted his desire for the emergence of a leader with knowledge, vision, and courage to make difficult decisions for the nation. Kishi's vision of rebuilding independent Japan with "control and order" led by strong leadership manifests the continuity in his basic political orientation (Hara, 1995: 127–28).

After his release from prison, Kishi set as his immediate goal overthrowing Shigeru Yoshida and shifted foreign policy away from dependence on the United States to an independent direction (Hara, 1995: 160). Kishi adopted a two-track tactic: top-level negotiations among conservative parties and a grassroots campaign to expand and consolidate the support base for the forthcoming new party. For the latter purpose, he formed a political association, the Japan Reconstruction Federation (*Nihon Saiken Doumei*) in April 1952. Met by poor public response, this plan failed (Hosokawa, 1986: 101–3). He then tried to found a new grand party by uniting conservative and some right-wing socialist forces, but in vain. Kishi's flirtation with socialists reveals both Kishi's legacy as a reform bureaucrat and the amorphous nature of Japanese political culture, which smoothed Kishi's political comeback even to the extent that some in business and government welcomed Kishi for his talent and expertise to be used in Japan's economic reconstruction (Hara, 1995: 152).

Kishi believed that the two-party system was best for Japan. As the first step, he founded a new conservative party to pursue more nationalistic goals than Yoshida's, even as he managed to get elected as a member of the Liberal Party, headed by Yoshida in the general election in April 1953 (Shioda, 1996: 233). After long-winded formal and informal negotiations with conservative forces, mutual squabbling, and sharing dissatisfaction with Yoshida, he managed to establish the Japan Democratic Party (JDP) in November 1953 and compelled Yoshida to resign in December 1954. JDP president Ichiro Hatoyama became prime minister and appointed many prewar politicians to his cabinet. Kishi became secretary-general of the new JDP. Hatoyama sought to shift foreign policy to an independent line and normalized relations with the Soviet Union.

Meanwhile, Kishi's merger effort was facilitated by the expansion of the leftist forces in the February 1955 election, which increased the incentive to unite among the alarmed conservative forces. Kishi was also helped by external pressure forged by himself. During his meetings with Dulles in Washington in August 1955, Kishi managed to secure U.S. Secretary of State Foster Dulles' endorsement of unification of conservative forces to build a strong and stable Japan as a bulwark against communism (Hara, 1995: 175). The reunification of the socialist parties in October 1955 gave the final push. About a month later, on November 11, 1955, the conservative parties were also united to give birth to the Liberal Democratic Party. Kishi became secretary-general of the new party (Hosokawa, 1986: 131).

After Prime Minister Tanzan Ishibashi, who succeeded Hatoyama briefly, resigned because of poor health, Kishi became prime minister in February 1957. After the general election of May 1958, Kishi formed his second cabinet and embarked on the long-embraced project of restoring true independence to Japan by eliminating the Occupation syndrome (i.e., a deeply ingrained sense of subservience to, and dependence upon, the United States) prevalent among the Japanese. This was the central theme that drove Kishi's political life after the war. Although he believed that the United States–Japan partnership was necessary for Japan's economy and security, he felt it essential to remove the psychological and institutional remnants from the Occupation era to achieve true partnership (Shioda, 1996: 287).

Domestically, Kishi continued "reverse-course" policies to dismantle the excesses of the Occupation reforms started by Yoshida and Hatoyama, by re-concentrating political and administrative power to the national government in such areas as police administration and education. But his autocratic political style provoked strong fear of reviving an antidemocratic order of the prewar vintage among the Opposition, labor unions, teachers' unions, and the media (Hara, 1995: 204). In particular, a Police Duties Law Amendment Bill, which Kishi introduced in 1958, provoked massive strikes and demonstrations, press critiques, and Opposition boycott of the Diet (Shioda, 1996: 316) to force him to shelve it.

To build the sound social economic foundation, another pillar of independence, Kishi introduced a system to foster small and medium industry (by incorporating socialist ideas), the national pension, and the minimum wage systems (Ohinata, 1985: 185–88; Kitaoka, 1995: 144). These policies may not match his hawkish image but are consistent with Kishi's ideological inclination toward national socialism before the war and his latent paternalism.

To make Japan truly independent internationally and conduct autonomous foreign policy, Kishi felt it necessary to revise the Constitution and the United States–Japan Security Treaty, both imposed by the Americans after Japan's defeat. He set three pillars of Japan's foreign policy: (1) to work for world peace through the United Nations; (2) to enhance Japan's relationship with the United States; and (3) to cooperate with Asian nations (Kitaoka, 1995: 135).

To enhance the alliance with the United States, Kishi planned a meeting with President Eisenhower to discuss the security treaty revision and directed concrete arrangements. Kishi had preliminary meetings with the U.S. Ambassador to Japan, Douglas MacArthur II, at least seven times to discuss the issue (Hara, 1988: 106). The input through the ambassador had significant impact on Dulles (Hara, 1988: 189). To enhance his clout at the negotiating table in Washington as a leader of Asia, Kishi made a six-country trip in Southeast Asia in May (Hiwatashi, 1990: 151). In Japan critics often equated Kishi's Asia policy with a revival of the East Asian Co-prosperity Sphere idea, which would provoke anti-Japanese sentiments among Asians. Kishi himself, however, noted after the trip that many of the Asian leaders were more impressed by, and even grateful to, Japan's standing up against the West despite the obvious lack of natural resources in the Pacific War (Kishi, 1983a: 315).

To show to Dulles, who had once rejected Japan's request to revise the security treaty by saying that Japan did not have the power to be an equal partner to the United States (Hiwatashi, 1990: 154), that Japan had the will and ability to build enough defense capability to qualify as an equal partner of the United States, Kishi ordered the Self-Defense Agency to draft a long-term defense plan, making personal inputs in the process (Shioda, 1996: 299). While Kishi saw the revision as a means to increase Japan's independence of action without increasing Japan's defense commitments, the Opposition criticized it for perpetuating and increasing danger of Japan's involvement in unwanted war started by the United States. The most troublesome, however, were the anti-mainstream factions within the LDP that began mounting open criticisms of Kishi in the hope of replacing him with their own leaders (Stockwin, 1999: 52).

What precipitated the massive protest in the street was Kishi's decision to ram through the treaty in the Diet on May 19, 1960, to ensure its automatic ratification on June 19, the day that Eisenhower was scheduled to visit Japan. The Opposition fanned the public fear that he might subvert democratic institutions and procedures altogether (Stockwin, 1999: 52). On June 15 a female student was killed in the clash between a swelling demonstration and police outside the Diet. On June 16, in the atmosphere of crisis and social unrest, Kishi canceled Eisenhower's visit to Tokyo. Four days after the House of Councilors ratified the treaty automatically on June 19, Kishi announced his resignation.

The demonstrators dispersed peacefully and quickly. The succeeding Hayato Ikeda government downplayed security issues and launched the national income-doubling plan for the new decade. Returning to the Yoshida line, Ikeda concentrated on economic growth with minimum spending on defense (Nakamura, 1995: 160). Labor leader Kaoru Ota (1976: 165) observed that underlying "an unfathomable and tremendous mobilization" were a deep-seated discontent and insecurity despite (or rather because of) rapid economic growth and "the old war scars" still unhealed in the memories of the masses.

## ANALYSIS

In what follows, I first summarize Kishi's successes and failures before, during, and after the war. Next, I examine where Kishi's leadership impact should be located in Jean Blondel's (1987: 88–97) typology through time. The final section evaluates the utility of Blondel's typology in understanding and predicting political behavior of Kishi as a national leader.

### Success and Failure

Kishi succeeded in reaching the apex of power and revising the treaty but failed in maintaining power to pursue his ultimate goal of constitutional revision. Kishi's unusually quick rise to power is generally attributed to his outstanding ability to observe the political currents and extensive human and financial ties with the business community built during his tenure at MCI (Kitaoka, 1995: 131; Kusunoki, 2000: 284). Also, his knowledge and expertise acquired before and during the war as planner and implementer of the control economy gave him valuable qualifications as a manager of the postwar version of the "national mobilization system," which required superefficient use of the scarce resources just as during wartime (Kusunoki, 2000: 284). Kishi had a clear vision of where to head and concrete ideas about policies required for the reconstruction of Japan and was convinced of the need to found a strong leadership system to carry out these policies (Kitaoka, 1995: 131).

It is doubtful if, as Kitaoka (1995: 131) argues, Kishi's ability to grasp the needs of society explains Kishi's postwar rise to power. Rather, Kishi's rise was mainly due to his superior strategic thinking and Machiavellian tactics coupled with sheer luck (his rivals either fell ill or died suddenly to vacate the prime ministership to him). The success part reveals the continuity in the elite political culture and structure during the early 1950s from prewar Japan, the environment suited for Kishi's political maneuvering.

In contrast, his quick fall from power reveals his inability to grasp the needs of society and changes in the mass political culture and in the distribution of power within the polity. It reveals that the radical institutional reforms imposed by the Occupation had wrought substantial changes by 1960 in the attitude and behavior of the mass public, the media, and students. Kishi miscalculated the power of these actors to mobilize the extra-parliamentary protest movement by highlighting his authoritarian political style of prewar vintage. His failure to recognize changes in the distribution of power in the political system had led Kishi to concentrate on the power game played by the regulars of the prewar era—the members of the government and opposition parties, the bureaucracy, the business community, and other organized interests—in disregard of the players who were gaining force outside the old power center.

### The Evolution of Kishi's Leadership

Blondel (1987: 3) defines political leadership as "the power exercised by one or a few individuals to direct members of the nation towards action." Before and during the war, Kishi exercised such power through three phases. First, as a junior bureaucrat, he played the role of adjuster in introducing and implementing an industrial rationalization policy from Germany, while at the same time playing the role of manager who worked to consolidate Japan's industrial order. Then, in Manchuria he exercised such power as an innovator to experiment with various new policies to transform the agrarian land into a model, controlled industrial economy. Finally, as MCI vice-minister and minister and MM vice-minister, he played the role of a reformist to transform Japan's free market economy into a controlled economy geared for war mobilization instead of profit maximization.

In terms of Dimension I, Kishi's goal and impact shifted from moderate change to large change, while in terms of Dimension II, Kishi's goals and impact shifted from a specialized scope (industrial rationalization) to moderate scope (the total economic system). At stake in his mind was national survival, but his impact was of moderate scope, rather than wide scope.

After the war, Kishi engineered a series of political changes that shaped the framework and basic rules, formal and informal, of the postwar party politics: (1) uniting the conservative parties into the LDP, eventually to solidify the so-called one and one-half party system; (2) shaping the basic factional lineups and organizational principles of the LDP (Masumi, 1995: 2); (3) establishing the policy-making pattern dominated by the internal political dynamics of the LDP; and (4) setting a precedent of a party presidential election in which each faction competes for a majority support for its candidate by freely distributing money and perfunctory promises of party and government posts in secret (Shioda, 1996: 275). In terms of policies, he took initiatives in (1) pushing "reverse-course" policies; (2) introducing the first series of social programs; and (3) consolidating the United States–Japan security alliance to build the foundation that made possible the total mobilization of the country's resources for economic growth in the 1960s.

In Dimension I, Kishi's goal was clearly for change, as in pushing "reverse-course" policies, revising the United States–Japan security treaty, and advocating constitutional revision, but it was change within the framework of the existing liberal democracy and the market economy internally and within the framework of the alliance with the United States internationally. Therefore, his goal should be defined as "moderate change." In Dimension II, his goal falls in the "wide scope" category, as his impact encompassed the nation as a whole. His thoughts extended further to encompass Asia as a natural unit of forming a regional community with Japan as a leader (Shioda, 1996: 289). To combine the two dimensions, he falls in the category of paternalists/populists.

## Utility of Blondel's Typology

Kishi's overall leadership impact, with moderate change and wide scope, falls into the paternalists/populists category. Does this categorization capture the central features of Kishi's leadership? Although in the past Kishi has seldom, if ever, been labeled as paternalist, the answer is positive in regard to the paternalist part, if paternalism means "the principle or practice of managing or governing individuals, businesses, nations, etc. in the manner of a father dealing benevolently and often intrusively with his children" (Random House, 1998: 1421). Kishi's definition of leadership as leading, not following, public opinion reveals his fundamental paternalism, which is anchored in the *shishi* ethos inculcated in him during his adolescence. Such paternalism perhaps helps explain his introduction of the small and medium enterprise laws, the national pension program, and other social policies as prime minister.

Was he a populist? Not in his image and style. If, however, populism means the political philosophy to connect to the common people in pursuing political goals rather than according with traditional party or partisan ideologies, his political behavior reveals elements of populism in his proclivity to form new movements to mobilize grassroots support, as in the case of the *Sonjo Doshi Kai* before the end of the war and the Japan Reconstruction Federation in 1952.

Was the environment conducive to the paternalists/populists category of leadership? In the prewar environment, external pressure was threatening national survival, while national pride and discontent were both high among the populace. The intense external pressure worked to convert domestic mass discontent into hostility directed externally, especially against the United States. At the elite level, for younger bureaucrats, civil and military, external pressure emanating from the United States and its allies and the unification movements in China worked as a catalyst to energize their discontent into emotionally charged reform movements. In this environment, Kishi's actions as a leader of reform bureaucrats inevitably had some populist connotation of rectifying capitalists' excesses.

The postwar environment was dominated by economic difficulties and ideological conflict percolating under the over-arching cold war confrontation. But it was also a "period of national renewal comparable with the Meiji period" (Stockwin, 1999: 36), which was filled with challenges and opportunities, a good combination to stimulate the *shishi* spirit within Kishi. External pressure was not threatening national survival per se, but, in the eyes of many conservatives, U.S. dominance was eroding national pride and independence, whereas communism was threatening internal order. Thus, the earlier postwar environment also had elements receptive to paternalist/populist leaders able to guide the reconstruction of the nation's economy and the restoration of a respectable status in the world.

How helpful is Blondel's typology in understanding and predicting the political behavior of Kishi as a national leader? It was useful in identifying general characteristics of Kishi, while at the same time delineating his multilayered character and the evolutionary process of his leadership impacts through time along the changes in the amount of authority and power endowed in him.

The basic weakness of the typology lies in the ambiguity in the definition of nine categories as ideal types. Besides providing examples, it does not specify behavioral characteristics of each category. It is, therefore, difficult not only to predict political behavior but also to decide in which category Kishi fell, savior or paternalist, redefiner or reformist, when he attempted to restructure the economy in order to preserve the existing political structure with a clear vision of Japan to defend, reestablish, and maintain.

Also, leadership impacts would differ significantly with the leaders' skill and power of mobilization. But Blondel's two dimensions fail to capture the leaders' ability to mobilize, the third phase in Tucker's (1995a: 18) leadership analysis (though they can capture Tucker's first and second phases, diagnosis and prescription). After the fall of Saipan, Kishi was called on to lead the anti-Tōjō movement, cast in the role of a savior in Blondel's scheme, but he was neither a charismatic orator nor a thinker. His leadership derived essentially from his technical and tactical decision-making ability rather than ideological or visionary power to inspire and mobilize enthusiastic followers—the very character that we usually associate with saviors. Perhaps this is why he was unsuccessful in his national movement attempts. Blondel's framework would be strengthened if it accommodated this dimension.

The nature/contents/tenacity of leadership impacts are another dimension that needs to be supplemented. Kishi's leadership impact encompassed the two distinct political systems, authoritarian and democratic, but built with remarkable continuity in their foundation of the political economy. One of the unique features of Kishi's leadership derives from his role as a chief architect of this foundation. Skeptical of the necessity or legitimacy of the private property system, Kishi accepted capitalism and market economy as a fundamentally more efficient system than the totally planned/controlled economy. While opposing the total control of the economy, Kishi created an amalgam of an economic system skillfully designed for total mobilization of the resources for the single national goal. Before and during the war, this goal was war production. In postwar Japan, it was economic growth. In a way, Japan's postwar "economic miracle" was achieved with the full utilization of the basic concepts and organizations of the control economy developed under Kishi's direction for wartime mobilization. In this respect, Kishi may be regarded as one of the founding fathers of Japan's postwar system, which is variously called "Japan, Inc." (Kobayashi, 1995: 183–84), "the 1940 system" (Noguchi, 1995: 7), or "the bureaucratically managed developmental state" (Johnson 1982: 164). Blondel's typology does not capture these ubiquitous aspects of leadership impacts, but it is a useful framework to start comparative analysis of leadership impacts.

## NOTE

1. *Zaibatsu* is a prewar business combined with interlocking directorates and a common family ownership base, which was disbanded by the Occupation reform but revived into *keiretsu* (organizational linkage), which, without a family ownership element, revolves around a corporate bank with cross-stockholding between the constituent companies.

Chapter 11

# When and Why Do Hard-Liners Become Soft? An Examination of Israeli Prime Ministers Shamir, Rabin, Peres, and Netanyahu

Yael S. Aronoff

## INTRODUCTION

With the end of the cold war, nations and groups that served as surrogates in the superpower conflict have lost the support of their former patrons, and thus new opportunities have arisen to shift formerly intractable positions and solve seemingly irreconcilable conflicts. It is important, therefore, to examine how and why "hard-line" political leaders change their attitudes and policy predispositions toward an international enemy in response to new information. As Lebow and Stein suggest, we know "surprisingly little about why, how, and when leaders initiate dramatic change in foreign policy" (Lebow & Stein, 1993: 95).

My focus in this analysis is on Israeli prime ministers Yitzhak Rabin, Yitzhak Shamir, Shimon Peres, and Benjamin Netanyahu.[1] All four of these prime ministers were hard-liners in that they were afraid that accommodation would be interpreted as weakness, and they viewed the opponent as monolithic and as having unlimited aims (Snyder & Diesing, 1977: 297–310). All were consequently against negotiating with the Palestine Liberation Organization (PLO) and the creation of a Palestinian state. In response to perceived changes on the part of the PLO and in the region, Rabin and Peres of the Labor Party underwent a radical change of attitude and policy, recognized and reached an agreement with the PLO by signing the Oslo Accords on September 13, 1993, and laid the groundwork for what is likely to become a Palestinian state. Prime Ministers Shamir and Netanyahu of the Likud Party did not undergo such a change in their image of the PLO and attempted to undermine the changes initiated by Rabin and Peres.

Examining these four prime ministers side by side is especially interesting since each served under largely similar circumstances: all served after the collapse of the Soviet Union, the *intifada* (the Palestinian uprising that began in December 1988 and continued through the initial stages of the peace process), the Gulf War, and changes within the PLO, thus controlling for a number of variables.

## HYPOTHESES AND CONCEPTUAL APPROACH

The goal of this study is to explore plausible explanations as to why certain leaders are more likely than others to perceive changes in the opponent and in the regional environment. It moves between three separate, but related, ways to describe individual cognition and attitude: ideology (drawing on Alexander George's work on the operational code); individual time horizons (derived from Jervis' use of the rate and magnitude of incoming information); and cognitive openness and complexity. In moving between these three theories, I want to capture the dynamic between cultural and individual psychology, by situating a leader's individual cognitive makeup (cognitive complexity, time horizon) within a larger, cultural context (the ideology shared by all members of the leader's political group). Ideology is key in explaining the different goals pursued by different leaders, which, in turn, influence the extent to which each leader changes. To explain the different rates and ways in which attitudinal change occurs in leaders who hold the same ideology, however, one can turn to the leaders' perceptions of time and cognitive rigidity.

### Ideology

For the purposes of my project, I define ideology as a more specific and rationalized interpretation of the political culture made by competing groups that justifies their interests, articulates their goals, and gives them legitimacy (Aronoff & Aronoff, 1996). Ideology is thus a prism through which leaders form images of the enemy and their consequent policy preferences. Ideology can shape beliefs both through its particular content and in the intensity with which the individual adheres to that content.

Since all four figures treated in this study were highly influenced by their respective ideologies, I focus on the ideologies' *content*, as opposed to the intensity of the leaders' beliefs alone. I thus examine ideology in much the same way that Alexander George defines and examines the "operational code," as a "general belief system about the nature of history and politics" (George, 1969). Where George posits several key questions that one needs to ask in order to define the parameters of an operational code, I focus on three components of ideology that are crucial to explaining both changes in the image of the enemy and resultant shifts in policy preferences: the ideology's "time horizon"; the relative compatibility or incompatibility of the ideology's central goals with that of the enemy; and its perception of the world as generally harsh or friendly. I define ideology's "time horizon" as the relationship between time and the achievements of central goals built into the logic of the ideology itself.

An ideology with an extended time horizon—one that perceives its struggle as extending into the distant future—could then encourage a perception that a strategy failing in the short term will win "in the next hundred years." I argue that if a leader's ideology inculcates the belief that "time is on one's side," he or she is less likely to reassess strategies that do not seem to be working in the short run and is thus less likely to change his or her image of the enemy. If, as some suggest, change is motivated by perceived failures, then to the extent that failing strategies are not perceived as such by leaders having an extended time frame, these leaders will be less likely to change.

In addition, hard-liners whose stance is linked to ideological goals that directly conflict with those of the enemy are less likely to change their image of an enemy or reach an agreement with an enemy because this would mean giving up on ideological goals. Finally, if the world is perceived as being inherently against "us," one is more likely to perceive conflict with an opponent as unchangeable.

## Time Horizon

Ideology, as I analyze it here, deals with the leader's participation in collective ways of viewing the world. As is clear in this study, however, leaders with the same political ideology also will differ in the ways and rates at which they change their image of an enemy in similar circumstances. Thus, to explain these differences, one must turn to individual factors, such as an individual's time horizon and the structure (as opposed to the content) of one's beliefs—one's relative openness and cognitive complexity.

In discussing a leader's "time horizons," I am analyzing two separate, but related, ways in which individuals think about time in relation to events, actions, and goals. The first kind of time horizon, as discussed above, is the way that the ideology views time in relation to the achievement of the ideology's goals. The second kind of time horizon, which I am discussing here, pertains to the percentage of time that each leader devotes to thinking of the past, the present, or the future. Whether a leader refers more to the past, the present, or the future in trying to understand events and to shape decisions will affect possibilities for and rates of change toward an enemy. I argue that leaders who devote a large amount of time to thinking about a conflict-ridden past, referring to the past for lessons for events in the present, will be less likely to change their image of the enemy.

This hypothesis has most often been analyzed at the level of groups and states, with the conclusion that when groups rely too heavily on the particular history of a dispute, at the expense of analysis of present changes and future possibilities—what Debrah Larson (1997: 25) calls the "heavy hand of the past"—this can inhibit change and progress. However, I am emphasizing the individual or personality implication of this phenomenon. Vertzberger (1990: 321) argues that some individuals have a greater propensity than others to view the past as a living reality with which to evaluate the present, while Jervis (1976: 331) has argued that some individuals use what he calls "the representativeness heuristic" to find similarities between present and past events and make (often misplaced) generalizations. When the individual not only dwells on the past but has an archaic or totemic (as opposed to linear) notion of time, he or she associates the present enemy with all other enemies, even in the ancient past. The past is an immediate part of the present, while the future is perceived in almost messianic terms, very distant and separated from the present by dramatic rupture (Aronoff, 1989: 137). Individuals who operate under this notion of time are less likely to expect and thus perceive change, and the image of a hostile enemy is magnified to mythical proportions.

While previous scholarship has argued that an emphasis on the past can limit a leader's attention to disconfirming information, there has been less theoretical attention paid to an individual's emphasis on the present or on the future and how this relates to possibilities for change. I argue that a leader who spends a greater percentage of time focused on the present is more likely to revise his or her image of the opponent than someone who dwells on the past but does so more gradually than a leader of the same ideology who is focused on the future. Focused on the present, he or she is more likely to react to events than to initiate change and is more influenced by particular dramatic events. Alternatively, a leader who dwells on the future is more likely to respond quickly to perceived changes and even initiate change, while particular dramatic events are subsumed within a vision of broad future trends and thus are less influential. A leader who analyzes the information as it comes in each day is slower to grasp broader trends of change than is a leader who emphasizes the future. Jervis has analyzed how, when discrepant information arrives gradually, it is likely to go unnoticed (Jervis, 1976: 308, 309).

Instead of looking at the rate of incoming information, I look at the way that it is perceived. If information is looked at primarily on a day-to-day basis, gradual changes are more likely to be overlooked. This may also imply that leaders who emphasize the present are more likely to react to dramatic, disruptive events that break with the pattern of day-to-day information, as opposed to initiating dramatic changes. If a leader, however, spends a greater percentage of his or her time thinking of the future, he or she is more involved in imagining a future that is different from the past and therefore is more likely to view the opponent as changeable. This leader not only reacts incrementally to daily changes in the environment but is more likely to create dramatic changes in response to perceived future trends. At the same time, individual dramatic events may be downplayed in importance, in favor of these perceived broad trends.

### Openness and Complexity

Finally, I analyze the influence of the *structure* (as opposed to content) of individual thinking on attitude change. There is extensive theoretical literature relating the relative openness of a leader's cognitive system and his or her attention to information. Rokeach characterizes a belief system as "open" to the "extent to which the person can receive, evaluate, and act on relevant information received from the outside on its own intrinsic merits, unencumbered by irrelevant factors in the situation arising from within the person or from the outside" (Rokeach, 1960: 57, 403). Related to openness is the complexity of one's cognitive system, which refers to the degree of differentiation that an individual shows in describing people and ideas (Hermann, 1987c: 12). The hypothesis to be tested, based on Holsti's predictions (Finlay et al., 1967: 23), is that the more open and cognitively complex the structure of a leader's thinking, the more likely the leader is to adapt to new information and change his or her image of the enemy.

### METHODOLOGY

This study uses George's method of structured, focused comparison of cases where data are collected on the same variables across units. I broadly follow George's procedures of congruence and process tracing in order to show the explanatory power of beliefs, first to establish consistency between beliefs and decisions and second to trace the steps in the process through which given operational code beliefs influence the assessment of information (George, 1979: 105). I rely heavily on more spontaneous communications by the leaders—on my own interviews (see Appendix 11.1), television and newspaper interviews, and party central committee meetings as opposed to prepared speeches, since the latter are less likely to reveal "genuine" attitudes (Hermann, 1977: 460).

## CASE STUDIES

### Ideology

The rationales for the four prime ministers' early hard-line positions were heavily influenced by their respective ideologies. Shamir constantly and explicitly spoke of ideology as a way of organizing one's life. He joined the *Betar Zionist Youth* movement, headed by Vladimir Zeev Jabotinsky, at age 14. He has argued that Jabotinsky left behind him a clear-cut ideology with Greater Israel at its core (Greater Israel refers to territorial boundaries that include the entire West Bank) and that "today Jabotinsky's name and spirit are kept alive mostly through the Likud Party" (Interview with Shamir, 1998; Shamir, 1994: 9).[2] In 1937 Shamir joined the *Irgun Zvai Leumi* (National Military Organization) and described it as "a combat formation made up of volunteers bound by a nationalistic and militant idealism" (Shamir, 1994: 19). Netanyahu was also highly influenced by Likud ideology, instilled in him by his father, who was an ideologue of Revisionist Zionism (Halevi, 1998: 12). Rabin's sister related that Labor's values were reflected in their home, school, and youth group (Interview with Rahel Rabin, 1998). Peres was sworn into the *Haganah* at age 15 and later worked closely with and admired Israel's first prime minister and Labor Party leader, David Ben-Gurion.

One crucial component in understanding the role of ideology in attitude change is the time horizon built into the ideology itself. Likud ideology, in part, acted as an obstacle to revision of its members' hostile image of the PLO in that it involved a long, optimistic time horizon in regard to the struggle to gain all of Greater Israel. Shamir and Netanyahu were optimistic that religious settlements on the West Bank would eventually leave much of the territory in Israeli hands. Looking to future generations, Shamir envisions building more Jewish schools outside Israel, which would result in another 5 million Jews emigrating to Israel, prompting the Palestinians to give up on statehood (Interview with Shamir, 1998). Given the logic of this position—that "time was on their side"—Shamir and Netanyahu had less incentive to revise policies that seemed ineffective in producing progress. Unlike Shamir and Netanyahu, Rabin and Peres increasingly believed that time was against Israel. In 1991 Rabin said that "in my eyes, the window of opportunity for the advancement of peace at the end of 1989, beginning of 1990, was wider and bigger than today (Party, May 1991: 11).[3] Likewise, Peres argued that Israel does not have the time to learn slowly because of the accelerating strength of the anti-peace forces (Peres, 1993: 159, 197).

A second crucial component in understanding an ideology's role in facilitating or inhibiting attitude change is the compatibility or incompatibility of the ideology's central goals with that of the enemy. Rabin

and Peres' Labor ideology took a general notion of security—not necessarily tied to any particular territory—as its centerpiece. Thus, as long
as security concerns were addressed, Labor ideology allowed Rabin and
Peres to be more flexible on territorial concessions. Peres claimed that
Ben-Gurion understood that partition based on a realistic compromise
was inevitable (Peres, 1993: 166). After the Six-Day War, Rabin claimed
that Israel would be willing to trade newly acquired territory for peace.
For Shamir and Netanyahu, on the other hand, Likud ideology was
based on specific territorial goals, namely, to keep the whole Land of
Israel. Shamir wrote that upon Israel's creation much of the Land of
Israel was severed. I have done all I could, in various ways, in the intervening years to help rectify this distortion to which I can never be
reconciled, and to prevent others like it" (Shamir, 1994: 26). Therefore,
Shamir and Netanyahu's ideology inhibited revision of their image of
the Palestinians, since to do so would necessarily threaten their goal of
the Greater Land of Israel.

Likud ideology also was an obstacle to revising the image of the PLO
in that it perceived a more permanently hostile world than did Labor
ideology. Dennis Ross (special Middle East coordinator for the State Department) claimed that Netanyahu's central worldview was that Israel
faced a hostile world (Interview with Ross, 1999). Likewise, Shamir
claimed that "we have a lot of enemies, more enemies than friends . . .
besides the Arabs" (Interview with Shamir, 1998). Shamir was quick to
castigate even representatives of friendly countries as anti-Israeli and
called James Baker "the new hangman for the Jewish people" (Arens,
1995: 60). Rabin and Peres shared the perception of an unfriendly world
earlier in their lives, but not to the same visceral degree as Shamir and
Netanyahu, and they were more disposed to perceiving changes. In a
meeting of the Labor Party after the United Nations (UN) resolution
equating Zionism with racism, Rabin did not say anything accusatory
about countries that voted for the resolution (Party, November 1975: 10–
17). In Rabin's first speech as prime minister in 1992, he claimed that
"the world is no longer against us." Peres claimed that the world no
longer hated the Jews (Peres, 1998: 10).

### Individual Time Horizon

While ideology helps explain the capacity (or lack thereof) for changing one's image of the enemy, individual time horizons also play a role,
both in reinforcing one's image of the enemy and in explaining differences in rates and mechanisms of change for those leaders holding the
same ideology. Shamir and Netanyahu continually referred to the past,
even the ancient past, and claimed that "history, more or less, repeated
itself" (Shamir, 1994: 69). For Shamir, there was little difference between

the PLO and the Roman legions: Shamir argued that Arafat should not be supported because "we have to learn a lesson from our ancient history dating back to the period before the destruction of the Second Temple . . . in the end, it was the Romans who destroyed the Jewish State." He criticized the Camp David Accords for being "written in a style which reveals nothing of the past, as though the conflicts referred to were equally the fault of all sides and recent." He believed that, historically, countries have used "the slogan of peace as a deliberate lie, a camouflage for the true objective which was conquest and occupation" (Shamir, 1996: 66, 69). Israeli ambassador to the United Nations, Dore Gold, claimed that Netanyahu also focused on the past (Interview with Gold, 1999). Netanyahu's book *A Place among the Nations*, often refers to the past and derides the "fashionable ahistoricism prevalent today" (Netanyahu, 1993: 29).

Rabin, on the other hand, was a "guarded analyst of the present," obsessed by details and thus more open to perceiving change in the environment (Savir, 1998: 25). However, his emphasis on the present enabled only a relatively slow rate of change. It also led him to be highly influenced by recent dramatic events. In explaining his assessment of politics abroad, he emphasized the situation today and how it may be different tomorrow (Party, November 1974). In undertaking the first steps toward a peace agreement, he refrained from dealing with the final status issues and suppressed any thought about them (Inbar, 1999: 153; Auerbach, 1995: 292, 308). This orientation toward the present contributed to what those who were close to him have described as his incremental thinking and his style of "muddling through" (Peri, 1996: 360, 361).

In stark contrast to Shamir and Netanyahu, Peres has said that "life is not made of repetitions, but of mutations of progress . . . the Lord gave us eyes in our foreheads so that we could go forward . . . life is moving faster than our intellectual capacities. We are always late" (Peres, 1998: 178). In his books, articles, and speeches he spent the most time talking of the future and virtually no time talking about the past. This is exhibited even in the titles of his books, such as *For the Future of Israel* and *The New Middle East*. Peres claimed that "our vocation is to see things that may happen and not to analyze things that have already happened" (Peres, 1993: 71) and that "we must forget the past for the sake of the present since the world is in perpetual change" (Peres, 1993: 3). For him, more important than present events is what he sees as the future trend toward international relationships based on economics rather than military might (Peres, 1993: 20, 66, 77, 96). In explaining his change toward the PLO, he has said that "I felt the world was changing around us . . . that in the future there would be not wars but competition" (Interview with Peres, 1997). Peres' focus on the future influenced him to change his image of the PLO at a faster rate than Rabin.

## Structure of Cognitive System

The different rates of change among those who exhibited significant change can also be partially explained through the relative rigidity of a leader's mind. Of the four, Peres is the most open, and Shamir, Netanyahu, and Rabin were more rigid. In attempting to evaluate a leader's openness or rigidity, one crucial question to ask is, "To what extent does he have qualities that lead him to receive a rich stream of advice and information?" (Burke & Greenstein, 1990: 266). Shamir admits that he can be disrespectful toward the opinions of others and has often rejected information that would require him to question his opinion of the PLO. For example, when some American Jewish intellectuals called upon him to accept a peace plan proposed by George Shultz, he dismissed their opinions as amateurish, and a minority view (Shamir, 1994: 4, 179). Shamir denounced Baker's remarks made before the American–Israel Public Affairs Committee as "useless" (Baker, 1995: 119, 122). His wife described him as very closed and as making his decisions alone (Landau, 1981). His foreign minister claimed that he at times would not hear him out (Arens, 1995: 128). Shamir accused those willing to make territorial compromises as hating their own people and as unpatriotic (Interview with Shamir, 1988).

Netanyahu was highly suspicious of opinions emanating from what he considered to be the Israeli establishment and elite, whom he hated. For Netanyahu, the Oslo "betrayal" was the ultimate expression of the Left's immorality. He inherited a deep feeling of persecution from his father, who was convinced that the Hebrew University did not hire him to teach after the 1930s because of his right-wing activism. His father felt that Likud leaders had betrayed Jabotinsky's teachings, and Netanyahu regarded his Likud colleagues with that same contempt (Halevi, 1998: 13, 14). Therefore, Netanyahu had a difficult time listening not only to members of the opposition but to those of his own party. Netanyahu was in continual conflict with his ministers, several of whom quit. He dismissed his defense minister, Yitzhak Mordechai, accusing him of having political agendas when Mordechai cautioned of impending conflict because of the stalled peace process. He ignored his chief of staff, Amnon Shahak, who warned that if the peace process slowed down, the army would have to prepare for a Palestinian uprising. In 1998 Netanyahu dismissed a *Shin Bet* (internal security) assessment that the Palestinian Authority was making a serious effort to fight terror and an analysis by the military intelligence chief, Moshe Ya'alon, that the peace stalemate was leading toward a blowup in the territories (Susser, 1998: 15–16).

Like Shamir, with whom he personally got along, Rabin was capable of changing his mind but leaned toward rigidity. Rabin grew up in an ideological family, spent 30 years in the army, and tended to view things in black or white (Interview with Sarid, leader of the more dovish Meretz Party, 1998; Peri, 1996: 377). He tended to view both the internal and external environment in simplistic, two-dimensional ways and differentiated between "good guys" and "bad guys" (Auerbach, 1995: 304–5). Rabin's sister claims that he was very stubborn and that it was very difficult for him to change his mind (Interview with Rahel Rabin, 1998). Ephraim Inbar's interviews of some of Rabin's longtime friends confirm this (Inbar, 1999: 5). Rabin was known for dismissing other opinions. For instance, in one Labor Party meeting in which he was discussing the Gulf War, he said that whoever did not understand his analysis of U.S. involvement did not know the United States, whoever did not understand his analysis of Iraqi motives simply did not understand the realities, and whoever thought Israeli restraint in reaction to an Iraqi missile attack on Israel was negatively affecting Israeli deterrence did not understand what deterrence was (Party, 1991: 1, 11, 15). Rabin did not rely heavily on advisors because he felt confident about his own knowledge and because he was uncomfortable communicating with others (Inbar, 1999: 146–52; Interview with Rahel Rabin, 1998).

In contrast to the other three prime ministers, Peres was the least rigid and changed his mind often in his life. For instance, in the mid-1970s he supported religious settlements in the West Bank, while later viewing them as an obstacle to peace. He prided himself on being a visionary who comes up with new ideas. For instance, he proudly wrote that as a youth working in an agricultural kibbutz, he urged them to consider industry—this, he recalled, "was like talking in the synagogue about eating pigs' feet" (Peres, 1998: 186). He is an avid reader and loves to befriend intellectuals. Peres had the most complex representations of the Palestinian conflict between 1995 and 1997, Rabin less so, and Netanyahu tended toward low complexity (Sylvan, 1998). Peres' relative cognitive complexity contributes to explaining why he changed his image of the PLO more quickly than did Rabin. He also had the most collegial advisory system as prime minister, allowing group problem solving and debate with multiple and conflicting perspectives (George, 1980: 157). He had a team of nine, all under the age of 40, who brainstormed together, and he was particularly influenced by his deputy foreign minister, Yossi Beilin, who initiated the Oslo talks on his own. Peres' ability to weigh alternative options and search for creative solutions contributed to the extent and rate of his changes.

## Different Perspectives of and Lessons Drawn from the *Intifada* and the Gulf War

The prime ministers' differing ideologies and personalities gave them differing perspectives on the same dramatic events, with significant implications for their image of the PLO and for their policy preferences toward resolving the conflict with the Palestinians. Rabin's Labor ideology, combined with his orientation toward the present, led him to be highly influenced by the *intifada*. The *intifada* revealed to Rabin the necessity of politically resolving the conflict with the Palestinians. Rabin attempted to quell the uprisings by "breaking their bones," but eventually he came to respect the Palestinians for taking charge of their fate (Peri, 1996: 354, 356). According to his chief of staff, Eitan Haber, Rabin realized that Israel could not do anything against children throwing stones, and the negative influence that it had on soldiers and the suffering of the Palestinians influenced him to seek peace more quickly and with greater concessions than he was once willing to make (Interview with Haber, 1997). In contrast, the *intifada* did not lead Peres to change his image of the Palestinians, so much as it confirmed his belief that a peace process was needed to resolve the overall conflict (Peres, 1993: 55, 58–60; Party, March 1991: 10). In his books, he barely mentioned the *intifada*, and when specifically asked how the *intifada* influenced him, he offered no suggestions (Interview with Peres, 1997).

The combination of the *intifada* and the Gulf War only strengthened Shamir and Netanyahu's views that peace was impossible. Shamir did not differentiate the popular uprising from previous acts of terrorism and wrote that "it was a continuation of the war against us," which changed nothing because Israel had faced "a hundred years of *intifada*" (Shamir, 1994: 180, 182). Because his ideology contained a long time horizon, he did not view Israel's "short-term" failure to end the *intifada* through military means as a failure because he thought that the Palestinians would eventually give up. Likewise, Netanyahu argued that the goals of the *intifada* were "to drive the Jews from every inch of Israel" rather than from the West Bank alone (Netanyahu, 1993: 165).

Shamir and Netanyahu did not see the weakening of the PLO in the wake of the Gulf War as an opportunity to reach an agreement in the face of the growing threat of *Hamas* (a Palestinian Islamist movement opposing the recognition of Israel) but rather as a positive end in itself. In contrast, the Gulf War served to highlight for Rabin and Peres the need for peace and the opportunity to pursue it with a weakened PLO, although they focused on different lessons from the war. According to Eitan Haber, Rabin was horrified when, for the first time in all of Israel's wars, 500,000 Israelis fled Tel Aviv because of a few Scud missiles, which killed one person. From that, Rabin "understood that Israel was tired from wars and its ability to stand was weaker" (Interview with Haber, 1997). This substantiated his view that time was not on Israel's side (Peri, 1996: 367).

While the events changed Rabin's view of Israeli holding power, for Peres the Gulf War confirmed his prior perception of future trends, including the growing threat of countries on Israel's periphery as opposed to its immediate territories. It also emphasized for Peres the decreased centrality of territory for a state's security in the age of missiles (Peres, 1996: 63; Party, August 1990: 20).

### Images of the Enemy

Drawing on Snyder and Diesing's (1977) definition of hard-line perceptions of an enemy—believing that the enemy views accommodation as weakness, seeing the enemy group as monolithic and having unlimited aims—it is clear that Peres and Rabin's ideology and individual time horizons enabled them to change their hard-line image of the PLO, while Shamir and Netanyahu retained their image of the PLO as monolithic and as seeking the destruction of Israel. Peres claimed that opportunities were missed because Israelis and Arabs "were blinded, making us incapable of changing our images of either 'them' or ourselves" and that he has changed his image of the PLO (Peres, 1993: 2; Interview with Peres, 1997). Rabin began to change his image of the PLO before Oslo, but Rabin began to respect Arafat only when Arafat took action against terrorism (Peri, 1996: 364).

In contrast, Netanyahu remained distrustful of the Palestinians' acceptance of Israel and of their motivations for negotiation (Sontag, 1999). Shamir perceived no changes in the enemy and saw every hostile Arab act as interconnected with a long history of hostility toward Israel. He argued that the "Arab riots of the 1920s, 1930s and 1980s are interconnected. Arab terrorism did not start with the founding of the Palestinian Liberation Organization (PLO) in 1964. . . . Neither the mission nor the target has changed" (Shamir, 1994: 19, 70). While Rabin and Peres increasingly revised their perception of PLO goals—gradually coming to believe that the PLO recognized that the destruction of Israel was not achievable—Netanyahu and Shamir were (and still are) convinced that the PLO remains bent on Israel's destruction. Netanyahu wrote that the "PLO is committed, sinews and flesh, tooth and nail, to the eradication of Israel by any means" and that peace is merely used by the Palestinians as a "tactical intermission in a continuing total war" (Netanyahu, 1993: 233, 337). Shamir argued that "those Arab groupings which do not recognize our right to live in the Land of Israel also do not recognize our right to live in part of the Land of Israel" and that "it is time we learned to believe our enemies when they say that they wish to destroy us. Who, after all, believed Hitler when he wrote in *Mein Kampf* that he would destroy all the Jews of Europe if he ever got the chance?" (Shamir, 1994: 93). When asked whether he believed that the PLO's recognition of Israel in the Oslo agreement means that they are settling for an area next to, not instead of, Israel, his response was, "That is impossible" and that Arafat cannot be trusted (Interview with Shamir, 1998; television Interview with Shamir on Israeli television, December 7, 1997).

Interestingly, based on Shamir and Netanyahu's characterizations of PLO peace gestures as merely tactical maneuvers while the long-term goal remains the same, we can see the flip side of the long-term "time horizon" of Likud ideology described above: seeing the conflict as stretching forward and backward in time and thus being willing to make short-term sacrifices for the sake of long-term goals, Shamir and Netanyahu attribute this same long-term view of the conflict to the PLO opponents.

By 1990 Rabin and Peres saw a stark difference between the PLO and *Hamas*, whom they viewed as more extreme than the PLO. Rabin feared that lack of progress in negotiations with the PLO would strengthen *Hamas* (Party, July 1990: 6). Rabin's speeches reflected a shift toward seeing *Hamas* specifically, as opposed to Palestinians as a whole, as central to his image of the conflict (Sylvan, 1998: 12–13). Rabin also came to view the PLO as less of a threat than Iraq (Party, January 1991: 16; Peri, 1996: 365–66). Rabin preferred to reconcile with the Palestinians so that neighboring countries would not be used as staging grounds for Iraqi and Iranian activity. Similarly, Peres said, "I definitely decided to pursue the peace process when I reached the conclusion . . . that Yasir Arafat had become so weak that he might fall" and that Arafat's disappearance "was a greater danger than his existence" (Peres, 1998: 74–75).

In contrast, Shamir and Netanyahu maintained a more monolithic image of the Palestinians due to their ideologically driven desire to hold on to the West Bank, their view of a hostile world, and their perception that the Palestinians were unchangeable due to their historical behavior. They believed that the PLO and *Hamas* were working together to achieve the same goals (Interview with Shamir, 1998; Netanyahu, 1993: 165). On an Israeli televised interview of Shamir and Peres, Shamir claimed that all the Palestinians want to destroy Israel. Peres answered, "There are those [who do] and there are those [who do not]," to which Shamir replied, "[T]here are no 'those,' they all want to destroy us" (Television Interview, 1997). Netanyahu has quoted PLO representatives who claim that the PLO and *Hamas* have the same goals but differ as to whether to get there in stages or in one blow. He also believes that today's "moderate could be tomorrow's radical, courtesy of a coup, an invasion, or mere intimidation" (Netanyahu, 1993: 224, 339).

Rabin and Peres increasingly differentiated between the PLO and *Ha-*

*mas*, partially due to the fact that they had a lower standard than did Shamir and Netanyahu for evidence of good faith, because this would not require sacrificing central ideological goals and because they were not immersed with the history of the conflict. Rabin and Peres often ignored Palestinian hostile public statements, while Shamir and Netanyahu publicized them as representative of true motivations. According to Netanyahu, the PLO has a history of proclaiming its moderation and denying terrorism while engaging in it (Netanyahu, 1993: 207). He also stressed Palestinian violations of agreements as proof of their bad faith (Susser, 1998). In contrast, Rabin argued already in 1974 that Israel should not focus on what Sadat says in any particular speech and accepted as an unavoidable fact that "there is opposition. If there were no opposition, there would not have been 26 years of war between the Arab world and Israel" (Party, September 1974: 6, 21, 22). Likewise, Rabin generally gained confidence in the Palestinian Authority and complained that the headlines about the stabbing of several youths (by Palestinian terrorists) had been three times the size of the headlines in the papers at the outbreak of the Six-Day War (Peri, 1996: 368). Peres also claimed that the majority of Palestinians opposed terrorism, that Arafat was fighting terrorism, and that one should not focus on what Arafat says (Peres, 1996: 60; 1993: 14).

## CONCLUSION

Although changes within the PLO and in the regional and international context are necessary elements in explaining the Oslo agreements between Israel and the PLO, they are not sufficient: it is clear that the perceptions of individual leaders can make a significant difference in reaching agreements like Oslo. The differing ideologies of the four Israeli prime ministers had a significant impact on their images of the enemy, their perception of and reaction to the *intifada* and to the Gulf War, and ultimately on their ability to reach an agreement with the Palestinians. Of the factors discussed in this study—ideology, time horizon, and cognitive rigidity—ideology seems predominant in determining a capacity for changing one's image of the enemy, being the only one of the three variables that divided the two prime ministers who changed their image of the PLO from the two that did not. Therefore, the predictions emanating from Alexander George's work on the operational code prove to be robust in explaining which hard-liners are more likely to change their image of an enemy. Shamir did not alter his image of the Palestinians, while Netanyahu only marginally revised his image of certain elements of the PLO but did not alter his overall image.

The long-term, optimistic time horizon built into Likud ideology predisposed Shamir and Netanyahu to hope for increased Jewish emigration and for the Palestinians to give up on statehood. They did not perceive Israel's military response to the *intifada* as a failure requiring political solutions, as did Rabin. Likud ideology's emphasis on the territorial Greater Land of Israel inhibited them from perceiving change in the Palestinians, since to do so would lead to a conflict of goals. The Gulf War and the *intifada* only emphasized to them the hostility of the Palestinians and did not lead them to think that a solution was any more possible or urgent.

At the same time, however, Netanyahu and Shamir did ultimately make changes due to both American and domestic pressures. Although it is clear that Shamir would not have been able to make the concessions necessary to reach an agreement with the Palestinians, he did undergo some changes—specifically, he negotiated in Madrid in 1991 with Palestinians receiving instructions from the PLO. Similarly, Netanyahu ultimately made territorial compromises in Hebron and agreed in the Wye Memorandum, signed by himself, Arafat, and President Clinton in October 1998, to carry out withdrawals from the West Bank called for under the Oslo Accords. However, Netanyahu implemented only one of the three phases outlined in the memorandum, not withdrawing from the total amount of territory agreed upon. Although acting to varying degrees as spoilers to the Oslo Accords, Shamir and Netanyahu made shifts that, while not producing foreign policy changes as significant as those produced by Peres and Rabin, kept them from standing completely still in the face of changes. Their tactical changes ultimately had significant, if unintentional, political consequences, since they paved the way for broader public support for negotiating with Palestinians and accepting the Oslo Accords. This also suggests further hypotheses for research: hard-liners whose image of the enemy does not change will be motivated only by outside and internal pressure to make tactical foreign policy changes to appease this pressure. Hard-liners whose image of the enemy does change are more likely to make more significant foreign policy changes that are less motivated by international pressure.

Labor ideology, in contrast to Likud, centered on a notion of security that was able to adapt to changing circumstances by not hinging on specific territorial goals. It also had a more short-term time horizon in regard to the Palestinian conflict, perceiving that time may not be on Israel's side, and did not stress the image of Israel standing alone among nations. Due to these factors, Rabin and Peres were more amenable to revising their image of the Palestinians and policy preferences: they were able to reassess the role of the PLO in the wake of the closing of the Jordanian option; their originally monolithic approach to the Palestinians evolved into a perception that *Hamas* posed a greater threat than the PLO; they were able to learn from and react to new circumstances such as the *intifada* and the Gulf War (albeit in different ways); they gradually shifted focus from the Palestinians to perceiving greater regional threats from Iraq and Iran. The specific government coalitions and growing domestic support allowed Rabin and Peres' preferences, as expressed through the secret Oslo negotiations, to become policy as the Israeli Parliament voted to sign the Oslo agreements (Aronoff and Aronoff, 1998).

The analysis of the individual time horizons of the prime ministers provided greater empirical verification for previous analyses (such as Vertzberger's, 1990), suggesting that individuals who focus to a greater extent on the past are less likely to reevaluate a hostile image of an enemy. Both Shamir and Netanyahu thought of present events most readily in terms of the past and thus viewed the enemy as unchangeable, and they did not reassess their image of the PLO as a consequence of the *intifada* or the Gulf War. The hypotheses tested in regard to present and future time orientation revealed that these different individual time horizons can help explain differing rates and mechanisms of change for those leaders holding the same ideology.

Leaders who focus most on the present, receiving information about ongoing changes in small increments, are slower to perceive overall shifts and thus are slower to implement changes. Consequently, Rabin was slower to shift his attitudes and policy preferences than Peres. For instance, Rabin accepted the notion of negotiating with the PLO only after the process had already begun and had achieved results. Peres was more apt to look at future trends—perceiving that in the future, for example, in the age of missiles, security would become less dependent on territory, while increased regional economic cooperation would enhance security. Perceiving these trends as well as the strengthening of *Hamas*, Peres was intellectually ready to negotiate with the PLO more than a decade before Rabin and before the *intifada* and the Gulf War (although he dared not voice this readiness in public for political reasons) (Peres, 1993: 20; Interview with Beilin, 1997). Rabin, whose orientation toward the present de-emphasized the importance of future trends, learned to a greater extent from trial and error throughout the *intifada* that military force was failing to produce a solution. In addition, while the Gulf War merely confirmed Peres' view of future trends, Rabin was shocked that Israelis were fleeing Tel Aviv, and thus the war underscored for him the urgency for making peace.

The structure of individual cognitive systems on their own was not able to explain why some hard-liners changed and others did not. In some ways this study runs counter to the predictions of some theories that propose a high correlation between openness, cognitive complexity, and change: Rabin was relatively rigid yet eventually changed his image of and policy preferences toward the PLO. Netanyahu and Shamir's relative rigidity led them to dismiss information that contradicted their images and thus reinforced the influences of their ideology and individual focus on the past. However, the flexibility of Rabin's ideology, combined with his orientation toward the present, enabled him to change despite his relative rigidity.

This study suggests that the content of beliefs as defined by a political ideology may be a more significant predictor of change than the structure of one's beliefs (although the two are not entirely independent). While using a comparative case study and process tracing was useful in analyzing the factors addressed, since only four cases were analyzed, this study points to a need for further research. It would be fruitful to test these hypotheses in additional cases and with a variety of methods in order to verify their generalizability.

## APPENDIX 11.1: INTERVIEWS BY THE AUTHOR

Beilin, Yossi. August 12, 1997, Tel Aviv.

Gold, Dore. June 2, 1999, New York.

Haber, Eithan. July 27, 1997, Tel Aviv.

Peres, Shimon. August 5, 1997, Tel Aviv.

Rabin, Rahel. July 7, 1998, Kibbutz Menarah.

Ross, Dennis. August 6, 1999, Washington, D.C.

Sarid, Yossi. May 5, 1998, Jerusalem; July 5, 1998, Tel Aviv.

Shamir, Yitzhak. July 5, 1998, Tel Aviv.

Labor Party Meetings, Labor Party Archives.

Leadership Bureau. September 29, 1974; November 7, 1974; November 27, 1975; August 9, 1990, Document #182; January 31, 1991, Document #278.

Central Committee. July 26, 1990, Document #177; March 27, 1991, Document #1053; May 13, 1991, Document #1111.

## NOTES

1. This research is based on extensive review of archival material and interviews conducted by the author in Israel, as well as memoirs and hundreds of speeches over the past 30 years. Due to length restrictions, much of the supporting evidence could not be included. For further evidence and argumentation see author's unpublished dissertation, "Making the Impossible Possible: When and Why Do Hardliners Become Soft?" (August 2001).

2. Interviews conducted by the author are cited as (interview, date). For full citation, see Appendix 11.1.

3. Statements made by Peres and by Rabin in Labor Party committees will hereafter be cited as (Party, date, page number). This information was collected from the Labor Party Archives in *Beit Berl*, Israel, and translated from Hebrew into English by the author.

# Chapter 12

# Predicting the Performance of Leaders in Parliamentary Systems: New Zealand Prime Minister David Lange

John Henderson

## INTRODUCTION

When David Lange led the Labour Party to victory in New Zealand's 1984 general election, he ended his center-left Labour Party's nine years in opposition. At the age of 43, he became the country's youngest prime minister in the twentieth century. In 1987, following a period of radical reform in economic policy and a change of direction in foreign policy, Lange again led Labour to victory at the polls, winning re-election with an increased majority and becoming the first Labour prime minister to win a second term since 1949. Yet just two years later, in August 1989, he shocked the country when he resigned as prime minister following a long and bitter dispute over economic policy with his minister of finance, Roger Douglas. As I have observed elsewhere (Henderson, 1992), for Labour supporters, Lange's period as prime minister will be remembered for both triumph and tragedy. The triumph was in the area of foreign policy with the establishment of a nuclear-free New Zealand (Lange, 1990). The tragedy was the self-destruction of the Labour government over disagreements regarding the pursuit of a "new right" economic policy that reversed the center-left direction pursued by previous Labour governments.

This chapter seeks to assess the impact of Lange's personality on these extraordinary years in New Zealand politics. As director first of Lange's policy Advisory Group and later of the Prime Minister's Office, I was in a unique position to observe events and assess Lange's performance as prime minister. It was a fascinating experience for a political scientist with an interest in political psychology. However, I should note that during most of the time I was preoccupied by the events of the day and did not consciously seek to apply any of my earlier political science training. Perhaps I should have, but somehow it didn't seem right to mix official duties with academic interest; in any case, there just simply wasn't time.

But I have now been long free of any official obligations, and I am now working on a wider academic account of my experiences of working for the third Labour government and particularly the linkages—or rather lack of connections—between the theory and practice of politics. A point that I seek to demonstrate in this chapter is that the analysis of personality does shed light on the actions of key politicians and in this way contrasts with so much of the political science discipline, which seems to have little practical relevance to the "real world" of politics.

The theoretical basis of this chapter is taken from the writings of Duke University political psychologist James David Barber. As with the subject of this analysis, the choice of theory is also rooted in my past experience. During the early 1970s I was fortunate to have Barber as a course instructor and supervisor of my doctoral thesis. With the self-inflicted demise of President Richard Nixon dominating the news media, these were exciting years for students of leadership personality. Barber's book, *The Presidential Character: Predicting Performance in the White House* (1992), was receiving a lot of attention, especially as Barber claimed, with considerable justification, that he predicted the collapse of the Nixon presidency.

In drawing on Barber's work for the analysis of a New Zealand prime minister, it must be acknowledged that Barber made no claim that his framework of analysis could be applied to other political systems outside the United States. I have made some past modest attempts to apply Barber to New Zealand politicians (Henderson, 1974, 1978, 1992) and found that it works quite well. His framework is commendable—and unusual—in that it is largely jargon-free and easily comprehensible. For the purposes of this study his framework also has the advantage of providing rigor and organization to the analysis and a degree of objectivity that would otherwise be difficult for a participant in the political process to achieve.

Barber's typology has the advantage of simplicity and the employment of easily recognizable variables. It is based on two questions relating to the leaders' participation in politics—how much energy or activity they devote to politics and how they feel about their political life. Barber argues that these two dimensions—activity and affect—are the central features of anyone's "orientation to life" and are central to understanding the personality of politicians. Regarding the activity dimension, Barber observes: "In nearly every study of personality, some form of the active-passive contrast is critical; the general tendency to act or be acted upon is evident in such concepts as dominance-submission, extraversion-introversion, aggression-timidity, attack-defence, fight-flight, engagement-withdrawal, approach-avoidance." Similarly, the "affect" dimension relates to fundamental questions about orientation toward life in general and politics in particular—"whether the person seems to be optimistic or pessimistic, hopeful or skeptical, happy or sad." The question that Barber asked of U.S. presidents was: "Relatively speaking, does he seem to experience his political life as happy or sad, enjoyable or discouraging, positive or negative in its main effect?" (Barber, 1992: 8–9). Do the leaders have a positive or negative view of their political life? Are they happy in their work, or is it a burden that must be borne?

The answers to these two questions on activity and affect produce what Barber calls a "general mapping scheme," with four character types: active-positive, active-negative, passive-positive, and passive-negative. Barber acknowledges that the boundaries between these types are far from watertight. Political leaders, like anyone else, display differing degrees of activity in their chosen profession and satisfaction with the amount of effort they put into their jobs. Barber demonstrates that the two dimensions produce four types of "presidential character," which have their roots in the psychological literature (Barber, 1992: 8–11).

As the title of Barber's major work suggests, the whole point of his approach is to predict the performance of U.S. presidents. Barber seeks to demonstrate that with each of four types identified above goes a certain pattern of behavior, which, in turn, can be traced to basic motivations for entering politics. From examining politicians' life history, important clues can be established about how they are likely to perform should they obtain high office. Barber seeks to demonstrate that presidential character is established in childhood, their "worldview" in adolescence, and their political style by their early political successes (Barber, 1992: 5–6). However, the focus of this chapter is not on Lange's early life character formation but on the effect of personality factors on his style of operating, as this is what I was able to observe. As Barber acknowledges, origins are less important than the results (Barber, 1988: 125).

## LANGE'S ACTIVITY LEVEL

How much energy did Lange put into his political role, especially the task of prime minister? Does he belong at the active or passive level of political involvement? There appears to be little doubt that Lange belongs in the passive category. But this does not mean that I accept the view of some of his critics within and outside the party that he was lazy. When circumstances required it—for instance, during "crisis" periods—he would work for as long as was necessary to deal with an issue. But it was true that Lange did not, as the more active types tend to do, devote all his energies to the pursuit of political goals. He displayed what I regard to be a refreshing ability to distance himself from the more frantic devotion of some of his colleagues (for instance, Deputy Prime Minister Geoffrey Palmer) for work and third-ranking minister Mike Moore for political intrigue). But Lange's more passive approach did ultimately prove costly in maintaining his political standing. He was simply not prepared to put the time in and lobby colleagues around the clock to keep the job of prime minister. From Lange's point of view, the job wasn't worth that level of total commitment. There were other aspects to life to be pursued and enjoyed.

An important factor having a very direct effect on Lange's activity level was his health. Lange had since childhood been grossly overweight. As a big man, he tired easily. In 1980 he underwent a stomach stapling operation, which did succeed in drastically reducing his weight, but he remained large. In 1988 he had heart trouble and was successfully treated for angina. But health factors continued to place restrictions on his activity level.

Lange's attitude toward his work is further evidence of his passive nature. Even as prime minister he was at times bored. He hated the routine work of signing mountains of correspondence—and occasionally (and unwisely, from the point of view of those who had carefully drafted the letters) broke the monotony by adding handwritten comments at the bottom of letters. He at times found committee—and even cabinet—meetings boring and would sometimes get up and leave the meeting, without making it clear when, or if, he would return. He didn't like having to sit in one place for a long period. His attention span could be short and may have seemed to verge on rudeness for some visitors. He would sit behind his desk talking to a staff member or political colleague and then, without warning, spin around on his chair and tap on his computer, ignoring his visitor. No rudeness was intended. Lange had the ability and intelligence to deal with several issues at once, and he simply assumed that others would understand. He particularly loathed formal occasions when he was "trapped" by the protocol of the seating arrangements.

As has already been noted, Lange was capable of bursts of sustained effort and rose to the occasion during periods of crisis. For instance, during the currency crisis that greeted Labour's election in 1984, the bombing of the anti-nuclear Greenpeace protest vessel *Rainbow Warrior* in Auckland harbor by French government agents the following year, two Fiji military coups in 1987, and other political and natural disasters, he put in long hours of work and thrived on the excitement. He also was greatly "energized" by foreign travel, although, given the choice, his preference was to enjoy himself at fun parks rather than attend the seemingly endless formal VIP receptions. (This account is based on the author's observations.)

Barber demonstrates that patterns of leadership behavior are developed long before gaining high political office. In Lange's case there were clues to his passive behavior during his school days and in his early legal and political careers. Those who knew or worked with him were impressed by his obvious intelligence and abilities, while noting that he seldom drew fully on them. His biographer recorded that at school and university Lange "persistently performed below capacity," although he performed superbly (gaining a first-class honors degree in law) when he put his mind to it (Wright, 1984a: 17). Contemporaries from school, university, law practice, and politics have recalled how Lange seemed to be able to coast along and then, when the pressure came on, to move, seemingly without great effort, into overdrive. Lange, while justifiably rejecting suggestions that he was lazy (with the implication that he neglected his duties) has nevertheless confirmed the wide variations in his energy levels. "There were days of crisis when I would have worked more than twenty hours. There were other days, I would have worked, formally, about four hours. And there were some days when I would deal with questions, lie down on the couch, and go to sleep in the office" (McMillan, 1993: 19).

Lange's ability to put in bursts of work when it was absolutely necessary provides a partial answer to the question of how passive types of leaders ever gain top political positions. Barber's more complete answer is that they are put there by others who seek to use them for their own purposes. Referring to two of his examples of passive U.S. presidents (William Howard Taft and Warren G. Harding), Barber writes that they were thought to be "safe and controllable," as they were regarded to have "no particular convictions" and would do as they were told (Barber, 1992: 222).

Lange was elevated to high political office through the efforts of others who expected—mistakenly—that he, too, would be "controllable." He took pride in recalling that he never lobbied or engaged in aggressive self-promotion. Indeed, he claims to have discouraged attempts to promote him to party leadership. "I resisted for a long time the impulse of those who wanted to dispose of Bill Rowling and install me" (McMillan, 1993: 63).

Ironically, the group promoting Lange was led by Roger Douglas and made up of those who would later turn against Lange when it became clear that he did not share their views on neo-liberal economic reform. Lange was expected to provide a human face to the economic restructuring, not to contribute to the content of the policy.

Richard Prebble was a further key Labour politician promoting Lange—and later joined Douglas in seeking Lange's removal from office.

He gave as the reason that Lange should resign as leader the cruel analogy that he was never supposed to be more than the "show captain," the cruise-line skipper who looked like a captain, dressed like a captain, and sat at the head of the captain's table but in reality left the running of the ship to others. Lange was stung by the analogy and confided to the author: "Prebble is right—either I have to start running the show, or get out" (author's recollection). A few months later he resigned.

It is significant to note that after his resignation as prime minister, Lange admitted that he continued to find the prospects of a return to the party leadership attractive. But he recognized that if this was to happen, others would have to re-install him in the position. As before, he would not actively seek the leadership. He confided to a journalist:

I would love to be Prime Minister again. But it is a totally irrational and unreasonable expectation. . . . I mean, I do not . . . never did have . . . could not have the Machiavellian political capacity to cobble together, coerce, nobble, knee-cap, or personally destroy by vilification or exposure, people who did not agree with me, or what I wanted to do in a proper broadstream, well-meaning approach to politics. (McMillan, 1993: 63)

Lange decided not to seek re-election to Parliament. There was more to life than politics, and it is to this attitude toward political life that I now turn attention.

## POLITICS: A JOY OR BURDEN?

It will be recalled that Barber's second dimension relates to a political leader's "affect" toward politics—whether or not he enjoys his political life. It might seem that a political leader's passivity suggests a dislike for politics. But the test here is not the degree of political activity but how the leader felt about this activity (Barber, 1992: 8–9). In the case of Lange, I conclude that despite the fact that he willingly gave up high political office, he nevertheless greatly enjoyed the political stage. He is, in Barber terms, a "passive-positive."

But why do those with a passive approach to politics nevertheless accept high office? How do they remain in office, apparently without effort? Barber argues that passive-positive types are drawn to politics through their search for affection and need to attract the approval of others. They remain in office by delegating their authority—trusting others to do much of their work. They are the "political lovers"—the "nice guys who finish first, only to discover that not everyone is a nice guy." Referring to Taft (a presidential passive-positive), Barber wrote: "He was from the start a genial, agreeable, friendly, compliant person, much in need of affection" (Barber, 1992: 8–9).

Politics is by definition a social activity that involves mixing with other people. Part of the draw card to political activity is the desire to be part of a group or movement. Meeting with individuals and groups and addressing crowds from the platform or television studio are a key part of the job and provide an opportunity to win public approval.

Lange's attraction to the community service aspect of politics fitted his ideal of why he embarked on a political career. In his maiden parliamentary speech he declared that his goal was "to create a society where people feel committed to each other . . . when they realise they have a duty to their brothers, where the fruits of such a society are seen in the love, the charity, and the compassion of the people" (*New Zealand Parliamentary Debates*, 1977: 145). In doing this, he was carrying on the work that he did as a "poor man's" lawyer and his father's service to the underprivileged as a doctor. As Lange later explained: "You meet all the powerless, all the moneyless and the hopeless. And you think about it, and get mad about it" (Wright, 1984b: 16). When Lange felt that his government was no longer committed to these goals but had been hijacked by the economic right to serve the interests of business, he resigned.

However, what most attracts the passive-positive to public service is not ideology but the drama of politics—the lure of the political stage on which to affirm and win the affection and support of others. Barber found that passive-positive presidents gained pleasure from "performing and pleasing people" (Barber, 1992: 487–88). For Lange it was the drama of politics that attracted him. It was an extension of the stage on which he excelled as a lawyer. His considerable legal reputation was based on his wit and power of oratory rather than a comprehensive grasp of the legal intricacies of the case. So, too, in politics. In this respect there was little difference between the public and private Lange. He reveled in the sheer joy of being center stage and "performed" with his stream of jokes as much in private as in public (author's recollection).

In seeking public approval, passive-positives develop finely tuned skills of reading their crowd and playing on its emotions. Lange would not appreciate the comparison, but his skills as a "great communicator" are similar to those of U.S. president Ronald Reagan (whom Barber classifies as belonging to this passive-positive type). Reagan "through the years had developed a remarkable sensitivity to small and larger audiences, learning just how to charm and divert them toward an appreciation of himself. . . . from childhood on he had been attuned to play acting" (Barber, 1988: 23). Lange has himself reflected, somewhat cynically, on his ability to play the emotions of his audience—how he could exercise power that was "darn near demagoguery. I have driven people to the point where I've seen tears coming to their eyes, by flicking [*sic*] to them, wafting in front of them verbally and by body language expressions of things from the past which move them" (Wright, 1984b: 16).

Lange took the dramatic side of politics very seriously. He worked hard at preparing for major television interviews and speeches. Although he was a natural television performer, he nevertheless took part in tutoring and workshops designed to help him perfect his television style.

What Barber wrote of U.S. presidents and the show business dimension of politics has considerable relevance to Lange:

The President as star brings his audience together in their admiration of him, lets their glamorization of him flow freely around the hall, where, for a moment at least, all experience simultaneously the common joy of his presence. The transformation of a middle aged politician into a glamorous star is a mysterious process, one perhaps best understood by the managers of rock groups. (Barber, 1992: 486)

One of Lange's most experienced press secretaries used the same analogy of a pop star to explain Lange's sudden change in energy levels and his ability to work and woo an audience. Others have likened his ability to perform when required to that of a prize-fighter. Up until the moment that Lange moved onto the stage, he would seem ill-prepared and distracted. But once on the stage, the lights and the applause provided the stimulation and energy for a superb performance. Lange delighted in the response. After one key address to an international audience during a time when he was under criticism at home, he took great reassurance from the long applause—and confided to staff: "I needed that" (Author's recollection). So, too, did his staff. As one key staffer commented, "You can hate him for ten small mistakes and then love him for that great speech" (Wright, 1984a: 141).

While passive-positives gain general satisfaction and pleasure from their political work, there is one aspect that they hate: the disharmony, conflict, and rejection that are also inevitably part of the political process. Barber noted how their dislike of discord made them reluctant to confront opponents. They feel threatened by conflict—"and particularly conflict at close quarters" (Barber, 1992: 223) between political colleagues or staff. They seek harmony, and to avoid disputes or bad news.

Certainly, Lange reflected this desire to avoid conflict. As has already been noted, he was not prepared to "fight" for his own promotion in politics. After his selection as Labour's leader, he made it clear that he saw his role as promoting consensus and conciliation within his party and country. This was the purpose of the national summit held soon after Labour's election. But the "Rogernomics" (named after the minister of finance, Roger Douglas—the New Zealand version of Reaganomics) neo-liberal economic reforms that followed brought conflict, not consensus. Lange came to differ greatly with Douglas over the pace and extent of the economic reforms, but he was very reluctant to directly confront him. When staff organized private meetings to discuss the differences, the two men avoided controversial topics. When these differences reached the cabinet, Lange would at times fail to use material that staff had prepared to support his case and sometimes leave the meeting rather than openly argue points of difference. Similarly, with staff Lange would seek to avoid those whose work he found unsatisfactory or in whose company he felt uneasy. He seldom openly differed with staff or political colleagues.

## POLICY AND POLITICAL IMPLICATIONS

Barber warns that the danger with passive-positive presidential types is that their desire to avoid conflict and win affection leaves them vulnerable to the manipulation of others. For passive-positives, major disappointments are likely. The danger is that they tend to focus on performance rather than substance, and the question of judgment is transformed into a question of appreciation (Barber, 1992: 222–23). There is little doubt that Lange paid a political price for his use of humor and love of the dramatic. He insisted, against the wishes of key advisors, on holding long press conferences in which he clearly enjoyed debating and amusing the parliamentary press gallery. His weekly press conferences became known about the parliamentary buildings as the "best show in town" and were crowded affairs attended by both journalists and political staff. But as Lange's political fortunes waned, the media increasingly portrayed him as a frivolous prime minister who did not take his job seriously. In 1988 he played into the hands of his critics by allowing himself to be photographed lying in long grass. It was all good fun, but the photos, which appeared in *Time* and on the front pages of major newspapers, portrayed a figure more interested in clowning around rather than exercising prime ministerial leadership. It was an unfair, but nevertheless damaging, portrayal.

But there were also major achievements that required the skillful use of the prime ministerial office. Passive-positive types are good at bringing people together, and Lange demonstrated this by hosting a summit conference of major interest and community groups soon after taking office. But the consensus was not to last. Lange found himself spending more and more of his time trying to hold his party together in the face of deep divisions over economic policy.

The Labour government's anti-nuclear policy is an interesting policy example, because it would seem to be out of character for a passive prime minister to spearhead such a major change in New Zealand foreign policy. But it is significant to note that, true to form for the passive-positive type, Lange initially sought a compromise by suggesting that nuclear-powered, but not-armed, ships be allowed entry to New Zealand ports. The compromise was designed to appease the U.S. Navy, but the very hostile reaction from the party was a hard lesson that, if he wanted to keep the leadership, he must not compromise Labour's anti-nuclear policy.

Lange went on to champion the anti-nuclear policy, even though it brought New Zealand into conflict with the United States, which held to its "neither confirm nor deny" policy on nuclear ship visits. When Lange persisted with the policy, New Zealand was excluded from the ANZUS (Australia, New Zealand, United States) security alliance. Lange believed very strongly that nuclear weapons posed a threat rather than provided security to the South Pacific. His powerful advocacy extended his political stage to include the international media and speaking circuits, including the Oxford Union debate. He thrived on the attention, as any passive-positive would, but his willingness to be at the heart of controversy is not characteristic of the type.

Lange could also claim credit for the controversial launching of the economic reforms that began the process of restructuring the New Zealand economy. He recognized the need to restore life into an economy stifled by government regulations—extending to both wage and price controls introduced by the previous administration. But Lange found that initiating reform was much easier than determining its pace and scope.

Lange delegated economic policy to his minister of finance, Roger Douglas. But having relinquished control of such a key part of his administration, Lange was not able to reassert his authority when policy differences emerged. Lange believed that Douglas was taking the neoliberal reforms too far and too fast and hurting the very people whom Labour was in power to protect. When, in the late 1980s, Lange sought—in a manner typical of a passive leader—to institute a "breathing space" in the economic reform process by calling time-out for a "cup of tea," he found himself largely isolated. However, history would prove that his political judgment was correct. Labour was overwhelmingly defeated in the 1990 general election.

Lange has identified his handling of Rogernomics as the greatest shortcoming of his administration. "It was a failure not to have accepted Roger Douglas' resignation when it was offered on a number of occasions, and not to have mustered the support to eliminate his convictions early" (McMillan, 1993: 38). Lange's distaste for conflict—characteristic of the passive-positive type—prevented him from taking this early action. As a colleague commented:

It's a lonely job, and when things are evenly balanced you sometimes have to make the decision to go straight down the middle. This means everyone hates you. You can't get too close to anyone and you have to be your own counsellor. But that was not David Lange's style. He liked people, and liked to be liked. And that was a problem. (McMillan, 1993: 39)

It is a problem that characterizes the leadership of passive-positive types.

A further related problem was Lange's reluctance to work behind the scenes to build up a coalition that could resist the "Rogernomics" economic policy. Others in cabinet and the Labour Party parliamentary caucus shared Lange's views, but Lange was reluctant to actively enlist their support. This was partly due to the fact that this group was made up mainly of the Left of the party, which had earlier opposed Lange's takeover of leadership from Bill Rowling. Even after Douglas resigned over Lange's opposition to his policies, Lange was unable to bring this group, which largely shared his policy views, together under his direction to ensure a change in economic policy.

Others who know Lange well have confirmed that his inability to lobby caucus for what he believed in was a major political weakness. His biographer recalls that former fellow Auckland Labour Member of Parliament (MP) and cabinet minister Michael Basset commented in 1984—long before he turned against Lange—that his "passivity" was his "deficient political streak." "He will not lobby on his behalf. His style too can work against him." Lange's biographer commented. "The plotting and persuasion of political maneuvers are not Lange's forte" (Wright, 1984a: 121, 129).

Lange took his distaste of lobbying and aversion to conflict to extraordinary lengths. In 1989 he did not directly inform his caucus colleagues that if they insisted on re-electing the by then former finance minister Roger Douglas to cabinet, he would resign. He later reflected: "I had to go. I assumed that would be obvious to members of the caucus, but a lot of them didn't see it that way" (McMillan, 1993: 39).

## THE MAKING OF A PASSIVE-POSITIVE

Barber employs a life history approach to establish the origins of each of his four types of presidential character. He found that the passive-negative type typically came from families where they were the center of attention and often spoiled. An analysis of the degree to which Lange followed this pattern will have to await further study. However, the account of his biographer suggests that Lange was not overly indulged (Wright, 1984a: 5–7). His mother spent most of her time on her social work—with her attention on other people's children rather than her own.

Nevertheless, it seems clear that young David, the oldest of four children, was the favorite of his father and, indeed, of the wider community in which he grew up. His father's medical practice, with the surgery in the family home, meant that there were always lots of people around. Young David was often the center of attention, and this gave him a sense of confidence. As he said in his maiden speech to Parliament, "Where I was bought up we had no doubts. We knew without a doubt we would have a home. We knew we could achieve what we set out to do" (*New Zealand Parliamentary Debates*, 1977: 145).

David Lange grew up feeling a sense of obligation toward his father and the community. At times he felt guilty that most of the time he did not fully extend himself and use his many talents. He commented that his father's achievements "hung over me" (*New Zealand Parliamentary Debates*, 1977: 76). In his maiden speech to Parliament he spoke of his need "to account to the host of people who were involved in my upbringing, who have a part of me. If I let them down it is a condemnation of me. They will show it, and I will feel it" (*New Zealand Parliamentary Debates*, 1977: 76).

Perhaps the major factor in Lange's childhood and evolving personality was his sensitivity over his size. From an early age David Lange was grossly overweight. His biographer concluded that concern over his size "frequently made him prefer his own company." He portrays Lange as, in many ways, a lonely figure who turned "from sociable sporting activities with his peers to a more thoughtful introspective life." "There is a space inside David, again probably because of his size, that could not be touched." Lange's sharp wit was a means of deflecting the teasing of other children. "Joking initially deflects pain and eventually becomes a source of sustenance" (Wright, 1984a: 20, 41, 100).

Lange later reflected on the defense strategies used by obese people.

You develop a whole technique of living and presentation when you are fat, where you have to master that adversity, and you have to excel in some areas—either in charm, or wit, or intelligence or expertise or power or something—so that you cease to have your enormous impediment be the whole focus of people's views of you, and you carry it in some other way. (*Auckland Star*, November 23, 1982)

His sister Margaret recalled how he sought to compensate for his size "[b]y being funnier, by being more fluent, by being adventurous, not being a follower" (Wright, 1984a: 21).

Lange used humor as a form of withdrawal. It enabled him to avoid having to focus on serious subjects that might provoke hostility and argument. He avoided forming close relationships. His biographer recorded the views of his school contemporaries on the habit that Lange developed during his teenage years. "He would flit from one subject to another with impressive speed and intellectual dexterity, but not necessarily relating to the person he was with. He had no close friends, and his intellectual detachment caused him to be alone much of the time." (Wright, 1984a: 21). In this respect Lange reflected some of the characteristics of one of Barber's passive-positives, Taft, who had "many friends, no intimates" (Barber, 1992: 175).

## CONCLUSIONS: TRIUMPH OR TRAGEDY?

The objective of this chapter on Lange's term as prime minister has been to explain, not to render judgment. But on the two central features of Lange's administration I expect history will treat him favorably. He will be remembered for entrenching New Zealand's anti-nuclear policy and, with it, a much more independent foreign policy. It is significant that when the National government replaced Labour in 1990, it did not seek to change the anti-nuclear legislation and, indeed, once again took up Lange's anti-nuclear crusade with opposition to French nuclear testing in the Pacific.

Lange will also be remembered for launching, then curtailing (mainly) the extremes of Rogernomics' free-market economic policy. Without Lange's intervention—albeit at times fumbling and uncoordinated—Douglas would have continued to dismantle the welfare state that the first Labour government had in the 1930s done so much to establish. For Labour to have continued to follow Rogernomics would have meant political oblivion. (The party that Douglas formed to "finish the job," the Association of Consumers and Taxpayers' [ACT] poll ratings have seldom made double figures.) Against the achievements of the anti-nuclear policy and derailing the Rogernomics juggernaut, criticisms of Lange's work habits seem petty and insignificant. What does it matter how Lange handled, or failed to handle, matters of routine, when he could rise to the occasion on key issues that really mattered? Furthermore, in human terms, there is something attractive about a politician who employs humor rather than spite and who is not motivated primarily by a drive for power. Of course, views will differ on whether or not Lange's "achievements" were in the best interests of New Zealand. But few will argue with the conclusion that without Lange the outcomes would have been different.

The use of the Barber framework demonstrates that Lange's leadership performance was, in good part, generally predictable in terms of its style and outcome. Lange, in broad terms, fits the passive-positive type. But while he was put in the leadership position by others, he proved to have a mind of his own in key aspects of economic and foreign policy.

For Lange the relinquishing of high office was not a personal tragedy. Indeed, he felt considerable relief about ending the politics of division and conflict, which was so contrary to his political character. While he missed the excitement that goes with high office, he has been able to continue to be active in public life as a political commentator, public speaker, and television performer. He continues to have many opportunities for public appearances and engaging in what passive-positives do so well—winning the appreciation and affection of the crowd.

This chapter has demonstrated that a framework developed to analyze U.S. presidents can be usefully applied to leadership in parliamentary systems. Barber's objective was to help inform the American voter of what to look for in casting their vote for president. In the New Zealand parliamentary system the choice of prime minister is made by the members of Parliament of the governing party. As political colleagues, MPs are in a much better position than voters to make an assessment of the capabilities of aspiring leaders. Barber's insights could help this process. But increasingly, New Zealand politics, in line with most other parliamentary systems, is becoming more presidential, especially at election time, when attention focuses on the leader. The concern of the party is, not unexpectedly, to choose a leader who will maximize the party's popular support on Election Day. The leader's ability to provide effective management of the governing process tends to be of secondary concern.

Barber's work shows that the overall style of leadership is predictable. He has further demonstrated that successful leadership requires the coming together of the leader and the times (Barber, 1980). Passive-positive types excel when the public yearning is for reassurance. As Barber notes, "[F]or a people in search of community, they provide a refreshing hopefulness, and at least some sense of sharing and caring" (Barber, 1992: 223). The danger is that their distaste of conflict leads them to overlook the harsh reality that much politics is conflictual. What was predictable, using Barber's insights, was that Lange would provide unifying leadership to a society that was becoming increasingly torn by conflict. But equally predictable was Lange's unwillingness to remain leader when his own government's economic reforms were causing further deep rifts within his own party and society at large.

## ACKNOWLEDGMENT

Earlier versions of this chapter were presented to the Australasian Political Studies Association Conference, University of Melbourne, Australia, September 26–28, 1995, and the 22nd Annual Scientific Meeting of the International Society for Political Psychology, Amsterdam, Netherlands, July 18–21, 1999.

Chapter 13

# Self-Presentation of Political Leaders in Germany: The Case of Helmut Kohl

Astrid Schütz

## INTRODUCTION

This chapter uses the social psychological theory of self-presentation to analyze political leadership and present a case study focused upon German chancellor Helmut Kohl. It suggests a taxonomy of self-presentational strategies in the domain of politics and then presents two empirical approaches to the analysis of self-presentation in politics. Content analysis allows an identification of self-presentational strategies in political campaign communication, while the effect of self-presentational strategies on observers is evaluated with experimental analysis. Kohl's style of self-presentation and his leadership are evaluated, and the utility of this particular approach is discussed.

Theories of self-presentation in social psychology have largely been based upon the seminal work of Erving Goffman, and a host of empirical studies have been conducted to advance those models (see, e.g., Baumeister, 1982; Leary, 1995; Schlenker, 1980; Tedeschi et al., 1971). Several classifications of self-presentational tactics have been promoted (e.g., Jones & Pittman, 1982; Snyder et al., 1983; Tedeschi & Reiss, 1981); with few exceptions these derive from laboratory studies of self-presentational behavior (see Nezlek & Leary, 2001).

Schütz (1993) has shown that self-presentation theory is useful in the analysis of political communication, especially in light of the fact that self-presentation has become an important factor in electoral campaigns. In the age of televised political campaigning, media-conveyed images of top candidates and their self-presentational styles have become crucial in creating the candidates' public image and influencing voter decisions

(Klingemann & Taylor, 1977; Norpoth, 1979). Modern technology enhanced this ability; most politicians are more likely to advertise their personalities than give detailed accounts of their views on various issues.

## SELF-PRESENTATIONAL STYLE IN POLITICS

In previous research designed to analyze the self-presentation styles of leaders, including Ronald Reagan, George Bush, Bill Clinton, Helmut Kohl, Johannes Rau, and Oskar Lafontaine, during election campaigns and/or political scandals (Laux & Schütz, 1996; Schütz, 1993, 1999), three general categories of self-presentation were distinguished: assertive self-presentation, aggressive self-presentation, and defensive self-presentation (Schütz, 1993, 1998a). Assertive self-presentation consists of active, but not aggressive, efforts to build positive impressions. This represents the attempt to look good by presenting a favorable image. Aggressive self-presentation includes domination or derogation of others in an attempt to try to look good by making others look bad. Politicians who are characterized by this style of self-presentation attempt, by attacking others and presenting themselves as superior, to convey desired impressions of themselves or to dominate the debate and promote favored issues and causes. Defensive self-presentation becomes necessary when the desired identity has been threatened or damaged. Schütz (1998a) distinguishes various strategies of defensive self-presentation characterized by how much wrongdoing an actor admits. Such defensive strategies have been applied in a variety of scandals, including a recent analysis of Bill Clinton's defensive self-presentation during "Monicagate" (Schütz, 1999).

These different styles of self-presentation evoke quite distinct impressions and have specific advantages as well as risks. Defensive self-presentation, for example, may be effective in removing negative impressions but does not normally create favorable impressions. Assertive self-presentation is an important tool for the purpose of establishing positive impressions and raising one's social profile. It is an important method for the creation of the desired impression, although its use includes the risk of presenting a vainglorious or pretentious image. Aggressive self-presentation can be effective in conveying an image of potency, áuthority, or superiority. It can also be used to reduce the credibility of the source and thus minimize the impact of criticism. A concomitant risk exists with the use of aggressive self-presentation: the speaker may be perceived as unfair or rude.

## ANALYZING SELF-PRESENTATION IN CAMPAIGN COMMUNICATION

Schütz (1993) used a content analysis of campaign communication to identify and compare specific tactics within each of these three styles of self-presentation in a variety of circumstances.

### Method

Content analysis aims at reducing complexity in verbal behavior by grouping verbal statements into categories. The classical strategy records a statement's manifest content as the frequency of specific words or terminology. Other approaches have focused upon the latent or psychological meaning of statements and coded for its presence. This chapter utilizes the latter strategy in a form of qualitative content analysis. As a research technique, qualitative content analysis is capable of "making replicable and valid inferences from data to their context" (Krippendorf, 1990: 21). Approximately seven hours of videotaped material from the 1987 federal election campaign interviews and debates were analyzed for this research. The 1987 federal election campaign was Kohl's third election for the office of chancellor and represented the middle of Kohl's political career. By this point in his career he had established himself as an influential and accepted political force. In 1987 Helmut Kohl's competition was Social Democrat Johannes Rau, a politician with an image of righteousness, nicknamed "Brother John."

The three supercategories described above were used to categorize interviews and debates: assertive, aggressive, and defensive self-presentation. In addition, prior analyses of the Ronald Reagan and Walter Mondale campaign debates (Laux & Schütz, 1996) indicated the presence of more fine-grained categories that are useful in the analysis of campaign communication. The set of categories that resulted from the Reagan–Mondale analyses was adapted and refined for use in the analysis of campaign communication between Kohl and Rau. Two coders were trained to understand and apply the category system. Interviews and debates between the two candidates were transcribed and coded; interrater agreement between the two coders proved to be satisfactory (70%).

### Results

Sixteen categories of self-presentation were ultimately distinguished. Some of these categories were based on earlier taxonomies, such as the one used by Jones and Pittman (1982). Others were derived from the current material or adapted to fit the context of self-presentation in politics. The categories are briefly described here.

Three variants of aggressive self-presentation were observed: (1) criticizing the question or the questioner or determining the topic of discussion; (2) belittling the opinions of the opponent or insisting on one's own opinion; and (3) attacking the rival.

Five variants of defensive self-presentation were observed: (1) denial (e.g., the politician denied that an incident detrimental to his or her reputation had occurred); (2) reframing (e.g., the politician interpreted an unfavorable event in a different way or gave it a less negative interpretation); (3) avoiding blame (e.g., the politician justified his or her own behavior with superior goals). The two other defensive tactics were present when the politician defended against an attack upon his or her party or the people with whom he or she associates. These included (4) "defending one's own party" (e.g., the politician did not re-establish his own image but he tried to present a favorable image for the party or group with which he or she is associated, thereby strengthening his or her own image); and (5) "cutting off reflected failure" (Snyder, 1985) (e.g., the politician in question did not try to justify the behavior of people or group with which he or she is associated but attempted to disassociate from negatively evaluated individuals or negatively evaluated behavior).

Eight categories were distinguished within the domain of assertive self-presentation. Five of the categories refer to the effort to present a favorable personality; three refer to the effort to present favorable abilities. The five "favorable personality" categories include (1) exemplification (e.g., emphasizing moral values [see Jones & Pittman, 1982]); (2) ingratiation (e.g., emphasizing the nice, polite, friendly, and likable aspects of the personality); (3) the "I am your man" category (e.g., an emphasis upon the attempt to present one's self as a true representative of the peoples' interest, a person who appears to be "just like us" in the eyes of average voter); (4) "self-disclosure" (e.g., candidates disclose something personal and private about themselves, indicating with their candid disclosure that they have nothing to hide and so may be trusted [see Jourard, 1964]); and (5) "showing fairness" (e.g., the politician attempts to present himself or herself as a fair opponent by refusing to attack his rival).

The attempt to promote the presence of favorable abilities was accomplished in three ways: describing laudable goals, promoting the self, and providing some proof of favorable abilities. The three "favorable abilities" categories include (6) "presenting goals" (e.g., talking about specific plans or promising particular policies if the candidate were elected); (7) "self-promotion" (e.g., claiming competence in politically relevant issue areas or demonstrating competence by providing detailed information about politically relevant issue areas [see Jones & Pittman, 1982]); and

(8) "providing proof" (e.g., supporting an argument or claim to power by referring to political status or past achievements).

The above-described categories were used to compare self-presentation for Johannes Rau and Helmut Kohl. On average, Kohl showed more assertive and aggressive self-presentation than Rau. He also scored highly in the "favorable abilities" categories and in the "I am your man" category, with attempts to demonstrate that he was the true representative of the people. Furthermore, regardless of whether journalists' questions implied criticism or not, Kohl used aggressive self-presentation more frequently than Rau: criticizing the journalists and their questions more frequently, redefining the topic under discussion, insisting upon his own views, and belittling divergent opinions. He frequently labeled journalists as "devious" and declared that he did not intend to talk about a particular issue but insisted upon speaking about another matter.

These results might be explained by Rau's position as challenger in the campaign. Rau's self-presentation may have been necessarily defensive in order to respond to criticism and successfully defend his own position. As a result, his self-presentation style would lack aggressive and assertive elements primarily because of the particular position that he occupied in the campaign itself. If Rau must continually defend himself against criticism, it may be predictable that his use of statements designed to either build a favorable image of himself or attack his rival would occur less frequently.

## EFFECTS OF DIFFERENT STRATEGIES OF SELF-PRESENTATION

Research has indicated the presence of individual differences in styles of self-presentation (e.g., Arkin, 1981). There is, however, little research on the effectiveness of distinctive strategies of self-presentational behavior. This line of thought may be useful, however, as research has indicated that presentation strategies have complex effects. For example, an overstatement of one's abilities (e.g., Jones & Pittman, 1982) or an underemphasis of one's abilities may each have negative effects. Likewise, studies have shown that comparing oneself positively with others can have either positive (Merten, 1991) or negative effects (Schütz, 1998b).

Three self-presentation strategies can be distinguished, according to Schlenker and Leary (1982). One can assertively and directly describe one's positive attributes, one's abilities, and one's achievements. Overt self-praise may, however, result in appearing boastful, and thus negative impressions may outweigh positive impressions. So, an alternative strategy would be the understatement of one's qualities and an attempt to seem modest in one's self-description. However, this may not be effective in increasing audience awareness of the scope of one's abilities. The third strategy is both aggressive and indirect. Rather than pointing out one's positive qualities, one attempts to disparage the competitor, in an effort to enhance one's own image. Attacking others can create an image of potency or superiority, but it is also associated with the risk of being perceived as rude or unfair.

## Method

Schütz (1998b) presents the results of research based upon evaluations of the performance of the top candidates in 1990 for the chancellery in Germany and designed to determine the effects of various self-presentational strategies. Videotaped scenes of debates were presented to observers who judged the self-presentation of each of the candidates. Forty-three students at Bamberg University, enrolled in a class on communication research, participated in the study. Participants were exposed to six scenes from two televised political talk-shows featuring the two top candidates for chancellery: the Social Democratic challenger Oskar Lafontaine and the Christian Democratic incumbent chancellor Helmut Kohl.

Three scenes, lasting approximately two minutes each, were also selected from campaign interviews. These were chosen only if they dealt with self-relevant questions and created a form of predicament for the candidate (see Schlenker, 1980); that is, the politician had to respond to criticism or an embarrassing question. In addition, each of the three scenes per candidate was selected only if it was comparable in terms of content and critical impact on the candidates. Scenes were evaluated by a team of three raters. In the first pair of scenes the two candidates were asked to self-evaluate their physical attractiveness. In the second pair of scenes they were each confronted with criticism that had been uttered by their respective rival. The third pair of scenes dealt with response to a public criticism of problems that had manifested in each candidates' policies. The similarity of scene-pairs created a control for context and, as such, allowed for the observation of different strategies used in reaction to similar stimuli and supported an analysis of the impact of those strategies on an audience.

After participants had viewed each scene, they were asked to evaluate the politicians' performances. Rather than have participants rate candidates on pre-constructed dimensions, participants were asked to answer open-ended questions about their impressions of each candidate. Participants were then asked to note the verbal and nonverbal candidate behaviors that led to their impressions. This approach allowed for a qualitative analysis of responses, preferred because it enhances access to self-generated dimensions, which are assumed to more accurately strike the observer as important with regard to a specific scene (see Schütz & DePaulo, 1996). Scenes were presented in alternating order. A coding scheme of self-presentational categories was set up with reference to a sample of the responses. Two independent raters then coded the participants' answers; inter-rater agreement was significant (88%).

## Results

The participants' evaluations of politician performances varied along two dimensions; that is, there was variance in respondent judgments of candidates' self-presentation as self-assured or arrogant, and variance existed in judgments of how aggressive or committed candidates were in their endeavors. Some favorable self-descriptions were evaluated as self-assured; others, as arrogant. Likewise, some performances were judged as committed, while others were judged as aggressive. The purpose of the study was to distinguish between positive and the closely related negative impressions and to find out which behaviors stimulated these positive or negative impressions. Variance was found to be largely unrelated to political partisanship.

Overall, Lafontaine was described as self-assured and competent more frequently than was Kohl. Alternatively, Kohl was described as arrogant and aggressive more frequently than Lafontaine. That assessment prevailed even among supporters of Kohl's party, the Christlich Demokratische Union (Christian Democratic Union [CDU]). Despite the fact that non-supporters' views on this question were more pronounced, a wide variety of viewers, regardless of their political standing, observed something in Kohl's conduct that they interpreted as arrogant. Participants' answers to open-ended questions indicated that the impression of arrogance was related to Kohl's highly positive self-description as well as his resolute and repeated rejection of criticism.

In addition, Kohl's pronounced habit of interrupting journalists was evaluated as aggressive. Lafontaine was perceived as having a more subtle style when rebutting criticism: keeping his calm, using irony, and showing confidence nonverbally (e.g. smiling), thus receiving more positive evaluations in this category. Kohl's heated and personal attacks against Lafontaine were predominantly interpreted as negative. However, Kohl's style of self-presentation was generally interpreted as more committed than Lafontaine's. Apparently, behavior that seems aggressive also at times evokes the impression of commitment.

In summary, Kohl's habit of describing himself in highly positive terms, his proclivity to brush off criticism, and his attacks on journalists and opponents were regarded as aggressive. However, this strategy of self-presentation was also regarded as committed, confirming results reported in Merten (1991), who noted that Kohl's aggressive style of self-presentation also creates positive impressions of strength.

## ANALYZING SELF-PRESENTATION IN POLITICAL LEADERS: AN EVALUATION

Self-presentation theory has many attributes as a means for analyzing the behavior of political leaders. As an at-a-distance method, it can be used in conjunction with content analysis and/or laboratory methodology to determine relationships between self-presentation style, public perception, and electoral success. Associations also exist between self-presentation strategy, public perception, and electoral success. However, the method does have certain disadvantages; advantages and disadvantages are summarized below.

### The Analysis of Self-Presentational Strategies

Self-presentation theory proves to be a useful framework for the analysis of campaign behavior. Although general categories used in the analyses were derived from earlier classifications based on laboratory studies used to analyze an American election campaign, these were found to successfully cross the cultural divide to provide insights into the tactics and patterns of self-presentation in German election campaigns. Additionally, categories seemed rather stable across different campaigns (see Laux & Schütz, 1996). It is, however, probable that the use of the method may require the addition of new categories if it is to account for typical behavior patterns found in political campaigning across other, more diverse cultures.

The analysis of self-presentation techniques has utility along two separate dimensions. While politicians may certainly be interested in predicting the effects of their presentational behavior on viewers, specifically in order to improve their political performance, the method is also useful for voters who may want to better understand campaign strategies and at least potentially recognize manipulative efforts at impression management.

The micro-analytic approach to self-presentation analysis that has been presented also has advantages and disadvantages. As a micro-analytic strategy, it allows for the identification of unique elements of self-presentation. However, if the goal is to understand an individual politician's overall strategy, for building a career and maintaining power, content-analytic and laboratory techniques need supplementation with more macro-analytic approaches that may, for example, rely upon interpretations from biographers, who observe the politician's behavior and decisions from a broader perspective. Insights from biographical sources are used in the next section to expand and enhance the self-presentation analysis.

## The Analysis of Self-Presentational Effects

The content-analytic and laboratory studies presented above were capable of identifying interactions between a politician's self-presentational style or strategy and viewers' perceptions. However, the identification of behaviors and their relationship to public impressions are only one aspect of the larger study of personality and its effect on political behavior. Demographic studies have focused upon voters' overall evaluations of a candidate (e.g., Brettschneider, 1999; Kepplinger & Rettich, 1996), and experimental studies have evaluated self-presentational effects (e.g., Schlenker & Leary, 1982), but each has its own limitations.

Although the research conducted for this chapter utilized a more naturalistic experimental approach—using scenes that had naturally occurred (instead of fabricating material that systematically varied on critical factors)—this approach does not allow for the imposition of strict controls to reduce the possibility of confounding factors. For example, even though results indicated that partisanship had no effect on respondent evaluations, it is possible that the likability of candidates (as perceived by the viewer) and other aspects of overall impressions as well as affective components of the verbal and non-verbal communication (Abelson et al., 1982) may have contributed to viewer evaluations. Further, the current research necessarily relied upon observers' subjective statements regarding which factors had caused their specific impressions, despite the existence of known limitations to viewers' insight into their own cognitive processes (Nisbett & Wilson, 1977).

Accuracy in the evaluation of factors that had affected impressions would have required an evaluation of systematic co-variation. An experimental study with artificial material would have given us the option of controlling for other factors and systematically varying self-presentational tactics, but we preferred the naturalistic strategy as a trade-off made for the sake of external validity. A host of studies on self-presentation in the laboratory already exists; however, results cannot unhesitatingly be applied to an analysis of the effects of campaign communication. Therefore, the naturalistic approach seemed warranted in this particular study.

The micro-analytic strategy used in this research could be supplemented by (1) a larger sample of scenes leading to a more complete analysis of overall self-presentational qualities in the two candidates; (2) a more macro-analytic approach using demographic results and the analysis of voters' motives; and/or (3) a comparison of content-analytic and laboratory studies with biographical analysis. Although possible, a larger sample of scenes was not utilized in this research in favor of providing a detailed account of the detrimental or favorable effects of the behavior presented in scenes that were chosen, and, although certainly important, the use of demographic information to supplement this research with comparative analysis will be reserved for later studies. Here, the micro-analytic approach is supplemented with relevant biographical information. The intersection between biographic findings and micro-analytic findings is presented below as a valuable and important adjunct to this line of research.

## THE PUBLIC PERSONALITY OF A POLITICAL LEADER: HELMUT KOHL

A more over-arching view into the character of Helmut Kohl requires the introduction of biographic information in the analysis. Self-presentation style is one component of the political personality of Helmut Kohl; however, by accessing biographic sources, we can expand and elucidate the overall picture. This section presents biographical information, describes major events in Kohl's political career, and then integrates the above-described micro-analytic findings to create a fuller picture of Kohl's public personality, emphasizing styles of self-presentation and leadership.

### The Political Career of Helmut Kohl: An Overview

Helmut Kohl was born in 1930 at Ludwigshafen, a medium-sized town on the river Rhine. In postwar Germany young Helmut Kohl had an astonishing political career. By the age of 39 he had been elected as Germany's youngest prime minister in Rhineland-Palatinate.

Kohl participated in six federal election campaigns as a candidate for the chancellorship. His party was successful in four of them. Here is a brief outline of these campaigns with emphasis on Kohl's self-presentation and image (for a more detailed biographic analysis, see Schütz, Hertel, & Schulze, 2001). In 1976 Kohl ran for chancellor against Social Democrat Helmut Schmidt. At the time chancellor Helmut Schmidt was very popular.

In 1975 *Newsweek*'s (May 26, 1975, cited in Vogel, 1990: 104–5) commentary on Kohl's style mentioned: "His wooden speeches are no match for Schmidt's sharp-tongued performances on the rostrum. And what Kohl's supporters see as pragmatic patriotism, his critics interpret as undiluted provincialism." That election was lost but was nevertheless a relative success for Kohl and his party since they were able to garner more votes than in the previous election.

In 1980 Kohl's rival, Franz Josef Strauss, was chosen as the conservative candidate and then suffered a severe loss against Social Democratic chancellor Helmut Schmidt. As a result of a vote of "no confidence," Schmidt had to leave office in 1982; shortly thereafter, Kohl was elected chancellor. In 1983 Kohl's self-presentational strategies were typical of an incumbent. He largely ignored his opponent and used his position to stage events that portrayed him as a competent statesman. In 1987 Social Democrat Johannes Rau became Kohl's challenger. As noted in the study presented above, Kohl used a more aggressive and assertive self-presentation than Rau. Rau seemed preoccupied with the necessity of defending himself, which then dominated his self-presentation (rather than more assertive styles of self-presentation). In that election the Sozialdemokratische Partei Deutschland (Social Democratic Party) [SPD] lost a considerable number of votes compared with the preceding election, and the CDU/ Christlich Soziale Union (Christian Social Union) [CSU] were able to continue their coalition with the Freie Demokratische Partei (Free Democratic Party [FDP]).

In 1990, during the first parliamentary election after German reunification, Social Democrat Oskar Lafontaine was chosen as Kohl's opponent. Early in the campaign Lafontaine had a very positive image when compared to that of the incumbent chancellor, but as the campaign progressed, and as noted in the study described above, Kohl was rated significantly more aggressive and arrogant than was Lafontaine. During early stages of the campaign Kohl received lower approval ratings than Lafontaine. Kohl's final success was attributed to the perception among a majority of voters that he was the architect of the reunification of Germany.

In 1994 Kohl ran for the office of chancellor for the fifth time. His opponent was Rudolf Scharping. Scharping was generally viewed as "OK but not great." Kohl evoked a bipolar reaction from the electorate, with extremely positive as well as extremely negative ratings. As polling day approached, Kohl's image improved, and his party won the election again.

In 1998 Kohl, who had held office for a record period of 16 years, was not re-elected. Kohl's party suffered a clear loss of votes, and the "eternal chancellor" Kohl was replaced by Gerhard Schröder, a challenger who had been called a media event and an expert at self-presentation (Kugler, 1999). Throughout the campaign Kohl received lower evaluations than his rival on most dimensions (Brettschneider, 1999). Gerhard Schröder was elected federal chancellor after having worked out a coalition agreement with the Green Party.

About a year after Kohl's electoral loss, a party finance scandal dramatically affected his image. Despite his defeat in the fall of 1998, Helmut Kohl was still regarded as a "chancellor of superlatives." He still enjoyed high approval in Germany and abroad and was voted one of the 10 "greatest Germans" of all time (*Newsweek*, December 31, 2000). However, in November 1999 the former CDU treasurer Walther Leisler Kiep came under suspicion for tax evasion. When he provided evidence that the money in question had been a donation to the CDU, Helmut Kohl became deeply entangled in a scandal that led to his resignation as honorary chairman of the party in January 2000. During the summer of 2000 a parliamentary inquiry was initiated to find out whether these cash donations had influenced decisions during Kohl's 16 years in power.

### Self-Presentational Styles as Traits

In July 2000 Kohl testified before a parliamentary committee investigating the party finance scandal. Kohl's presentation of himself during these hearings sheds some light on the traits that compose his more complete personality profile. Personality traits represent the building blocks of personality theory. They are considered to be constructs that can be inferred from the consistency of individual behavioral responses to a variety of situations (Pervin & John, 1997). If behavior is relatively stable over time and across situations, we conclude that an underlying trait shapes that person's interpretation of situations and his or her responses to stimuli. The following discussion focuses upon Helmut Kohl's habitual styles of self-presentation and traits that emerged as relevant to self-presentation. Three habitual patterns of self-presentation were present for Helmut Kohl: (1) lack of self-criticism, (2) aggressive response, and (3) sitting out. Kohl has often been criticized for his conceit and a seeming absence of self-criticism. Results from the laboratory study described earlier in this chapter confirmed that this perception also existed among respondents viewing scenes from the campaign. As was discussed, respondents in this particular study found that Kohl's self-description was too positive and lacked elements of self-criticism.

His behavior during the scandal was typical of this self-presentational style. In a televised interview Kohl admitted that he had violated the Campaign Fund Act by accepting $1 million in illegal campaign funds, but then proceeded to explain that his behavior was justified because he had pledged not to reveal the names of the anonymous donors. He denied that the donations were bribes and said that he used the money to help the Conservative Party expand in the former German Democratic Republic (GDR). He would then often redirect the discussion to focus upon his own historic achievements. His demeanor suggested that he considered his unethical behavior to be a minor problem and felt that the issue was not worth the turmoil. The German press fumed at this apparent self-righteousness and called Kohl's obstinacy at placing his word of honor above the law unbearable, arrogant, and obdurate, made worse by his lack of respect for democratic rules and clearly indicating that he had been in power for so long that he had lost touch with reality. Even the conservative *Die Welt* wrote that Kohl had governed with "the arrogance of a feudal baron" (CNN, June 30).

This type of behavior reflects self-concept as well as self-presentation. Kohl appeared completely convinced of the legitimacy of what he said and reacted with anger at any hint of criticism, indicating that patterns of self-presentation and self-deception may have merged, creating a proclivity to discount criticism while simultaneously presenting highly positive images of the self.

Kohl's typically aggressive response to criticism is the second habitual pattern of self-presentation. In the studies that have been conducted, Kohl's style of self-presentation proved to be rather belligerent. During the scandal, the same pattern of belligerence in response to criticism emerged as Kohl was confronted with allegations of wrongdoing. He frequently called criticism of his behavior or attitude "devious" and depicted himself as a victim of conspiracy that was aimed at destroying his life work. He claimed that political rivals were responsible for this "unprecedented attempt to defame me, to criminalize me, and to cast the fifteen good and successful years we had in a dark light" (CNN, June 29). Kohl responded to criticism with counter-attacks. He accused the media of unprecedented defamation and claimed that the ruling Social Democratic Party was not in a position to accuse him of breaking the law because it had acted in a manner that was contrary to the constitution on past occasions (ABC News, June 6, 2000).

The third pattern, "sitting out," is indicated by Kohl's refusal to give in when even fellow party members demanded that he should reveal the names of the donors. He insisted that he could not do that because he had given his word of honor that donors would remain anonymous. The "sitting out" pattern is one in which the individual uses stubborn refusal as a counter-measure. During his political career Kohl was repeatedly successful in getting his way simply because he insisted upon his particular position until his opponents were worn out. Kohl returned to this successful "sitting out" behavior during this scandal and again used the tactic to his advantage. After more than eight months of turmoil, the general public began to tire of the whole affair. By the summer of 2000, the press was reporting that support for Kohl within the party, which was at a record low in the spring, when official parties for his 70th birthday were actually canceled, was rising again.

## Self-Presentation a Key to Political Success?

Kohl has been not only the country's longest-serving chancellor since 1945 but also the longest-serving leader in any of the Western democracies. While self-presentation is an important factor in modern political communication, it is not everything. In the case of Helmut Kohl this analysis indicates that self-presentation is not the only key to understanding why he was able to stay in power so long.

Contrary to his successor, Gerhard Schröder, Helmut Kohl has never been considered to be a master of self-presentation, and this may have been one of the reasons that he was so often underrated. In 1979 *The Guardian* (February 8, 1979, cited in Vogel, 1990: 168–69) wrote that even some of his friends felt that he lacked the caliber to be chancellor. When he was about to become chancellor, the *Times* described him as "the colorless man from the sticks" with a "bland bespectacled face" (September, 27, 1982, cited in Vogel, 1990: 201). Kohl's reputation as a clumsy and provincial politician may, however, have been the reason that ordinary people regarded him as one of their own. His sometimes awkward way of speaking and his weight problems were more familiar to the man in the street; people perceived him as one who might understand them (Schütz, 1993). Furthermore, he was able to convince voters that he was the best representative of their interests. Helmut Kohl has never been very popular, but he has surprising political instinct. Leinemann (1994) argued that Kohl has a feeling for people's desires, weaknesses, and sentimentalities.

What other factors may have been relevant to Kohl's success as a political leader? The relationship between the leader and the electorate is only one aspect of leadership. Another crucial aspect of leadership is the leader's position within the political organization. Various sources maintain that Kohl was a master within that realm. His style of leadership within the party and his manner of obtaining and retaining loyalty were both crucial in the explanation for his longevity in office. Kohl built a network of loyal followers from within the party. Many of those were people whom he had helped to obtain positions of power.

Biographer Clemens (1994: 41–42) noted that "the number of top CDU officials who owed their careers at least in part to Kohl grew.... His network was impressive." Even while Kohl was being heavily attacked during the politics-and-money-scandal, he was still influential within his own party. At one point in the investigation, it became clear that a conservative member of the parliamentary inquiry committee investigating the scandal had secretly briefed Kohl about the progress of the investigation. Observers have asserted that he dominated the party through numerous close relationships at all levels. The term "Kohl system" was frequently used by the media to describe a situation where dissenters were marginalized, and innovation rarely occurred (Pflüger, 2000).

## ANALYZING SELF-PRESENTATION AND PERSONALITY PROFILING

This chapter has focused on Kohl's public self, that is, impressions left on observers, and his actual self as revealed in a sample of campaign scenes and statements. Self-presentation as the aspect of a leader's personality that is projected to the general public represents an important component of a leader's personality. How, then, does the analysis of self-presentation relate to the profiling of a leader's personality? The term "personality" usually refers to the characteristics of a person that account for consistent patterns of feeling, thinking, and behaving (Pervin & John, 1997).

With a view to analyzing personality at a distance, the behavioral aspects of the personality are most easily accessible. Still, there are a variety of different facets to a person's behavior. For example, people behave differently when they are alone, rather than in the company of others. Baumeister and Tice (1986) have distinguished four selves: (1) the public self (i.e., how one is known to others), (2) the private self (i.e., how one perceives oneself), (3) the actual self (i.e., how a person actually behaves), and (4) the ideal self (i.e., how one would like to be). The actual self may differ from the self-concept due to self-deception and may differ from the public self because of self-presentation and observer biases. All of these aspects are true inasmuch as they describe part of a person's personality, but they may still diverge.

The analysis of political leaders is limited by restricted access to information. In the current research, leaders were analyzed from the perspective of televised behavior during interviews and debates. Even with broader access to more direct and personal information, one can expect that divulged information will be edited according to self-presentation concerns. That is, most information will give the analyst access to the public self rather than either the private or actual self. The analysis of the actual self is possible only with an evaluation of the leader's behavior, insofar as it is observable.

Occasionally, unintended slips may provide interesting additional information; however, generally we must deduce characteristic features of the personality from what the leader says about himself or herself, and it is to be expected that these self-descriptive statements will be censored for self-presentational purposes. The application of self-presentational theory to the analysis of political leaders' behavior has proved to be productive. The analysis of self-presentation provides useful information on one important aspect of a leader's public personality. However, a fuller picture of a leader's personality requires that this type of micro-analysis be supplemented with biographical information and other methods designed to provide an enhanced context for the observed behavior.

## ACKNOWLEDGMENT

I would like to thank Tobias Schulze and Janine Hertel for their extensive literature searches on Helmut Kohl's biography.

Chapter 14

# The Comparative Psychoanalytic Study of Political Leaders: John McCain and the Limits of Trait Psychology

Stanley A. Renshon

## INTRODUCTION

Selecting good leaders is the linchpin of a successful democracy. Not surprisingly, then, citizens and scholars both have turned their attention to trying to understand what makes good leaders. What are the personal and professional standards by which one can reasonably evaluate candidates for high political office? Is every personal characteristic of a leader a matter of political concern, and, if not, which are, and why? Even if we agree that certain personal qualities do have important implications for how a leader approaches and carries out his or her responsibilities, the question remains: How are we to discern them without relying on candidates' views of themselves? After all, as the public has become more concerned with the personal qualities of its leaders, they, in turn, have become increasingly sophisticated in presenting themselves as they would prefer to be seen, rather than as they are.

These matters have ceased to be solely an American concern. The rise of globalization has resulted in a fundamental shift in the status of democracies. Simply put, there are more of them. Whether it is the former communist states of Eastern Europe, the former authoritarian states of Latin America or the Pacific Rim, or the still as yet unrealized aspirations for democracy in countries like China or regions like the Middle East, the trend is clear. Democracy is in the ascendancy.

Yet, America has exported not only the ideals of democracy but also its strategic tools (Scammel, 1997). Chief among these have been the image and the capacity to define and shape it. President Clinton's chief media advisors, James Carville and Paul Belgala, were Israeli prime minister Ehud Barak's advisors during his election campaign. American techniques have been adapted and used in no less an anti-American country than Iran (Schneider, 2000). Mexico's new president, Vincente Fox, whose campaign included focus groups, sophisticated polling strategies, and advisors like Dick Morris, was quoted as saying (in Moore, 1999), "We are going more and more the route of the US. Have charisma and look good on TV, and you can become president."

The globalization of American campaign techniques indicates, for citizens and scholars alike, the difficulties of breaching the image to gauge the leader. This dilemma surfaces repeatedly in the assessment of political leaders. It arose, for example, in the 2000 U.S. presidential campaign when a story broke about one of the main Republican contenders, John McCain. Senator McCain, it was said, had a temper and perhaps a very large one. Was it true? If so, why did it matter?

These kinds of questions have traditionally been approached in the psychological study of leaders via the theory of traits. In this chapter, building on work I've done on American presidents (Renshon, 1996a, 1996b), I argue against relying on trait theory to analyze political leaders in one country or cross-culturally. Instead, I propose a framework for the analysis of the psychology and performance of political leaders in democracies making use of comparative psychoanalytic theory.

The word "framework" is central to my purpose here. In using it, I want to make clear that I am not presenting a theory of leadership psychology and performance that can then be applied without effort elsewhere. On the contrary, the framework is just that, a set of categorical elements that require detailed observational data with which to give meaning to them and chart their associations.

In the sections that follow, I first ask: Why not trait theory? I then present the example of Senator John McCain's temper. It illustrates why answering the most central questions of political leadership assessment in a democracy, domestically or cross-culturally, cannot rely on trait theory. Rather, for a theory of leaders and performance to be useful, it must be conversant with the facts that place traits in a larger psychological perspective. I then present an alternative framework for the comparative psychological study of political leadership and assess its possible usefulness and limitations. I do so with a theoretical eye on the question of the framework's cross-cultural applicability. The examples draw on my work with American presidents and candidates, but my purpose is to ask whether and how the lessons learned there may be useful elsewhere. I begin with an examination of trait theory, the chief rival to the kind of framework proposed herein.

## CROSS-CULTURAL LEADERSHIP PSYCHOLOGY: WHY NOT TRAIT THEORY?

What is the best way to understand a leader's interior psychology? The most common approach is to focus on a trait or traits, which can be understood as related to the particular aspects of a leader's personality that are deemed important. A basic question with which to begin is: Which ones?

Not surprisingly, given different interests and approaches, the list of important traits varies. Winter (cf. 1994b) argues that the traits of achievement, power motivation, and affiliation are what is important to know about every leader. Steve Rubenzer et al. (2000) make use of the so-called big five measures of personality to rate presidents. Those five and their definitions are neuroticism (a sliding scale including impulsiveness and depression), extraversion (warmth, assertiveness), openness to experience (dreams, new ideas, or new values), agreeableness (modesty, honesty), and conscientiousness (order, self-discipline). Recently, Fred Greenstein (2000) has proposed his list of six characteristics important in the rating of presidents: (1) their proficiency as communicators, (2) their organizational capacity, (3) their political skill and (4) vision, (5) their cognitive style, and (6) their emotional intelligence, defined as the degree to which a president is able to "manage his emotions and turn them to constructive purposes."

Some proponents argue their trait lists are useful universally. Perhaps, but being able to assign numbers to characteristics does not in itself make them relevant or important. Power motivation, to take a trait from Winter's listing, is clearly important, but so, too, are a leader's ideals, commitments, and the level of fidelity to them, which are completely ignored. These are found nowhere in his list. In Greenstein's (2000) trait set there are no elements of motivation and no reference to the inner psychology that fuels every one of us. The same could be said for the so-called big-five theory.

There are also questions of measurement associated with most trait theories. Winter measures political speeches (e.g., inauguration and State of the Union addresses) as if they reflected a leader's innermost psychology and not primarily their political calculations. I have heard him begin professional talks with a plea to "stipulate the problems of measurement" involved in his studies and then go on to present his findings as if that were not relevant. This cannot do.

"Big-five" measurements are equally problematic. Why is extraversion defined in terms of assertiveness and warmth? The latter would seem to fit much more with a definition of "agreeableness," the fourth trait. Why are honesty and modesty the operational definitions of "agreeableness"? How are they related? Why not just measure "friendliness"? Finally, no clinician and no theory with which I am familiar define neurotic psychology in terms of impulsiveness and depression. Obsessive personalities, for example, are ordinarily squarely placed in the "neurotic" continuum of psychological functioning, but they are hardly impulsive. So, do both being impulsive and not being impulsive equally qualify for placement in this category? If so, it's not very useful.

Or consider Greenstein's (2000) list of traits, specifically, "emotional intelligence." He uses this term as an overall assessment for the many elements of a leader's inner psychology and how they work (or don't work) together. Yet, "emotional intelligence" as a term is simply not up to the task of providing adequate substantive understanding of the key elements that are subsumed under that term.

"Emotional intelligence" is, of course, Daniel Goldman's (1995) popular psychology term derived from education professor Howard Gardner's ideas on "multiple intelligences." Gardner (1983) started with seven such "intelligences"—music, math, language, social practice, naturalism, insight into others, and self-insight. While the idea is educationally and political appealing (everyone is a prodigy in some area), evidence for it is scant. Nor have matters been helped by the expansion of the list over time. Gardner (1999) now has added at least one and possibly three new "intelligences" (naturalist, spiritual, and existential). I'm reminded here of the early trait theorists who, in their enthusiasm for the idea, posited a separate one for each behavior. I have strong doubts that "emotional intelligence" is the best descriptive or theoretical tool by which to plumb the understanding and implications of a president's or any leader's psychology. Managing your emotions is certainly significant, but it is even more important to be clear about what emotions you are trying to manage.

Trait theories are not alone, of course, in having to deal with the ambiguities, trade-offs, and practical difficulties of measurement and inference. However, in the hands of its most enthusiastic practitioners they run the risk of overly confident self-certainty. Steve Rubenzer, the organizer of the big-five study of presidents noted above, is quoted (in Kaufman, 2000; emphasis added) as saying, "The mission for our project has been . . . bring a new perspective to questions where there has been a lot of debate, *but not a lot of objectivity or science* in the discussion."

He appears to believe that because his raters assigned numbers to the questionably valid or relevant categories that they were given, their study is "objective" and "scientific." Of course, the raters were not trained in psychology. Therefore, their placement of a president into psychological categories represents a large leap of untrained speculation. Moreover, the study's admonition to its raters to consider the characteristics of the presidents whom they rated only before they entered office is naive, to say the least. They hope that post hoc will prove to be emotionally neutral proper hoc, but it is a reflection on their understanding of how psychology operates that they could count on this to bolster objectivity. Quantification without theory is a form of numerology.

## CONSTRUCTING PSYCHOLOGICAL UNDERSTANDING: THE CASE OF SENATOR JOHN McCAIN'S TEMPER

One critical insight of psychoanalytic theory is that the elements of an individual's psychology are related to each other in patterned ways. A second, key insight is that these patterns develop over time. These two core insights represent the foundation of the framework that I advocate in this chapter. From this foundation, several specific questions emerge. What are the basic psychological elements that define this person? How are they connected with other elements of his or her psychology? What is their importance to what political leaders do? Lastly, how are these elements located in the person's developmental history? These questions take time and hard work to fully answer. Yet, often questions arise about the psychology of a political leader that cannot await decades of scholarship to resolve. One test of a framework in those circumstances is: Does it help us to gain some substantive traction on the issues of leadership psychology and their implications?

In this section I briefly examine the questions that arose around the temper of Senator John McCain, Republican candidate for the presidency. I do so not in the expectation that the analysis will provide a definitive profile of his psychology. Rather, I hope to demonstrate the ways in which trait theories falter and how a more broadly psychologically framed analysis can raise and help to resolve some important and time-pressing issues.

More specifically, once the fact that McCain had a temper was established, a number of very important questions remained on which trait theory provides little, if any, help. What is the nature of McCain's temper? Is it worse than that of others, even those who have led the country? How does his temper fit in, if it does, with other parts of his psychology? Finally, what are the implications of his temper should he be elected president?

John McCain had been a U.S. Senator from Arizona for 18 years and, before that, a congressman. He was well known for having been shot down over North Vietnam and survived five and a half harrowing years as a prisoner of war (POW), enduring three years of solitary confinement and periods of torture.

McCain's status as a war hero and straight-talking maverick in a campaign framed by the hunger for authenticity and passion among the voting public propelled his candidacy and his rising poll numbers. But a story in McCain's home state newspaper, the *Arizona Republic*, quoted the state's governor, Jane Dee Hull (a fellow Republican), as describing

McCain as someone prone to fly off the handle (Broder, 1999a, 1999b). Others who have had dealings with him in both Arizona and the Senate confirmed that he did, indeed, have a large temper and often could be publicly humiliating to those with whom he disagreed. For example, in his column George Will (1999) detailed several instances of McCain's temper outbursts that had been reported long before the issue arose in the presidential campaign. He quoted the *Atlantic Monthly* (December 1985): "Just after the July 4 recess, as freshman Joe Barton was walking down the center aisle of the House to cast a vote, he found himself in the middle of an angry cross fire of epithets between Democrat Marty Russo, of Illinois, and Republican John McCain, of Arizona. Seven-letter profanities escalated to twelve-letter ones and then to pushes and shoves before the two were separated."

Will then went on to quote other Republican senators who said that many of McCain's outbursts are not about matters of policy ("gross injustices") but rather about his personal pique. They spoke off the record with astonishing asperity about McCain, they expressed doubts—if not conviction—that his temper is evidence of a temperament unsuited to the presidency. The disqualifying flaw, they said, is a self-righteousness that makes McCain disdain the motives of those who differ with him.

At this point his temper became a campaign issue (Mitchell, 1999b). The testimonial evidence seemed to provide evidence that McCain did, indeed, have a temper and that it often took a publicly abusive form with colleagues. Yet, not everyone agreed that he had a temper worth worrying about. McCain himself provided his own explanation for his temper, saying that yes he had one; however, "I have gotten angry at people. And I will continue probably to get angry when I see an injustice done. I feel that, as I say, people who are not represented and people who are not well treated, particularly in the legislative process, deserve that kind of attention. And I'll continue to give it" (ABC transcript, 1999).

In other words, his anger is justifiable and in the service of a good cause. How would trait theory handle that assertion?

Complicating questions about McCain's temper was the subtext, his long and difficult POW experience. Some, including McCain himself, saw the temper issue as a character attack designed to raise questions about his emotional stability and suitability for the presidency. Chuck Hagel, Republican senator from Nebraska and supporter of McCain, is quoted as seeing the temper issue "as a not-so-subtle attempt to make a point that McCain's service to his country, five and a half years in a prisoner of war camp, means he is not stable enough to be President of the United States" (quoted in Mitchell, 1999a).

Do McCain's angry outbursts stem from his years as a prisoner of war? Is it righteous anger in the service of his constituents, or something else? How would trait theory help us to resolve these questions? It can't, really. In reality, neither explanation proved a good fit with the evidence. The angry outbursts that many described were only indirectly, if at all, related to constituents left out of the process or not being well treated and appear to have more to do either with McCain being frustrated in his own policy wishes or, alternatively, some other, more personal reason.

Moreover, there is strong evidence that his temper predates his POW experience. In his autobiography, McCain (1999) refers to his "outsized temper" as an infant and says that "when I got angry, I held my breathe until I blacked out." He further recalls that a doctor told his parents to drop him into a bathtub of cold water when he had these outbursts. Obviously, if McCain had this level of "temper" as an infant, his POW experience could hardly be the primary cause of it.

What this biographical revelation does suggest are a temperament that is vulnerable to noxious stimuli and a difficulty in either calming himself or allowing others to do so. On the other hand, although McCain sometimes provoked his North Vietnamese captors, he was clearly able to control the enormous emotional stresses associated with his circumstances. So, it is also possible that the POW experience left McCain feeling that he no longer had to contain himself, having earned the right not to do so during his years of captivity. Does trait theory help to resolve these issues? No, it would not even undertake the analysis necessary to raise them.

Interestingly, to combat "rumors" of his psychological suitability growing out of his POW experience, McCain released over 1,500 pages of his medical records, including post-POW psychological evaluations. These records were generally consistent with the view of his having come through his ordeal in fairly good emotional shape. A statement released by the director of the Center for Prisoner of War Studies, which evaluated McCain, said, in part, "Senator McCain had never been diagnosed with or treated for a psychological or psychiatric disorder.... He has been subject to an extensive battery of psychological tests and following his last examination in 1993, we judged him to be in good physical and mental health." Less prognostically valid, given the evidence of his post-POW political career, they wrote, "Mr. McCain also learned how to control his temper and not become angry over insignificant things" (Altman, 1999).

Of course, being judged in "good mental health" is not the same as understanding the elements that constitute a person's psychology, which is precisely the set of questions at the heart of "character issues." The report did provide some important clues for the analyst seeking to assemble a portrait of McCain's psychology. It details McCain's "preoccupation" with getting out from under the shadow of his father (a highly successful admiral and commander of U.S. forces during the Vietnam

War), which he felt his experiences as a POW finally allowed him to do. It also details his increasing rebelliousness, doing poorly academically and behaviorally at the Naval Academy, a "rebel without a cause," as McCain described it. Both are consistent with McCain's descriptions of himself and observations of him by others.

The picture that emerges is of a person with above average intelligence whose ambition is both framed and shaped by a famous and highly successful father who was at sea and away from home for long periods of time. Expected to follow in his father's (and grandfather's) footsteps of going to the Naval Academy, he did, but rebelliously. There, he accumulated many demerits, but not enough to be expelled. He also did poorly academically, but not poorly enough to be asked to leave. Generally, he led a somewhat wild and undisciplined life (given his surroundings) of parties and attractive women, by which he made clear that he was the anti-McCain McCain, a rebel and maverick.

Not surprisingly, these are two terms that McCain uses to describe himself and his chosen style of political leadership. Others agree. A not atypical profile of McCain says that he has clearly "established himself as a maverick messenger." That same profile notes that McCain's favorite television program is *Maverick*, starring the antihero character played by James Garner (Rogers, 2000). In an interview, McCain was asked who, besides veterans and students, he plans to recruit to his cause, and he answered, half smiling, "Oh, iconoclasts, mavericks, cranks, all of those are part of the coalition we're building here" (quoted in Goldberg, 1999).

Interestingly, the psychological reports that McCain released did corroborate some of these formulations by characterizing him as a "histrionic personality." Although that personality syndrome does appear in the *Diagnostic and Statistical Manual of Mental Disorders* (DSM-IV), of the American Psychiatric Association (1994), its more immediate interest here is what it describes. According to the DSM-IV, a histrionic personality is one that desires and usually calls attention to oneself by excessive or otherwise unusual actions. The purpose is to gain center stage and call attention to oneself. Clearly, McCain's chosen political role as rebel and maverick is consistent with a psychology that likes to call attention to himself as different and therefore worthy of notice. A large temper, rarely contained, is also consistent with someone whose interpersonal style is to stand apart from others and often against them when his views are not the preferred and accepted option. Would the "big-five" trait theory be able to develop these kinds of relationships? No.

Finally, there is the inconsistency between McCain's maverick and truth-telling status and what a critic might call an all-too-ordinary political career. McCain was implicated, along with four other senators, in an influence-peddling attempt (the Keating Five scandal), which resulted in a probe and reprimand by the Senate Ethics Committee. As chairman of the powerful Senate Commerce Committee, McCain was given large campaign contributions by a number of large companies interested in securing his approval of their plans, a fact acknowledged by him.

When McCain appeared with Democratic presidential hopeful Senator Bradley to discuss campaign finance reform, he said, "I believe I probably have been influenced because the big donor buys access to my office and we know that access is influence" (quoted in Kuntz, 1999). Shortly thereafter, letters emerged that McCain had written on behalf of large campaign contributors to the Federal Communications Commission (FCC) in an attempt to help his contributors (Labaton, 2000a, 2000b). So, the analysts must certainly entertain the hypothesis that the strength of McCain's commitment to his maverick stance, defined primarily in this campaign as a man of honor who is beyond influence peddling, is possibly related to the blemish on his record for having admitted that he wasn't.

These formulation are, of course, very preliminary. They do, however, demonstrate the ways in which different pieces of evidence can be used to assemble a tentative picture of how particular psychological elements are linked to each other and form part of a package. What they do not answer, however, is the question: So what?

Certainly, chronic temper outbursts toward those with whom one works lead to a decreased ability to work well with them. On the other hand, anger can be an effective tool for chief executives if Neustadt (1960) is correct about others' always gauging the seriousness of the president's commitments and the consequences for opposing him.

Certainly, discussions of McCain's temper have not harmed him with voters. Some have taken the position by one New Hampshire voter: "I'd rather have a commander-in-chief that loses his temper, than a wuss" (quoted in Rogers, 2000). A Republican consultant not affiliated with either the Bush or McCain campaigns said, "Most Americans do not expect their presidents to be Casper Milquetoasts. They also don't want him flying off the handle at inappropriate times. And whether or not this matters depends on the example that Senator McCain offers to the American people" (quoted in Mitchell, 1999b).

Expectations that McCain would get testy when confronted with his own not wholly consistent attempts to champion campaign finance reform while writing letters on behalf of large contributors did not materialize, although several commentators did notice the somewhat inappropriate smile that seemed frozen in place when he was asked about these issues (James, 1999; Mitchell, 2000). Still, a highly volatile temperament, even if held in check publicly, would be inconsistent with arriving at solid judgments on matters large and small and might well have an adverse impact on a president's ability to form the coalitions necessary to pass legislation or gather public support.

This showed up several times during the course of the primary campaign. At one point McCain ran an angry ad against George W. Bush accusing him of "twisting the truth like Clinton." Many found the ad hard-hitting but inflated, harsh, and rhetorically overheated (Marks, 2000). William Bennett (quoted in Bruni, 2000), who advised both candidates, said that the ad crossed the line between "fair play and unwarranted warfare." Republicans anxious to gain the White House could be excused for worrying that one of their candidates was neutralizing a very powerful issue for the fall campaign. Shortly after the negative response to these ads, McCain promised, again, to conduct a positive campaign.

In retrospect, that ad also revealed something about John McCain's psychology that destroyed his campaign. Questions had already been raised about his temper and temperament. That ad revealed a person who would lash out, in a very personal and overcharged way, against someone who he thought had wronged him. He had already done so, but the incident was not widely reported or discussed.

In December 1999 McCain's campaign finance reform was attacked by a group, Americans for Tax Reform (ATR). According to the report (Neal, 1999),

The McCain campaign struck back in highly personal terms with a blistering attack on ATR and its president, Grover Norquist, calling him "one of Washington's most notorious special interest group leaders" whose only concern was that "the soft money spigot flowing into his group's coffers" would be cut off. But McCain, who is leading Texas Gov. George W. Bush in New Hampshire polls, didn't stop there. He attacked Norquist's character, saying he had lobbied in the past for the "Marxist" president of the Republic of the Seychelles and "against a government crackdown on Internet porn."

So, when he lashed out again, for a third time, against the "evil" influence of Jerry Falwell and Pat Robertson with highly personal, overheated charges, the transition from hero to hothead was consolidated (Von Drehle, 2000).

## TRAIT THEORY REVISITED: WHERE IT FALTERS

The discussion of Senator McCain's temper brings into sharper focus some drawbacks to trait theories of political leadership. If trait theories cannot adequately address these issues within one culture, it is difficult to see how they would do so cross-culturally. There are at least seven areas where trait theory does not help to improve the quality of our understanding of political leadership.

## What Is the Trait? The Problem of Description

This seems like the most basic question and one that, in McCain's case, is easily answered. Yes, McCain shows his displeasure, but is it anger, rage, annoyance, exasperation, irritation, indignation, resentment, hatred, or some combination? These terms are not synonymous. Anger differs from rage, and resentment differs from indignation. Each of these terms reflects different aspects of a person's psychology and stands in different relationships to other aspects of the psychology of the person who exhibits them. So, we can say that McCain has a temper, but our work is not finished by saying so.

## What Is the Trait? The Problem of Cause

Specifying what we mean by "temper" involves some consideration of its psychological nature. In distinguishing, say, rage from exasperation, we are distinguishing not only one trait from another but one psychological constellation from another as well.

Some observers speculated that McCain's expression of displeasure came from a streak of self-righteousness. McCain said that it came from legitimate anger at others' mistreatment. It could as well have derived from a tendency to impatience or inflated self-confidence or importance or as a bolstering device for a lack of self-confidence (why can't they see what's so obvious to me?). Without attempting to sort through these different possibilities and see the extent to which other evidence is or is not consistent with a formulation, we are left with a characterization disconnected from substantive, validated meaning.

## The Relationships of Traits to Other Aspects of Character and Interior Psychology

The relationship of a trait to other aspects of a leader's psychology is related to but separable from the problem of cause noted above. There the question was: What, exactly, is this trait's meaning, given the different ways that it can be understood? Here the question is: Having gained some understanding of the nature of the trait, how is it connected to other important aspects of the leader's psychology?

An emphasis on the importance of a single trait is a form of reductionism—trying to explain too much with too little. An isolated trait, though important, can't tell us much. McCain's temper seemed related to his self-image as a "maverick" and a heroic "truth-teller." Some evidence emerged of an "attention-seeking" element in his psychology. How these elements are connected to each other in a larger psychological package is ordinarily far removed from the interests or theoretical means of trait theory.

It is important to know not only *if* psychological characteristics are related to each other, but *why*. Trait studies can tell us something about the first, but not much about the second. When Winter (1994b: 126) profiled the 1992 presidential candidates on their affiliation, power, and achievement scores, he found that President Clinton scored high on achievement, above average on affiliation, and moderate, increasing to high, on power motivation. Leaving aside questions of measurement and validity (Clinton has been characterized by many as having a high need for affiliation), one does not know and cannot tell why these three traits come together like this for Clinton and why they have a very different configuration for Ross Perot and Bush.[1]

### The Relevance of Circumstances

Trait-based explanations assume that the affect of a trait is equally important across situations. Yet, McCain appeared to express his temper when he wasn't getting his way or was frustrated that other people didn't see things as he did. So his temper was circumstantial. However, the nature of the circumstances gives a strong clue to the nature of his temper and the way it is connected with other parts of his psychology.

Ordinarily, trait theory, which assumes that traits, in order to be traits, must be consistent across circumstances, misses an important theoretical and practical point. Circumstances themselves can be useful theoretical clues in understanding a leader's psychology. The difference between episodic and chronic displays of temper certainly matters. So would the fact that a leader with a temper, like Dwight Eisenhower, learned to curb it.

### What's Important?

John McCain had a temper. So have many presidents. Eisenhower's temper did not appear to adversely affect his performance either as Supreme Allied Commander in World War II or as president. Bill Clinton's problems in his presidency seemed to have nothing to do with his temper and a lot more to do with the relationship between his ambition and his values.

Trait-based explanations are not helpful in choosing among characteristics, except in obvious cases. Of course, it is better to have a temperamentally balanced leader in power than one who isn't. But what if the leader has a temper and a vision, or no temper but poor political skills? What traits are more important? Why? Answering such questions requires a theory of leadership performance, not traits.

### The Relationship of Traits to Political Performance

Sometimes it's easy to see the connection between the trait and desirable political skills. A highly volatile temperament, even if held in check publicly, would be inconsistent with arriving at solid judgments on matters large and small. It might, as well, have an adverse impact on a leader's ability to form the coalitions necessary to pass legislation or gather public support. On the other hand, a leader who gets angry and remembers why is someone you might cross only after thinking about it.

McCain was not the only candidate or leader to have a temper. George Washington, Andrew Jackson, Ulysses S. Grant, Theodore Roosevelt, Warren G. Harding, Harry Truman, Dwight D. Eisenhower, Lyndon B. Johnson, and William Clinton all had a tempter (Vinciguerra, 1999; Greenstein, 1982; Renshon, 1996a). Some of these men are considered great leaders; others, above average; and others, not that good. Clearly, temper by itself has to be considered in relationship to other characteristics. But which ones? Trait theory does not tell us.

### Where's the Theory?

Trait-based evaluations fail to build a more comprehensive and theoretical view of psychological functioning and leadership performance. There are things that are important for a leader to be; there are others for which he need only be capable. Trait-based evaluations fail to distinguish these or to make clear the circumstances in which a trait might be crucial or merely preferred. Trait-based evaluations are not necessarily wrong, just ad hoc.

### CROSS-CULTURAL LEADERSHIP PSYCHOLOGY: A PROPOSAL

Four basic questions can be raised regarding any leader's psychology. First, what are the most basic elements that most accurately characterize a leader's psychology? Second, how are those elements related to each other? Third, how did this psychology develop? Fourth, how is this psychology manifested in performance?

So, if not traits, which theory provides the best chance to answer the four basic questions of any leader's psychology? In my view, the answer is comparative psychoanalytic theory. I use the adjective "comparative" to describe the psychoanalytic theory that I recommend for a simple reason. Psychoanalytic theory no longer means only Freudian psychology.

To be sure, the basic elements of the topographical and structure models that Freud outlined remain relevant to varying degrees to most, if not all, psychoanalytically framed theories. But to equate psychoanalytic theory solely with the work of Freud at this time would be analogous to equating classical music solely with Mozart. A serious and trained student of psychoanalytic theories would have to be conversant with the developments of ego psychology, object relations theories, interpersonal and relational theories, and the various forms of self psychology. It is the only theory of psychological functioning that focuses on broad patterns of motivation and the more specific patterns of personality and behavior that develop from it.

One advantage of such a theory would be that it provides a theoretical link by which any particular personality trait might be more firmly anchored in a deeper understanding of its role in the person's overall psychology. In doing so, it might also provide some insight into the ways in which particular traits, viewed in the context of a person's overall psychology, affect or might be more usefully viewed in relationship to responsibilities of office. A strong intelligence embedded in, and shaped by, a strong motivation to do "what's right" will differ from one embedded in a motivation structure dominated by self-interest.

The theoretical framework that I developed (Renshon, 1996a, 1996b) for the analysis of presidential candidates and other leaders was guided by several considerations. Among these were (1) to put forward a theory of character psychology that focused on its nature and specific content, rather than argue its importance primarily on its dynamic functioning, (2) to develop a theory whose use did not require information normally available, if at all, only in a psychotherapeutic setting, and (3) to develop a framework in which the theory of character and psychological functioning could be directly and plausibly linked with the analysis of presidential performance.

### The Character-Performance Framework

The framework developed in Renshon (1996a) and applied to President Clinton (Renshon, 1996b) and later to Republican presidential candidate Robert Dole (Renshon, 1998) drew on a theory of character with three major elements: ambition, integrity, and relatedness.[2] The three basic elements of the psychological part of the framework—ambition, fidelity to values tempered by humility, and interpersonal relations—are not new discoveries on my part. They have a long and deep theoretical tradition in psychoanalytic theory. My more modest contribution was to recognize these elements as essential building blocks of character and to chart the ways in which they can be connected to each other and to leadership performance.

Ambition, fidelity to values, and how people relate to others are all domains of human experience that are accessible and understandable, in large part, because they define core elements of most persons' daily lives. We must all figure out what we want to do in life (our ambitions) and refine the skills that will help us realize these ambitions if we are to be successful.

Every person must develop principles for navigating life's inevitable, but often unclear or difficult, choices. Some aspire to the high ideals but fail to put them into practice. Others are guided primarily by self-interest but present their choices as if they weren't. A smaller number struggle to maintain fidelity to their ideals even when it is difficult to do so.

Finally, every person exists and lives in a sea of others. Others are our friends and our enemies, our allies and our competitors, and our most trusted and intimate relations, thus becoming a profound source of fulfillment or regret. We may move toward, away, or against others or stand apart from others, but we cannot avoid them. Whether internalized within our psychologies because of experience or as a consequence of ongoing relationships, they are as central to our emotional lives as oxygen is to our physical life.

Aren't these three elements and their placement together in a framework of character in reality a theory? Yes, to some degree, of course. Anytime you take elements and place them together in a rubric, you have engaged in some theoretical work. What, then, is the difference between an analysis that purports to provide a theory of the psychology of leaders and one with the more modest objective of providing a framework? Just this: a theory presents a specific set of relationships that it argues are true. A framework presents a set of important elements whose actual content and relationships are the matters to be determined. The analysis presented herein therefore combines deductive and inductive strategies.

The framework presented herein is derived from psychoanalytic theory, but it does not require of people using it that they train and buy a couch. The terms that provide the structural scaffolding for the framework are relatively straightforward and purposely meant to be so. The evidence that allows us to gauge the specific ways in which these categories have developed for specific leaders is, as it must be, a matter of public record. So, although the framework can be described as psychoanalytic, its use does not depend on one's being a psychoanalyst or on any special insight into unconscious motivation. On the contrary, the framework specifically and purposefully avoids any such speculations for the very good reason that they are often wrong and, worse, unnecessary.[3]

Filling in the framework for the analysis of a leader's psychology is only one part of the theoretical and data-gathering work that it is necessary to do. The other consists of specifying a framework for the analysis of leadership performance. Elsewhere, I have proposed two fundamental dimensions of the tasks of those who govern democracies-leadership and decision making, with the quality of judgment that a leader brings to his or her tasks, rather than procedure, being the focus of the latter. Here, too, theory enters into the selection of these two as primary. Yet, here again, having used theory to tell us what the important categories are, it is still necessary to gather and evaluate the concrete data which allows us to assess the effectiveness of a specific leader's performance.

It may be possible to eventually develop character "types" from this framework, but that is not its purpose or the use made of it. Rather, using the framework requires determining in each particular case just how the character elements are related, individually and in combination, to the essential elements of a leader's performance.

This approach has its advantages and its limitations. Among the former I would count that it makes fewer a priori assumptions and demands on the researcher to reach closure. One problem with Barber's (1992) typology, as George (1974) pointed out, is that one is forced to choose *a* category in spite of the fact that some presidents (e.g., Eisenhower) appeared to span them. With this framework, each element requires the reality of data to give it meaning, and any particular package of elements represented by an individual's psychology is a matter that emerges from the data, not from placement in a category.

The framework also does not make or require a priori assumptions about the way(s), if any, that each or several of the character elements are related to the twin pillars, as I view them, of presidential performance—judgment in decision making and political leadership. The framework, then, is just that—it requires data to transform each element category from a theoretical container to an empirically based description. It requires as well a capacity to appreciate and understand the implications of different individual characteristics, in relation both to the other character elements and then to the elements of presidential performance.

Like every other such effort, this one, too, has several drawbacks. All psychoanalysts accept the existence of unconscious motivation, the importance of early experience as a foundation of an individual's psychology, and the view that individuals develop stable and understandable patterns of adult functioning that reflect how they have been able to integrate their experiences, skills, and circumstances. Yet, there is not a single psychoanalytic theory. Some focus on the primacy of childhood; others stress adulthood. Some focus on the internalization of object representations; others stress the importance of interpersonal relations. Some still view motivation through the prism of instinctual drives; others view it through the lens of what it takes to develop and maintain a coherent, vital sense of self. Greenstein's (1969) well-taken point is as relevant for different kinds of psychoanalytic theory as it is more generally for theories of psychological functioning.

To issues with the theory within its own discipline, one must add those issues that have arisen from its use in political analysis. Some have borrowed the concepts without due concern for their larger theoretical foundation. Some have applied its theoretical elements in a manner that borders on caricature. In these efforts, the child not only is father to the man but is viewed, in fact, as the man. Others have written as if a president's performance could be reduced to his or his interior psychology. Few have measured up to the theoretically sophisticated and contextually sensitive analysis by the Georges (1956) of the impact of Woodrow Wilson's formative childhood and adult experiences on his substantial political accomplishments and his equally striking defeats.

### Applying the Framework: For Whom?

The theory underlying the framework of analysis developed in Renshon's (1996b) work focused on the selection of American presidents. Yet, it was not intended to be a theory of "presidential character." So, the question arises: is it applicable elsewhere?

Let us begin with the three character elements—ambition, integrity, and relatedness. Are these elements useful (if they are) only in thinking about presidents? Are they useful in understanding other political roles? Would we want to know something about the ambitions and skills that do or don't accompany them, in thinking about House members, senators, or prime ministers? What of newly elected president Olusegun Obasanjo of Nigeria; would we be interested in his ideals, values, and capacity to have fidelity to them? Would this be of some interest to us were we to study movement leaders or political activists? Finally, what of a person's stance toward interpersonal relations? Would it be useful to examine whether a leader in Chile felt it important to move toward, against, away, or apart from others? At least preliminarily, the answers to these questions would appear to be yes.

In some respects, that answer is not surprising. Those elements were developed in the hope that they would be a useful way to understand *anyone's* basic interior psychology. Therefore, if the hoped-for promise of these elements proves itself, there is no reason that they should not shed light on a wide range of political roles. Just how much light each or any shed is, of course, a matter to be determined by their actual application. Since the framework leaves the specific impact an open question to be resolved by the process of application, it cannot be asserted a priori.

Consider the importance of ambition in presidential candidates. I (Renshon, 1996b) argued that the nature of the modern presidency and the motivation needed to obtain it made high ambition more of a given than a variable. Even Ronald Reagan, whose somewhat passive executive style in the presidency has been much commented on, spent many years and much time reaching for that office.

The uniformly high ambition of modern presidential candidates results in focusing more attention on the other two character elements as possible sources of useful distinctions. Certainly, the specific ideals and values of candidates would seem to be a more variable and therefore more useful tool for drawing useful distinctions. The capacity for, and realization of, fidelity to their ideals and values would certainly seem to be an important and distinguishing character element.

Of course, the fact that modern presidential candidates are mostly highly ambitious still leaves open the questions of what these skills are and whether they support or impede a person's ambition. It is possible that one's skills support the level of one's ambitions, are greater than one's ambitions, or don't measure up to one's ambitions. Also, the assumption of high ambition in the presidency leaves open the issue of the relationship between skills and ambition, on one hand, and *political* performance, on the other.

This brings us to a second important point about the framework. The relationship of its two major elements, character and performance, is contingent. Character is a constant. That is, the theory begins with the view that ambition, character integrity, and relatedness are a central part of anyone's interior psychology, regardless of the political roles being analyzed. Yet, the reverse is not true.

Different roles call on character psychology differentially. One of Bill Clinton's ambition-supporting skills was his verbal facility, certainly important for a political career and particularly important to the leadership performance dimension of the modern presidency. Bob Dole, on the other hand, had a number of skills to support his ambition, but articulateness was not among them (Renshon, 1998). In a governing context in which "going public" is one key tool of presidential leadership, inarticulateness is a terminal disability. Yet, public articulateness as an ambition-supporting skill was clearly less important in Dole's role as Senate minority/majority leader than it was for his attempt to gain the presidency.

The framework begins with the view that essential performance characteristics of different political roles will be a variable. I characterized the two chief dimensions of presidential performance as judgment and leadership. Are these two equally important for judges and members of Congress or Parliament? That remains to be seen. One might argue that "leadership" or judgment is important in both these public roles and perhaps others as well. However, judicial, congressional, or parliamentary "leadership" would seem to be different from each other, and both differ from leadership in the presidency. Leadership within the Court may differ as well. Leadership in the Supreme Court is related, in part to influencing one or a few other justices or being looked to for the depth of vision and articulation of your opinions. Appellate court judges rely more on the latter. Just as each character element requires understanding in the context of a specific individual, each element of performance to which it is tied requires the same.

What is the particular relationship between the three character elements and non-presidential political roles? How do issues of relatedness play out in judicial, congressional, or parliamentary roles? Is a character style that entails moving toward others rather than, say, standing apart from them more consistent with good performance in each role? Such questions can be answered only by gathering and evaluating data.

Is this framework truly useful cross-culturally? Would the three elements of character help us to understand political roles in, say, India or Brazil? What of their relationship to leadership performance? Both sets of elements, their nature and their measurement, are deeply embedded in the cultures within which they operate.

Many theories of psychology have run into cross-cultural questions. Is the Oedipus complex universal? Are Erik Erikson's "eight stages of man" too closely tied to a particular historical period and "too Western" as well? Can Trobriand Islanders be motivated by a need for "self-actualization"?

The three elements put forward here might well fall victim to the same questions. Ambition, fidelity to one's ideals and values, and relatedness might prove culturally or historically insular as well. There is the risk that we might analyze others by standards that have little or different meaning to them. Obviously, it's necessary to ascertain whether the categories have meaning in the cultural context in which they will be applied. However, this won't resolve all the questions that must be addressed. Sensitivity to the interplay between culture and interior psychology leads to the issue of the data and evaluation that would allow us to place individuals within these three characterological frames.

The problem can be illustrated with a question: How does one gauge the degree of ambition in Japan? In that culture the direct expression of self-interest and striving to stand out at the expense of others are taboo. How, then, would one assess the relationship between ambition and political performance there? What does political leadership mean in such a cultural context? These and related questions will have to be addressed and resolved before the framework can be usefully applied outside of the content for which it was developed.

## CONCLUSION

The psychological analysis of leaders is likely to persist, in spite of all of its controversies and difficulties, for two very fundamental and critical reasons. First, the underlying psychology that motivates how leaders see and try to shape the world is related to their exercise of the power that they are given. If we want to understand what they do, we had better have useful theories of why they do it (Renshon, 2000). Second, variations in the psychology that leaders bring to their positions affect what they will, won't, or can't do. There is an enormous practical set of implications to leaders' level of ambition and the skills (or lack thereof) that accompany them, their ideals and values, their capacity to have fidelity to them and how they truly feel, beneath the public displays, about the many kinds of relationships with which they must contend.

It is hard to imagine that any theoretical stance that does not require of its practitioner that he or she be immersed in the details of a leader's ongoing life will bring the level of confidence in one's theoretical understanding or validity required by this critical task. Many years ago Lasswell (1930: 1) observed, that "political science without biography is a form of taxidermy."

Since he wrote those words, developments in psychoanalytic theory and its increasingly sophisticated application in a variety of settings have brought us to the point where we might well add to Lasswell's observation: analyzing leadership performance without the tools of modern psychoanalytic theory is like assessing the performance of a Grand Prix race car designed without wheels. It can be done, but it is unlikely to result in much theoretical or substantive mileage.

## NOTES

1. Beyond the question of how traits are connected to each other lie problems with the assumption of equivalence. The assumption of equivalence is found in the logic of inquiry that underlies trait analysis, especially comparative trait analysis. Basically, it assumes that a high power motivation score for, say, Richard Nixon is the same as a high power score for Bill Clinton. I would not agree that Clinton has a high need for power in the conventional understanding of that term in political psychology research (Lasswell, 1948). But even if the two had similar power motivation scores, the nature of that "need," its connection with other interior psychological elements, and therefore its implications for presidential performance would differ dramatically and therefore consequentially. Or consider the trait of achievement motivation. By Winter's measure (1994b: 126), Clinton scores high on this need, and in this case I believe that the score accurately reflects the psychology. However, what exactly does it mean that Clinton, or any president, scores high on achievement motivation? One problem here is that given the length and intensive nature of seeking the office, any person who campaigns and gains the presidency has already demonstrated substantial personal and political ambition. What, then, does a high (or low) score on achievement motivation mean in this context? It makes some sense to distinguish personal political ambition from policy ambition, although in many presidents they become intertwined. For Clinton, high achievement motivation is not, I ar-

gue, easily satisfied with modest or even with what would be for many substantial achievement. Rather, what Clinton has in mind when he considers his own ambitions is something on a much larger scale.

2. Some will recognize that these formulations follow the imprint of later developments in psychoanalytic theory, self-psychology, object relations theory, and ego psychology.

3. Recently, one well-known analyst and his collaborator (Lifton & Mitchell, 1996) "explained" the unconscious conflicts that led President Truman to drop two atomic bombs on Japan. Another (Volkan et al., 1997) thought it possible to make us privy to the unconscious thoughts that Richard Nixon's mother had early in her marriage about her son.

# References

ABC Transcript. (1999). *Good Morning America: Interview with John McCain.* November 3.

Abelson, R. P., Kinder, D. R., Peters, M. P., & Fiske, S. T. (1982). Affective and semantic components in political person perception. *Journal of Personality and Social Psychology, 42,* 619–30.

Admon, T. (1987). Mehakim lebibi [Waiting for Bibi]. *Ma'ariv,* April 24, 22–24.

Adorno, T., Frenkel-Brunswik, E., Leninson, D., & Safrod, R. N. (1950). *The authoritarian personality.* New York: Harper.

Altman, L. K. (1999). Release of McCain's medical records provides unusually broad psychological profile. *New York Times,* December 6, A26.

Aluf, B. (1996). David Agmon yetaem bein ozry rosh hamemshala [David Agmon will coordinate Prime Minister's assistants]. *Ha'aretz,* October 10, 6.

American Psychiatric Association. (1994). *Diagnostic and statistical manual of mental disorders* (4th ed.). Washington, DC: Author.

Andeweg, R. B. (1993). A model of the cabinet system: The dimension of cabinet decision-making processes. In J. Blondel & F. Müller-Rommel (Eds.), *Governing together* (pp. 23–42). New York: St. Martin's Press.

Arens, M. (1995). *Broken covenant: American foreign policy and the crisis between the US and Israel.* New York: Simon & Schuster.

Argaman, Y. (1987). Netanyahu veshodedey hateva ha'avuda [Netanyahu and the raiders of the lost ark]. *Bamahane,* October 13, 46–48.

Arkin, R. M. (1981). Self-presentational styles. In J. T. Tedeschi (Ed.), *Impression management theory and social psychological research* (pp. 311–35). New York: Academic Press.

Aronoff, M. J. (1989). *Israeli visions and divisions: Cultural change and political conflict.* New Brunswick, NJ: Transaction Publishers.

Aronoff, M. J., & Aronoff, Y. S. (Summer/Fall 1996). Explaining domestic influences on current Israel foreign policy: The peace negotiations. *The Brown Journal of World Affairs*, 3, 83–101.

Aronoff, M. J., & Aronoff, Y. S. (1998). Domestic determinants of Israeli foreign policy: The peace process from the declaration of principles to the Oslo II interim agreement. In R. O. Freedman (Ed.), *The Middle East and the peace process: The impact of the Oslo Accords* (pp. 11–34). Gainesville: University Press of Florida.

Ashri, E. (1996). Hu ligleg al kol haarahim shel aavat moledet [He scorns every value of love of country]. *Ha'aretz*, May 29, 2.

Associated Press. (1999). *Siberian governor uses police to keep out fired TV, radio executives*. January 23.

Atkinson, J. W. (1982). Motivational determinants of thematic apperception. In A. J. Stewart (Ed.), *Motivation and Society* (pp. 3–40). San Francisco: Jossey-Bass.

Atlas, J. (1990). Understanding the correlation between childhood punishment and adult hypnotizability as it impacts on the command power of modern "charismatic" political leaders. *Journal of Psychohistory*, 17, 309–18.

*Auckland Star*. (1982). November 23.

Auerbach, Y. (1995). Yitzhak Rabin: Portrait of a leader. In D. J. Elazar & S. Sandler (Eds.), *Israel at the Polls 1992* (pp. 283–320). Lanham, MD: Rowman & Littlefield.

Baker, J. A. (1995). *The politics of diplomacy*. New York: G. P. Putnam's Sons.

Baker-Brown, G., Ballard, E. J., Bluck, S., de Vries, B., Suedfeld, P., & Tetlock, P. E. (1992). The conceptual/integrative complexity scoring manual. In C. P. Smith (Ed.), *Motivation and personality: Handbook of thematic content analysis* (pp. 401–18). New York: Cambridge University Press.

Ballard, E. J. (1983). Canadian prime ministers: Complexity in political crises. *Canadian Psychology*, 24, 125–29.

Ballard, E. J., & Suedfeld, P. (1988). Performance ratings of Canadian prime ministers: Individual and situational factors. *Political Psychology*, 9, 291–302.

Barber, D. (1987). *Gliding on the lino: The wit of David Lange*. Auckland: Benton Ross.

Barber, J. (1991). *The prime minister since 1945*. Oxford: Blackwell.

Barber, J. D. (1980). *The pulse of politics: Electing presidents in the media age*. New York: W. W. Norton.

Barber, J. D. (1988). *Politics by humans*. Durham, NC: Duke University Press.

Barber, J. D. (1992). *The presidential character: Predicting performance in the White House* (4th ed.). Englewood Cliffs, NJ: Prentice-Hall.

Barnea, N. (1997). America aheret [A different America]. *Yediot Aharonot*, November 28, 2.

Bashan, T. (1995). Kah nizal Bibi Netanyahu [How Bibi Netanyahu was rescued]. *Ma'ariv*, May 19, 4–5, 7, 10.

Bass, B. M. (1981). *Stogdill's handbook of leadership: A survey of theory and research*. Englewood Cliffs, NJ: Prentice-Hall.

Baumeister, R. F. (1982). A self-presentational view of social phenomena. *Psychological Bulletin*, 91, 3–26.

Baumeister, R. F., & Tice, D. M. (1986). Four selves, two motives and a substitute process self-regulation model. In R. Baumeister (Ed.), *Public self and private self* (pp. 63–75). New York: Springer.

Benziman, U. (1993). Haolam alpi bibi [The world according to Bibi]. *Ha'aretz*, June 30, 4.

Benziman, U. (1996). Mi haish [Who is the man]. *Ha'aretz*, June 7, B3.

Benziman, U. (1997a). Bedikat rekamot [Tissue examination]. *Ha'aretz*, November 28, B3.

Benziman, U. (1997b). Tohelet zemano shel hasheker [The life expectancy of a lie]. *Ha'aretz*, November 21, B3.

Benziman, U. (1997c). Haim Netanyahu yepol? [Will Netanyahu fall?]. *Ha'aretz*, November 14, B3.

Benziman, U. (1997d). Lohama psihologit [Psychological warfare]. *Ha'aretz*, October 17, B3.

Benziman, U. (1997e). Lo rhoe [See not]. *Ha'aretz*, March 7, 3.

Binion, R. (1993). *Love beyond death: The anatomy of a myth in the arts*. New York: New York University Press.

Binion, R. (2000). Psychohistory's false start. *Clio's Psyche*, 6, 133, 138–39.

Blondel, J. (1980). *World leaders*. London: Sage.

Blondel, J. (1987). *Political leadership*. London: Sage.

Blondel, J., & Müller-Rommel, F. (1993). *Governing together*. New York: St. Martin's Press.

Bollas, C. (1992). *Being a character: Psychoanalysis and self experience*. New York: Farrar, Straus, & Giroux.

Bolsover, G. H. (1956). Aspects of Russian foreign policy, 1815–1914. In R. Pares & A.J.P. Taylor (Eds.), *Essays presented to Sir Lewis Namier*. New York: St. Martin's Press.

Brettschneider, F. (1999). Kohls Niederlage: Kandidatenimages und Medienberichterstattung vor der Bundestagswahl 1998 [Kohl's defeat: Images of candidates and media coverage prior to the federal election in 1998]. In P. Winterhoff-Spurk & M. Jäckel (Eds.), *Politische Eliten in der Mediengesellschaft: Rekrutierung, Darstellung, Wirkung* [Political elites in a media society: Recruiting, presentation, and appeal] (pp. 65–97). München: Verlag Reinhard Fischer.

Brezki, N. (1997). Bibi model 87 [Bibi: Model '87]. *Ma'ariv*, August 22, 42–44.

Broder, D. S. (1999a). For McCain, no place like home for controversy. *Washington Post*, November 28, A1.

Broder, D. S. (1999b). McCain's past comes back to haunt him. *Washington Post* (weekly ed.), December 6, 13.

Bruni, F. (2000). Bush and McCain, sittin' in a tree, D-I-S-S-I-N-G. *New York Times*, February 9, A14.

Burch, M. (1995). Prime minister and cabinet: An executive in transition. In R. Pyper & L. Robins (Eds.), *Governing the UK in the 1990s* (pp. 15–42). New York: St. Martin's Press.

Burch, M., & Holliday, I. (1996) *The British cabinet system*. London: Prentice-Hall.

Burke, J. P., & Greenstein, F. I. (with the collaboration of Berman, L., & Immerman, R.). (1990). *How presidents test reality: Decisions on Vietnam, 1954 and 1965*. New York: Russell Sage Foundation.

Burns, J. F. (1999a). As Iran's reformer speaks, anti-reformers sit and scowl. *New York Times*, September 30, A3.

Burns, J. F. (1999b). Iranian evokes mood of '79, rebuking US and liberals. *New York Times*, November 4, A10.

Burns, J. F. (2000a). Many reformers ruled off Iran ballot. *New York Times*, January 20, A6.

Burns, J. F. (2000b). Its voters have spoken. Now meet Iran's gunmen. *New York Times*, March 19, 16.

Byars, R. S. (1972). The task/affect quotient. *Comparative Political Studies*, 5, 109–20.

Byars, R. S. (1973). Small-group theory and shifting styles of political leadership. *Comparative Political Studies*, 6, 443–69.

Carlyle, T. (1841). *On heroes, hero-worship, and the heroic*. London: Fraser.

Carneiro, R. L. (1970). Scale analysis, evolutionary sequences, and the rating of cultures. In R. Naroll & R. Cohn (Eds.), *A handbook of method in cultural anthropology* (pp. 834–71). New York: Natural History Press.

Cartwright, D., & Zander, A. (1968). Leadership and performance of group functions: Introduction. In D. Cartwright & A. Zander (Eds.), *Group dynamics* (pp. 301–17). New York: Harper & Row.

Clarke, M. (1992). *British external policy-making in the 1990s*. Washington, DC: Brookings Institution.

Clemens, C. (1994). The chancellor as manager: Helmut Kohl, the CDU and governance in Germany. *West European Politics*, 17, 28–51.

Cohen, S. F. (1999). "Transition" is a notion rooted in U.S. ego. *New York Times*, March 27.

Colton, T. J. (1995). Boris Yeltsin, Russia's all-thumbs democrat. In T. J. Colton & R. C. Tucker (Eds.), *Patterns in post-Soviet leadership* (pp. 48–74). Boulder, CO: Westview Press.

Converse, P. E. (1964). The nature of belief systems in mass publics. In D. E. Apter (Ed.), *Ideology and discontent* (pp. 206–61). New York: Free Press.

Conway, L. G., III, Suedfeld, P., & Tetlock, P. E. (2001). Integrative complexity and political decisions that lead to war or peace. In D. J. Christie, R. V. Wagner, & D. Winter (Eds.), *Peace, conflict, and violence: Peace psychology for the 21st century* (pp. 66–75). Englewood Cliffs, NJ: Prentice-Hall.

Cotton, H. (1985). *India in Transition*. Delhi, India: B. R. Publishers.

Cox, C. (1926). *The early mental traits of three hundred geniuses*. Stanford, CA: Stanford University Press.

Dansereau, F., Jr., Graen, G., & Haga, W. J. (1975). A vertical dyad linkage approach to leadership within formal organizations. *Organizational Behavior and Human Performance*, 13, 46–78.

Davis, G. (1975). Theodore Roosevelt and the Progressive Era: A study in individual and group psychohistory. In L. deMause (Ed.), *The new psychohistory* (pp. 245–305). New York: Psychohistory Press.

deMause, L. (1975). The independence of psychohistory. In L. deMause (Ed.), *The new psychohistory* (pp. 7–27). New York: Psychohistory Press.

deMause, L. (1982a). The psychogenic theory of history. In L. deMause (Ed.), *Foundations of psychohistory* (pp. 132–46). New York: Creative Roots.

deMause, L. (1982b). Historical group-fantasies. In L. deMause (Ed.), *Foundations of psychohistory* (pp. 172–243). New York: Creative Roots.

deMause, L. (1988). "Heads and tails": Money as a poison container. *Journal of Psychohistory*, 16, 1–18.

deMause, L., & Ebel, H. (Eds.) (1977). *Jimmy Carter and American fantasy*. New York: Psychohistory Press.

Demick, B. (1999). Last week's rioting shows deep discontent in Iran. *Seattle Times*, July 18, A20.

Derksen, J. (1995). *Personality disorders: Clinical and social perspectives, assessment and treatment based on DSM-IV and ICD-10*. New York: John Wiley.

Dille, B. (2000). The prepared and spontaneous remarks of Presidents Reagan and Bush: A validity comparison for at-a-distance measurements. *Political Psychology*, 21, 573–85.

DiRenzo, G. J. (1974). *Personality and politics*. New York: Doubleday.

Dixon, W. J. (1994). Democracy and the peaceful settlement of international conflict. *American Political Science Review*, 88, 14–32.

Doek, N. (1997). Zila Netanyahu, isha hazaka [Zilia Netanyahu, strong woman]. *Yediot Aharonot*, March 11, 2.

Doherty, M. (1988). Prime-ministerial power and ministerial responsiblity in the Thatcher era. *Parliamentary Affairs*, 41, 49–67.

Donley, R. E., & Winter, D. G. (1970). Measuring the motives of public officials at a distance: An exploratory study of American presidents. *Behavioral Science*, 15, 227–36.

Doyle, M. W. (1986). Liberalism and world politics. *American Political Science Review*, 80, 1151–69.

Elgie, R. (1993). *The role of the prime minister in France, 1981–91*. New York: St. Martin's Press.

Elman, M. F. (1995). The foreign policies of small states: Challenging neorealism in its own backyard. *British Journal of Political Science*, 25, 171–217.

Elman, M. F. (1997). *Paths to peace: Is democracy the answer?* Cambridge, MA: MIT Press.

Elovitz, P. H. (2000). The partial success and bright prospects of psychohistory. *Clio's Psyche*, 6, 133–38.

Erikson, E. H. (1950). *Childhood and society*. New York: Norton.

Eysenck, H. J., & Eysenck, M. W. (1985). *Personality and individual differences*. New York: Plenum Press.

Eteshami, A. (1995). *After Khomeini: The Iranian second republic*. London: Routledge.

Faber, C. F., & Faber, R. B. (2000). *The American presidents ranked by performance*. Jefferson, NC: McFarland.

Fehr, B., Samson, D., & Paulhus, D. L. (1992). The construct of Machiavellianism: Twenty years later. In C. D. Spielberger & J. N. Butcher (Eds.), *Advances in personality assessment*, vol. 9 (pp. 77–116). Hillsdale, NJ: Lawrence Erlbaum.

Feldman, A. B. (1952/1959) Lincoln: The creation of a cult. In A. B. Feldman (Ed.), *The unconscious in history* (pp. 28–52). New York: Philosophical Library.

Feldman, O. (2000). *The Japanese political personality: Analyzing the motivations and culture of freshman Diet members*. New York: St. Martin's Press.

Finlay, D. J., Holsti, O. R., & Fagen, R. R. (1967). *Enemies in politics*. Chicago: Rand-McNally.

Freud, S. (1921). Group psychology and the analysis of the ego. In S. Freud, *The standard edition of the complete psychological works of Sigmund Freud 18* (pp. 65–143). London: Hogarth Press and Institute of Psycho-Analysis.

Galili, L. (1995). Haish shemazkir lay or lama hu roze et hashilton [The man who reminds the chirman why he wants power]. *Ha'aretz*, March 16, 2.

Galili, O. (1993). Bou lo nedaber al ze [Let's not talk about it]. *Ha'aretz*, December 31, 26.

Gardner, H. (1983). *Frames of mind: The theory of multiple intelligences*. New York: Basic Books.

Gardner, H. (1999). *Intelligence reframed: Intelligences in the 21st century*. New York: Basic Books.

Geddes, B. (1990). How the cases you choose affect the answers you get: Selection biases in comparative politics. *Political Analysis, 2*, 131–52.

George, A. L. (1969). The "operational code": A neglected approach to the study of political leaders and decision making. *International Studies Quarterly, 23*, 190–222.

George, A. L. (1974). Assessing presidential character. *World Politics, 26*, 234–82.

George, A. L. (1979). The causal nexus between cognitive beliefs and decision-making behavior: The "operational code." In L. S. Falkowski (Ed.), *Psychological models in international politics* (pp. 95–124). Boulder, CO: Westview Press.

George, A. L. (1980). *Presidential decisionmaking in foreign policy*. Boulder, CO: Westview Press.

George, A. L. (1988). Presidential management styles and models. In C. W. Kegley, Jr. & E. R. Wittkopf (Eds.), *The domestic sources of American foreign policy: Insights and evidence* (pp. 107–26). New York: St. Martin's Press.

George, A. L., & George, J. L. (1956). *Woodrow Wilson and Colonel House: A personality study*. New York: John Day.

Giddings, P. (1995). Prime minister and cabinet. In D. Shell & R. Hodder-Williams (Eds.), *Churchill to Major* (pp. 30–70). Armonk, NY: M. E. Sharpe.

Gilat, M. (1997). Rosh hamemshala bikesh hakira vehistabeh [The prime minister asked for investigation and got into trouble]. *Ma'ariv*, February 21, 2–3.

Golan, A. (1995). Ad habeirot shishtok [Let him be silent until the elections]. *Ha'aretz*, February 7, 2.

Goldberg, C. (1999). A holiday offers good news for McCain. *New York Times*, November 12, A28.

Goldman, D. (1995). *Emotional intelligence*. New York: Bantam Books.

Gordon, M. R. (1996). The kingmaker: Alexander Lebed, from war hero to populist politician. *New York Times*, June 18.

Goren, B., & Berkowitz, E. (1996). Mi ze? [Who is he?]. *Ha'ir*, June 21, 34–43, 86–87.

Granatstein, J. L., & Hillmer, N. (1999). *Prime ministers: Rating Canada's leaders*. Toronto: HarperCollins.

Grayevski, M., Las, A., & Kampner-kryin, M. (1997). Tik Sara Netanyahu [Sera Netanyahu's file]. *Yediot Aharonot*, December 12, 12–25, 90.

Greenstein, F. I. (1969). *Personality and politics: Problems of evidence, inference and conceptualization*. Chicago: Markham.

Greenstein, F. I. (1982). *The hidden hand presidency*. New York: Basic Books.

Greenstein, F. I. (1987). *Personality and politics* (2nd ed.). Princeton, NJ: Princeton University Press.

Greenstein, F. I. (2000). *The presidential difference: Leadership style from FDR to Clinton*. New York: Free Press.

Guo J. (1993). *Mao Zedong de wannian shenghuo* [Mao Zedong's life in his old age]. Beijing: N.p.

Hadley, E. M. (1970). *Antitrust in Japan*. Princeton, NJ: Princeton University Press.

Halevi, Y. K. (1998). His father's son. *Jerusalem Report*, February 5, 12–16.

Hanrieder, W. F., & Auton, G. P. (1980). *The foreign policies of West Germany, France, and Britain*. Englewood Cliffs, NJ: Prentice-Hall.

Hara, Y. (1988). *Sengo nihon to kokusaiseiji* [Postwar Japan and international politics]. Tokyo: Chuo Koronsha.

Hara, Y. (1995). *Kishi Nobusuke*. Tokyo: Iwanami Shoten.

Hardy, T. (1978). *The dynasts: An epic-drama*. London: Macmillan (Original work published 1903–1908).

Harel, I. (1997). Hayamin hayav legalot aharayot ulehapil et Netanyahu [The Right should show responsibility and bring Netanyahu down]. *Yediot Aharonot*, October 24, 11.

Hargrove, E. (1989). Two conceptions of institutional leadership. In B. Jones (Ed.), *Leadership and politics* (pp. 57–83). Lawrence: University Press of Kansas.

Hellberg-Hirn, E. (1998). *Soil and soul: The symbolic world of Russianness*. Aldershot, UK: Ashgate.

Heller, M. (1985). *Mashina i vintiki: Istoriia formirovaniia sovetskogo cheloveka* [Machine and bolts: A formative history of the Soviet man]. London: Overseas Publication Interchange.

Helms, L. (1996). Executive leadership in parliamentary democracies: The British prime minister and the German chancellor compared. *German Politics*, 5, 101–20.

Henderson, J. (1974). The childhood origins of political struggle: An interpretation of the personality and politics of a New Zealand radical. *Political Science*, 26, 2–19.

Henderson, J. (1978). Muldoon and Kirk: Active-negative prime ministers. *Political Science*, 30, 111–14.

Henderson, J. (1992). Labour's modern prime ministers. In M. Clark (Ed.), *The Labour Party after 75 years* (pp. 98–117). Wellington: Victoria University Press.

Hennessy, P. (1986). *Cabinet*. Oxford: Basil Blackwell.

Hermann, M. G. (1979). Who becomes a political leader? Some societal and regime influences on selection of a head of state. In L. S. Falkowski (Ed.), *Psychological models in international politics* (pp. 15–48). Boulder, CO: Westview Press.

Hermann, M. G. (1980a). Explaining foreign policy behavior using personal characteristics of political leaders. *International Studies Quarterly*, 24, 7–46.

Hermann, M. G. (1980b). Assessing the personalities of Soviet Politburo members. *Personality and Social Psychology Bulletin, 6,* 332–52.

Hermann, M. G. (1980c). Comments on foreign policy makers' personality attributes and interviews: A note on reliability procedures. *International Studies Quarterly, 24,* 67–73.

Hermann, M. G. (1983). Handbook for assessing personal characteristics and foreign policy orientations of political leaders. *Occasional Papers.* Columbus, OH: Mershon Center.

Hermann, M. G. (1984a). Personality and foreign policy decision making: A study of 53 heads of government. In D. A. Sylvan & S. Chan (Eds.), *Foreign policy decision-making: Perceptions, cognition, and artificial intelligence* (pp. 53–80). New York: Praeger.

Hermann, M. G. (1984b). Validating a technique for assessing personalities of political leaders at a distance: A pretest. Report prepared for Defense Systems, Inc. as part of Contract DSI-84–1240.

Hermann, M. G. (1985). Validating a technique for assessing personalities of political leaders at a distance: A test using three heads of state. Report prepared for Defense Systems, Inc. for Contract DSI-84–1240.

Hermann, M. G. (1986). Effects of speech and interview materials on profiles of leaders at a distance: A validation exercise. Report prepared for Defense Systems, Inc. as part of Contract DSI-85–1240.

Hermann, M. G. (1987a). The effects of translation on profiles of leaders at a distance. Report prepared for Defense Systems, Inc. as part of Contract DSI-86–1240.

Hermann, M. G. (1987b). Assessing the foreign policy role orientations of sub-Saharan African leaders. In S. Walker (Ed.), *Role theory and foreign policy analysis* (pp. 161–98). Durham, NC: Duke University Press.

Hermann, M. G. (1987c). *Handbook for assessing personal characteristics and foreign policy orientation of political leaders.* Columbus: Ohio State University, Mershon Center.

Hermann, M. G. (1988). Validating a technique for assessing personalities of political leaders at a distance: Profiles of 12 leaders from the same culture. Report prepared for Defense Systems, Inc. as part of Contract DSI-87–1240.

Hermann, M. G. (1989). *Defining the Bush presidential style: Mershon Center Memo.* Columbus: Ohio State University.

Hermann, M. G. (1999). *Assessing leadership style: A trait analysis.* Columbus, OH: Social Science Automation, Inc.

Hermann, M. G. (2000). An addendum: Making empirical inferences about elite decision making politically relevant. *The Political Psychologist, 5,* 24–29.

Hermann, M. G., & Hermann, C. F. (1989). Who makes foreign policy decisions and how: An empirical enquiry. *International Studies Quarterly, 33,* 361–87.

Hermann, M. G., & Kegley, C. W., Jr. (1995). Rethinking democracy and international peace: Perspectives from political psychology. *International Studies Quarterly, 39,* 511–33.

Hermann, M. G., & Kogan, N. (1977). Effects of negotiators' personalities on negotiating behavior. In D. Druckman (Ed.), *Negotiations: Social-psychological perspectives* (pp. 247–74). Beverly Hills, CA: Sage.

Hermann, M. G. (Ed.) (with T. W. Milburn). (1977). *A psychological examination of political leaders*. New York: Free Press.

Hermann, M. G., & Preston, J. T. (1994). Presidents, advisers, and foreign policy: The effects of leadership style on executive arrangements. *Political Psychology, 15*, 75–96.

Hermann, M. G., & Preston, T. (1999). Presidents, leadership style, and the advisory process. In E. R. Wittkopf & J. M. McCormick (Eds.), *The domestic sources of American foreign policy: Insights and evidence* (pp. 351–68). Lanham, MD: Rowman & Littlefield.

Hermann, M. G., Preston, T., & Young, M. (1996). Who leads can matter in foreign policymaking: A framework for leadership analysis. Paper presented at the annual meeting of the International Studies Association, San Diego.

Hiwatashi, Y. (1990). *Sengo seiji to nichibei kankei* [Postwar politics and Japan–US relationship]. Tokyo: Tokyo Daigaku Shuppankai.

Holsti, O. (1970). The operational code approach to the study of political leladers: John Foster Dulles' philosophical and instrumental beliefs. *Canadian Journal of Political Science, 3*, 123–57.

Holsti, O. R. (1977). The "operational code" as an approach to the analysis of belief systems. Final report to the National Science Foundation. Grant no. SOC75-15368.

Horowitz, R. (1992). Alilot bibi basayeret [Bibi's legend in the special unit]. *Hadashot*, December 4, 6–8.

Hosokawa, R. (1986). *Kishi Nobusuke*. Tokyo: Jiji Tsushinsha.

House, R. J., Spangler, W. D., & Woycke, J. (1991). Personality and charisma in the U.S. presidency: A psychological theory of leader effectiveness. *Administrative Science Quarterly, 36*, 364–96. http://tehran.stanford.edu/khatamistory.

Huskey, E. (1999). *Presidential power in Russia*. Armonk, NY: M. E. Sharpe.

Ihanus, J. (1994). Zhirinovsky and the swaddled Russian personality. *Journal of Psychohistory, 22*, 187–97.

Ihanus, J. (1999). Water, birth and Stalin's thirst for power: Psychohistorical roots of terror. *Journal of Psychohistory, 27*, 67–84.

Ihanus, J. (2000). Interdisciplinary futures. *Clio's Psyche, 6*, 161–62.

Inbar, E. (1999). *Rabin and Israel's national security*. Baltimore: Johns Hopkins University Press.

Iroshnikov, M., Protsai, L., & Shelayev, Y. (1992). *The sunset of the Romanov dynasty*. Moscow: Terra.

Iwami, T. (1994). *Showa no yokai* [Showa's monster]. Tokyo: Asahi Sonorama.

James, C. (1999). Debate gives boxing another black eye. *New York Times*, December 4, A14.

James, S. (1999). *British cabinet government*. London: Routledge.

Janis, I. (1972). *Victims of groupthink: A psychological study of foreign-policy decisions and fiascoes*. Boston: Houghton Mifflin.

Jervis, R. (1976). *Perception and misperception in international politics*. Princeton, NJ: Princeton University Press.

Johnson, C. (1982). *MITI*. Tokyo: Charles E. Tuttle.

Jones, B. (1985). Mrs. Thatcher's style of government. In B. Jones (Ed.), *Political issues in Britain today* (pp. 1–15). Manchester, UK: Manchester University Press.

Jones, E. E., & Pittman, T. S. (1982). Toward a general theory of strategic self-presentation. In J. Suls (Ed.), *Psychological perspectives of the self* (pp. 231–63). Hillsdale, NJ: Erlbaum.

Jones, G. W. (1991). The study of prime ministers: A framework for analysis. *West European politics: Special issue on West European prime ministers*, 14, 1–8.

Jourard, S. M. (1964). *Transparent self*. Princeton, NJ: D. van Nostrand.

Kaarbo, J. (1997). Prime minister leadership styles in foreign policy decision-making: A framework for research. *Political Psychology*, 18, 553–81.

Kaarbo, J., & Hermann, M. G. (1998). Leadership styles of prime ministers: How individual differences affect the foreign policymaking process. *Leadership Quarterly*, 9, 243–63.

Kääriäinen, K. (1999). Religion and the Russian elite. In E. Helander (Ed.), *Religion and social transitions* (pp. 56–68). Helsinki: University of Helsinki, Department of Practical Theology.

Kartsev, V., & Bludeau, T. (1995). *Zhirinovsky!* New York: Columbia University Press.

Kaspit, B. (1997). Misheu yepol veze lo ani [Someone will fall and it won't be me]. *Ma'ariv*, April 2, 12–13.

Kaspit, B., & Kfir, I. (1997a). *Netanyahu: Haderekh el hako'ah* [Netanyahu: The road to power]. Tel Aviv: Alpha Tekshoret.

Kaspit, B., & Kfir, I. (1997b). Neshotav shel bibi netanyahu [Bibi Netanyahu's women]. *Ma'ariv*, June 6, 22–28.

Kaufman, M. (2000). Profiles offer a peek inside the presidential psyche. *Washington Post*, August 7, A7.

Kavanagh, D. (1994). A Major agenda? In D. Kavanagh & A. Seldon (Eds.), *The Major effect* (pp. 3–17). London: Macmillan.

Kepplinger, H. M., & Rettich, M. (1996). Publizistische Schlagseiten. Kohl und Scharping in Presse und Fernsehen [Negative public images. Kohl and Scharping in the papers and on television]. In C. Holtz-Bacha & L. L. Kaid (Eds.), *Wahlen und Wahlkampf in den Medien: Untersuchungen aus dem Wahljahr 1994* [Elections and campaigns in the media: Studies from the election year 1994] (pp. 80–100). Opladen: Westdeutscher Verlag.

Kernberg, O. (1975). *Borderline conditions and pathological narcissism*. New York: Jason Aronson.

Kernberg, O. (1980). Adolescent sexuality in the light of group processes. *Psychoanalytic Quarterly*, 49, 27–47.

Kernberg, O. (1985). *Internal world and external reality*. New York: Jason Aronson.

Kim, H. (1996a). Tov layehudim, ra laisraelim [Good for the Jews, bad for the Israelis]. *Ha'aretz*, October 8, 3.

Kim, H. (1996b). Hu zarich lehiot mapainik kedei lehazliach [He has to be a Mapainik in order to succeed]. *Ha'aretz*, June 7, 2.

Kim, H. (1997a). Dogli, mogli vemelech hajongel [Dogli, mogli and the king of the jungle]. *Ha'aretz*, November 14, B2.

Kim, H. (1997b). Hakonspirator hagadol [The big conspirator]. *Ha'aretz*, November 7, B2.

Kim, H. (1997c). Me bead hisol halikud, sheyarim et yado [Who wants to eliminate the Likud Party, raise your hand]. Ha'aretz, October, 31, B2.

Kimhi, S. (1999). Psychological profiles of political leaders using behavior analysis. Paper presented at the International Society of Political Psychology 22nd Annual Scientific Meeting, Amsterdam, Netherlands.

King, A. (1985). Margaret Thatcher: The style of a prime minister. In A. King (Ed.), The British prime minister (pp. 96–140). Durham, NC: Duke University Press.

King, G., Keohane, R. O., & Verba, S. (1994). Designing social inquiry: Scientific inference in qualitative research. Princeton, NJ: Princeton University Press.

Kishi, N. (1983a). Kishi Nobusuke kaikoroku [Nobusuke Kishi's memoir]. Tokyo: Kosaido.

Kishi, N. (1983b). Waga seishun [My youthhood]. Tokyo: Kosaido.

Kishi, N., Yatsugi, K., & Ito, T. (1981). Kishi Nobusuke no kaiso [The recollection of Nobusuke Kishi]. Tokyo: Bungei Shunjusha.

Kitaoka, S. (1995). Kishi Nobusuke: yashin to zasetsu [Kishi Nobusuke: Ambition and frustration]. In A. Watanabe (Ed.), Sengo nihon no saishoutachi [Postwar prime ministers of Japan] (pp. 121–47). Tokyo: Chuo Koronsha.

Klingemann, H. D., & Taylor, C. L. (1977). Affektive Parteiorientierung, Kanzlerkandidaten und Issues [Party orientation, candidates and issues]. Politische Vierteljahrsschrift, 18, 301–47.

Kobayashi, H. (1995) Cho kanryo [Superbureaucrats]. Tokyo: Tokuma Shoten.

Kohut, H. (1971). The analysis of the self: A systematic approach to the psychoanalytic treatment of narcissistic personality disorders. New York: International Universities Press.

Kohut, H. (1977). The restoration of the self. New York: International Universities Press.

Kohut, H. (1978). The psychology of the self. New York: International Universities Press.

Kohut, H. (1985). On leadership. In C. Strozier (Ed.), Self psychology and the humanities (pp. 51–94). New York: W.W. Norton.

Krippendorf, K. (1990). Content analysis. Beverly Hills CA: Sage.

Kugler, C. (1999). Wie verkaufen sich die Kanzlerkandidaten? Schröder und Kohl und die "Jahrtausendwahl" [How do chancellor candidates advertise themselves? Schröder, Kohl, and the "millennium election"]. In C. Schicha & R. Ontrup (Eds.), Medieninszenierung im Wandel: Interdisziplinäre Zugänge [The media as a stage: Recent developments] (pp. 181–98). Münster: ikö-Publikationen.

Kuntz, P. (1999). McCain's financing stance recalls keating-five role. Wall Street Journal, December 17, A16.

Kusunoki, S. (2000). Retsuden: Nihon kindaishi [A series of biographies: Modern Japanese history]. Tokyo: Asahi Shinbunsha.

Labaton, S. (2000a). McCain urged FCC action on issue involving supporter. New York Times, January 6, A1.

Labaton, S. (2000b). Issue for McCain is matching record with his rhetoric. New York Times, January 7, A16.

Lambeth, B. S. (1996). The warrior who would rule Russia. Santa Monica, CA: Rand Corporation.

Landau, D. (1981). Moderate extremist . . . and his very discreet wife. *Jerusalem Post Magazine*, January 16, 1.

Lange, D. (1990). *Nuclear free: The New Zealand way*. Auckland: Penguin Books.

Larson-Welch, D. (1997). *Anatomy of mistrust: U.S.–Soviet relations during the cold War*. Ithaca, NY: Cornell University Press.

Lasswell, H. D. (1930). *Psychopathology and politics*. Chicago: University of Chicago Press.

Lasswell, H. D. (1948). *Power and personality*. New York: Norton.

Laux, L., & Schütz, A. (1996). *Wir, die wir gut sind. Die Selbstdarstellung von Politikern zwischen Glorifizierung und Glaubwürdigkeit* [Self-presentation of politicians between glorification and credibility]. München: Deutscher Taschenbuch Verlag.

Leary, M. (1995). *Self-presentation. Impression management and interpersonal behavior*. Madison, WI: Brown.

Lebow, R. N., & Stein, J. G. (1993). Afghanistan, Carter, and foreign policy change: The limits of cognitive models. In D. Caldwell & T. J. McKeown (Eds.), *Diplomacy, force, and leadership: Essays in honor of Alexander L. George* (pp. 95–128). Boulder, CO: Westview Press.

Lehman, H. C. (1953). *Age and achievement*. Princeton, NJ: Princeton University Press.

Leinemann, J. (1994). Helmut Kohl [Helmut Kohl]. In W. von Sternburg (Hrsg.), *Die deutschen Kanzler. Von Bismarck bis Kohl* [German chancellors. From Bismarck to Kohl] (pp. 457–67). Frankfurt: Fischer Taschenbuch Verlag.

Leites, N. (1951). *The operational code of the Politburo*. New York: McGraw-Hill.

Leites, N. (1953). *A study of bolshevism*. New York: Free Press.

Levine, J. M., & Moreland, R. L. (1990). Progress in small group research. *Annual Review of Psychology*, 41, 585–634.

Li, Y. (1991). *Zai Mao Zedong shenbian shiwunian* [Fifteen years beside Mao Zedong]. Hebei: People's Press.

Li, Y. (1994). *Waijiao wudai shangde xinshongguo lingxiu* [New China's leaders on the diplomatic stage]. Beijing: Foreign Languages Education Press.

Li, Y. (1998). Taped interview on September 4.

Li, Z. (1994). *The private life of Chairman Mao*. New York: Random House.

Lifton, R. J., & Mitchell, G. (1996). *Hiroshima in America: A half century of denial*. New York: Avon Books.

Lindholm, C. (1990). *Charisma*. Oxford: Blackwell.

Little, G. (1988). *Strong leadership*. Oxford: Oxford University Press.

Maddi, S. R. (1989). *Personality theories: A comparative analysis* (5th ed.). Chicago: Dorsey Press.

*Mao Zedong nianpu* [Mao Zedong chronology]. (1993). Edited by the Office of Documentary Studies, the Central Committee of the CCP, vol. 1. Beijing: Documentary Press of the CCP Center.

*Mao Zedong waijiao wenxuan* [Selected works of Mao Zedong on diplomacy]. (1993). Beijing: Documentary Press of the CCP Center.

Maoz, Z. (1998). Realist and cultural critiques of the democratic peace: A theoretical and empirical re-assessment. *International Interactions*, 24, 3–89.

Marks, P. (2000). McCain launches a new salvo. *New York Times*, February 9, A14.

Markus, Y. (1992). Gonev laem et hamiflaga [Stealing the party from them]. *Ha'aretz*, August 14, 1.

Markus, Y. (1996). Shuvo shel Netanyahu [The return of Netanyahu]. *Ha'aretz*, March 1, 1.

Markus, Y. (1997a). Arbaa lekahim mimashber ahad [Four lessons from one crisis]. *Ha'aretz*, November 30, 1.

Markus, Y. (1997b). Im Bibi, rak bekoah [With Bibi, only by force]. *Ha'aretz*, June 24, 1.

Martin, L. (1997). *The antagonist: Lucien Bouchard and the politics of delusion*. New York: Viking.

Masumi, J. (1995). *Contemporary Politics in Japan* (trans. L. E. Carlile). Berkeley: University of California Press.

Mawdsley, E., & White, S. (2000). *The Soviet elite from Lenin to Gorbachev: The Central Committee and its members, 1917–1991*. Oxford: Oxford University Press.

Mayntz, R. (1980). Executive leadership in Germany: Dispersion of power or "Kanzlerdemokratie"? In R. Rose & E. N. Suleiman (Eds.), *Presidents and prime ministers* (pp. 139–70). Washington, DC: American Enterprise Institute for Public Policy Research.

Mazlish, B. (1972). *In search of Nixon: A psychohistorical inquiry*. New York: Basic Books.

Mazlish, B. (1976). *Kissinger: The European mind in American policy*. New York: Basic Books.

Mazlish, B., & Diamond, E. (1979). *Jimmy Carter: A character portrait*. New York: Simon & Schuster.

McCain, J. (1999). *Faith of my fathers*. New York: Random House.

McCann, S.J.H. (1992). Alternative formulas to predict the greatness of US presidents: Personological, situational, and zeitgeist factors. *Journal of Personality and Social Psychology, 62*, 469–79.

McClelland, D. C., Atkinson, J. W., Clark, R. A., & Lowell, E. L. (1953). *The achievement motive*. New York: Appleton-Century-Crofts.

McDaniel, E., & Lawrence, C. (1990). *Levels of cognitive complexity: An approach to the measurement of thinking*. New York: Springer-Verlag.

McMillan, N. (1993). *Top of the greasy pole: New Zealand prime ministers of recent times*. Dunedin: McIndoe.

Merten, K. (1991). Django und Jesus: Verbal-Nonverbales Verhalten der Kanzlerkandidaten im Bundestagswahlkampf 1987 [Django and Jesus: Verbal and nonverbal behavior of the candidates for chancellor in 1987]. In M. Opp de Hipt & E. Latniak (Eds.), *Sprache statt Politik* [Language instead of politics] (pp. 188–210). Opladen, Germany: Westdeutscher Verlag.

Milani, F. (1999). Lipstick politics in Iran. *New York Times*, August 19, A21.

Mischel, W. (1977). The interaction of person and situation. In D. Magnusson & N. S. Endler (Eds.), *Personality at the crossroads* (pp. 333–52). Hillsdale, NJ: Lawerence Erlbaum.

Mishne, J. M. (1993). *The evolution and application of clinical theory: Perspectives from four psychologies*. New York: Free Press.

Mitchell, A. (1999a). McCain exhorts his party to reject campaign system. *New York Times*, July 1, A17.

Mitchell, A. (1999b). Temperament issue poses test for McCain. *New York Times*, November 5, A12.

Mitchell, A. (2000). GOP candidates redirect their fire toward democrats. *New York Times*, January 8, A9.

Mitofsky, W. J. (1996). Exit polling on the Russian elections. *Public Perspective* (August–September), 41–44.

Mollon, P. (1996). *Multiple selves, multiple voices: Working with trauma, violation and dissociation.* Chichester: John Wiley & Sons.

Moore, M. (1999). In selling of candidates, Mexico tries US way. *Washington Post*, November 5, A25.

Müller, W. C., Philipp, W., & Gerlich, P. (1993). Prime ministers and cabinet decision-making processes. In J. Blondel & F. Müller-Rommel (Eds.), *Governing together* (pp. 223–56). New York: St. Martin's Press.

Nakamura, T. (1995). Ikeda Hayato. In A. Watanabe (Ed.), *Sengo nihon no saishoutachi* [Postwar prime ministers of Japan] (pp. 149–74). Tokyo: Chuo Koronsha.

Nakatani, T. (1974). *Senji gikaishi* [Wartime history of the Diet]. Tokyo: Minzoku to Seijisha.

Neal, T. M. (1999). Tax reform group attacks, McCain fires back. *New York Times*, December 26, A32.

Netanyahu, B. (1993). *A place among the nations: Israel and the world.* New York: Bantam.

Netanyahu, B. (1995). *Makom tahat hashemesh* [Place under the sun]. Tel Aviv: Yediot Aharonot.

Netanyahu, B. (1996). *Ma'avak bateror* [Fighting terrorism]. Tel Aviv: Yedioth Aharonot Books & Chemed Books.

Netanyahu sipur haim [Netanyahu life story]. (1956). *Yediot Aharonot*, June 21, 6–13.

Neustadt, R. (1960). *Presidential power and modern presidents.* New York: Free Press.

*New Zealand Parliamentary Debates.*

Nezlek, J. B., & Leary, M. (2001). Individual differences in self-presentational motives in daily social interaction. Manuscript submitted for publication.

Nisbett, R., & Wilson, T. D. (1977). Telling more than we know: Verbal reports on mental processes. *Psychological Review*, 84, 231–59.

Nobody gave you the right to rifle through my biography! (1994). *Washington Post*, March 6, 5A.

Noguchi, Y. (1995). *1940 nen taisei* [The 1940 System]. Tokyo: Toyo Keizai Shinposha.

Norpoth, H. (1979). Kanzlerkandidaten: Wie sie vom Whler bewertet werden und seine Wahlentscheidung beeinflussen [Political candidates: How they are evaluated and how they influence voting behavior]. In M. Kaase (Ed.), *Wahlsoziologie heute* [Sociology of political elections today] (pp. 198–221). Opladen: Westdeutscher Verlag.

Norton, P. (1994). *The British polity.* New York: Longman.

Ohinata, I. (1985). *Kishi seiken 1241 nichi* [The Kishi administration's 1241 days]. Tokyo: Gyosei Mondai Kenkyujo.

Oren, A. (1997). Yerivim veamitim [Rivals and colleagues]. *Ha'aretz*, October 24, B5.

*Ot pervogo lica: Razgovory s Vladimirom Putinym* [From the first person: Discussions with Vladimir Putin]. (2000). Moscow: Vagrius.

Ota, K. (1976). *Tatakai no nakade* [Amid the struggle]. Tokyo: Chuo Keizaisha.

Pancer, S. M., Brown, S. D., & Barr, C. W. (1999). Forming impressions of political leaders: A cross-national comparison. *Political Psychology*, 20, 345–68.

Pancer, S. M., Hunsberger, B., Pratt, M. W., Boisvert, S., & Roth, D. (1992). Political roles and the complexity of political rhetoric. *Political Psychology*, 13, 31–43.

Peres, S. (1993). *The new Middle East*. New York: Henry Holt & Co.

Peres, S. (Summer/Fall 1996). Vision and reality. *Brown Journal of World Affairs*, 3, 57–63.

Peres, S. (1998). *For the future of Israel*. Baltimore: Johns Hopkins University Press.

Peri, Y. (1996). Afterword. In Yitzhak Rabin, *Yitzhak Rabin: The Rabin memoirs* (pp. 339–80). Berkeley: University of California Press.

Pervin, L. A. & John, O. (1997). *Personality: Theory and research* (7th ed.). New York: Wiley.

Pflüger, F. (2000). *Ehrenwort: Das system Kohl und der neubeginn* [The word of honour. The system Kohl and the recommencement]. München: Deutsche Verlags-Anstalt.

Plowden, W. (Ed.). (1987). *Advising the rulers*. New York: Basil Blackwell.

Porter, C. A., & Suedfeld, P. (1981). Integrative complexity in the correspondence of literary figures: Effects of personal and societal stress. *Journal of Personality and Social Psychology*, 40, 321–330.

Post, J. M. (1986). Narcissism and the charismatic leader–follower relationship. *Political Psychology*, 7, 675–88.

Post, J. M. (Ed.). *Profiling political leaders: Theory and practice*. Ithaca, NY: Cornell University Press.

Preston, T. (1996). The president and his inner circle: Leadership style and the advisory process in foreign policy making. Unpublished doctoral dissertation, Ohio State University.

Preston, T. (1997). "Following the leader": The impact of US presidential style upon advisory group dynamics, structure, and decision. In P. 't Hart, E. Stern, & B. Sundelius (Eds.), *Beyond groupthink: Political group dynamics and foreign policymaking* (pp. 191–248). Ann Arbor: University of Michigan Press.

Preston, T. (2001). *The president and his inner circle: Leadership style and the advisory process in foreign policy making*. New York: Columbia University Press.

Preston, T., & 't Hart, P. (1999). Understanding and evaluating bureaucratic politics: The nexus between political leaders and advisory systems. *Political Psychology*, 20, 49–98.

Quételet, A. (1968). *A treatise on man and the development of his faculties*. New York: Franklin (Reprint of 1842 Edinburgh translation of 1835 French original).

Random House. (1998). *Random House Webster's unabridged dictionary*. New York: Random House.

Reich, W. (1983). *Children of the future: On the prevention of sexual pathology* (with translations by D. Jordan, I. Jordan, & B. Placzek). New York: Farrar, Straus, & Giroux.

Renshon, S. A. (1996a). *High hopes: The Clinton presidency and the politics of ambition*. New York: New York University Press [1998 paperback edition, with new introduction, published by Routledge Press].

Renshon, S. A. (1996b). *The psychological assessment of presidential candidates*. New York: New York University Press [1998 paperback edition, with new introduction, published by Routledge Press].

Renshon, S. A. (1998). Analyzing the psychology and performance of presidential candidates at a distance: Bob Dole and the 1996 presidential campaign. *Journal of Leadership Studies*, 3, 253–81.

Renshon, S. A. (2000). Political leadership as social capital: Governing in a fragmenting culture. *Political Psychology*, 21, 199–226.

Riasanovsky, N. V. (1985). *The image of Peter the Great in Russian history and thought*. Oxford: Oxford University Press.

Ridley, N. (1991). *"My style of government": The Thatcher years*. London: Hutchinson.

Rogers, D. (2000). McCain mystery is whether voter love feast will last. *Wall Street Journal*, January 3, A20.

Rogow, A. (1970). *The psychiatrists*. New York: Putnam.

Rokeach, M. (1960). *The open and closed mind*. New York: Basic Books.

Rose, R. (1980). British government: The job at the top. In R. Rose & E. N. Suleiman (Eds.), *Presidents and prime ministers* (pp. 1–49). Washington, DC: American Enterprise Institute for Public Policy Research.

Rose, R. (1991). Prime ministers in parliamentary democracies. *West European Politics: Special Issue on West European Prime Ministers*, 14, 9–24.

Rose, R., & Suleiman, E. N. (Eds.). (1980). *Presidents and prime ministers*. Washington, DC: American Enterprise Institute for Public Policy Research.

Rozenblum, D. (1993). Geula derekh habivim [Redemption via the sewers]. *Ha'aretz*, March 5, B1.

Rozenblum, D. (1997). El haen [To nowhere]. *Ha'aretz*, October 19, B1.

Rubenzer, S., Faschingbauer, T. R., & Ones, D. S. (2000). Measuring presidential psychology. Paper presented at the annual meeting of the American Psychological Association, Washington, DC.

Russett, B. M. (1993). *Grasping the democratic peace*. Princeton, NJ: Princeton University Press.

Sampson, A. (1982). *The changing anatomy of Britain*. London: Hodder & Stoughton.

Santmire, T., Wilkenfeld, J., Kraus, S., Holley, K., Santmire, T., & Gleditsch, K. (1998). The impact of cognitive diversity on crisis negotiations. *Political Psychology*, 19, 721–48.

Savir, U. (1998). *The process: 1,100 days that changed the Middle East*. New York: Random House.

Scammel, M. (1997). The wisdom of the war room: US campaigning and Americanization. Cambridge, MA: Harvard University, Joan Shorenstein Center (Research paper R-17).

Schafer, M., & Crichlow, S. (2000). Bill Clinton's operational code: Assessing source material bias. *Political Psychology*, 21, 559–71.

Schlenker, B. R. (1980). *Impression management: The self concept, social identity and interpersonal relations*. Monterey, CA: Brooks/Cole.

Schlenker, B. R., & Leary, M. R. (1982). Audience's reactions to self-enhancing, self-denigrating and accurate self-presentations. *Journal of Experimental Social Psychology*, 18, 89–104.

Schlesinger, A. M. (1948). Historians rate the US presidents. *Life*, November 1, 25, 65–66, 73–74.

Schneider, H. (2000). Spin doctors in Iran reformists adopt US campaign tactics. *Washington Post*, February 18, A1.

Schram, S. (Ed.). (1992). *Mao's road to power: Revolutionary writings*, vol. 1. Armonk, NY: M. E. Sharpe.

Schroder, H. M., Driver, M. J., & Streufert, S. (1967). *Human information processing*. New York: Holt, Rinehart, & Winston.

Schütz, A. (1993). Self-presentational tactics used in a German election campaign. *Political Psychology*, 14, 471–93.

Schütz, A. (1998a). Assertive, offensive, protective and defensive styles of self-presentation: A taxonomy. *Journal of Psychology*, 132, 611–28.

Schütz, A. (1998b). Audience perceptions of politicians' self-presentational behaviors concerning their own abilities. *Journal of Social Psychology*, 138, 173–88.

Schütz, A. (1999). Techniken defensiver Selbstdarstellung: Die Äußerungen Bill Clintons zu seiner Affäre mit Monica Lewinsky [Tactics of defensive self-presentation: Statements of Bill Clinton concerning his affair with Monica Lewinsky]. In C. Schicha & R. Ontrup (Eds.), *Medieninszenierungen im Wandel: Interdisziplinäre Zugänge* [The media as a stage: Recent developments] (pp. 232–49). Münster: ik-Publikationen.

Schütz, A., & DePaulo, B. M. (1996). Self-esteem and evaluative reactions: Letting people speak for themselves. *Journal of Research in Personality*, 30, 137–56.

Schütz, A., Hertel, J., & Schulze, T. (2001). Rise and fall of a political leader. Helmut Kohl's style of self-presentation and leadership. Unpublished Manuscript, Chemnitz University, Germany.

Sciolino, E. (1998a). Iranians like their president's conciliatory remarks on US. *New York Times*, January 10.

Sciolino, E. (1998b). At Khomeini's tomb, Iran's president switches tune on US. *New York Times*, January 20.

Sciolino, E. (1998c). Iranian president paints a picture of peace and moderation. *New York Times*, September 22, A12.

Sciolino, E. (1999). For once, the veil that hides conflict slips. *New York Times*, July 18, sect. 4, 5.

Seldon, A. (1994). Policymaking and cabinet. In D. Kavanagh & A. Seldon (Eds.), *The Major Effect* (pp. 154–66). London: Macmillan.

Shalev, H., Kasptit, B., & Raat, M. (1996). Ani lo adam natul regashot, aval lo adam aosek bepinkasanut [I am not a man without emotions, but I do not do bookkeeping]. *Ma'ariv*, June, 28, 2–3.

Shamir, Y. (1994). *Summing up: An autobiography*. Boston: Little, Brown.

Shamir, Y. (Summer/Fall 1996). Israel and the Middle East today. *Brown Journal of World Affairs*, 3, 65–69.

Shavit, H. (1996). Mizrah tihon hadash? Eize raayon meshashea [New Middle East? What a ridiculous idea]. *Ha'aretz*, November 22, 18.

Shell, D. (1995). The office of prime minister. In D. Shell & R. Hodder-Williams (Eds.), *Churchill to Major* (pp. 1–29). Armonk, NY: M. E. Sharpe.

Sheng, M. (1998). *Battling Western imperialism: Mao, Stalin, and the United States.* Princeton, NJ: Princeton University Press.

Sheory, D. (1985). Haverim mesaprim al bibi [Friends talk about Bibi]. *Al-Hamishmar*, November 20, 7.

Shepherd, R. (1991). *The power brokers.* London: Hutchinson.

Shioda, U. (1996). *Kishi Nobusuke.* Tokyo: Kodansha.

Shiraev, E., & Zubok, V. (2000). *Anti-Americanism in Russia: From Stalin to Putin.* New York: Palgrave.

Sigelman, L., & Shiraev, E. (1998). The rational attacker in Russia? Negative campaigning and the 1996 Russian presidential election. Paper presented at the annual meeting of the International Society of Political Psychology, Montreal.

Simonton, D. K. (1977). Creative productivity, age, and stress: A biographical time-series analysis of 10 classical composers. *Journal of Personality and Social Psychology*, 35, 791–804.

Simonton, D. K. (1980). Land battles, generals, and armies: Individual and situational determinants of victory and casualties. *Journal of Personality and Social Psychology*, 38, 110–119.

Simonton, D. K. (1981). Presidential greatness and performance: Can we predict leadership in the White House? *Journal of Personality*, 49, 306–23.

Simonton, D. K. (1983). Intergenerational transfer of individual differences in hereditary monarchs: Genes, role-modeling, cohort, or sociocultural effects? *Journal of Personality and Social Psychology*, 44, 354–64.

Simonton, D. K. (1984a). Leader age and national condition: A longitudinal analysis of 25 European monarchs. *Social Behavior and Personality*, 12, 111–14.

Simonton, D. K. (1984b). Leaders as eponyms: Individual and situational determinants of monarchal eminence. *Journal of Personality*, 52, 1–21.

Simonton, D. K. (1985a). Intelligence and personal influence in groups: Four nonlinear models. *Psychological Review*, 92, 532–47.

Simonton, D. K. (1985b). The vice-presidential succession effect: Individual or situational basis? *Political Behavior*, 7, 79–99.

Simonton, D. K. (1986a). Dispositional attributions of (presidential) leadership: An experimental simulation of historiometric results. *Journal of Experimental Social Psychology*, 22, 389–418.

Simonton, D. K. (1986b). Presidential greatness: The historical consensus and its psychological significance. *Political Psychology*, 7, 259–83.

Simonton, D. K. (1986c). Presidential personality: Biographical use of the Gough Adjective Check List. *Journal of Personality and Social Psychology*, 51, 149–60.

Simonton, D. K. (1987a). Presidential inflexibility and veto behavior: Two individual-situational interactions. *Journal of Personality*, 55, 1–18.

Simonton, D. K. (1987b). *Why presidents succeed: A political psychology of leadership.* New Haven, CT: Yale University Press.

Simonton, D. K. (1988a). Age and outstanding achievement: What do we know after a century of research? *Psychological Bulletin*, 104, 251–67.

Simonton, D. K. (1988b). Presidential style: Personality, biography, and performance. *Journal of Personality and Social Psychology*, 55, 928–36.

Simonton, D. K. (1990). *Psychology, science, and history: An introduction to historiometry*. New Haven, CT: Yale University Press.

Simonton, D. K. (1991a). Latent-variable models of posthumous reputation: A quest for Galton's G. *Journal of Personality and Social Psychology*, 60, 607–19.

Simonton, D. K. (1991b). Predicting presidential greatness: An alternative to the Kenney and Rice Contextual Index. *Presidential Studies Quarterly*, 21, 301–5.

Simonton, D. K. (1992). Presidential greatness and personality: A response to McCann (1992). *Journal of Personality and Social Psychology*, 63, 676–79.

Simonton, D. K. (1993). Putting the best leaders in the White House: Personality, policy, and performance. *Political Psychology*, 14, 537–48.

Simonton, D. K. (1995). Personality and intellectual predictors of leadership. In D. H. Saklofske & M. Zeidner (Eds.), *International handbook of personality and intelligence* (pp. 739–57). New York: Plenum.

Simonton, D. K. (1996). PresidentsÇ wives and First Ladies: On achieving eminence within a traditional gender role. *Sex Roles*, 35, 309–36.

Simonton, D. K. (1997). Creative productivity: A predictive and explanatory model of career trajectories and landmarks. *Psychological Review*, 104, 66–89.

Simonton, D. K. (1998a). Mad King George: The impact of personal and political stress on mental and physical health. *Journal of Personality*, 66, 443–66.

Simonton, D. K. (1998b). Political leadership across the life span: Chronological versus career age in the British monarchy. *Leadership Quarterly*, 9, 195–206.

Simonton, D. K. (2000). Creative development as acquired expertise: Theoretical issues and an empirical test. *Developmental Review*, 20, 283–318.

Simonton, D. K. (in press). Predicting presidential greatness: Equation replication on recent survey results. *Journal of Social Psychology*.

Smith, E. E. (1968). *The young Stalin: The early years of an elusive revolutionary*. London: Cassell.

Smith, M. B. (1968). A map for the analysis of personality and politics. *Journal of Social Issues*, 24, 15–28.

Smith, M. J. (1999). *The core executive in Britain*. New York: St. Martin's Press.

Smith, S. (1988). Belief systems and the study of international relations. In R. Little & S. Smith (Eds.), *Belief systems and international relations* (pp. 11–36). Oxford: Basil Blackwell.

Snow, E. (1968). *Red star over China*. New York: Grove Press.

Snyder, C. R. (1985). The excuse: An amazing grace? In B. R. Schlenker (Ed.), *The self and social life* (pp. 235–61). New York: McGraw-Hill.

Snyder, C. R., Higgins, R. L., & Stucky, R. J. (1983). *Excuses: Masquerades in search of grace*. New York: Wiley.

Snyder, G. H., & Diesing, P. (1977). *Conflict among nations: Bargaining, decision-making, and system structure in international crises*. Princeton, NJ: Princeton University Press.

Solovyov, V., & Klepikova, E. (1995). *Zhirinovsky: The paradoxes of Russian fascism* (trans. C. A. Fitzpatrick in collaboration with the authors). London: Viking.

Sontag, D. (1999). Netanyahu sees enemies all around him. *New York Times*, April 23.

Sorokin, P. A. (1925). Monarchs and rulers: A comparative statistical study. I. *Social Forces*, 4, 22–35.

Sorokin, P. A. (1926). Monarchs and rulers: A comparative statistical study. II. *Social Forces*, 4, 523–33.

Specter, M. (1996). Russian leaders back Yeltsin in ouster of Lebed. *New York Times*, October 19.

Stavrakis, P. (1996). Russia after the elections: Democracy or parliamentary Byzantium? *Problems of Post-Communism*, 43, 13–20.

Stites, R. (1989). *Revolutionary dreams: Utopian vision and experimental life in the Russian revolution*. New York: Oxford University Press.

Stockwin, J.A.A. (1999). *Governing Japan: Divided politics in a major economy* (3rd ed). Oxford: Blackwell.

Stone, W. F., Lederer, G., & Christie, R. (Eds.) (1993). *Strength and weakness: The authoritarian personality today*. New York: Springer-Verlag.

Suedfeld, P. (1985). APA presidential addresses: The relation of integrative complexity to historical, professional, and personal factors. *Journal of Personality and Social Psychology*, 49, 1643–51.

Suedfeld, P. (1992). Cognitive managers and their critics. *Political Psychology*, 13, 435–53.

Suedfeld, P. (2000). Domain-related variation in integrative complexity: A measure of political importance and responsiveness? In C. de Landtsheer & O. Feldman (Eds.), *Beyond public speech and symbols: Explorations in the rhetoric of politicians and the media* (pp. 17–34). Westport, CT: Praeger.

Suedfeld, P., & Bluck, S. (1988). Changes in integrative complexity prior to surprise attacks. *Journal of Conflict Resolution*, 32, 626–35.

Suedfeld, P., Bluck, S., Ballard, E. J., & Baker-Brown, G. (1990). Canadian federal elections: Motive profiles and integrative complexity in political speeches and popular media. *Canadian Journal of Behavioural Science*, 22, 26–36.

Suedfeld, P., Bluck, S., Loewen, L., & Elkins, D. J. (1994). Sociopolitical values and integrative complexity of members of student political groups. *Canadian Journal of Behavioural Science*, 26, 121–141.

Suedfeld, P., & Coren, S. (1992). Cognitive correlates of conceptual complexity. *Personality and Individual Differences*, 13, 1193–99.

Suedfeld, P., & Epstein, Y. M. (1973). Attitudes, values, and ascription of responsibility: The Calley case. *Journal of Social Issues*, 29, 63–71.

Suedfeld, P., & Rank, A. D. (1976). Revolutionary leaders: Long-term success as a function of changes in conceptual complexity. *Journal of Personality and Social Psychology*, 34, 169–78.

Suedfeld, P., & Tetlock, P. E. (1977). Integrative complexity of communications in international crises. *Journal of Conflict Resolution*, 21, 169–84.

Suedfeld, P., & Tetlock, P. E. (1991). The roots of controversy. In P. Suedfeld & P. E. Tetlock (Eds.), *Psychology and social policy* (pp. 1–30). New York: Hemisphere.

Suedfeld, P., Tetlock, P. E., & Streufert, S. (1992). Conceptual/integrative complexity. In C. P. Smith (Ed.), *Motivation and personality: A handbook of thematic analysis* (pp. 393–400). Cambridge: Cambridge University Press.

Suslov, M. (1996–1997). Suslov's secret report on Mao, Khrushchev, and the Sino-Soviet tensions, December 1959. *Cold War International History Project* (Woodrow Wilson International Center, Washington, DC), 8–9: 244–48.

Susser, L. (1998). History repeating itself? *Jerusalem Report*, June 22, 14–16.

Sylvan, D. A. (1998). Assessing the impact of problem representation upon Israeli–Palestinian conflict and cooperation. Paper presented at the annual meeting of the International Society of Political Psychology, Montreal.

Tapsell, R. F. (1983). *Monarchs, rules, dynasties and kingdoms of the world*. New York: Facts on File.

Tedeschi, J. T., & Reiss, M. (1981). Impression management. In C. Antaki (Ed.), *Ordinary language explanations of social behavior* (pp. 271–310). London: Academic Press.

Tedeschi, J. T., Schlenker, B. R., & Bonoma, T. V. (1971). Cognitive dissonance: Private ratiocination or public spectacle? *American Psychologist, 26*, 685–95.

Tetlock, P. E. (1981). Pre- to post-election shifts in presidential rhetoric: Impression management or cognitive adjustment? *Journal of Personality and Social Psychology, 41*, 207–12.

Tetlock, P. E. (1983). Cognitive style and political ideology. *Journal of Personality and Social Psychology, 45*, 118–26.

Tetlock, P. E. (1984). Cognitive style and political belief systems in the British House of Commons. *Journal of Personality and Social Psychology, 46*, 365–75.

Tetlock, P. E. (1985). Integrative complexity of American and Soviet foreign policy rhetoric: A time-series analysis. *Journal of Personality and Social Psychology, 49*, 1565–85.

Tetlock, P. E. (1998). Social psychology and world politics. In D. T. Gilbert, S. T. Fiske, & G. Lindzey (Eds.), *Handbook of social psychology* (pp. 869–912). New York: McGraw-Hill.

Tetlock, P. E., Bernzweig, J., & Gallant, J. L. (1985). Supreme Court decision-making: Cognitive style as a predictor of ideological consistency of voting. *Journal of Personality and Social Psychology, 48*, 1227–39.

Tetlock, P. E., & Boettger, R. (1989). Cognitive and rhetorical styles of traditionalist and reformist Soviet politicians: A content analysis study. *Political Psychology, 10*, 209–32.

Tetlock, P. E., Peterson, R., & Berry, J. (1993). Flattering and unflattering personality portraits of integratively simple and complex managers. *Journal of Personality and Social Psychology, 64*, 500–511.

Tetlock, P. E., Skitka, L., & Boettger, R. (1989). Social and cognitive strategies for coping with accountability: Conformity, complexity, and bolstering. *Journal of Personality and Social Psychology, 57*, 632–40.

Tetlock, P. E., & Tyler, A. (1996). Churchill's cognitive and rhetorical style: The debates over Nazi intentions and self-government for India. *Political Psychology, 17*, 149–70.

't Hart, P. (1994). *Groupthink in government*. Baltimore: Johns Hopkins University Press.

Thomas, G. P. (1998). *Prime minister and cabinet today*. Manchester: Manchester University Press.

Thorndike, E. L. (1936). The relation between intellect and morality in rulers. *American Journal of Sociology*, 42, 321–34.

Tolstoy, L. (1952). *War and peace* (trans. L. Maude & A. Maude). In R. M. Hutchins (Ed.), *Great books of the Western world*, vol. 51. Chicago: Encyclopedia Britannica (original work published 1862–1869).

Treisman, D. (1996). Why Yeltsin won. *Foreign Affairs* (September/October): 64–77.

Tsurumi, K. (1970). *Social change and the individual*. Princeton, NJ: Princeton University Press.

Tucker, R. C. (1972). *The Soviet political mind: Stalinism and post-Stalin change* (rev. ed). London: George Allen & Unwin.

Tucker, R. C. (1990). *Stalin in power: The revolution from above 1928–1941*. New York: W. W. Norton.

Tucker, R. C. (1995a). *Politics as leadership* (rev. ed). Columbia: University of Missouri Press.

Tucker, R. C. (1995b). Post-Soviet leadership and change. In T. J. Colton & R. C. Tucker (Eds.), *Patterns in post-Soviet leadership* (pp. 5–28). Boulder, CO: Westview Press.

U.S. Census Bureau. (2000). International data base. Retrieved May 24, 2000 from the World Wide Web:http://www.census.gov/cgi-bin/ipc/idbrank.pl.

Vardi, R. (1997). *Bibi: Mi ata adoni rosh hamemshala?* [Bibi: Who are you, Mr. Prime Minister?]. Jerusalem: Keter.

Verter, Y. (1996a). Netanyahu mekanes et rashei hamosadot balikud lediun bedrahim leafagat hametihot batenua [Netanyahu gathered the head of the Likud Party to discuss ways of reducing tension]. *Ha'aretz*, September 2, 7.

Verter, Y. (1996b). "Netanyahu yeshalem beyoker al haitalelot be arbaat habekhirim," omrim balikud [Likud sources: "Netanyahu will pay high price for maltreatment of the four senior members."] *Ha'aretz*, June 17, 3.

Verter, Y. (1997). Netanyahu: Novil et israel leshnat alpaim um'ever la [Netanyahu: We will lead Israel to the year 2000 and beyond]. *Ha'aretz*, April 18, 3.

Vertzberger, Y. I. (1990). *The world in their minds: Information processing, cognition, and perception in foreign policy decision-making*. Stanford, CA: Stanford University Press.

Vinciguerra, T. (1999). Hell from the chief: Hot tempers and presidential timber. *New York Times*, November 7, 7.

Vogel, B. (1990). (Ed.). *Das Phenomen: Helmut Kohl im Urteil der Presse 1960–1990* [The phenomenon: Press commentary on Helmut Kohl 1960–1990]. Stuttgart: Deutsche Verlags-Anstalt.

Volkan, V. D., Itzkowitz, N., & Dodd, A. W. (1997). *Richard Nixon: A psychobiography*. New York: Columbia University Press.

Von Drehle, D. (2000). Trying to erase "evil": John McCain's rhetorical grenades have stirred anger in the GOP and raised allegations that he is exploiting religious differences. *Washington Post*, March 2, A7.

Walker, S. G. (1977). The interface between beliefs and behavior: Henry Kissinger's operational code and the Vietnam War. *Journal of Conflict Resolution*, 21, 129–68.

Walker, S. G. (1983). The motivational foundations of political belief systems: A re-analyis of the operational code construct. *International Studies Quarterly*, 27, 179–201.

Walker, S. G. (1990). The evolution of operational analysis. *Political Psychology*, 11, 403–18.

Walker, S. G. (1995). Psychodynamic processes and framing effects in foreign policy decision-making: Woodrow Wilson's operational code. *Political Psychology*, 16, 697–717.

Walker, S. G. (2000). Role identities and the operational codes of political leaders. Paper presented at the annual meeting of the International Society of Political Psychology, Seattle.

Walker, S. G., & Schafer, M. (2000). The political universe of Lyndon Johnson and his advisors: Diagnostic and strategic propensities in their operational codes. *Political Psychology*, 21, 529–43.

Walker, S. G., Schafer, M., & Young, M. D. (1998). Systematic procedures for operational code analysis: Measuring and modeling Jimmy Carter's operational code. *International Studies Quarterly*, 42, 175–90.

Walker, S. G., Schafer, M., & Young, M. D. (1999). Presidential operational codes and the management of foreign policy conflicts in the post–cold war world. *Journal of Conflict Resolution*, 43, 610–25.

Walker, S. G., & Watson, G. L. (1992). The cognitive maps of British leaders, 1938–39: The case of Chamberlain-in-cabinet. In E. Singer & V. Hudson (Eds.), *Political psychology and foreign policy* (pp. 31–58). Boulder, CO: Westview Press.

Wallace, M. D., & Suedfeld, P. (1988). Leadership performance in crisis: The longevity-complexity link. *International Studies Quarterly*, 32, 439–51.

Wallace, M. D., Suedfeld, P., & Thachuk, K. L. (1993). Political rhetoric of leaders under stress in the Gulf crisis. *Journal of Conflict Resolution*, 37, 94–107.

Wallace, M., Suedfeld, P., & Thachuk, K. (1996). Failed leader or successful peacemaker? Crisis, behavior, and the cognitive processes of Mikhail Sergeyevitch Gorbachev. *Political Psychology*, 17, 453–72.

Waltz, K. N. (1967). *Foreign policy and democratic politics: The American and British experience*. Boston: Little, Brown.

Ward, D. (1975). Kissinger: A psychohistory. In L. deMause (Ed.), *The new psychohistory* (pp. 69–130). New York: Psychohistory Press.

Watson, G. & McGaw, D. (1980). *Statistical inquiry*. New York: John Wiley.

Weber, E. U., & Hsee, C. K. (2000). Culture and individual judgment and decision making. *Applied Psychology: An International Review*, 49, 32–61.

Weller, P. (1985). *First among equals*. Sydney: George Allen & Unwin.

Wendt, A. (1999). *Social theory of international politics*. Cambridge: Cambridge University Press.

White, S., Rose, R., & McAllister, I. (1996). *How Russia votes*. Chatham, NJ: Chatham House.

*Who said what when: A chronological dictionary of quotations*. (1991). New York: Hippocrene Books.

Will, G. F. (1999). The politics of sanctimony. *Washington Post*, November 14, B7.

Winter, D. G. (1973). *The power motive*. New York: Free Press.

Winter, D. G. (1983). *Manual for scoring motive imagery in running text*. Middletown, CT: Wesleyan University Press.

Winter, D. G. (1987). Leader appeal, leader performance, and the motive profiles of leaders and followers: A study of American presidents and elections. *Journal of Personality and Social Psychology*, 52, 196–202.

Winter, D. G. (1991a). Measuring personality at a distance: Development of an integrated system for scoring motives in running text. In A. J. Stewart, J. M. Healy, Jr., & D. J. Ozer (Eds.), *Perspectives in personality: Approaches to understanding lives* (pp. 59–89). London: Jessica Kingsley Publishers.

Winter, D. G. (1991b). A motivational model of leadership: Predicting long-term management success from TAT measures of power motivation and responsibility. *Leadership Quarterly*, 2, 67–80.

Winter, D. G. (1992a). Content analysis of archival data, personal documents, and everyday verbal productions. In C. P. Smith (Ed.), *Motivation and Personality: Handbook of Thematic Content Analysis* (pp. 110–25). New York: Cambridge University Press.

Winter, D. G. (1992b). Personality and foreign policy: Historical overview. In E. Singer & V. Hudson (Eds.), *Political psychology and foreign policy* (pp. 79–101). Boulder, CO: Westview Press.

Winter, D. G. (1993). Power, affiliation, and war: Three tests of a motivational model. *Journal of Personality and Social Psychology*, 65, 532–45.

Winter, D. G. (1994a). *Manual for scoring motive imagery in running text* (Version 4.2). Ann Arbor: University of Michigan, Department of Psychology.

Winter, D. G. (1994b). Presidential psychology and governing styles: A comparative psychological analysis of the 1992 presidential candidates. In S. A. Renshon (Ed.), *The Clinton presidency: Campaigning, governing, and the psychology of leadership* (pp. 113–34). Boulder, CO: Westview Press.

Winter, D. G. (1997). Measuring the Motives of Bill Clinton and Saddam Hussein. Unpublished manuscript, University of Michigan, Ann Arbor.

Winter, D. G. (2000). Measuring the motives of political actors at a distance. Unpublished manuscript, University of Michigan, Ann Arbor.

Winter, D. G., & Carlson, L. (1988). Using motive scores in the psychobiographical study of an individual: The case of Richard Nixon. *Journal of Personality*, 56, 75–103.

Winter, D. G., Hermann, M. G., Weintraub, W., & Walker, S. G. (1991). The personalities of Bush and Gorbachev measured at a distance: Procedures, portraits, and policy. *Political Psychology*, 12, 215–45, 457–64.

Winter, D. G., & Stewart, A. J. (1977). Content analysis as a method of studying political leaders. In M. G. Hermann (Ed.), *A psychological examination of political leaders* (pp. 27–61). New York: Free Press.

Woldendorp, J., Keman, H., & Budge, I. (1993). Special issue: Political data 1945–1990. *European Journal of Political Research*, 24.

Wolf, M. (1970). Child training and the Chinese family. In M. Freeman (Ed.), *Family and kinship in Chinese society* (pp. 37–62). Stanford, CA: Stanford University Press.

Wolfers, A., & Martin, L. W. (Eds.). (1956). *The Anglo-American tradition in foreign affairs*. New Haven, CT: Yale University Press.

Woods, F. A. (1906). *Mental and moral heredity in royalty*. New York: Holt.

Woods, F. A. (1913). *The influence of monarchs*. New York: Macmillan.

Wortman, R. S. (1995). *Scenarios of power: Myth and ceremony in Russian monarchy*, vol. 1. Princeton, NJ: Princeton University Press.

Wright, V. (1984a). *David Lange: Prime minister*. Wellington: Unwin.

Wright, V. (1984b). David Lange. *New Zealand Listner*, July 7.

Wu, X. (1991). *Huiyi yu huainian* [Recollection and remembrance]. Beijing: The Party School of the CC of the CCP Press.

www.Number-10.uk.

www.Parliament.uk.

www.russiaworld.com.

www.SocialScience.net.

Xu, Y. (1992).*Jinmen zhizhan* [The battles over Jinmen Island]. Beijing: Chinese Broadcast-Television Publishers.

Yan, M. (1996). Rethinking the interruption of the 8th Congress's line. *Lilun daokan* [Theoretical guide], 7, 25–27.

Ye, F. (1988). *Ye Fi huiyilu* [Ye Fi memoirs]. Beijing: PLA Press.

Yeltsin, B. (1990). *Against the grain: An autobiography* (trans. M. Glenny). London: Jonathan Cape.

The Yeltsin-Lebed Alliances (Editorial). (1996). *New York Times*, June 19.

Young, H. (1991). *One of us*. London: Macmillan.

Young, M. D. (2000). Automating assessment at a distance. *The Political Psychologist*, 15, 17–23.

Yudin, P. (1994). Transcript of conversation with comrade Mao, March 31, 1956. *Far Eastern Affiairs*, 4–5, 134–44.

Zhirinovsky, V. (1993). *Poslednii brosok na yug* [The last push to the South]. Moscow: N.p.

Zhirinovsky, V., & Jurovicky, V. (1998). *Azbuka seksa: Ocherki seksual'noi kul'tury v rynochnom mire* [The ABC of sex: Reports on sexual culture in the market world]. Moscow: Politbyuro.

Zubok, V. (1996). *Inside the Kremlin's cold war*. Cambridge, MA: Harvard University Press.

# Index

# About the Editors and Contributors

OFER FELDMAN is Associate Professor of Social Psychology and Politics at Naruto University of Education, Japan. He is the author of numerous journal articles in the fields of political psychology and communication studies. In addition, he is the author of *Politics and the News Media in Japan* (1993), *The Japanese Political Personality* (1999), and two books in Japanese on political behavior. He is the editor of *Political Psychology in Japan* (1999) and is co-editor of *Politically Speaking* (Praeger, 1998) and *Beyond Public Speech and Symbols* (Praeger, 2000).

LINDA O. VALENTY is Assistant Professor of Political Science at San Jose State University. She has authored several journal articles and book chapters on the subject of political behavior and political psychology. She is the recipient of multiple research grants and has presented research at numerous national and international scholarly meetings. She serves as a reviewer for Prentice-Hall, Houghton Mifflin, and Wadsworth Publishing and is on the Executive Board of the Psycho-Politics Research Committee of the International Political Science Association.

YAEL S. ARONOFF recently accepted a teaching position at Hamilton College and has served as Javits Fellow in the Senate Foreign Relations Committee and as Assistant for Regional Humanitarian Affairs in the Pentagon's Office of Humanitarian and Refugee Affairs under the Office of the Secretary of Defense. Her publications have appeared in the *Washington Post*, *The Brown Journal of World Affairs*, *Lawyers Committee for Human Rights: Middle East*, and several edited volumes. Honors include the Columbia University Andrew Wellington Cordier Teaching Fellowship, the Columbia University President's Fellowship (1995–2000), and the prestigious Morris Abrams Award in International Relations (1998).

LUCIAN GIDEON CONWAY III has authored or co-authored eight articles, comments, and book chapters. He is on the editorial board of *Representative Research in Social Psychology* and has served as an ad hoc reviewer for the *Journal of Personality, Group Dynamics: Theory, Research, and Practice*, and *Personality and Social Psychology Bulletin*. While at the University of Montana he taught courses in Introductory and Biological Psychology. His varied interests include the complexity of thought, the origins of culturally shared beliefs (such as stereotypes), group processes, and political psychology.

DAVID EICHHORN has given poster presentations at the 1998 and 1999 Canadian Psychological Association Conferences and the third Annual Conference of the Association for the Scientific Study of Consciousness and spoke at the 26th International Congress of Psychology. He received a 1999 American Psychological Association Dissertation Research Award for his proposed research into the importance of considering person, environment, and task interactivity, as contrasted with mere co-occurrence, when predicting cross-time task success in changing environments. His focus is upon environmental psychology, but he also studies cognition, social cognition, and political psychology.

SHIGEKO N. FUKAI is Professor of International Politics at Okayama University, Japan. She has published numerous book chapters and articles in *World Politics, Current History, PS*, and *Asian Survey* in English and *Kokusai Seiji* and *Chuo Koron* in Japanese, among others. Her research interests include the role of non-state actors in the international regime formation and comparative politics with a focus on political leadership, policy making, and party politics in Japan.

JOHN HENDERSON is Head of the Political Science Department at the University of Canterbury, where he teaches New Zealand and Pacific Island politics. He has divided his career between teaching and working in politics; from 1985 to 1989 he was Director of the Prime Minister's Office during David Lange's term as prime minister. Earlier in his career, he worked for another Labour Party leader, Bill Rowling, about whom he published a biography, *Bill Rowling: The Man and the Myth*. He has since published several articles on New Zealand political leadership and plans to publish a biography on David Lange.

JUHANI IHANUS is Adjunct Professor of Cultural Psychology at the University of Helsinki. He has edited six books in Finnish and one in

Swedish and published articles and book chapters in English, Finnish, Swedish, German, and Russian on topics including psychohistory, cultural psychology, and clinical psychology, which he has connected especially with Russian studies and research on political leadership. In addition, he is the author of five scientific books in Finnish and one book in English, entitled *Multiple Origins: Edward Westermarck in Search of Mankind* (1999). He is a member of several editorial boards, including the *Journal of Psychohistory* and *H-Net/Psychohistory*, and is a Contributing Editor to *Tapestry*.

JULIET KAARBO is currently Associate Professor of Political Science at the University of Kansas. She was awarded a dissertation fellowship from the National Science Foundation Research Training Group on Cognition and Collective Political Decision Making. Her research and teaching interests include comparative foreign policy, political leadership and personality, and group dynamics. She has recently contributed articles to numerous journals, including *International Studies Quarterly*, *Political Psychology*, and *Leadership Quarterly*. She currently serves as co-editor of the *International Society of Political Psychology Newsletter* and as an officer in the Foreign Policy Analysis section of the International Studies Association.

SHAUL KIMHI is currently Assistant Professor of Psychology at Tel Hai Academic College, Israel. He teaches courses that include Introduction to Psychology, Abnormal Psychology, Social Psychology, Stress Management, and Personality Theories. His current research interests include psychological profiles of political leaders, living under conditions of continuous uncertainty in Israeli settlements along the border with Lebanon, and adjustment to military service among Israeli youth. He is a professional Psychologist Officer in the Israeli Defense Forces Reserves and served (1992–1995) as a special advisor to the army.

THOMAS PRESTON is Associate Professor of International Relations in the Department of Political Science at Washington State University. He is the author of numerous journal articles and book chapters in the fields of political psychology, foreign policy analysis, and security studies. His published works focus upon presidential leadership style, personality, bureaucratic politics, group dynamics, foreign policy decision making, and the design and use of policy simulations. In addition, he is the author of *The President and His Inner Circle: Leadership Style and the Advisory Process in Foreign Policy Making* (2001).

STANLEY A. RENSHON is Professor of Political Science, the City University of New York, and a certified psychoanalyst. He has authored more than 60 articles and seven books, including *Psychological Needs and Political Behavior, Handbook of Political Socialization, The Political Psychology of the Gulf War, The Clinton Presidency, The Psychological Assessment of Presidential Candidates,* and *Political Psychology: Cultural and Cross-Cultural Foundations.* His psychologically framed biography of Clinton, *High Hopes: The Clinton Presidency and the Politics of Ambition,* won the 1997 Richard E. Neustadt Award for the best book on the presidency and the National Association for the Advancement of Psychoanalysis' Gravida Award for the best psychoanalytic biography. He was a Research Fellow at Harvard's John F. Kennedy School (2000–2001), studying the role of character issues in the 2000 presidential election.

MARK SCHAFER is Associate Professor of Political Science at Louisiana State University. He teaches international relations and specializes in political psychology, foreign policy decision making, and conflict resolution. Schafer's research has been published in the *Journal of Politics, Journal of Conflict Resolution, International Studies Quarterly, Political Psychology, International Interactions,* and other scholarly outlets. Most of his research is in three areas: group decision making, the operational code, and personality correlates in foreign policy decision making.

ASTRID SCHÜTZ is Professor of Psychology at the University of Chemnitz, Germany. She is the recipient of scholarships and travel grants from the Fulbright Foundation, the Federation of German American Clubs, the Alexander-von-Humboldt-Foundation, and the German Research Foundation (DFG). She was a visiting scholar at the University of Virginia (1993/1994) and at Case Western Reserve University (1998). She is the author of numerous publications on self-esteem, self-presentation, self-defeating behavior, political psychology, and coping with stress and serves as a reviewer for journals in personality and social psychology.

MICHAEL M. SHENG is an Associate Professor of History at Southwest Missouri State University whose articles on China's foreign relations and the Chinese communism have appeared in numerous academic journals. His first book, *Battling Western Imperialism: Mao, Stalin, and the United States,* was published in 1998. He is currently working on a psychoanalytically informed biography of Mao.

ERIC SHIRAEV served on the faculty of St. Petersburg University until 1992. He now teaches political science at George Mason University and serves as a Research Associate at the Institute for European, Russian, and Eurasian Studies at George Washington University. He is an author, co-author, and co-editor of the following books: *The Russian Transformation*

(1999), *Anti-Americanism in Russia: From Stalin to Putin* (2001), *The Accent of Success* (2001), and *Introduction to Cross-Cultural Psychology* (2001).

DEAN KEITH SIMONTON is Professor of Psychology at the University of California, Davis. He has authored more than 200 publications, including such books as *Genius, Creativity, and Leadership: Historiometric Inquiries* (1984), *Why Presidents Succeed: A Political Psychology of Leadership* (1987), and *Origins of Genius: Darwinian Perspectives on Creativity* (1999), which received the William James Book Award from the American Psychological Association. Other honors include the Sir Francis Galton Award for Outstanding Contributions to the Study of Creativity, the Rudolf Arnheim Award for Outstanding Contributions to Psychology and the Arts, and the George A. Miller Outstanding Article Award.

PETER SUEDFELD is Professor of Psychology at the University of British Columbia, Canada, and Peter Wall Distinguished Scholar in Residence. He has published eight books and approximately 200 scientific articles and book chapters. Suedfeld is a Fellow of the Royal Society of Canada and many other scientific organizations. He has received the U.S. Antarctica Service Medal and the Canadian Psychological Association's Donald O. Hebb Award for distinguished contributions to psychology as a science. In 1998–1999, as President of the Canadian Psychological Association, he worked with M.E.P. Seligman to establish the joint American Psychological Association–Canadian Psychological Association (APA–CPA) Initiative on Ethnopolitical Warfare and is currently Vice President of the International Society of Political Psychology.

TANYEL TAYSI is a graduate student in Comparative Politics and International Relations in the Department of Political Science at Washington State University, Pullman, Washington. Her research interests include Middle East regional focus on Turkey and Iran, national identity, gender, political psychology, and security studies.

STEPHEN G. WALKER is a Professor of Political Science at Arizona State University. He has served as Vice President of the International Society of Political Psychology, as a co-editor of *International Studies Quarterly*, and on the editorial boards of *Political Psychology* and *International Interactions*. His research on the operational codes of political leaders as they relate to problems of crisis management has been funded by the National Science Foundation. He has published in several academic journals, including *World Politics, International Studies Quarterly, Journal of Conflict Resolution, Journal of Peace Research, Political Psychology,* and *Journal of Politics*.